THE *Heart* OF

Nonviolent

COMMUNICATION

25 KEYS
TO SHIFT FROM
SEPARATION TO
CONNECTION

STEPHANIE BACHMANN MATTEI

KRISTIN K. COLLIER

PuddleDancer
P R E S S

2240 Encinitas Blvd., Ste. D-911, Encinitas, CA 92024
email@PuddleDancer.com • www.PuddleDancer.com

The Heart of Nonviolent Communication:
25 Keys to Shift From Separation to Connection

© 2023 PuddleDancer Press
A PuddleDancer Press Book

PuddleDancer Press, Permissions Dept.
2240 Encinitas Blvd., Ste. D-911, Encinitas, CA 92024
Tel: 1-760-652-5754; Fax: 1-760-274-6400
www.NonviolentCommunication.com Email@PuddleDancer.com

Ordering Information
Please contact Independent Publishers Group, Tel: 312-337-0747; Fax: 312-337-5985;
Email: frontdesk@ipgbook.com, or visit www.IPGbook.com for other contact information
and details about ordering online.

Authors: Stephanie Bachmann Mattei and Kristin Collier
Copyeditor: Virginia Herrick
Indexer: Beth Nauman-Montana
Cover and interior design: Shannon Bodie (BookWiseDesign.com)
Cover source image: Shutterstock.com/Tai11

Manufactured in the United States of America
1st Printing, April 2023
♻ Printed on recycled paper
28 27 26 25 24   2 3 4 5 6
ISBN: 978-1-934336-42-7

Library of Congress Cataloguing-in-Publication Data

Names: Mattei, Stephanie Bachmann, author. | Collier, Kristin K., author.
Title: The heart of nonviolent communication : 25 keys to shift from separation to connection /
Stephanie Bachmann Mattei, Kristin K. Collier.
Description: Encinitas, CA : PuddleDancer Press, [2022] | Includes bibliographical references and index.
| Summary: "Do you want to learn how to express yourself honestly and compassionately? How to
live in choice rather than submit or rebel? These are two of the key distinctions that Marshall B.
Rosenberg, the creator of Nonviolent Communication, developed and taught as ways to reveal the
consciousness behind his visionary practice. This book invites you into a systematic exploration of
these key distinctions. Each chapter provides real-life examples from around the world alongside
contributions from brain science research and awareness of power dynamics and systemic
conditioning. Key by key, chapter by chapter, you'll collect understandings and practices that will
help you see every action and relationship anew. Nonviolent Communication is often introduced as
a model with four components-observation, feeling, need, and request. This is just the beginning.
At its heart lies a reverence for life based on awareness of interdependence, wholeness, and
power-with. With this consciousness, Nonviolent Communication reaches beyond interpersonal
conversations into the realms of spirituality, social change, and life-serving community. Use this
book as your key to moving toward the spirit of true connection" -- Provided by publisher.
Identifiers: LCCN 2022036115 (print) | LCCN 2022036116 (ebook) |
ISBN 9781934336427 (trade paperback) | ISBN 9781934336434 (ebook)
Subjects: LCSH: Interpersonal communication. | BISAC: SELF-HELP / Communication & Social Skills |
PSYCHOLOGY / Interpersonal Relations
Classification: LCC HM1166 .M357 2022 (print) | LCC HM1166 (ebook) |
DDC 302.2--dc23/eng/20220914
LC record available at https://lccn.loc.gov/2022036115
LC ebook record available at https://lccn.loc.gov/2022036116

ENDORSEMENTS OF
THE HEART OF NONVIOLENT COMMUNICATION

"Brilliant! This book is a major contribution to the literature on consciousness and social change. Especially in this era of increasing polarization, this book is an indispensable roadmap for returning to connection and wholeness."

—CHRISTOPHER K. GERMER, PHD, lecturer on psychiatry, Harvard Medical School,
and author, *The Mindful Path to Self-Compassion*

"Studying, practicing, and engaging with the deep learning available within this book can support unbinding from early limiting conditioning and finding some degree of choice. . . . I recommend this book to anyone who chooses to grow and learn and wishes to be free."

—FLORENCE MELEO-MEYER, Assistant Professor of the Practice, program director, Global Relations
and Professional Education Mindfulness Center, Brown University School of Public Health

"The authors bring us into connection with their heartfelt love, insights, and wisdom drawn from their deep experience with Nonviolent Communication and present us with this gift. The wisdom contained in this book is to be lived with by every NVC and mindfulness teacher."

—ALLAN GOLDSTEIN, UC San Diego Center for Mindfulness, Professional Training
Institute cofounder, MBSR teacher development and mentorship

"*The Heart of Nonviolent Communication* is masterfully written. . . . An essential tool for an embodied and relational Science of Connection. I will use this work in my teachings of Hakomi, MatrixWorks, and Soul-Force Leadership."

—MUKARA MEREDITH, MSW, CHT, author of *MatrixWorks:
A Life-Affirming Guide to Facilitation Mastery and Group Genius*

"Focusing on needs as the lens, the authors bring attention to multiple complex and challenging themes. . . . The authors make the distinction between power-with and power-over as a key to learning to use power—personal, role, and status—wisely and well."

—CEDAR BARSTOW, Certified Hakomi Trainer and Therapist, Doctor of Psychosocial Intervention,
founder and director of the Right Use of Power Institute

"This beautiful, in-depth, comprehensive elaboration of Marshall Rosenberg's work takes us far beyond NVC as a set of communication skills and illuminates its power to transform consciousness at a personal, institutional, and societal level. The book invites us and leads us toward the vision and the possibility of personal and collective liberation."

—JANET SURREY, PHD, Insight Dialogue teacher, clinical psychologist and Founding Scholar
of the Jean Baker Miller Institute at the Stone Center, Wellesley College

"This book carries an invitation to refine how I engage others and how I engage my own heart. . . . NVC is far more than a communication methodology. It rests on a philosophy of dignity and care that is expressed by how we speak and how we act."

—GREGORY KRAMER, author of *Insight Dialogue: The Interpersonal Path to Freedom* and
A Whole-Life Path: A Lay Buddhist's Guide to Crafting a Dhamma-Infused Life

"This is an important read for our day. . . . In a world that can feel contentious on a good day, we are led to bring out the best of who we are through both story and practice. . . . If you believe in a growth mindset for your life, I encourage you to read this book."

—ERIC DULL, pastor, United Lutheran Church

"A deep dive to explore the consciousness of Nonviolent Communication, providing invaluable insights for seasoned practitioners as well as new learners. Stephanie and Kristin carefully frame the connection between the spiritual basis of NVC highlighted by Marshall Rosenberg and the impact for social change so central to his vision of NVC in the world. I imagine Marshall's joy to read this book and to know that new generations continue to grow and deepen the gifts he has offered us."

—LUCY LEU, author of *Nonviolent Communication Companion Workbook* and coauthor of *Nonviolent Communication Toolkit for Facilitators*

"I don't know of any other resource that explores these fundamental aspects of Nonviolent Communication in such a thorough and accessible manner.... I'm excited to recommend this book to both students and fellow trainers of Nonviolent Communication alike. We can all learn from the nuanced understanding they bring to Marshall Rosenberg's radical vision of personal and social transformation through the practical spirituality of Nonviolent Communication."

—OREN JAY SOFER, CNVC certified trainer and author of *Say What You Mean*

"*The Heart of Nonviolent Communication* is a pivotal body of work.... By engaging with power differences, privilege, and patriarchy as both concepts but also realities we live with, the book brings NVC to the most significant questions of our times. The inclusion of voices of NVC practitioners from all over the world demonstrates how the process evolves beyond its original context and stays deeply, profoundly relevant."

—MANASI SAXENA, CNVC certified trainer and CNVC board member; founder, enCOMPASSion

"The authors illuminate key distinctions foundational not only to the practice of NVC, but also to enhanced clarity and awareness of our intentions ... , the choices we may make in life, and the impact of such choices on others."

—PENNY WASSMAN, CNVC certified trainer and assessor

"The authors offer you a clear path toward developing relationships that are based on interdependence, wholeness, and power-with, and open the door to authenticity and compassion. Detailing the key distinctions of the NVC process reveals the true power that awaits you. Step in and revel in it!"

—MARY MACKENZIE, CNVC certified trainer; author, *Peaceful Living*; cofounder, NVC Academy

"I trust that those reading this work will come away with both an intellectual understanding of each key differentiation and a sense of inspiration on how to apply that understanding to their lives. I plan to recommend this book to each of my candidates for NVC certification."

—ROXY MANNING, PHD, CNVC certified trainer and assessor, licensed clinical psychologist

"By deeply and expansively exploring the key distinctions, they provide us all with clarity and insight that will enhance our journey into the heart of nonviolence. The personal stories will inspire each of us to see how these important distinctions can be immediately applied in everyday life."

—JIM MANSKE, CNVC certified trainer and assessor, author of *Pathways to Nonviolent Communication*

CONTENTS

FOREWORD

by Miki Kashtan

That Nonviolent Communication can be linked to a set of key differentiations came to us directly from Marshall Rosenberg. He often used them in response to a question or comment, to emphasize what he saw as a developmental step in our human consciousness. Referencing a key differentiation was one way he grounded NVC in principles and took it beyond a communication technique, showing us how much transformation can hinge on changing just one word. As someone who has been exploring ways to apply the principles and practices of NVC to individual and collective liberation over many years, both spiritually and politically, I have found those moments of transformation to be pivotal to my own integration of NVC, and of nonviolence more broadly, into my being.

We will never know what Marshall's full list of key differentiations consisted of, because he never put it in writing. What we have is a list of twenty-five key differentiations put together by a team of people who were preparing materials for those pursuing trainer certification from the Center for Nonviolent Communication.

This is the foundation of what this book offers. Inside, you will find the key differentiations organized into a meaningful sequence that can be followed as a whole or engaged with in specific meaningful chunks.

Each chapter takes one key differentiation and fully lays out its significance for the journey of individual liberation. And often, also, what it means for collective liberation.

In reading this book, I am struck in particular by what I experience as the authors' extraordinary gentleness in making a case for why we would want to move across the trajectory from one side of each key differentiation to the full capacity for choice and togetherness that it points to. Stephanie and Kristin went far and wide in their research and exploration and still managed to rigorously integrate everything they found into the shift in consciousness that NVC emerges from and is a practice for. The result is an open invitation for each of us to apply our own discernment as we investigate and uncover, through engaging with this book, what each of the key differentiations holds within it.

An In-Depth Journey

When my late sister Inbal and I were working with the key differentiations as part of the BayNVC Leadership Program in the 2000s, we often suggested that participants, especially those who were pursuing trainer certification, write a paragraph about each key differentiation as part of their learning. While we recognized the depth of the consciousness shift that each key differentiation pointed to, I never envisioned just how much could be found in each of them until I read what Stephanie and Kristin created. They have taken this exploration beyond anything I could have imagined possible.

Each chapter in this journey rests on a deep grappling with a foundational aspect of what it means to be human in a world such as ours. The engagement that you are about to embark on spans many layers, including emotional, spiritual, conceptual, and political, as well as looks squarely at the material and economic bases of human social reality that give rise to the global challenges we are facing. This level of integration is deeply needed, making this book a gift for anyone who wants guidance on how to respond to our current global crises—whether internally, together with others, or systemically.

What is in this book goes well beyond what you might find in NVC workshops. Stephanie and Kristin have engaged with vast bodies of literature in many disciplines, distilling and reframing much that supports our understanding about why NVC "works." Each element of each key differentiation is explored in depth, along with the transition from one side to another, what it may mean, and how it may come about. Each chapter concludes with a summary of key points, a story that illustrates the significance of the distinction, and a practice in support of it. This book is a true companion on the journey.

Beyond the Either/Or Trap

One of the key mechanisms that continues to sustain and reproduce several thousand years of inner and outer systems designed within scarcity, separation, and powerlessness is either/or thinking. Given how deeply this thinking is embedded within us, a focus on key differentiations could very easily lend itself to an either/or framework and thus reinforce separation by blatantly or subtly framing one element of each pair as better than the other. For example, moralistic judgments would be framed as wrong while value judgments would be seen as right; talking about strategies would be considered suspect and talking about needs the thing to do; using power-over would be seen as shameful and only power-with acceptable; and so on and so forth for each and any of the key differentiations.

This is not the path that Stephanie and Kristin took. This book is not a prescription for how to be or how to live. Instead, Stephanie and Kristin bring extraordinary care and thoroughness to an exploration of a journey, a trajectory of opening to new possibilities and ways of understanding ourselves, life, and the systems within which we live. In this way, they demonstrate their commitment to one of the core principles of NVC: that every word, thought, or action is an attempt to serve life, even if it turns out to be misguided or fraught with impacts on ourselves, others, or the whole. We remain human, our dignity intact, throughout this entire book.

It is all too easy to use spiritual principles in a way that bypasses the complexities of our human experiences. All too easy, when we are in the grip of strong emotion and want to stay true to our experience, to forget our deep commitment to nonviolence and spiritual practice. Stephanie and Kristin, in their unwavering attention to nuance and complexity, show us, here, how NVC can support integration of these principles beyond any either/or proposition. This is a spiritual practice deeply grounded in honoring the fullness of our human experience.

Of Power, Privilege, and Systems

In addition, this is a book that can bring relief to anyone who's been longing for NVC to be framed and held within a deeper understanding of systems of domination. In particular, this book shares a clear vision of how such domination systems—whether patriarchy as a whole or any of its more virulent offshoots, such as capitalism or racism—shape the conditions we find ourselves in and the different starting points and challenges that our social locations present to the journey of liberation.

I am particularly appreciative of how Stephanie and Kristin navigated one of the more difficult key differentiations: fear of authority and respect for authority. What makes this challenging is the very concept of authority, which so deeply evokes the coercive nature of power-over. Any system that depends solely on fear of authority to continue functioning will sooner or later collapse; only systems which function based on respect for authority, absent any fear, have the capacity to continue functioning indefinitely. This gives deeper significance to this distinction in a time of global collapse.

Stephanie and Kristin's discussion of this complex distinction brings forth, with depth and rigor, questions that we all will face on the path of liberation: How can we free up the human spirit to release the automatic association of authority with coercion?

Releasing fear of authority is a potent personal journey toward reclaiming the power of natural authority. Transforming the systemic conditions that reinforce this fear is a whole other layer of liberation, that goes far beyond the individual. Our conditioning, born of shaming and coercion, leaves us with many limitations and confusions, which this book explores with grace. I see it thus as a contribution to thinking about both the possibilities and the limitations of such individual liberation journeys.

It is all too easy to engage with NVC, and with the key differentiations in particular, purely as a conflict resolution process or as a tool for personal growth, or to see the systemic lens as an add-on. One of the gifts this book offers is that it grounds the psychological, individual, and spiritual in the material and social conditions of our lives. The systemic lens is fully integrated, inviting us into a deep grappling with our own and others' experiences of living in a world where some people's needs matter more than others'. Inviting us to consider what it would take, individually and collectively, to shift such deeply ingrained patterns.

The Genius of NVC

When I was first asked to write the foreword to this book, I didn't dream that I would be writing a foreword to a book that I would first become part of shaping. This book, like every book, is truly the work of a community. Given the content of the book, how this unfolded is relevant, as it points to some key aspects of NVC and how the authors live it. So I want to end by sharing a bit about my experience in this process. I believe that moral integrity is a pivotal aspect of what we are asked to live into in these times, and I want to highlight how the authors modeled it in spades.

To begin, during the course of my involvement with this book, there was not a single comment of mine that the authors didn't engage with. This was something I found deeply moving. And while all my conversations, explorations, and deep ponderings were entirely with Stephanie, I know that every word of this book emerged from a committed collaboration between Stephanie and Kristin. This book is thus an example of what can emerge when mutual trust is present.

Not only that, even on topics which we initially grappled with and had divergent views on, every exchange stimulated a deeper inquiry. I watched as Stephanie and Kristin found ways of integrating new insights through living into the spirit of collaboration—which is of course core and central to the consciousness shift this entire book is about. In each case, often with a light touch and a very few words that actually made a huge difference, Stephanie and Kristin found solutions and pathways to convey what we had collaboratively shed light on. Working together became an exercise in depth and humanity and provided us all with multiple opportunities to deepen intimacy and reverence for life.

It is the genius of NVC, I believe—in both the principles and the unique forms of relating that NVC engenders—that made it possible for each of us to give and receive feedback while deepening our connection and collaborating on making meaning in the world. In this way, the process of the book was integral to the outcome, as we modeled with and to each other what the book is about. I continue to treasure the receptivity, humility, generosity, and courage that I experienced in working with Stephanie and Kristin. This is NVC in action.

INTRODUCTION

Shortly after his family moved to Detroit, Michigan, when he was nine, Marshall B. Rosenberg's parents asked him to stay inside the house for four days. Outside, one of the worst race riots of its time was unfolding in that hot summer of 1943.[1] Acute racial marginalization in the work environment, unsafe living conditions, and unequal access to services and goods contributed to this profound social unrest. The violence only subsided after president Franklin D. Roosevelt sent in six thousand army troops with automatic weapons.

Young Marshall pondered in shock how people could resort to violence and harm one another based on the color of their skin. Conversely, he noticed how his uncle would come every day to joyfully care for Marshall's grandmother, who was unable to care for herself. The contrast between these formative experiences provided a powerful and painful education for Rosenberg.

Juxtaposing our human capacity to contribute to one another's well-being with our capacity to engage in violence, Rosenberg started to ask himself existential questions. What allows people to stay connected to the joy of contributing? And what happens to human beings that interferes with their capacity to see one another's humanity and turns them to violence?

Years later, Rosenberg studied clinical psychology, mentored by Carl Rogers. Then, looking for answers beyond this field, he plunged into studying comparative world religions. Rosenberg came to realize that because the vast majority of humans were socialized within systems of domination, this disconnection was not an aberration: it was

1

commonplace. Recognizing this pervasive harm, he looked for ways to reclaim a connection with what he saw as our human nature—our desire to contribute to one another's well-being.

Exploring some of the factors that would support humans in staying connected to compassion, he identified three main aspects: language, thinking, and the strategies we rely upon to meet our needs. Based on the historical principles of nonviolence, Nonviolent Communication emerged, in Rosenberg's words, as "an integration of a certain spirituality with concrete tools for manifesting this spirituality in our daily lives, our relationships, and our political activities."[2]

Rosenberg developed the basic process of Nonviolent Communication (NVC) in the 1960s. As the practice of NVC evolved, Rosenberg began to explore illuminating crucial contrasts, such as requests and demands, power-with and power-over, and life-connected and life-disconnected mindsets. Across decades of investigation, application, and teaching, Rosenberg distinguished many such core distinctions. Understanding these key distinctions, he realized, was foundational to the practice of Nonviolent Communication. Bringing attention to these differentiations shed light on the transformative nature of the NVC process as a way of life. He envisioned NVC as offering much more than merely an approach to communication. Rosenberg began to call these *key differentiations*. They are also referred to as *key distinctions* or, in this book, simply *keys*, and we use all of these terms here.

The key distinctions support clarity and meaning. For example, if we fully understand the distinction between making a demand and making a request, we will be able to choose the communication in line with our values. Likewise, exploring the other contrasts will provide us with a means to reconnect with our capacity for awareness and choice. Socialization based on control and punishment disconnects us intrapersonally and interpersonally from the wisdom of our bodies, our feelings, and our needs. By discerning how socialization interferes with our core humanness, we can realign to the deeper truth of our feelings and needs. We are empowered to reclaim our wholeness and stay in our personal power.

As we learn to embrace apparent opposites, however, our consciousness grows more inclusive. "Without contraries is no progression," writes the poet William Blake.[3] We believe Rosenberg offered us the key differentiations in the spirit of this inclusive consciousness, beyond the social construct of right and wrong, beyond mutually exclusive either/or alternatives. By offering us stimulating contrasts to engage with, he left us with concrete tools to cultivate more conscious ways of living. Engaging with these contrasts, we can discern what contributes to life and choose consciously.

The History of the Key Differentiations

Unfortunately, Rosenberg did not publish a book specifically on the topic of the key differentiations. Stephanie sought dialogue with many senior trainers certified through the Center for Nonviolent Communication (CNVC) to learn as much as she could about the history of the key distinctions. The consensus she gathered is that Rosenberg shared the key differentiations during live trainings. "All learning is a process of making keener and keener key differentiations," some trainers recall him saying.

In one of many dialogues with certified trainer Lucy Leu, Stephanie learned that initially there were fewer than twenty key distinctions. Miki Kashtan, CNVC certified trainer and Stephanie's mentor, shared with her a draft of key differentiations that had been left unfinished by Rosenberg. It is substantially different from the list that is now offered in the CNVC Certification Preparation Packet.[4] Just as the NVC process has evolved, so have the key differentiations themselves.

Social Programming and the Key Differentiations

The key differentiations present two ways of relating to ourselves, others, and life. Generally, one is unconscious, based on conditioning—how we have been trained to think, feel, and behave in socially acceptable ways.

This programming is determined by our personal history, education, family culture, and social location. The latter includes factors such as gender, race, social class, age, physical ability, religious affiliation, sexual orientation, and geographic location. The other approach intentionally cultivates needs-based awareness. "To practice NVC, it's critical for me to be able to slow down, take my time, to come from an energy I choose, the one I believe that we were meant to come from, not the one I was programmed into,"[5] Rosenberg said. Juxtaposing one idea with another, the keys invite us to discern the paradigm we are operating from. We can then begin to realize how it has affected our relationship with ourselves, others, and the planet.

Clarity about our states of mind—thoughts, perceptions, feelings, and needs—supports mindful self-understanding. As we begin to recognize the causes and conditions that influence these mind states, radical transformation can occur.

Over time, the intentional practice of NVC allows for temporary states of mind to become more stable traits of mind. And while deep social transformation requires massive change in the institutions and systems that govern our lives, such change is not likely to come about without at least some of us engaging in the process of personal transformation. As we step into fully owning our personal power, we can join a greater collective power. Together, we have the capacity to direct social change toward more life-giving systems.

By naming our conditioned mind states and the needs-based awareness we want to cultivate, the key differentiations contribute to compassion for the ways we are neurologically wired and socially conditioned. We have chosen to include some research in neuroscience. In our experience, such resources support understanding and compassion for ourselves and others.

Our brains operate quite differently when in a state of regulation, a responsiveness characterized by calm, contented, and caring creativity, than they do when in a reactive mode of functioning referred to as dysregulation[6] (due, for example, to stress, trauma,[7] and social conditioning).

Awareness of regulated and dysregulated brain states can give context to our experience and help us bring empathy to it. Our NVC practice calls us to honor our experiences, mediated by our minds, with all their life-supporting qualities and life-disconnecting conditionings.

Rosenberg distilled the relational practice of NVC into two simple questions that awaken connection with ourselves and others: "What's alive in us?" And, "What can we do to make life more wonderful?"[8] An exploration of the key differentiations supports us in staying attuned to these questions that invite aliveness and reciprocity. Nurturing a needs-based awareness is the driving force of the NVC process and is ubiquitous in all the key distinctions. It guides us to a life of greater compassion within ourselves and with others.

Psychiatrist Bruce Perry points out, "Being born a human being does not ensure a child will become humane. Humans become humane. The capacity to care, to share, to listen, value, and be empathic—to be compassionate—develops from being cared for, shared with, listened to, valued, and nurtured."[9] The key differentiations, processes, and principles of NVC support the mind, heart, body, and spirit as we journey from human to humane.

The key differentiations, processes, and principles of NVC support the mind, heart, body, and spirit as we journey from human to humane.

Finally, the key distinctions support us in becoming more aware not just of our internal experience, but also of the impact of our choices on others. As we wrote this book for example, we not only attuned to our intentions around word choice and content, but also actively sought readers who would let us know how our choices affected them. We are immensely grateful to Miki Kashtan in particular and to many others for making time to share their honest feedback, insights, and experience regarding our work. Staying connected to our intentions while also staying open to the impacts of our words, we have drawn power from integrating personal introspection with communal feedback. Such learning and interplay have shaped the book. We will doubtless continue to grow as we receive the feedback of our readers. Balancing intention and impact, we deepen our awareness of interconnection.

The Two Wolves

Western-educated minds[10] typically default to the apparent clarity of dichotomies like good/evil or internal/external. Our hearts, by contrast, allow us to go beyond those polarities toward a deeper understanding of nonduality. Our inquiry into the key differentiations encourages immersion in this flow between mind and heart, integrating the affective and the cognitive.

When we approach the key distinctions from a cognitive standpoint and do not meet them at the heart level, the contrasts may paradoxically reinforce the right/wrong mentality we have internalized. As long as this dichotomous lens remains unexamined, the keys will not support the radical transformation of consciousness we believe was Rosenberg's vision. They will at best provide only peripheral change. It is vital that we tune into the habits of our conditioned minds if we intend to shift from a state of separation, fear, scarcity, and domination to a state of interconnectedness, trust, sufficiency, and partnership. For example, as long as we engage with the key differentiations as a contrast between right and wrong, empathy will always be the right choice and sympathy always the wrong one. A systematic investigation with the support of the key differentiations allows us to discern how our minds are conditioned and helps us intentionally choose where to place our attention. The keys become a tool for cultivating personal and collective liberation.

These differentiations offer an opportunity for us to "meet" ourselves anew, beyond dichotomies. They invite us to open our minds and hearts in an exploration that allows for the unconscious to become conscious. This inquiry begins by honoring polarities. These conditions allow for the whole, including and transcending its parts, to gradually emerge.

We both enjoy a legend of unknown origin about an elder who spoke with his grandson one evening about a battle that goes on inside human beings. He said, "My son, there is a conflict between two 'wolves' inside each one of us. One is a hurting wolf, a wolf who experiences pain in the form of anger, jealousy, envy, sorrow, guilt, shame, resentment, and self-pity. The other wolf is connected to its heart and experiences joy and peace, love and kindness, empathy and compassion." The grandson thought about it for a while and then asked, "Which wolf wins?" The old man looked into his grandson's eyes and replied, "The one you feed."[11]

From a perspective informed by the practice of NVC, we recognize that both wolves in this story are attempting to meet needs. Yet one is suffering and contributes to great distress. The wolf connected to compassion is able to see beyond the behavior of the hurting wolf and recognize its innate beauty. This wolf's loving presence empowers it to be a catalyst of healing and transformation. The hurting wolf may slowly disarm its heart from self-protective mechanisms

Holding both wolves with compassion, we can choose to feed the wolf who is connected to its heart as it bears witness to the alienation of the other.

and find freedom. The care for one wolf directed toward the other wolf inside of us integrates our experience so we may touch inner peace while embracing both wolves.

As we approach every one of the twenty-five key differentiations, we are thus invited to open ourselves to both parts of the key distinction. Holding both wolves with compassion, we can choose to feed the wolf who is connected to its heart as it bears witness to the alienation of the other. As this process unfolds within, we integrate what matters most. Cultivating self-understanding we create the conditions for healing to unfold. The more we heal, the more we allow ourselves to step into our power.

Language, Power, and Transformation

When we fine-tune our awareness around habitual thinking patterns and conditioned forms of self-expression, evidence of our enculturation slowly emerges. From that awareness, we can make choices to progressively release thoughts, language, and strategies that do not serve life. At the same time, only interdependently within community can we muster the support to change the existing social order that continues to impinge on us. As physicist and social reformer Robert W. Fuller writes, "Only when enough people arrive at this state can the existing consensus collapse and a new one rise in its place."[12]

In his later years, as Rosenberg fine-tuned the NVC process to support integration, he described the practice as having three levels of creating peace: within ourselves, with others, and in the transformation of "the structures we've created—corporate, judicial, governmental, and others—that don't support peaceful, life-enriching connections between us."[13] We appreciate his clarity and understanding that these aspects are interconnected in a practical spirituality that is "transformative" because it moves us collectively toward wanting to serve life and create life-giving systems.[14]

Rosenberg acknowledged that unless we become active agents of social change, all the personal healing of the heart and mind would not support the healing of humanity. "If I use Nonviolent Communication to liberate people to be less depressed, to get along better with their family, but do not teach them, at the same time, to use their energy to rapidly transform systems in the world, then I am part of the problem. I am essentially calming people down, making them happier to live in the systems as they are, so I am using NVC as a narcotic."[15]

Rosenberg identified four dimensions of social change: *the story*, the basic cultural paradigm we live within; *the structures* we create, which determine who makes decisions around distribution of resources and protection; *the language* we are taught that molds our minds; and how we *use power*, which is meant to respond to the question of what power we use to influence life.[16] We take Rosenberg's words to heart, and our exploration of the key distinctions actively carries further his passion for social transformation through systemic applications. NVC is rooted in a paradigm in which all human needs matter, and we are invited to cultivate an ever-expanding awareness of who is included in the "all."

Rosenberg chose "nonviolent" to describe his approach to communication as a path toward compassion and justice.[17] He also used the word *life-alienating* to distinguish between societal conditioning that fosters oppression and the life-affirming consciousness he intended to advance. Even though these words do not per se convey a direct observation, they capture an overarching set of ideas and collection of human experiences. The naming of these topics contributes to our facing them.

In fact, our brains are often unable to register a concept or an experience if it is not named. Having specific words to describe experience shapes our quality of attention. In the Russian language, for example, there are individual words for light blue and dark blue—none for "blue" in general. Studies show that Russians perceive a line that is crossed in gradation between light and dark blue as if they were discerning these as different colors. English speakers, by comparison, see these gradations only as shades of one color and have no specific words to clarify what is light and dark blue.[18]

In this book, we intentionally use words such as privilege, power differential, systemic oppression, and patriarchy to describe manifestations of domination systems. We acknowledge that these words can trigger a subtle sense of uneasiness or even overt discomfort in some of us. All words are labels and as such have the potential of contributing to disconnection depending on the context of the communication. And, words are also powerful instruments to symbolize and communicate meaning. As such they can contribute to setting the conditions for awareness and learning. Rosenberg defines violence as a tragic attempt to meet needs. Is that an evaluation that creates division or is it rather a powerful way to awaken compassion? As Fuller writes, "Once you have a name for it, you see it everywhere."[19] Historically, when we started to name gender and race,[20] we also began to speak to inequity and injustice. As a global society, we have yet to adequately address power imbalances that result in misuse and abuse of power and consequent violence.

There is power behind any form of inherited privilege. Privilege is linked to greater access to resources based on social constructs such as race and/or gender. This power can be leveraged to bring liberation to those under the knee of domination systems. Such a stand contributes to the safety of all humanity. We firmly believe that silence in the face of social inequities is a passive endorsement for them to continue. Millenia of domination systems cannot be undone without the conscious efforts of those of us in positions of privilege and power. We address these complex topics within every key differentiation, hoping that this book as a whole is a step toward supporting the fierce and compassionate deconstruction of patriarchy[21] and the conscious choice to cultivate a life-giving awareness. As two White authors, we aim to use our privilege to contribute to all beings. We hope that in specifically naming some of the systems of domination Rosenberg referred to, we may contribute to empowering all of us to clearly identify these social dynamics. Awareness can support us in tending to more needs, creating greater safety and dignity for all.

Rosenberg addressed "domination systems" directly, drawing inspiration from the work of theologian Walter Wink[22] and social systems scientist Riane Eisler.[23] Domination systems concentrate power and resources in the hands of the few people at the top of a pyramidal social structure, while its weight is shouldered by the massive population at the base. Everyone involved is conditioned to think in ways that support such systems.

"On the one hand, I see it as our task to free ourselves and our personal environment from the violence in our language and in our thinking. And on the other hand, it is our task to change the power structures that conditioned us in the first place and that continually produce the misfortune that we are fighting," Rosenberg said. In his view,[24] domination systems require four foundational elements:

1. Suppression of the self—internalized oppression, being disconnected from our own experience and truth.

2. Moralistic judgments based on right/wrong dichotomous thinking.

3. A language that denies choice by using words like should/
    shouldn't, have to/ought, and "makes me feel."

4. The concept of "deserving."

Because language shapes and reinforces our minds,[25] Rosenberg
named these elements and the domination systems themselves. Many
of the key distinctions directly address these constituents of the mind,
language, and systems.

As we become more aware of the ways in which our minds are
shaped by language and how we are programmed to express ourselves,
we can consciously choose to cultivate a new way of thinking and speaking. This transformation from conditioning to intentionality becomes
a revolutionary act that has the potential to shift our understanding of
what it means to be fully human.

Training the Mind/Heart System

We are always training the mind, whether intentionally or unintentionally.
Brain structure and function are experience-dependent. Learning and
practicing Nonviolent Communication with the key distinctions allow us
to harness the power of self-directed neuroplasticity.[26] We can then make
the most of what the practice of NVC has to offer as an intentional training of the mind. By deciding how to use the mind/heart and where to
focus our attention, we influence our brain structure and function.

As we learn to make clear observations, develop an awareness and
language with which to describe feelings and needs, and make requests
that value what's important to all involved, we are literally resculpting
our brains. Four of the twenty-five key distinctions explore how these
components—observations, feelings, needs, and requests—operate
intrapersonally, interpersonally, and in community.

This book is offered as a possible guide for the journey of liberation
from socialization to conscious awareness of choice. It is "a" guide, not

"the" guide. We hope that this book may support an odyssey deeper into your own heart and the heart of your NVC practice. We imagine that some of you may at times disagree with our understanding of NVC. We welcome you to engage in a process of discernment with curiosity, to find your own truth. In our experience, a willingness to explore beyond our present understanding allows for learning, choice, and clarity about what matters most to us.

Dialogue with others offers the gift of clarifying what is important to us by opening us to new perspectives. Indeed, we trust that further inquiry and discussion, especially when prompted by disagreement with this book, will contribute to ideas and strategies within our communities that will serve in new and enhanced ways.

What Is in This Book

This book is divided into five parts, with a chapter for each key distinction. In general, the side of the key that represents habit and conditioning is explored first. But in a few instances, we believe clarity and meaning are enhanced by beginning with the life-affirming side of the key. Each chapter has developed its own path, to be fully itself, as if it were an individual essay. Yet key differentiations intertwine with one another, and their meaning is amplified in the context of the others. Those newer to learning NVC may benefit from reading the book in the existing order. We have arranged it to systematically explore NVC concepts within the chapters, each in preparation for what follows.

Part 1, Fundamentals, contains five chapters which we identify as the building blocks of the consciousness we aim to cultivate in our NVC practice. We begin with a study of life-connected and life-disconnected mindsets, as the practice of Nonviolent Communication is geared toward enriching life. The following key, discerning the distinction between moralistic and value judgments, explores how our conditioned way of thinking and right/wrong mentality lies at the foundation of violence. This chapter includes strategies to transform those judgments into needs awareness. An exploration of the key that focuses on interdependence invites us to realize that our needs are inextricably intertwined with the needs of others. Power-with and power-over examines power in general and in specific applications. More options around the use of power can be found in Part 4. Finally, the Fundamentals include a key that examines how choice can rebalance the paradigm of coercion and obedience or rebellion instilled by millennia of patriarchal conditioning.

Part 2 focuses on the four components of NVC practice—observations, feelings, needs, and requests. In this cluster, you will also find a key differentiation concerning idiomatic and classical NVC language—a topic which directly relates to the NVC model of communication.

Part 3 clusters the key differentiations that point to the options for connection, including "being" giraffe and "doing" giraffe,[27] self-empathy, empathy, and compassionate honesty. These keys can support nurturing an inner sense of safety, connection, and wholeness. The integration of these options can be experienced as a path toward a healthy sense of self-connection, inherent power, and awareness of interdependence. Practicing the options in Part 3, we are less likely to misunderstand compassion as being nice and love as giving up and giving in.

Part 4 considers options for using power, depending on the paradigm we operate from. Various ways to use force are explored, as well as respect for and fear of authority. Self-discipline is juxtaposed with obedience. In Part 5, Further Applications, you will find several keys that offer strategies and insights to deepen and integrate the practice of NVC.

We are immensely grateful to all the people who have shared their Walking the Talk narratives at the end of each chapter. They bring the key distinctions to life, capturing unique and personal ways of embodying the NVC process in the real world, in the moment. Some names and identifying characteristics have been changed in some of these stories.

Each chapter closes with a practice. These practices are scaffolded from simpler to more complex. They aim to support us in a mind-body experience of the keys. As you venture forth in your reading and integration, we hope you enjoy the journey with a playful heart and mind.

Our Hopes for Liberation

We have been learning, living, and sharing NVC for more than two decades. We were "empathy buddies" in the Parent Peer Leadership Program[28] in 2006 and continued sharing empathy weekly for years. Since then, Stephanie has become a certified trainer and an assessor, while Kristin has continued to share NVC regionally and in her social skills work with children on the autism spectrum. During Stephanie's certification journey, her assessor, Penny Wassman, strongly encouraged Stephanie to publish her writings on the key differentiations. Once certified, Stephanie continued to explore the key distinctions with fellow CNVC trainers, as well as with her NVC students and CNVC trainer candidates. After a joyful reunion in Italy and after reading Kristin's memoir, Stephanie invited her to join in this project. Kristin's writing skills and partnership in idea development helped make this book a reality.

In these key differentiations, we find the inspiration to cultivate and methodically practice a consciousness that embraces unity among all living beings. It is our hope that this treatise kindles an inquiry in you, stimulating more intentionality and choice in your life. In our experience, these keys unlock a door to freedom, social justice, personal peace, and collective liberation. We aim to walk through it together, in harmony with the earth and all creatures that belong to her.

PART I
FUNDAMENTALS

In this section, we have clustered some of the key differentiations that address foundational aspects of the consciousness we seek to cultivate when embracing the practice of NVC. Recognition of our basic interconnection and mutuality supports healing for both individual and collective trauma. For millennia, our minds and hearts have been unconsciously trained to believe in and operate from a sense of separation and aloneness. Consequently, our brains tend toward the apparent ease of dichotomous thinking and strive for control. (On page 457, you will find an overview of some core aspects of brain and mind states linked to the consciousness paradigm we are accustomed to.)

In these first five keys, we explore a different paradigm—one that can support a world where everyone's humanity is fully honored and everyone's needs truly matter.

1

LIFE-CONNECTED AND
LIFE-DISCONNECTED MINDSETS

I have set before you life and death . . .
Therefore choose life.

—DEUTERONOMY 30:19

One of the most foundational key distinctions explores life-connected and life-disconnected[1] mindsets. With this key, we can discern the energy we are coming from and direct it in a life-serving way. Nonviolent Communication, also called "a language of life," supports our connection to the life energy in and around us. The more we become aware of this key, the more we can rely on it to inform the way we communicate.

A life-disconnected viewpoint is based on and reinforces perceptions linked to separation, scarcity, and powerlessness. A life-connected approach is grounded in interconnectedness, wholeness, and partnership. Theoretical physicist Albert Einstein is said to have remarked that "the most important decision we make is whether we believe we live in a friendly or hostile universe." If we believe the universe is hostile, we will strive to control life. If, on the other hand, we believe in a friendly universe, we will relax into trusting life. As the mind shapes the world

17

we inhabit, what are the large-scale consequences of what we are unconsciously transmitting from generation to generation when we choose a friendly or hostile—life-connecting or life-disconnecting—approach to life?

This key distinction helps us awaken to the paradigm we are operating from and discern whether it serves life or not. We tend to be unaware and to frame whatever we experience in ways that maximize the possibility of matching

A life-disconnected viewpoint is based on and reinforces separation, scarcity, and powerlessness. A life-connected approach is grounded in interconnectedness, wholeness, and partnership.

and reinforcing our worldview. Our NVC practice challenges us to grow in ways that support authenticity and freedom in our communication. Cultivating this intentional awareness empowers us to make mindful choices, moment by moment, in relationship to ourselves and all life.

The Life-Disconnected Mindset

When we operate from a life-disconnected state of being, we view the world through a dichotomous lens—right/wrong, appropriate/inappropriate, I/other, either/or. This perspective keeps us in the illusion of separation. Unaware of these constructs, we blame, criticize, praise, and compare. The life-disconnected mindset is expressed in the language we use, which perpetuates social conditioning. Studying the relationship between language and violence, Rosenberg wrote, "Life-alienating communication both stems from and supports hierarchical or domination societies."[2] Imprisoned in our own minds, we perceive power to lie outside ourselves. Our minds become agitated, our actions motivated by fear of punishment or desire for rewards.

A life-disconnected viewpoint stimulates us to react in keeping with conditioned patterns, seeking strategies to protect ourselves, often at the cost of many other needs. This can lead to additional life-alienating choices, as we seek to meet our needs in isolation, without the support of self-connection and community.

The Four Ds of Disconnection

Rosenberg pinpoints the tragic expression of unmet needs in the Four Ds of Disconnection: *demands, diagnosis, denial* of responsibility, and *deserve* mentality. The Four Ds are illustrated below:

- *Demand*: If you don't buy a hybrid or electric car, then I won't be traveling with you!
- *Diagnosis*: One problem with this team is that they don't take action fast enough!
- *Denial* of responsibility: The divorce is all my husband's fault. I tried to make it work!
- *Deserve* mentality: We deserve the truth about what's in our food!

Sometimes, we make *demands* when we are at our wit's end and can picture no other way to meet our needs. When we make demands from such a disempowered state, we grow increasingly resentful. Relationships deteriorate.

On the other hand, when we perceive or actually have power over a person or group of people, our demands—even if intending to educate—can stimulate fear. Goodwill plummets. Even if we do get the result we want, it is usually delivered out of the fear of punishment rather than a sincere desire for cooperation or alignment with a shared purpose.

Diagnosis in the form of judgments, labels, or criticism statically defines what people "are" and stimulates defensiveness and/or shame. Viewing the other person as the problem does not help meet anyone's needs. Such a diagnosis may alienate people from each other and negatively affect collective power. Shame, defensiveness, or possibly violence are likely to arise. Opportunities for meaningful connection, understanding, and problem-solving among people with different viewpoints and experiences may be lost.

When we *deny* our part of responsibility, we again forfeit the power we have personally, interpersonally, and socially. When we abdicate responsibility for whatever we do have power to influence, we unwittingly contribute to our own disempowerment.

The *deserve* mentality implicitly links our behavior to punishment and reward. A deserving mentality fosters a mindset of separation, categorizing some as worthy and others as unworthy. Entertaining such a mentality also objectifies others, and fuels unhealthy dynamics of submission or rebellion. Our ability to think and respond outside of these patterns is severely challenged. Fear motivates our behavior.

The Four Ds' driving force is linked to a perceived disconnection from our own personal and collective power. The Four Ds are a tragic expression of unmet needs. Yet we can find value in hearing their wake-up call, alerting us to the untapped power of what we value most.

A Mask for Protection

Connection and disconnection to life stem from the way we relate with and talk to ourselves. We all long to be seen in the beauty that we often do not fully trust is within us. We may try to present ourselves in ways that we subconsciously believe will ensure love and belonging. In doing so, we project a persona that we think is somehow better than what we believe we are. The word *persona* derives from the ancient Greek theater word for mask. We may wear our masks especially when feeling vulnerable, as they protect us from facing the pain and fear we hold inside. But others cannot see our humanity beneath this cover. Sadly, the more we wear our masks, the more we lose touch with our authenticity.

> STEPHANIE: When I first became an assessor, I did not expect to be inundated with Italian trainer candidates, yet I was the only mother-tongue Italian assessor. As prospective candidates emailed daily, a part of me unwittingly began projecting a competent persona that held everything together and knew exactly what to do.

I did not allow myself to feel any insecurity or agitation in this new position. I consistently made myself available to candidates who wanted to talk with me, even if I felt overwhelmed. "You have to be available," I thought. "That's what a good, caring assessor does. They support candidates whenever needed."

"If you say no, they won't like you!" I told myself. "You'll be criticized. You are the only Italian assessor. Who else should they turn to?"

I *had* to prove to myself that I was competent. At the same time, I doubted myself. "Will I be able to transmit the integrity of Marshall's teachings? Am I willing to ask of myself whatever I ask of a candidate?" Projecting a sense of expertise, I unconsciously tried to compensate for my fear of not being good enough.

With the loving input of some persistent fellow trainers, I realized how nervous I felt to find myself suddenly immersed in this new work. I listened to their feedback carefully and investigated my own experience. With compassion, I recognized I had projected competence in an unconscious attempt to meet my needs for belonging, trust, and love. I witnessed these self-protective mechanisms and compassionately confronted my fears.

True healing began as I tapped into deeper levels of my authentic self and shared my truth with others. I became less absorbed with my self-image and more present to myself and the candidates I love to serve. I also started to balance time for self-care with the number of candidates I took on.

Cultivating Life-Connected Awareness

Life-serving consciousness is ever present in a friendly universe. When we commit to a practice of nurturing trust in the essential goodness of life in and around us, we cultivate faith that we are all doing the best we can, given the inner and outer resources we perceive we have in the moment. Nurturing such trust can be an act of radical transformation within and without.

The process of NVC, embraced in ever-growing depth, becomes a spiritual practice that allows us to rest in a consciousness that is greater than our own. When we attune ourselves to partnership with the entire cosmos, we are not alone. The source of life pulses powerfully through us and every living being.

The more we embrace a life-affirming perspective, the more we realize that we cannot embrace life without embracing death as well, both literally and figuratively. Choosing life entails cultivating an awareness of death. When life and death are seen from a paradigm of interconnectedness rather than separation, our connection with needs starts to flow with some grace.

> The more we embrace a life-affirming perspective, the more we realize that we cannot embrace life without embracing death as well.

Death is represented in the ends of things as we know them, whether we perceive that we have had closure or not. When we refuse to accept death as part of life, we turn our backs on grief. The unwillingness or inability to grieve obstructs our personal and collective well-being. Life-connected and "death-connected" are inseparable. The practice of Nonviolent Communication aims to support our connection to life, which includes honoring death. Becoming aware of our resistance to what is unpleasant or painful, we can stretch—and then, if possible, invite some relaxation into our authentic experience. Then mourning becomes a way to engage with all life.

As a daily relational practice, this key distinction inspires us to connect with the universal energy of life underneath our habitual patterns of thought, speech, and action. Our tendency to judge ourselves, others, and life itself in terms of right or wrong has been ingrained in us. We may personally, or as a culture, judge certain needs as shameful, inappropriate, or utterly unacceptable.

Sometimes life-disconnecting conditioning interferes with our life-affirming intentions. We have internalized the pyramidal structures of domination systems we have been exposed to. To our disbelief, we may find that we unwittingly place some needs at the top of our personal unspoken hierarchy, consistently valuing them over and above other needs. In our understanding of the NVC process, there is no actual hierarchy of needs, though our lifelong experiences of pyramidal conditioning often lead us to rank our needs in such a hierarchy.

> KRISTIN AND STEPHANIE: As women, for example, we have been socialized to quickly connect with the need for contribution, while putting needs for self-care and self-expression at the bottom of our cultural ranking system. "Good women don't have personal needs; they thrive on taking care of others," has been, and at times still is, a stereotypical undercurrent of our personal and professional lives.
>
> After learning NVC, we both began to discover the ways that conditioning had shaped our internal hierarchies. Incrementally, we shifted from the habit of unconscious conditioning to making choices based on conscious connection with needs.

It takes practice and repetition to notice the movement of consciousness between the poles of life-disconnected and life-affirming. With self-compassion and perseverance, we can learn to redirect our attention toward life-serving consciousness, rather than defaulting to the conditioning associated with personal history, family upbringing, cultural beliefs, social circumstance, and systemic framework, for example.

Relating to the Thinking Mind

When shifting the paradigm we operate from, it is helpful to become familiar with our mind states and with aspects of the thinking mind. A mind trained by the domination system races to label life experiences as static dichotomies or opposites—exciting/boring, worthwhile/worthless, wonderful/horrible. When the thinking mind mediates sensory experiences by classifying and categorizing our world, this process distances us from our intimate, direct experience. Yet life is dynamic, emerging moment by moment. While we may want some relationships and experiences to be permanent to support a sense of predictability, the only predictable aspect of life is change itself.

As we grow aware of our connection to life, we learn to observe, acknowledge, and investigate the mind without identifying with its proliferation of thoughts. We attune to the energy we share with all living beings, resting in the web of interconnectedness. This quality of consciousness springs from a willingness to deconstruct much of our mental conditioning, so we can touch what deeply matters to us.

When we acknowledge our power to connect with our needs, we are free to ask ourselves, "How do I manifest this need right here, right now?" That question is born in self-responsibility. It reshapes our mental landscape completely, as we move from expecting others to meet our needs to reconnecting with the intrinsic quality of the needs we care about. Our mindset shifts from grievance to a more life-serving orientation. From there, we can compassionately and courageously touch our vulnerability. As we relax into the need, we discover actions that help us experience more of what deeply matters to us.

Touching Our Wholeness

When we relate to our needs in life-serving ways, our core wounds slowly come to light, providing us with opportunities for healing. This revelation invites integration among different parts of ourselves and empowers us to reconnect with a deeper sense of who we are.

We all have within us the power to "meet"—encounter, acknowledge, and welcome—needs in this way. Opening our hearts and minds allows us to welcome strategies that embrace our own and others' needs, holding an awareness of both short- and long-term perspectives. We embrace the joy of giving and receiving. This flow then ripples outward to contribute to a collective consciousness that aims at serving a wider net of life. Moved to serve others, we do so in the spirit of interdependence, knowing that beyond our personal experience of needs—mine and yours—this energy is universal.

An Open Heart for Present and Future

Understanding this key distinction is helpful in finding compassion for ourselves and others, too. Rosenberg reminds us that all life-alienating behavior is a tragic expression of unmet needs. We are affected in varying degrees by conditioning and by collective and individual experiences of trauma, whether it is childhood trauma linked to patriarchy,[3] capitalism, communism, or climate collapse, to name a few. Remembering that life-alienating behaviors are "tragic expressions of unmet needs" can help us recognize the humanity in ourselves and others instead of believing the labels or judgments we might have. We can then cultivate a life-giving stance in the face of what we perceive as life-alienating choices.

The behavior of children and adults with trauma histories or neurodiversity may be perceived as "life-alienating." For example, children who are fostered or adopted often take things that do not belong to them without permission. This is usually labeled as "stealing." Typically, the behavior is an attempt to soothe the internal stress linked to underlying unmet needs for safety, security, and belonging. Understanding the behaviors that link to these needs empowers caregivers to approach children with compassion, inviting them to seek regulation in safe relationships. Helping youth to find behaviors that meet their needs with consideration of other people's needs, also empowers them and supports the community at large.

A Systemic Lens on This Key Differentiation

Exploring what is labeled as "stealing" invites us to consider what is socially acceptable and what is judged unacceptable. The human constructs of acceptable/unacceptable, disconnected from needs, are life-dissociating. When tensions and violence escalated in the United States between the Native Americans and colonial settlers, two peace treaties, the Fort Laramie Treaties of 1851 and 1868, were signed between the United States Government and the Oceti Sakowin (a.k.a. Sioux) Nation. Nonetheless, the US government unilaterally annexed native land protected under those treaties in 1877. In 1980, the Supreme Court ruled in the *United States v. Sioux Nation of Indians* case that the US had illegally appropriated the Black Hills. This, too, could be seen as "stealing." The US then offered the Oceti Sakowin over 100 million dollars, which they did not accept, maintaining the land had not been for sale. The Black Hills have yet to be returned to the Oceti Sakowin Nation. Their people have not accessed ancestral lands for the sustenance of life for generations.

Grounding our collective response in care for humanity may move us toward a more equitable distribution of resources as we repair the harm done by European colonialism.

The more we integrate the practice of NVC, the more we are encouraged to listen for needs rather than talking. Both are essential. Yet, to express ourselves effectively, we are called to observe our inner dialogue. That inner pause empowers us to choose words that reflect a life-connected stance.

By bringing our attention to the mind's predisposition to protect itself with the armor of conditioning, we can turn a compassionate eye on ourselves as well as the people around us when we hear words we find life-alienating. This key distinction invites us to find the quality of the need hidden like a pearl within a shell clamped tightly shut. Trusting that vital needs are there, we can avoid the temptation of shutting down ourselves. Instead, we can remain open to connecting with the life energy of wholeness and beauty in ourselves, others, and the world.

SUMMARY

- This key distinction helps us to relate with understanding to our thinking mind. Differentiating between life-connected and life-disconnected mindsets, we deepen our experience of needs and find clarity and compassion for ourselves and others.

- Connecting to the wholeness of needs, we can touch the power of what we deeply value, even if not manifested currently in our outer experience, and live from that integrity.

- Cultivating such intentional awareness empowers us to make mindful choices moment by moment, in our relationships with ourselves and all life.

- Grounding ourselves in a collective life-giving consciousness moves us toward a more equitable distribution of resources.

WALKING THE TALK:
A LIFE EXAMPLE FROM NEW ZEALAND

BY FILIPA HOPE, CNVC TRAINER

Māori are the First People of Aotearoa (New Zealand). As in the cases of most "first" people, colonization has stripped them of lands and rejected their culture. One impact has been a huge decrease in the number of te reo Māori—Māori language—speakers. Tragically, I, like most descendants of colonizers, have been conditioned to believe there is no value or relevance for the Māori language in the English-dominated world where "getting ahead" is the primary goal and measure of worth.

Last year during a workshop, I struggled to correctly pronounce, yet again, a Māori participant's name. I felt embarrassed, a disconnection to the flow of life within me. I realized that the thinking I'd been socialized to had affected my ability to live in alignment with my needs in the moment.

After the workshop, a Māori friend and mentor I am blessed to know offered her support to show me practices to build my pronunciation. She compassionately pointed out that free te reo Māori classes were available in my area. Through her kindness and wisdom, I was able to see through the veil of my conditioning what it meant to her that I was willing to try to learn. I felt so grateful to discover that I valued learning te reo Māori . . . so as to honor my own needs! Out of my experience of life-disconnection grew a life-connectedness within me that was reflected in my relationship with my dear friend.

I finally realized I had never taken the time to understand what the Māori language was for Māori—that it is an essential expression of their culture and their identity as a people. I had never questioned my belief that I was "walking my talk" because I did things like advocate for te reo Māori to be taught in school. I celebrated that my daughters had been taught in school proper pronunciation, some of the language, and valuing Māori culture. And yet, when I struggled to pronounce the Māori participant's name, I saw that my prior choice not to learn the language myself did not reflect at all what I valued.

How much I regretted that I had never really listened to *why* te reo Māori was important—from a Māori perspective. I connected with a deep longing to understand what they valued, and this longing opened my heart in a life-connected way. I imagined that learning more about the Māori language and perspective would support my sense of inter-connectedness and the valuing of something greater than myself.

I am committed to challenging my conditioning, and it has been heartbreaking and humbling to discover how dismissive I had been of the needs of the Māori people. I take a weekly night class to learn te reo Māori. It fills my needs to live in integrity, contribute to connection, and value the universality of needs as they live in all people, including me.

PRACTICE

Growing Awareness of Choice

Awareness is an inherent capacity that supports us in discerning when we operate from a life-connecting mind frame and when from life-disconnecting habitual conditioning. The goal of this practice is to cultivate choice and the ability to redirect attention when it drifts from the chosen object of focus, in this case physical sensations, without identifying with either. This is a meditation practice followed by questions for reflection.

Find a comfortable spot to sit on the ground, in a chair, or in some other position in which you can be both relaxed and alert. We invite you to read through the practice once before beginning. Then, in meditation, you can allow space between sentences to connect with your experience, moment by moment, with curiosity. You might also record yourself reading this practice slowly aloud so you can play back the meditation with eyes closed.

We imagine that you might spend ten to fifteen minutes on this practice, longer if you wish.

Taking the time you need to connect with whatever is present in the body-mind system, acknowledge any thoughts about the past, such as memories, and thoughts about the future, such as planning, that may be present. Gently invite the mind, just for now, to let go of these thoughts, and focus on the body. Notice the body's physical position, the touchpoints between certain body parts and surfaces that support its posture, and slowly find the part of yourself that is observing the body from the inside out.

Sensing how it feels to inhabit this body, open awareness to any physical sensations such as heat or coolness, tingling or numbness, tension or a sense of relaxation. What is there to notice? Invite awareness to witness these sensations without forcing or judging anything.

When thinking arises, acknowledge it with care, then bring the mind back to physical sensations. What are you experiencing? Are those sensations pleasant? Unpleasant? Neither?

Sinking into the awareness of comfort and discomfort, observe your experience without judging it. You may be aware of the movements that breathing produces in the body, the chest expanding and contracting, the abdomen inflating with each in-breath and deflating with each out-breath. You may be aware of the heart beating. You may or may not experience energy glowing, pulsating, or otherwise making its presence known in your body. Whatever you experience in this moment is fine.

Whenever you notice the mind moving away from body sensations and thinking instead, say to yourself, "This, too, is a moment of mindfulness." Neither scolding nor identifying with the thought, gently and firmly redirect the mind to physical sensations again. This is an intentional shift of awareness; you are empowering yourself to direct your attention rather than being directed by the thinking mind.

REFLECTION

~ What was your experience with this practice? Did you enjoy it?

~ What did you notice whenever you touched thoughts? What were some of the physical sensations that stood out for you?

~ How could the skill of consciously choosing where to place awareness support well-being and a deeper connection to life?

2

VALUE JUDGMENTS AND
MORALISTIC JUDGMENTS

There is nothing either good or bad,
but thinking makes it so.

—SHAKESPEARE

B ringing awareness to our human tendency to judge and evaluate, Rosenberg calls attention to the key distinction between moralistic judgments and value judgments. From that awareness, a choice arises: We can either appraise a situation based on right/wrong thinking, moralistic judgment, or we can choose to make a value judgment, grounding our assessment in a recognition of human needs. When we channel our energy into a value judgment, we anchor ourselves in what really matters to us. Then we are more likely to remain open to the variety of ways in which these needs could be satisfied.

Moralistic Judgments

For a variety of reasons ranging from evolutionary purposes to internalized conditioning, we automatically assess what we come in contact with as pleasant or unpleasant, an opportunity or a threat. After that initial appraisal, we typically approach what we like and distance ourselves from what we do not like, whether it is another person, an experience, or even some part of ourselves. As most of us are socialized into cultures based on right/wrong thinking, we habitually label what is pleasant as "good" or "right" and what is unpleasant as "bad" or "wrong," thus forming moralistic judgments.

Judging Ourselves, Judging Others

Rosenberg suggests that a moralistic judgment is a tragic, life-alienating expression because it increases our sense of separation, elicits defensiveness in the person whose behavior is concerning us, and creates self-loathing if we are judging ourselves.

> KRISTIN: In my twenties, my father had a heart attack. While he recovered in his hospital bed, I told him angrily that I wasn't surprised, because smoking and drinking so much was terrible for his health! He became defensive and some tension arose between us. Years later, he found himself saying the same things to his father in a similar circumstance. Then my dad told me that he understood that my response to his heart attack stemmed from fear and care, which totally resonated with me.

A moralistic judgment is a fixed and rigid evaluation based on a dichotomized worldview. The person or the action is often perceived as always or never being a certain way. If we identify with and believe our thoughts as if they were fact, our ability to see the bigger picture beyond that particular interaction is compromised.

Moralistic judgments dehumanize the person judging as much as they dehumanize the person being judged. In fact, the very process of judging reinforces the right/wrong mentality that is then unconsciously and indiscriminately applied to oneself. In other words, by practicing judgment of others, we implicitly reinforce that very concept of good/bad. Accordingly, we will view ourselves through that same lens. The converse is also true; the more we judge ourselves, the more we judge others. Even viewing moralistic judgments as wrong and value judgments as right will paradoxically reinforce that dichotomous way of thinking!

The lens is an apt metaphor to describe how our observations may be affected by the subconscious moralistic conditioning that colors much of what we see. Over the course of our lifetime, this lens is molded by underlying conceptual templates—beliefs, operating assumptions, and mindsets—through which we perceive ourselves, others, and the world. Those templates, drawn from past experiences, act as filters. When we gaze at the world through our lens, the templates are sometimes activated, and we operate from a state of identification with those filters.

We often inadvertently judge in others what we struggle to see or accept in ourselves. When we catch ourselves doing this, we can witness the proliferation of moralistic judgments without believing them. There is a universal human need enshrined in every moralistic judgment. When we align ourselves with that essence of life, we may experience greater understanding, acceptance, and healing.

When something occurs that we do not like, we might make moralistic judgments as a self-protective measure. By labeling something that has occurred as fun or boring rather than connecting with our emotional response and the needs stirred in us, we disconnect from our personal experience. Instead, we channel a burst of energy, equal to the forcefulness of our resistance to pain, toward more judgments and reactive behaviors. While this burst of energy may feel empowering in the moment, it magnifies the challenge of reconnecting with ourselves and others. The energy of separation and punishment often embedded in a judgment also prevents us from attending to our pain.

Equally tragic, the moralistic judgments we speak to our children often become internalized by them as core beliefs. These beliefs are pervasive patterns of thinking, usually subconscious, static, and overgeneralized about ourselves, others, and the world that can accompany us for a lifetime. Those unrecognized and unexamined beliefs strongly affect our inner monologues. Peggy O'Mara, a parent educator, once said, "The way we talk to our children becomes their inner voice."[1] As adults, we can usually trace our own limiting beliefs—fears about being unlovable, unworthy, or not belonging—to some message we internalized while young. It is ironic that limitations are planted in us in this way. Parents often have the best intentions when they speak from a place of moralistic judgment.

> The moralistic judgments we speak to our children often are internalized by them as core beliefs.

Disguising Moralistic Judgments as NVC Practice

Judgments can point to cherished values of ours, can even be expressed in terms of human needs, and still come from a right/wrong mindset.

STEPHANIE: When I heard about migrant children being detained and caged in freezing facilities at the United States border with Mexico, I expressed myself using the language of NVC, yet my mind still entertained strong moralistic judgments against the administration. Watching the news, I said to my husband, "When I see those kids, sometimes just eighteen months old, caged, I feel outraged. I so value protection of human life, especially our little ones whose brains are particularly vulnerable to trauma! I will write to pressure elected officials to stop this!" I punctuated that request of myself by banging my fist on the couch. Righteously, I held onto the thought that this is a humanitarian crisis and this is criminal!

No doubt my facial expressions, tone of voice, and the intensity of my gestures transmitted my moralistic mindset. My husband put his arms around my shoulders. That alerted me that he was picking up on my whole-body communication much faster than any of the words I had used. That was my wake-up call. I paused and asked myself, "What is my state of mind right now?" I recognized that when overwhelmed with distress and grief, my mind is more likely to revert to right/wrong thinking. I took a few deep, cleansing breaths and realigned myself with my value for protecting life. I reconnected with my deep longing to value the lives of those I was perceiving as "enemies." I still took action, yet from a very different energy from that which arose in me first. And thankfully, my actions stemming from a value judgment did not come at a cost to my integrity.

The ability to track one's own state of mind, while remaining open to feedback, is essential in shifting from moralistic judgments to value judgments. Part of our inner work lies in transforming moralistic judgments into universal needs to the best of our abilities, before we express ourselves. If we are unable to do so, then we might aim to modestly recognize this and attend to the necessary repair work.

Value Judgments

As we cultivate our ability to shift from moralistic judgments to value judgments, we unearth our core perceptions, beliefs, and evaluations. We can start by entertaining the humbling idea that our appraisals may not be accurate (i.e., we may not have all the information). Observing our own thoughts, we can lessen our identification with our judgments and attachment to our views. With curiosity we can ask what we are telling ourselves. This brings us back to our own healing work. The more we are willing to see and embrace the pain we experience, the more we empower ourselves to also see and embrace the pain of others rather than judging them.

KRISTIN: I used to be a birth doula. I found that, instead of engaging in moralistic judgments, I could be more effective and stay fully present by feeling my emotions and honoring my needs with a value judgment.

When I caught myself beginning to think, "That obstetrician is pushing this mother to induce labor, and that's a terrible thing!" I paused to check in with myself. I noticed that I'd felt worried and confused when I heard the obstetrician recommending induction each of the three times she'd come by, after only five hours of labor. I realized—this is my value judgment—how important the health and well-being of the mother and baby were to me. Guessing these were values the obstetrician shared, I wanted to better understand her recommendations.

Transforming Our Thinking

Value judgments come from an awareness of the human needs that are alive in us. We can attune to these internal motivators when we catch ourselves responding automatically with a moralistic judgment. Instead of judging ourselves, we can choose to see our moralistic judgment as a wake-up call. Transforming our thinking, we can engage with what we value in order to remain connected with the flow of life in ourselves and others.

Our relationship to value judgments is susceptible to systemic conditioning.

How we relate to value judgments is still susceptible to systemic conditioning. This is inescapable—we assess and relate to our needs with a conditioned mind. The worldview we have been socialized into will affect how we relate to our values, such as freedom, autonomy, security, and belonging. Indigenous cultures generally have a worldview more centered on honoring all life, while Western societies emphasize a worldview that separates and prioritizes humans (and men in particular) above all other forms of life. For example, freedom in the Western world is understood as personal freedom: people are seen as operating separately and independently. In Indigenous societies, freedom is understood as collective, rooted in the interdependence of all life-forms. The Western mind translates autonomy related to children as the ability to stay by oneself or sleep alone, for example. By contrast, in most Indigenous cultures, autonomy is understood to be collective, as it revolves around the values and interests of the community.[2] Yet even these societies have not been spared from patriarchal and misogynous narratives.[3]

Moralistic judgments spawn and exhaust energy systemically in almost every arena. Let's take, for example, the judgments around the climate crisis. Environmental activists may see those working in the fossil fuel industries as ruining the planet—as "evildoers who don't care about Earth." Those working in the petroleum industry are angry at activists for being "dangerous and ill-informed," presuming they are out to disrupt jobs and the economy. These moralistic judgments on both sides breed an ever-deepening polarization.

In order to transform these moralistic judgments into value judgments, we look to the core needs beneath them. Activists valuing the diversity and vitality of life may see the work of those in the fossil fuel industry as "shortsighted" because research shows that countless species are put at risk by temperatures rising worldwide. The intensity of their judgment is proportional to the concern they feel for all life and their care for the individual and collective impacts on living creatures. People working in the fuel industry respond with equal concern. Many of them are concerned that the strategies proposed by the environmental movement would result in their own loss of work, that of people whose jobs rely on their industries, and in a decline in the standard of living overall.

Additionally, they may worry that dependence on other countries for fuel could interfere with meeting basic needs in the future. They might value self-reliance as a nation, grounded in a concern for safety and sustainability. Worried for the sustainability of their families and communities, the people in this industry fervently value life and want to be realistic about what is possible. This value of life is at the core of moralistic judgments on both sides, yet their chosen strategies to meet this need differ.

Imagine the ways we could unleash collaborative problem-solving if we uncoupled needs from strategies. That oppositional energy, once liberated, could be redirected toward solutions to the problem itself.

When we ground ourselves in the needs beneath moralistic judgments, fear starts to dissipate. As we focus on what we do want rather than what we do not, inner clarity begins to emerge. Acceptance and partnership naturally arise.

Cultivating Needs Awareness

Value-based judgments serve life because they acknowledge that the same life energy dwells in all of us. Value judgments honor the mind's capacity to bring order to experience. Rather than moralistically judging an experience good or bad, we are invited to appraise an experience by connecting with what we value. When we steer the mind in the direction of value judgments, we feel empowered to make requests of ourselves and/or others to nourish and expand our awareness of these qualities of life. We savor a deeper coherence between our needs and our actions. Value judgments are more likely to give rise to flexibility. They help us see more possible strategies that respond to the needs of all parties.

A value judgment is still a form of appraisal. We judge through the lens of universal needs while cultivating curiosity, rather than attachment to the way those needs may be met. Because they emerge from within us, value judgments are intrinsic and threaten any external establishment that seeks to impose order. In this regard, value judgments are a point of leverage for social change.

Understanding the key distinction between moralistic and value judgments empowers us to gain more self-awareness and cultivate compassion. We can train our minds to discern moralistic judgments from value judgments. Investigating with curiosity what really matters to us, we can slowly let go of our judgmental thoughts. This journey of self-awareness and the ability to focus our attention on needs are at the foundation of a life-giving consciousness.

SUMMARY

↭ This key supports us in realizing that we have the power to choose how we assess our experiences.

↭ We can intentionally explore our moralistic judgments based on right-and-wrong thinking and transform them into value judgments that acknowledge the needs we experience in the moment.

↭ Acknowledging that our appraisal may not be accurate, we can then carefully look at what we are telling ourselves.

↭ Connected to our value judgments, we stay open to the variety of ways in which they can be satisfied.

WALKING THE TALK:
A LIFE EXAMPLE FROM THE UNITED STATES

BY SEDA JANE COLLIER, KRISTIN COLLIER'S PARENTING PARTNER

My sister was in a serious car accident when her youngest son was about twelve years old. She spent three months in a coma, then seven years in a nursing home. My nephew struggled in those years, as extended family sought unsuccessfully to support him. At a crucial moment, a conservative, evangelical Christian family, "the Robinsons," agreed to foster my nephew. They took him in, and he adopted their religion, flourishing for the first time in years.

At the same time, my family weathered its own crisis. A year after my sister's car wreck, I came out as transgender. As my transition commenced, a family we held near and dear, also evangelical Christians, rejected me and my family. Transgender people became a hot topic then, and the news was filled with conservative Christians condemning us. I felt deeply hurt and found this rejection unfair. I left the faith myself for a short time. Although I'd started learning NVC, I judged these Christians as hypocritical and self-righteous.

Then my sister died. For the first time since transition, I returned to the rural Wyoming town where I'd been raised. I knew the Robinsons would be at my sister's funeral. Although I had only met them briefly once, I'd included them in my moralistic judgment against evangelical Christians. I suspected that their judgments of transgender people would be as deeply felt as mine of their faith.

Remembering what I'd learned in my practice of NVC, I let my anger in and found the needs underneath. I wanted to be seen as fully human, to experience compassion. And I wanted to be safe—not so much from the Robinsons as from people who sought to violently change the world to align with their perception of "God's plan." I got empathy from Kristin and held myself with care, treasuring my value judgments for safety, compassion, and being seen.

I realized I wasn't feeling compassion for the Robinsons. I then guessed they wanted the same love and consideration that I did. My heart opened in appreciation for them. I valued the care they had shown my nephew, which had anchored him emotionally and given him a fresh start. I decided to try to connect with them.

After the service, I approached the Robinsons and introduced myself. I saw their shoulders stiffen and they looked at each other, then down at the floor. This was as new to them as it was to me, and I guessed they worried about how to receive or understand me. I thanked them for loving my nephew. I expressed my gratitude, deeply honoring them, then watched as they relaxed. We had a short, pleasant conversation. I treasured them for their kindness and the good they did for my family. The moralistic judgments I held against them fell away, never to return.

PRACTICE

Welcoming Judgments, Befriending the Mind

We have daily opportunities to transform our moralistic judgments to value judgments. This practice is designed to offer a space in which to welcome moralistic judgments in order to embrace the intrinsic needs embedded within. This is a practice of meditative self-reflection. We invite you to find a quiet space in which to sit or find a position where you can be both relaxed and alert. We imagine this self-inquiry could last for fifteen to thirty minutes.

Begin by considering an event where you found yourself stimulated.

When a moralistic judgment comes to your attention through thoughts or perhaps through physical sensations in your body or breath, instead of resisting the judgment, invite a pause. Take a few deep breaths and then gently acknowledge that it is just a moralistic judgment.

Breathing into the judgment and your feelings about it, you might say: "I am more than my thinking. I can witness this judgment without getting lost in it or spinning a story around it."

Holding yourself compassionately, you may inquire, "What value is underneath this judgment?" Make space for discovering the need that wants acknowledgment. When you find it, breathe into it. Connecting with how precious this value is to you, you may experience yourself "meeting" that need, as one would meet a friend. You are now welcoming that quality of life, free from the moralistic judgments that spurred you to find it.

Experiencing this vital energy, stay with it for as long as you feel moved to; savor in your body-mind system the freedom from moralistic judgment. Is there a sense of openness? Of satisfaction? Of lightness?

Mentally return to the situation in which the moralistic judgment arose. Do you notice a shift within yourself? Do you have a request of yourself or someone else related to the need you discovered beneath the judgment?

Take a moment to thank yourself for engaging in this practice.

3

INTERDEPENDENCE AND DEPENDENCE/INDEPENDENCE

"To be" is always to "inter-be."

—THÍCH NHẤT HẠNH

The key distinction between interdependence and the dichotomy of dependence/independence directs our attention toward how we relate to life. This key offers us the opportunity to explore and apply a viewpoint that differs from mainstream Western culture. Our awareness of interconnection distinctly shapes the quality of our life on intrapersonal, relational, community, and societal levels. The perceptions and feelings we have about ourselves and others stem from our perspective on connection. As we integrate the spirit of interconnectedness that is essential to partnership, we find that this is a master key to many of the key differentiations.

We are presented here with two modes of relationship. The polarized forces of dependence/independence stem from the same unconscious paradigm of separation in which humans are not seen as inherently connected. This mode is rife with either/or thinking, a core symptom of the paradigm of separation. We either rely solely on other people or systems to meet our needs, with the understanding that they have access to resources that we do not, or we rely only on ourselves, perceiving ourselves as completely self-sufficient. Since Western conditioning directs us to believe that self-sufficiency leads to better chances of survival,[1] independence is upheld as the goal. In this viewpoint, dependence is associated with weakness and powerlessness.

> Our lives are inextricably intertwined with the lives of others. Life is sustained through interdependent relationships.

By contrast, nurturing an awareness that the same "Beloved Divine Energy"[2] moves through us all can awaken us to conscious interdependence. As this awareness grows, we recognize that we need others to meet our needs on a larger scale. Our lives are inextricably intertwined with the lives of others. Life is sustained through interdependent relationships.

Even trees connect with neighboring trees and share information through underground networks of fungi, according to the discovery of forest ecologist Suzanne Simard. In that way trees share information and nutrients supporting the health of the entire forest.[3] And unlike patriarchal systems, these trees create networks through which they pass nutrients to weaker trees to sustain them.

Awakening to the interconnectedness of life influences the choices we make. Growing our capacity for awareness, we make choices that embrace personal and communal needs. We empower ourselves to share power with others. Cultivating our commitment to conscious interdependence, we contribute to a world consciousness where everyone's needs matter.

Dependence and Independence

Dependence and independence are really flip sides of the same coin. Both, when accepted indiscriminately, can reflect a fear-driven, often shame-based approach. Whether we see ourselves as utterly dependent or independent, we likely feel alienated from ourselves, others, and from life itself.

When we see ourselves as dependent, the first connection that we may forego is with ourselves, shifting us into deeper powerlessness. We might experience no sense of agency and believe that our needs can be met by external forces alone. We may see ourselves and our communities as being incapable of meeting our needs.

For example, our capacity to connect with a sense of peace is born of early interactions that nourished inner peace. While the external experience of peace with others is essential to well-being, we can experience peace within, with ourselves, and with others.

When we see ourselves as completely dependent, we may also unwittingly "give in" or "give up" on many of our own needs, in hopes that some of our foundational needs, such as love and belonging, will be met. Likely acting from needs we are not conscious of, we might seek approval, a learned survival strategy to ensure belonging. In fact, we might not feel connected with that need nor see other ways it could be fully experienced.

On a larger scale, the "giving in" and "giving up" can emerge vis-à-vis established domination systems, such as those in health care, education, and justice. For example, there is enough food produced to feed everyone on the planet. Yet as many as 811 million people go to bed hungry each night.[4] We may "give in" or "give up" in the face of political and economic systems that yield such results. Perceiving ourselves as powerless, we may think we are unable to effect change. When survival is at stake, our peripheral vision dims. If we view ourselves as utterly dependent on a person or system holding the keys to the access of resources we need to survive, then we are more likely to submit toward that entity. Our connection to our personal power is severed.

Or, we might flip to the other side of the coin, in search of independence. Defined as self-sufficiency, independence is often confused with autonomy or freedom. In pursuit of independence, we typically forego our connection with others and aim for self-sufficiency. The mutuality of giving and receiving within the flow of life goes unrecognized in this worldview.[5]

Our core beliefs may have been shaped by the dominant paradigm that touts messages geared toward independence—"it's a jungle out there," and "every man for himself!" Notice that the gender stereotype embedded in these affirmations emphasizes that men, especially, are expected to not rely on others. Such "independence" is a heavy weight for many male-identified people and can create frustration to those who seek partnership with them.

All social structures determine allocation and access to resources. In the words of Miki Kashtan, "Every form of social organization includes in it implicit (or explicit) decisions about whose needs are prioritized, which needs are recognized and valued, and how resources are allocated towards meeting such needs."[6] One effective way to begin deconstructing domination systems is to look inward. Shedding light on deep-seated, internalized conditioning, we may better see how our actions contribute to the reinforcement of a paradigm of separation, scarcity, and choice-lessness. Beginning with such honest self-appraisal, we expand our capacity to assess these social structures as a whole.

Interdependence

All living beings are interconnected and play a variety of roles within the web of life, whether we are aware of it or not. The heart of the practice of NVC rests in faith that the same life force flows within every living being. Planetary scientist and stardust expert Ashley King confirms: "It is totally 100% true: nearly all the elements in the human body were made in a star and many have come through several supernovas."[7] This key differentiation invites us to cultivate a felt sense of the fundamental oneness of the whole cosmos and all its inhabitants.

Life is powerful. Every being is bestowed with personal power. There are no innate hierarchies that make us superior or inferior to one another, although

The heart of the practice of NVC rests in faith that the same life force flows within every living being.

we play different roles in this web of life. All phenomena, from weather to coral reefs, from world hunger to racism, are interdependent. They arise from countless causes and conditions and have a wide range of impacts on one another. Our so-called individual successes, too, are interdependent. As writer Malcolm Gladwell reminds us, these accomplishments are not of our own making; they are rather "a product of the world in which [we] grew up."[8] Influential factors may become visible only over time, and we cannot always trace their origins. "The butterfly effect" is the idea that the flutter of a butterfly's wings can touch patterns of weather across the planet. Small changes in some of the causes or conditions of countless systems can come together to create powerful results.

When conscious of interdependence, we touch a shared experience of intrinsic belonging. Our perceptions of scarcity, separation, and choicelessness are not inherent qualities of our being. They arise from the systemic environment, as well as our individual unhealed wounds. It is both an opportunity and responsibility to serve and enrich one another. When we acknowledge our intrinsic interconnectedness, we are moved to sharing resources. This connectedness is distorted when resources are withheld.

There are many intricate causes and conditions that uphold global power structures and dynamics and often factually limit access to resources for some.[9] On a personal level we may have a paralyzing belief that we are separate and cannot change the conditions that make us dependent on certain people or systems. Internalized powerlessness linked to systemic oppression can affect us to such a degree that we believe ourselves to be utterly dependent. This viewpoint may be based on concrete personal and systemic experiences. At the same time, we may have some power to transform, at least in part, this internalized power-lessness so as to reconnect to a sense of choice and agency. The impacts of such transformation may ripple out into wider society as collective power harnessed toward social change. When we turn our attention to the internal and external resources we do have, we are free to discover possibilities that could satisfy more needs. Awareness of our personal and collective power, even in the midst of structural disempowerment, threatens systems of domination. Any shift from scarcity, separation, and powerlessness toward trust in the flow of life, togetherness, and choice can help.

Recognizing Interdependence on a Larger Scale

No matter how small at first, our collective endeavors build momentum. In Nigeria, for example, between 1892 and 1960, Igbo women activists wrote multiple petitions to British authorities articulating their collective social and economic needs. This disenfranchised group took a stand and actively engaged male-dominated colonial institutions. These women succeeded in influencing the shaping of public policies within the empire.[10]

Power imbalances are ubiquitous. What we do with that reality is up to us. Sharing and creativity play critical roles in gathering resources to support oppressed groups. In 1965, Cesar Chavez and the National Farm Workers Association agreed to support Filipino American grape workers and encouraged a massive boycott, the Delano Grape Strike. While Filipino and Latino workers walked three hundred miles in nonviolent protest, churches and communities across the nation held masses and stopped buying grapes. This labor dispute effectively migrated from the fields to the cities.

Some workers wished to forcefully break ranks in the final years of this discord. Chavez then turned the focus of union efforts from heated conflict to the valuing of human life. In a personal fast that brought nationwide attention and political support, Chavez redirected all attention to his own willingness to suffer for the lives of many. Countless others felt moved to raise their voices in support and were heard. In 1970 the first union contracts with table grape growers were signed, protecting workers and providing benefits and better pay.[11] This is an example of structural power being counterposed by the collective power of noncooperation.

In other words, wherever there is unequal access to resources, we can widen our view with the lens of interdependence. With an eye toward communal resources, we expand our capacity to see possibilities and bring access and opportunity where before there were none. Dignity and social change toward an equitable and fair distribution of resources can then emerge from nonviolence.

When people whose agency, capacity to influence, and access to resources have been historically diminished step into personal and communal empowerment, there will likely be a dangerous backlash. In Latin America for example, one in every three women has experienced physical or sexual abuse at some point in her life.[12] Women who denounce this, such as Mazatec Indigenous leader Elisa Zepeda Lagunas, face harassment, threats, and even death.[13]

Herein lies a conundrum: How do we move toward interdependence in a way that protects those who have had their agency restricted? With the working understanding of interconnection outlined in this chapter, we posit that the empowerment of the oppressed relies on the awakening of groups with greater power. That power may be structural, political, economic, or social. In the United Nations global solidarity movement for gender equality, for example, strategies like the "#YearOfMaleAllyship Campaign" seek to engage men internationally in sharing stories about why equality matters to them.[14] A shift in mindset happens more quickly when allies work within their communities to embrace new paradigms.

Babies: Dependent or Interdependent?

Our perceptions of dependence and interdependence shape our lives from the time we are born. As we enter the world, we *are* vulnerable and dependent. Our survival is based on our caregivers' ability to meet our biological as well as our psycho-emotional and spiritual needs. As we age and are more actively socialized in the dominant paradigm, we learn to assign hierarchies and create dichotomies to describe our human connections.

In mainstream Western culture, we perceive the "dependence" of babies as powerlessness based on the dependent/independent dichotomy. As biologist and philosopher Humberto Maturana writes, "A baby is born in the operational trust that there is a world ready to satisfy in love and care all that he or she may require for his or her living, and is therefore not helpless."[15] Yet our perception of babies as helpless and powerless significantly impacts the relationships we have with ourselves and our young.

In fact, the interrelatedness between baby and parent is more complex than we may initially appreciate. The mutual interaction starts with conception. A number of changes occur in the expecting parent at neurobiological, hormonal, and psychological levels. Perinatal shifts in brain structure and function take place in order to facilitate successful caretaking.

Smiling, for example, is a complex, intimate communication within the parent/infant dyad. Science has investigated the neurophysiological "heart-opening" effects of a baby's smile on the caregiver. When we see our baby smile, the brain circuitry involved with pleasure becomes particularly active, maximizing survival of the baby and our species. As professor of neuroscience and author Lise Eliot explains, the natural turn-taking between mother and infant is an emotional exchange based on mirroring. It "helps the baby develop awareness of his own movements and expressions."[16] If the smile between a baby and caregiver is seen through the lens of interdependence, rather than dependence/independence, we can fully appreciate that both respond to each other, while sharing a neurochemical cascade of after-effects. When inter-being is fully experienced, "giver" and "receiver" are one and the same.

> **When inter-being is fully experienced, "giver" and "receiver" are one and the same.**

As with all binary thinking, one dichotomy is tied to another. Dependence/independence quickly associates with good/bad, a comparison which impacts the quality of relationship between a baby and its caregivers and the way we raise our children. A "good" baby in mainstream Western culture is one who does not cry much. Crying may be seen as a way in which babies "manipulate" their caregivers.

Our goal as parents in the dependent/independent mode is to teach our babies to calm themselves in order to become more independent, so we may let them cry without response from us. Parents may withhold the resources of comfort or food with the intention to teach the baby to self-soothe. However, from a neurobiological perspective, the baby's brain has not yet developed the structures that support self-soothing and will not until about age three.

As parents, we are also conditioned to prioritize the needs of adults over the needs of children. This power dynamic is typical in a system where children are raised in isolated nuclear families rather than communities.

By contrast, Indigenous societies with a precolonial, precapitalist worldview are geared toward interdependence. In those communities, a baby's cry is addressed quickly as a communication of needs, whether for nourishment, comfort, or something else. These societies are built around communities that share responsibility, ensuring many resources are available, enabling a higher level of responsiveness. This mode of parenting has informed a style many have come to know in the Western world as Attachment Parenting, a term coined by American pediatrician William Sears. In this model, the baby depends on the parent to meet basic survival and thriving needs, yet the relationship is valued in its mutuality. In fact, according to neuroscience, self-regulation—the ability to regulate one's own emotions—is learned by experiencing and registering in the body how regulation feels. That happens every time the parent soothes the baby. The caregiver and child's core relationship references constant interactions of mutual interdependent care rather than a power dynamic based on a perceived hierarchy of dependence/independence.

According to psychologist Howard Bath, co-regulation, the soothing presence of another in times of distress, can take many forms, typically involving "warmth, a soothing tone of voice, communication that acknowledges the . . . person's distress, supportive silence, and an invitation to reflective problem-solving."[17] We experience the need to give and receive such soothing throughout our lives. Hence, our capacity for *inner* peace is born from childhood interactions that nourished a sense of peace within us.

Growing Awareness

When we have the intention to consider everyone's needs with care, we grow an awareness of interconnection. While we are never certain about what is the highest good for anyone, ourselves included, every decision we make implicitly or explicitly affects life. The voice of another person may support us in seeing a fuller picture as together we find a path toward communal wisdom.

When we acknowledge that we are inherently interconnected, it becomes easier to stay in touch with our truth while staying open to the truth of another. Nothing can separate us from the web of life. Leaning into this awareness, we are less likely to objectify others by seeing them as strategies to meet our needs or as obstacles to satisfying them. And we are more likely to sense a mutuality between us, from the core of our being. In the words of Martin Buber,[18] we shift from the conditioned "I-I, I-It, It-It, We-We, and Us-Them" consciousness where the "other" is an object, to the "I-Thou" consciousness where "the other" is a mystery that calls us to open our hearts and recognize mutuality from the core of our being. From this state, which Zen monk and author Thích Nhất Hạnh calls "inter-being,"[19] we may find compassion for both ourselves and others.

As our awareness of inter-being grows, we might pause and consider how all external resources come from the earth—the wood our houses are built with, the fruit we eat, and the clothing we wear, to name a few. Or we might look at how our perspective on interdependence informs how we live. Money, for example, represents energy. Our awareness of the social impact of how we spend money is part of interrelationship.

When we purchase clothing, are we most concerned with how it looks, or whether it was made in a factory whose labor practices are humane? If we have the economic privilege to invest in the stock market, will we consider buying stocks in socially responsible funds even if returns might be lower?

While the relationship we have with our perceived or de facto privileges is extremely complex,[20] one factor to consider is that the more we are afraid of facing and/or losing privilege, the less we are willing to inquire about and grasp the impact of our choices. Do we dare to wake up to how our choices impact others? Massive accumulation of resources for some creates scarcity all around. While we may enjoy unlimited access to water, do we pause to remember that millions of people do not have enough? Do we consider that letting the faucet run affects our planet? Strategies to achieve comfort, a need prioritized in most capitalistic societies, often depend on the exploitation of resources and people. Interdependence invites us to engage in a constant, mindful investigation, as our individual and communal choices impact so many lives.

> **Massive accumulation of resources for some creates scarcity all around.**

Embracing Many Needs

Practice and repetition create new neural pathways. The more often we make choices that embrace many needs, the more likely we are to experience a sense of fluency in this practice of interdependent care. Our actions reflect our understanding that we share a communal well-being.

When opening up to interdependence, we accept responsibility to care for our own needs while making choices that tend to the needs of all. We are also willing to accept care from others and from the wider community. Indigenous people rooted in interdependent cosmologies traditionally value considering impacts of their decisions on the next seven generations. We might ask ourselves, "How can I authentically be in touch with what I value while maintaining connection with what's important to the other person/people?" We may initially experience a sort of inner tension as we stretch our willingness to strategically care for others outside the boundaries of self-interest. This tension, too, is born out of the paradigm of separation and antagonism between individual and society.

Integrating authenticity and belonging, we move away from a mentality where either your needs or mine will be met. Instead, we are called to cultivate our capacity to care for the needs of self and others as we weigh needs including and beyond our own.

Sharing Power, Building Community

Because interdependence leads us to coordinate a flow of resources according to needs, it slowly deconstructs the sense of competition and scarcity we have internalized. In this paradigm, which is just beginning to manifest in the world at large, empowerment of self and others is achieved in tandem. Understanding that we are all interrelated, we are more likely to maintain dialogue when challenges arise. Through dialogue, strategies that attend to the needs of everyone involved are more likely to emerge. Even the human needs of autonomy and freedom are held with awareness that all actions have wider impacts on ourselves, others, and the earth. While we often link individual freedom with unfettered consumption, we may choose to restrain our autonomy out of an understanding that such consumption comes at a huge cost to the well-being of other people and the planet. Paradoxically, our freedom grows as we interact with this wider net of interdependence by providing and asking for support.

Communities built around a shared purpose typically embody and manifest interdependence. They embrace practices of the commons, sharing resources more effectively by collaborating. Materials, skills, and efforts are harvested communally rather than depending on any one person or nuclear family. Gradually, such sharing reduces reliance on the market for material tools and, by extension, on extractive technologies.

Sharing power with others becomes a natural facet of interconnection within this consciousness of full partnership.

Interconnection is much more than an ideal or an intellectual exercise. Interdependence can be seen as a life orientation that calls for awareness of the countless ways we are interrelated. At a 2007 workshop, Rosenberg was noted to have said, "My need for food has never been fully met." When asked why, he replied, "Because for my whole life, there have always been people who are starving."[21]

We may become ever more cognizant of all the beings that support our lives and are affected by our existence. Our progressive integration of this key distinction can inform our choices and intentions to support the greater good. Stepping into our power within the dynamic of inter-being, we naturally empower others as we listen deeply to their needs, build intimate connections, and experience meaningful exchanges.

SUMMARY

- This key distinction can inspire us to become more aware of our worldview as it relates to interdependence or dependence/independence.

- Stretching to live our values, we can make choices that honor interdependence and embrace personal and communal needs.

- Awareness of interdependence can empower us to share power with others.

- A practice that integrates this distinction contributes, moment by moment, to a consciousness that honors everyone's needs.

WALKING THE TALK:
A LIFE EXAMPLE FROM THE UNITED STATES

BY CINDY BIGBIE, CNVC CERTIFIED TRAINER

Awareness of interdependence is perhaps the closest I have come to experiencing spirituality in the flesh. When I worked for Community Connections Restorative Justice, I lived this oneness on a regular basis with my team and the youth we served. It might have been the most unexpected place to do so—our judicial system! Yet there we were, Black people and White, young and old, those with wealth and those living in poverty, unveiling our interdependence. Collectively, we released these dichotomies that create more separation and result in violence. All our differences were at moments erased in that space we cultivated.

While running the restorative justice program, I put in place many strategies to model, teach, and embody interdependence. Many of the youth referred to us came from violent situations that had, ultimately, ended in arrest. Our program held the philosophy that violence occurs because of a power imbalance. So, ironically, we were "the system," using processes outside the norm of typical power-over structures.

During one-on-one case management with the youth, we often used the NVC empathy process. Typically, we asked the youth if they had anything they wanted to be heard about. Then we listened to their sharing while suspending both our opinions and advice. We found that giving these kids the opportunity to be fully heard was revolutionary in itself. We employed another strategy as well. When the youth didn't have anything to say, we asked whether they were willing to hear *us*. They always said yes. We then shared our feelings about something in our world, while the youth gave us empathy.

Writing this up, it sounds so simple. Yet empathy is not typically exchanged with youth in our Western mainstream culture, especially in a juvenile youth program where the adult is deemed a "professional." Nevertheless, we caseworkers shared about our lives as the teens practiced presence, reflected, and guessed our needs.

Once, a youth gave me empathy, and afterward, his eyes lit up with excitement, his face visibly different. All barriers had been broken. He wasn't young and me old, he wasn't the one in "trouble" and me the caseworker. We had reached beyond all those separations to be together—as one. No differences. I saw this quality of connection fostered repeatedly in many different circumstances with hundreds of "delinquents."

I am grateful to have been blessed with the deep, palpable love nurtured with these youth. Our success received national attention; youth leaving our program had a 12 percent recidivism rate as compared with an average of 76 percent within three years according to a Council for State Governments (CSG) Justice Center survey of thirty-nine states in 2015.[22]

And more than 30 percent of our youth actually returned to the program later as *volunteers* to support others. They didn't want to leave! In my mind, these statistics and the care we all experienced directly correlated with living in awareness of interdependence.

PRACTICE

Exploring Interdependence

There are many ways to weave the awareness of interdependence into our lives. The intention of this practice is to witness how we are interconnected with others. In particular, it asks us to reflect on the ways others have shaped the things we enjoy most about ourselves. This is a journaling practice. You will need a piece of paper, something to write with, and a quiet space. We invite you to allow fifteen to twenty minutes for this practice.

- ∿ Taking a seat, allow your body to settle. How does it feel to be in this body right now?

- ∿ Continue to quietly ground yourself by noticing the natural flow of your breath.

- ∿ Whenever you are ready, write down five qualities (inner resources) that you treasure about yourself.

- ∿ Notice how easy or challenging this is. We tend to take for granted our strengths and focus more easily on areas of potential change and growth.

- ∿ Now, one quality at a time, check in with yourself and connect some dots:
  - ○ Who first modeled that quality for you?
  - ○ What are some of the conditions that have allowed you to witness and strengthen that quality?
  - ○ Who touched your life in ways that led you to develop that quality? (You may or may not have appreciated them at the time.)

- ∿ Is there anything else that you want to acknowledge to yourself before bringing this exploration to a close?

4

POWER-WITH AND POWER-OVER

It seems to me that whereas power usually means power-over,
the power of some person or group over some other person or group,
it is possible to develop the conception of power-with, a jointly
developed power, a co-active, not a coercive power.

—MARY PARKER FOLLETT

The key distinction that compares power-over to power-with asks us to consider the wide range of needs we wish to meet as we engage with our power. Power is a universal human need that allows us to effect change in the world. Awareness of how we use power and which needs we are attempting to meet can support further empowerment, alignment, and integrity.

"Power-Over leads to punishment and violence. Power-With leads to compassion and understanding, and to learning motivated by reverence for life rather than fear, guilt, shame, or anger," Rosenberg says.[1] Power-over aims at producing a particular outcome by using power unilaterally to control behavior and nature's resources, whether consciously or unconsciously. We often aim to control life itself with a sort of dominion in regard to such things as cloning and genetic modification. It relies on top-down authority, obedience, and shame; decisions are nonconsensual in this paradigm.

Acting from a power-with consciousness, we use our power, skills, and resources to hold everyone's needs with care, prioritizing the needs of those who have historically had less access to structural power.[2] Focusing on connection and upholding the needs of everyone involved, Mother Earth included, we seek to meet needs with a natural flow of giving and receiving. Understanding the factors that contribute to our position of power enables us to more effectively honor ourselves and others in mutuality. As we bring awareness to power differentials, we increase our ability to tap personal and collective power. Healing personal, social, and historical wounds, we touch wholeness. From that groundedness, we enhance our participation in the power-with paradigm.

> Acting from a power-with consciousness, we use our power, skills, and resources to hold everyone's needs with care, prioritizing the needs of those who have historically had less access to structural power.

The Powers in Play

The word *power* evokes both fear and intrigue. People have lost their jobs and even their lives raising questions around power. The abuse of power spans recorded history in the form of imperialism, dictatorship, colonialism, apartheid, and slavery, for a start. Power dynamics manifest regardless of how much power we actually have. This may explain the phenomenon of workers being promoted to supervisory positions and suddenly treating other workers—including former coworkers—with the same power-over methods they previously despised.

We often mistakenly think that using power-over strategies corresponds to feeling powerful. Surprising as it may seem, however, domination and powerlessness regularly manifest as two sides of the same coin. They can both be our response to the traumatizing effects of oppression and abuse. When our fight response is utterly defeated, the energy reemerges as rage. Similarly, powerlessness is a thwarted flight response.

There is a dynamic of dominance and abuse that arises from not recognizing our objective power, feeling powerless, and then exploding into a traumatic rage. When we feel most powerless, we may end up resorting to the most overpowering of behaviors. Steven Wineman, author of *Power-Under: Trauma and Nonviolent Social Change*,[3] writes: "Power-under and conscious domination as responses to trauma are variations on the same theme. Both result from efforts to defend oneself against the overwhelming pain of helplessness caused by gross violations."[4]

In Wineman's view, understanding how power-under dynamics can manifest in the cycle of reenactment as powerless rage is essential in transforming overwhelming rage into "constructive" rage. According to Wineman, identifying powerless rage is essential "in order to develop strategies to both constrain the destructive face of rage and to mobilize rage politically in the service of humanization and egalitarian social change."[5]

The question is not how much power we have access to, but how we use the power we have. The culturally constructed habit of associating power with power-over haunts us even when we have small-scale power. There is both a personal and a political peril here. If we do not transform our relationship to power, then the moment we have access to more power—as an individual or as a formerly oppressed group—we are likely to repeat the cycle, using our newly accessed power over others rather than with them. This is the essential tragedy within the "power-under" dynamic that Wineman points to.

> The question is not how much power we have access to, but how we use the power we have.

"Power, when used responsibly and effectively, is the ability to impact and influence situations across diverse and unpredictable contexts with legitimacy (implied or explicit cooperation and agreement of others) for the greater good," writes international leadership consultant Julie Diamond.[6] The overarching question, then, is this: How can power be channeled in partnership toward life-affirming ends?

Miki Kashtan demystifies power in her book *Reweaving Our Human Fabric*. "Defining power, simply, as the capacity to mobilize resources to attend to needs, makes it neutral, in addition to being necessary," she writes.[7] When we realize that power is a human need, we are free to step up and explore effective ways to use it interdependently.

As Kashtan points out, it's important to take stock of our resources before mobilizing. Outer resources include education, money, connections, and technology. Inner resources are related to the mind or personal aptitudes, such as self-compassion, self-connection, affect-regulation, and specific abilities. They also include our willingness and capacity to transform negative core beliefs and heal our deepest wounds. This widens our windows of stress tolerance. There is an interplay between external and internal resources—the fewer external resources we have, the more likely we are to grow inner resources.

Our potential for power is ever present, yet at times, our realization of it may seem distant, even unreachable. Both misuse (under-use) and abuse (over-use), of power[8] lead to life-alienating impacts. Diamond writes that there is a "fatal mismatch that accounts for a great deal of power misuse: the gap between the power we feel and the power we have, between our self-perceived sense of power and our objective power."[9] When we do not acknowledge and engage the power we hold, others who depend on our leadership might feel confused and angry, needing clarity around role responsibilities and shared goals. Whether we choose to activate resources or not, both our action and inaction impact others. Interdependence is inescapable.

Personal Power

The internal locus of personal power is a state of mind. It is in our nature to influence the world, whether or not we are experiencing access to this power in the moment. Our ability to concretely impact our environment and to notice when we do, contributes to our sense of empowerment.

In our understanding, power is a need, a form of life energy, while control is a strategy to connect with a sense of power. Personal power is intrinsically sourced. It is built on the foundation of our earliest experiences of our primary caregivers' responses to us, as when a baby cries and is attended to. Human beings meet needs interdependently. And each of us has had different experiences that contribute to connection or disconnection with our power as we grew up.

Personal power draws from the well of our inner resources—self-awareness, mindfulness, emotional intelligence, and the strength of our spirituality, to name a few. The shape of our character and integrity in the moment contribute to our willingness to stand alone with this inner sense of knowing. The more we connect with our personal power, the freer we feel to step into vulnerability. Sometimes we are so rooted in our power that we are even prepared to give our lives to stay in integrity with our deepest values.

> **The more we connect with our personal power, the freer we feel to step into vulnerability.**

While we are born with an internal connection to our power, patriarchal socialization, primarily based on coercion and shame, leads us to disconnect from it. This internal connection can be intentionally rekindled and developed over the course of our lifetime. Concentration camp survivor and psychiatrist Viktor Frankl says, "Everything can be taken from a man but one thing: the last of the human freedoms—to choose our attitude in any given circumstances, to choose one's own way."[10] With this power, we change how we meet our environment by leveraging what we do have the power to change, starting with ourselves.

Relational Power

As we explore power related to roles, it is worth noting that we play up- and down-power roles[11] in the hierarchies inherent in patriarchal cultures. In up-power roles, we have more access to resources and exercise greater influence than do those in down-power roles. Those roles are linked to a particular context and environment. As we move through our days, we shift from up- to down-power and back again seamlessly. We are in up-power to those we supervise at work or serve in helping professions, and in down-power to those above us there. When we call our parents to ask for help with our kids' college tuition, we slip into a down-power role. As soon as we share this news with our children, we shift back to being in an up-power role. The kaleidoscope of responsibility and influence morphs according to needs and expectations within personal, professional, and systemic relationships everywhere we go and in almost everything we do. Cedar Barstow, founder of The Right Use of Power Institute, reminds us that awareness of power differentials is foundational to support safety and well-being for all.[12]

Role Power

Role power[13] relates to a position we play or hold in a particular context at a given time. These roles offer us opportunities for influence and come with responsibilities. Usually, such roles come through effort on our part such as extended study, running for an office, or providing an ongoing service. These roles may depend on recognition of some sort from others, in the form of awards, licensure or election, or other means. Many such roles are professions, including those of doctor, dog groomer, teacher, or politician. The power we experience in a role, additional to our baseline of personal power potential, is gone as soon as we step out of the role itself.

Rank or Status Power

Rank or status power enhances our personal and role powers. It is generally something given to us by others without any effort on our part; rather, it is associated with factors we were born into. Rank or status power is culturally conferred on the basis of religion, race, sex, socioeconomic status, physical abilities, and/or sexual orientation, to name a few. The experience of discrimination based on status may compound with intersectionality.[14]

The complexity of rank power shifts and changes as we move through the world. Because it relates to social values, in some cultures, elders enjoy up-status power, as they are revered for their life experiences and wisdom. In other cultures, elders experience down-status power because they slowly become less and less productive and more and more dependent on the care of others.

The negative impacts of status power differentials may be difficult for us to acknowledge when in up-status positions. We are unlikely to see or understand our own status in the intricate web of social disparities. That is part of the dynamic of privilege—we are blinded by it and do not see how we benefit. Most of us have experienced our status for a very long time and wear it closer than our skin.

Collective and Systemic Power

Power is magnified when a group comes together. Their collective power influences individuals and systems. A group of people may gather to protest the decision of a corporation. Their collective power may contribute to shifting the ways in which the corporation operates. While the people gather their power as a group, single individuals draw strength from collective actions.

Systemic power is related to collective power. Systemic power can address the needs of many or few and ranges from life-serving to life-alienating. Rank-related discrimination such as racism can be embedded in systems to an alarming breadth and depth. Systemic power determines the methods, validity, and scope of accessible knowledge in a way that reinforces the power of the dominant group. For example, some school districts in the United States (systems) have banned the subject of critical race theory from being taught. These systems are determining what information is accessible to students. Critical race theory is an academic movement initiated by civil rights activists. The theory examines how racism is embedded in legal systems and policies. Bills prohibiting it have even been passed in several states to regulate teachers and to maintain the status quo.

Collective power, directed toward changing policies and laws at all levels of government, is needed to protect the safety, health, and dignity of all. Becoming aware of the complexities of power differentials and how they play out in each and every relationship can support understanding and social justice.

Having explicit language to name power dynamics supports our awareness of the different types of power and addresses how power is used within those dynamics. Without a shared understanding and clear language around power use and dynamics, naming the problem becomes difficult. NVC and its focus on needs awareness offers invaluable contributions toward systemic change. It provides concrete maps to cultivate a consciousness beyond separation and choicelessness. Recognizing judgments as messengers of universal needs, we empower ourselves and one another to tap into the life force beyond binary, hierarchical thinking. Systemic change can emerge without further separating human beings from one another.

Power-Over

In power-over relationships, one person, group, or nation demonstrates an often-unexamined power over another. Dominance and coercion in the form of threats, force, punishments, and rewards, are used repeatedly and often without thought of alternatives. Coercion is engaged in varying forms and degrees. It can range from insidious structural means of control—for example, housing policies—to brute dominance, as in the case of war. Depending on the form and degree of coercion, the resulting damage to individuals, groups, and relationships will vary as well.

Power-over polarizes relationships and springs from a paradigm of separation. It may stem from an assumption that some people are less worthy than others. Those deemed more worthy, typically determined by cultural values, have greater access to power and resources and often blindly seek to achieve their own ends.

Power-Over and Parenting

The paradigm of separation embraces the moralistic judgments of right and wrong, elevating those who believe themselves to be in the "right" to a moral high ground. One assumption can lead to another. In the parenting arena, for example, adults enjoy greater physical stature, life experience, and access to resources. From that vantage point, we might believe that our judgment of what is good or bad is "better" than that of our child. Of course, we do have more capacity for discerning the impacts of particular choices as the brain reaches maturity at around age twenty-five. Yet choosing, out of mutual respect, to share information with our children as guidance and support differs from "knowing what is best for our kids."

In the power-over model, we dole out punishments and rewards, often in hopes of guiding our children. The "logical consequences" we enforce that induce shame, guilt, and fear are deemed by society at large to be beneficial and even necessary.

Surely, underlying needs motivate those choices, and some needs are met; our actions do at times contribute. This key distinction calls to our attention the life-alienating price of this contribution. Needs for safety, dignity, meaning, and connection—some of the primary needs responsible for nurturing our mental health—may go unmet.

Particularly in parenting, the consequences of our actions can last a lifetime. Therefore, exploring our intentions and their potential impacts can help us mindfully choose strategies to guide our children as they grow. When we "educate" our children with power-over, they do not typically experience access to their personal power. This lack of access at a formative age can impact their connection with personal power for the rest of their lives.

Power-With

Power is not a social construct. It is a human need. Power is a generative and creative "energy, a human drive to shape the world, influence others, and make an impact," writes Diamond.[15] Understanding that power is a need can help us find compassion for ourselves. Especially when we realize that we have related to the need for power in ways that did not

Power is not a social construct. It is a human need.

encompass the well-being of others, we can pause and hold ourselves and our socialization with care. Connecting with our need for agency, we might open our hearts and discover other needs we had intended to meet, such as contribution. With awareness, we can ground ourselves in these values as we shift toward relating to power with heart.

Power-with, founded in mutuality and respect, is based on the principle of equal dignity, regardless of functions. Using the skills of deep listening, empathy, and mindful self-expression without attachment to views, we open ourselves and become receptive to collaborative decisions. In self-awareness, we can observe how our beliefs, fears, and attitudes influence the way we show up in collaboration. We direct our creativity not only to meet needs and use power effectively, but also to enhance connection.

Power-with calls for transparency—communication, accountability, and open access to information and resources—as we foster collective action within families and organizations. Sharing power promotes social change incrementally as it counteracts millennia of historical power-over dynamics. Power-with moves the collective away from a domination culture based on control and fear. Mutual support and influence grow with our numbers and solidarity. Shared power is strengthened as we cultivate it. Individuals become more adept at accessing their personal power in supportive environments as the group summons energies and resources toward collective goals. As all stakeholders actively engage, cocreative power expands to reach across multiple sectors of government, corporations, and other community systems.

Power struggles easily arise when both parties believe the other has more power. In order to mitigate this tension, we can nurture trust that there are sufficient resources for all. We can also experience some sense of space and freedom as we connect with the understanding that while strategies are often in conflict, needs are rarely so. We do not have to agree to accept one another's perspectives as the work ensues. Giving up, giving in, and compromising are not considered life-affirming options as they do not address needs nor do they sustain the power-with paradigm.

Making the Shift

Since childhood, most of us have been conditioned to misuse or abuse power. Children form internal working models for relationships based on their experiences with their parents, other caregivers, and later teachers and on the information and stories they are exposed to through the media. The more authoritarian our family of origin and the culture we grew up in were, the more determination and persistence it takes to consciously shift toward a power-with approach.

We can compassionately cultivate an attitude of using power in mutuality by first noticing when we overpower ourselves. We might tell ourselves that we have to do or have certain things. We might even insist on having certain needs met in a certain way! Rosenberg suggests the practice of rephrasing our self-talk from "I have to," to "I choose to." He encourages us to acknowledge to ourselves the needs we are attempting to meet by choosing a certain strategy. Instead of saying, "I have to go to work," we can instead say to ourselves, "I choose to go to work because I value sustainability." We might name any number of values that move us—contribution, meaning, care, or whatever we connect with in the moment. When we align ourselves with our needs, we are inclined to act out of choice rather than fear.

We can also examine whether our means are consistent with our ends. While spanking has been proven to have harmful impacts regardless of our intentions, many of us still resort to hitting our children in order to teach them not to hit. Ultimately, hitting children is not the most effective way to support them in learning to regulate their feelings, modulate their actions, and be safe. And our behavior in such cases models neither emotional nor behavioral regulation.

On the collective level, bombing an abortion clinic because we value life manifests that same incoherence between means and ends. The more we cultivate an awareness of all the ways we can exercise our personal power, the less we risk acting from overwhelming rage (power-under).

When we commit to increasing our awareness of power imbalances in each and every relationship, we begin to shift in our relationship to power. We can seek to share power with those who are affected by our decisions. In partnering this way with a very young child, we can acknowledge their needs, invite them into brainstorming a solution, and hold the challenge in partnership. Those who do this with whole-hearted willingness to be influenced by their child discover, to their amazement, how often it is the child who comes up with solutions that work for all.

Every challenge provides an opportunity for learning and growth. Upholding self-determination with self-respect, we can sense into our body to check where our limits lie. What are areas where we can comfortably let our children make choices without instilling fear of punishment? What are the areas where we sense discomfort and want to ask for a dialogue? And finally, where can we not even imagine sharing power because we sense in our bodies now a level of constriction that is essential for us to honor? CNVC certified trainer Inbal Kashtan, our dear late mentor, writes, "Without understanding our own needs and mattering to ourselves, we are likely to find it very difficult to hold everyone's needs with care."[16] In partnership, we can be frank about such limits and share the needs behind them. More often than not, as the many articles written by Inbal Kashtan suggest, such conversations lead to surprising breakthrough results. And, if we end up making a unilateral decision in the end, we still have the option of sincerely mourning the impact and affirming the child's needs even if we do not know how to meet them.

KRISTIN: Our teacher team invites students to cocreate our classroom agreements so that we all have a sense of belonging and power in making decisions together. We, teachers, begin by asking, "What kinds of things in the classroom help you to feel comfortable and learn? Use all your senses—what do you like to hear or see, and how do you want to move or sit? What do you not enjoy?" While new students may not be accustomed to being asked these questions, we write all ideas down and with curiosity ask questions to better understand their needs.

When we look at nonnegotiable "school rules," like walking in the hall, we explore the needs behind these rules. "Why do you think we ask students to walk in the halls rather than run?" we ask. Students quickly assess that the rule is intended to support safety. We ask if they agree that the rule supports safety. "Well, what if a friend falls down and needs help at the other end of the hall? It seems like it would be more safe for him if I ran down the hall to help." In questioning safety, we can together imagine and problem-solve which strategies would work best in such dilemmas.

"What would be the consequences of such a dash?" we would ask.

"Well, I could help my friend, but I might run into someone else, though I probably wouldn't," they might answer.

"Do you think other students and teachers would understand that you were responding to an inner need for safety in not obeying that rule? If you explained afterward?" Students usually think a moment before they say yes, they imagine we would understand. This thought usually brings a smile, as they realize that the rules in such a classroom culture are there to serve relationships.

When the board of an organization invites all who will be affected by a decision into a discussion—dissenting voices included—this is a way of honoring everyone's needs. When power is shared in such decision-making, all participants are empowered.[17] Leadership and meeting facilitation rotations can support balancing power in mutuality while empowering those with less structural power. Sharing our power when we are in up-power roles and status is crucially linked to staying connected to our sense of personal power.

Repairing ruptures in relationships, especially those due to unawareness of power differences and dynamics, is another essential skill for making the shift to "power with." We can awaken to mutuality by being open to feedback about the impact of our actions, regardless of how life-affirming our intentions may have been. We can practice offering empathic understanding to those who may have been affected, and to ourselves for our limitations. We can take responsibility for the effects of our actions by expressing sincere regret.

As mentioned above, even when in down-power roles, our actions may stimulate great harm. Understanding this can actually support us staying in our power in life-giving ways. Regardless of our power role, we can learn from our "mistakes" and self-correct without losing our dignity through shame. Humility and self-connection enable us to undo both inner and outer power-over attitudes and behaviors. Expressing gratitude and appreciation to the people who help us see what we did not see supports us in staying connected to their humanity. This is another celebration of interdependence in action.

Expanding Awareness of Our Power

Understanding where our power comes from contributes to greater clarity and efficiency in its use. Such awareness also leads to fewer instances of embarking on a dialogue with an intention to share power, only to discover that others perceive us as exercising power-over.

In some sectors of our lives, we wield enormous influence. In other areas, we see ourselves as being at the mercy of various people or circumstances. This spectrum of experiences depends on personal and environmental variables. Whether we are affected by a migraine or are entering a room full of people we do not know, these variables influence our connection with power. Our ability to access personal power is affected by our neurobiological state. The more we stay connected with the prefrontal cortex, the more we can modulate emotions, consider possible consequences of our actions, and participate in attuned, empathic communications.

Access to our personal power is also affected by how aware we are of our beliefs about ourselves, others, and the world. If we associate power with power-over, we might decide we'd rather not have any. Such avoidance can be tragic, as power can be used in myriad ways to meet the needs of many.

Self-connection is linked to our capacity to make meaning of events and our implicit outlook on life. Disconnected from our power, we feel small and adrift. We may not perceive access to outer resources at our disposal in the moment. Environmental variables such as social and cultural norms will also affect the degree to which we experience role and rank power. When we understand the unique configuration of our power in the moment, we can decide what skillful measures to take in order to embrace our power-with practice.

If we are in a position of greater role and/or status power, we might acknowledge this power differential and use our resources to support others who are in a lower status or role. Our support could take many forms—mobilizing resources, amplifying their voices, or exploring their needs more deeply so that we can prioritize them in partnership.

Layers of rank, role, and even personal power are ultimately relational. They form a lens through which others see us and we see them. This key differentiation may support our discernment around what kind of power we are engaging in and its impact. Some of our most profound growth is achieved in the process of learning to use these powers in life-giving ways with awareness of interconnection.

Caring for Interdependence

As we learn to fully embrace our authenticity, we connect with our power in both heart and mind. In a power-with paradigm, we honor self-determination and weigh that with care for the well-being of other beings. Power-with involves the recognition that love naturally upholds equal dignity.

Exercising this degree of compassion for ourselves and others not only serves others directly; it may also inspire self-compassion in those around us. When we uphold mattering for ourselves and others, we are models; those around us may also realize they matter to themselves, and attune to the needs of the community. The means of power-with can fluidly support its own ends, enhancing intrapersonal, interpersonal, and systemic relationships.

Personal Healing: A Balm for the Collective

Power-with requires the bold commitment to seeing the unwavering wholeness and unconditional innocence of our own being. Personal and collective trauma[18] resides in our bodies. Healing our wounds, whether individual or intergenerational, is crucial if we want to shift from power-over to a paradigm of power-with. Otherwise, we unwittingly re-create systems of domination and oppression. Discussing the social context of trauma, educator and trauma professional David A. Treleaven writes: "We'll have been handed unearned privileges that keep us from seeing and validating the impacts of oppression and systemic trauma. We will have been conditioned to think about trauma as an individual tragedy instead of an event that's interconnected to larger systems of domination that shape our world. . . . Without this realization, we are living in virtually separate worlds and cannot bridge our realities. . . . We live inside of social and economic structures that are designed to respect and create safety and opportunity for

> Healing our wounds, whether individual or intergenerational, is crucial if we want to shift from power-over to a paradigm of power-with. Otherwise, we unwittingly re-create systems of domination and oppression.

some groups, while systematically disregarding others. This is a power-over model that shapes all our lives and perspectives, even when we have altruistic intentions."[19]

When we take responsibility for our healing, we empower ourselves to tend to our wounds personally and in community. Core beliefs grounded in a mindset of separation and deficiency can be unearthed. We may approach our fear and shame with compassion and care. In doing so, we expand our capacity for conscious choice rather than subconsciously passing on our wounds with reactive behaviors dictated by the blueprint of a domination system.

If personal healing is not attended to, the power-over dynamics still live inside us. We experience inner conflicts, as our conscious minds hold goals or values in conflict with the core beliefs and coping mechanisms of the subconscious. Parts of the mind can strive to overpower one another. The conscious mind may call on more willpower as the subconscious redoubles its efforts to get what it "needs" to experience safety.

In fact, information theory[20] tells us that the subconscious mind is exceedingly powerful. It has an extended capacity of processing eleven billion bits of information per second while the conscious mind only processes about fifty bits per second. The subconscious mind controls about 95 percent of our behavior.[21] In our understanding, healing and wholeness, which entail whole-brain integration, are crucial aspects of bringing partnership home.

Exploring the dynamics around power-over and power-with supports personal empowerment. This can lead to collective healing and empowerment. Together, we can strengthen the fabric of our common humanity and create a sustainable future that is equitable for all of us and for the earth.

SUMMARY

> ✎ Exploring power differentials based on role and status, for
> example, helps us become aware of the many ways we may
> unwittingly use power over others.

↶ Balancing intention and impact, and focusing on interdependence, we can learn to connect with and nurture our personal power.

↶ By learning and healing, personally and collectively, we can develop our inner resources and expand access to our power, allowing for enhanced participation in the power-with paradigm.

↶ Awareness of collective and systemic power helps us identify dynamics of domination that contribute to the use of power-over, whether we were aware of it or not. Unearthing these subterranean structures is essential to foster a more life-giving and sustainable world.

WALKING THE TALK:
A LIFE EXAMPLE FROM MEXICO

BY ELISABETTA SCHIAVON, CNVC TRAINER CANDIDATE

have been living for twenty years in Chiapas, Mexico. After almost a decade of working in partnership on responsible tourism with Indigenous communities, a cooperative of artisan women, *Mujeres Sembrando la Vida* (Women Sowing Life) asked me to offer a training on Nonviolent Communication, as they were experiencing some conflicts within their community. Contrasting emotions percolated in me—gratitude for the trust we had built together over the years, joy in being offered the opportunity to contribute . . . and also trepidation and deep concern. I noticed my body stiffening; I realized that I was afraid to give a training that might, despite my best intentions, contribute to abuses of power.

I am aware of my status power as a Western, White, middle-class person with many years of schooling. I live in a country marked by deep social inequalities and wounds linked to colonialism that have yet to be healed—Chiapas, in particular, has a 76.4 percent poverty rate (2018)[22] and a large population of historically marginalized Indigenous people. "How can I build a space for dialogue based on shared power, when there is such an implicit power differential?" I wondered.

When Stephanie, my CNVC certification assessor, told me that she was considering making a trip to Chiapas, I noticed my body relax.

"Surely, she knows how to manage this issue and offer the course from a consciousness of power-with!" I thought. Only later did I realize how much I had shifted into a down-power role. In passing all agency over to my assessor, I lost more confidence in my own abilities and experience.

Most painful of all, I realized that I had also put the Indigenous group in a collective down-power position, seeing them only as the recipients of a knowledge that came from outside. I didn't wish to perpetuate the violent power-over monologue of the Western White world. I asked myself to stay anchored in my body, rooted in my experience and my personal story. A curiosity awakened in me about their perspective. I wanted to honor their experience and enjoy the precious gift of mutual learning.

I continue to investigate how to share Nonviolent Communication as a "liberation praxis," borrowing a term of Brazilian educator Paulo Freire. I long to support the awakening of personal and collective power, based on a paradigm of interdependence between people and the rest of the living world.

Now, especially when facilitating an event with Indigenous people, I open the meeting by inviting a dialogue around our intentions for the gathering. Hearing everyone's hopes supports the cocreation of a safe space with room for all voices to be spoken and for a shared understanding of our common purpose to emerge.

I also like to transparently name some of the impacts of our social location and consequent internalized power differences and how they affect me and our relationship. I make room for mourning, then clarify that I uphold an intention for mutual understanding and learning to arise.

Finally, I consistently rely on people's feedback as my compass. Feedback helps me to stay present while cocreating a space of safe exploration, moment by moment. Together, we choose the direction we want to follow, manifesting power-with in action. I aim to support an exchange where there is no giver and no receiver, but a mutual inquiry on how to restore our full humanity.

PRACTICE

Reflecting on Power

Awareness and self-reflection provide opportunities for us to shift in our use of power so that it better aligns with our values. This practice supports self-inquiry about a situation in which you experienced your power. It can help you discern what kinds of power you connected to and how they were used in the context of the situation. It can also support your inquiry into what kinds of power others were connected with and whether the power used in the situation addressed all the needs in play. This is a practice of self-reflection that could be done internally in a quiet space, or, if you prefer, as a journaling exercise with a keyboard or pen and paper. We anticipate that this practice will take twenty to forty minutes.

- Think of a time when you experienced having power and effectively influenced some change, however small.

- How did you experience your power—body sensations, emotions, thoughts?

- What needs were you seeking to meet?
  - Were those needs met?
  - Which needs would you guess were not considered or addressed to the fullness you would have liked?

- What kinds of power contributed to this change—personal, role, or rank?

- What resources did you have access to? Inner? Outer? Both?

- What kinds of power did others involved in the situation have?

~ Did you utilize your power individually or collectively? Or both?

~ Did your use of power align with your values?

~ Were relationships enhanced as you engaged with power?

~ What impacts did you like and not like in the change you brought about?

- Self-empathy and/or empathy from a trusted friend could be supportive if uncomfortable feelings arise.

~ Understanding the layers of your power in the course of this self-reflection, is there anything you would have done differently?

~ Would you describe the power you engaged with as power-with or power-over?

~ How are you relating to yourself now? Are you relating to the different parts of yourself with a power-with mindset, or are there self-judgments? Is one part of your mind exercising power over another?

5

CHOICE AND SUBMISSION/REBELLION

It is difficult to find traction
on the gravel hills of habit.

—GREGORY KRAMER

The key distinction that explores choice and submission/rebellion highlights the power involved in choosing. Choice is the act of making a decision connected to self-determination. Recognizing that we have choice in how we respond to any situation, even when we cannot control the circumstances or environment, is foundational in the practice of NVC. Awareness of choice is key to personal power. Conversely, not having agency and choice are the hallmarks of powerlessness.

Submission and rebellion are linked to our biological and conditioned fight/flight/freeze survival response.[1] When we perceive that the demands of life are greater than our available resources, the flight/freeze responses of submission and the fight response of rebellion are triggered. These stress responses are the body-mind reaction to danger; they are not intentionally chosen.

Choice, in contrast, can be achieved when we connect with what matters to us deeply. Cultivating a sense of choice begins outside of the crisis moment. Growing awareness of ourselves, our resources, and our surroundings, we can learn tools for self-regulation that help us develop the ability to choose. When we have clarity about what is really essential for us at any given moment, we are empowered to make choices, think, and act in ways that are consciously connected to our needs.

Submission and Rebellion

Submission and rebellion usually arise from a place of reactivity. We define reactivity as any inner emotional movement and consequent outer behavior when we do not experience ourselves as having choice. Reactivity is linked to the inner biological dynamic of approach or withdrawal, either clinging to or resisting emotions we scarcely recognize. In reacting, we have no space for self-compassion and self-regulation. Responsiveness, on the other hand, comes from an awareness of needs and interconnection.

The experience of powerlessness from which we react may in itself stem from and trigger trauma. Whether we perceive a physical or emotional threat, the burst of arousal and cascade of stress hormones in our brain is similar, and we may in fact confuse the two. Discerning physical threats from emotional threats supports self-regulation. In acknowledging this distinction, we can step back into our power, gradually navigating back toward safety.

Both submission and rebellion are founded in and fueled by dichotomous thinking. Rather than addressing needs and consciously holding an awareness of resources and potential impacts, we react by either complying with what we believe someone else demands, or by refusing. In either case, our thoughts, actions, and verbal responses are reactive.

Patterns of submission are often an attempt to maintain relational and social stability within hierarchical orders relating to gender, age, and ethnicity, to name a few. Rebellion

Patterns of submission are often an attempt to maintain stability within hierarchical orders, such as those relating to gender, age, and ethnicity.

can be grounded in a hunger to prove oneself to others. While both submission and rebellion attempt to meet needs, these reactions often drain the vital energy from relationships on personal and community levels.

Submission

When we submit, we may do so to try to ensure our safety and security. Or we perceive that submission will support us in getting at least some of our needs met without bringing consequences we cannot accept. Indeed, we may consciously choose to submit if our life is threatened or we seek to meet other crucial needs like belonging. Such threats may be real or perceived.

When we underestimate our own power and overestimate the power of the other person/group, the part of the brain associated with the rapid detection of threats in the environment (the amygdala) gets activated. Our reactivity escalates in direct proportion to the powerlessness we perceive; the brain falls into dysregulation. When in that brain/mind state, we do not have access to our power even if we are in an up-power role. In fact, role power does not automatically transfer into "feeling powerful." How connected we are to our own power affects our ability to wield it.

"Power is a state of mind," leadership consultant Julie Diamond reminds us.[2] This is why we enjoy Inbal and Miki Kashtan's definition of power as "the capacity to mobilize resources to attend to needs." Even if we have access to resources, without the capacity to mobilize them, we remain powerless.

Submission, as a reaction, can be associated with a flight response.[3] Depending on the state of our autonomic nervous system, we may temporarily lose access to our prefrontal cortex as we attempt to respond to a perceived threat. When the stress response is chronically activated, and we perpetually submit, our entire organism gets depleted. It is worth noting that many of us are repeatedly stimulated by situations that are not actually life-threatening, such as seeing a red traffic light. Certain targeted groups live in a chronic state of survival due to the violence of systemic inequity. If we regularly conform in a state of duress, seeking physical safety or belonging, our compromised connection with authenticity and autonomy harms our physical, mental, and emotional health.

The internalization of moralistic judgments, in the form of core beliefs, can lead to submission. We may judge, blame, or shame ourselves, believing that an external authority knows what is best for us. Submission can also lead to learned helplessness. Resigned to a state of perceived powerlessness, we may consider ourselves inconsequential and unable to take an active role in the situation.

When we fear authority figures, we habitually submit to what they ask of us, in an attempt to meet needs for safety and security. We may please and obey authority rather than consciously making choices connected to needs and our own moral compass. Whenever, in a group, we do not recognize our collective power, we can spiral into further powerlessness, bringing tragic consequences to a group

Submission and rebellion usually arise from a place of reactivity. In contrast, responsiveness comes from an awareness of needs and interconnection.

that may be at a disadvantage to begin with. Patterns of submission and rebellion can thus become entrenched and further disempower individuals and communities.

Rebellion

Rebellion stems from the same survival response as submission does. Perceiving that we have inadequate resources to meet the situation, the brain goes into a state of distress. Distress can manifest as either chaos or rigidity. When in a state of chaos, the brain goes into hyperarousal (fight/flight stress response) and we lose the ability to modulate our emotions and regulate our behavior. When the freeze response kicks in, the brain enters a state of rigidity (hypoarousal) while we seek to excessively control the situation at hand. We resist authority, whether individual or collective. Reacting to protect our needs for autonomy, self-respect, and choice, we try desperately to connect with our personal and collective empowerment. We lash out verbally or physically, trying to regain a sense of agency or control. Ironically, that is when the brain falls into deeper dysregulation.

Historically, violent rebellions and revolutions have seldom led to stable democratic regimes where governance and power are shared, at least to some extent, with the people. Political scientist Robert Dahl states that stable democracies "are more likely to result from rather slow evolutionary processes than from the revolutionary overthrow of existing hegemonies."[4] Rebellion, stemming from an unintegrated brain state, can result in significant chaos and/or rigidity on the systemic level. Violent revolutions or dictatorships are examples of systemic chaos or rigidity. Political scientists Erica Chenoweth and Maria Stephan write that "the transitions that occur in the wake of successful nonviolent resistance movements create much more durable and internally peaceful democracies than transitions provoked by violent insurgencies."[5]

Choice

Three main obstacles may prevent us from connecting with our sense of choice: unawareness, inability to self-regulate in interdependence, and unwillingness or incapacity to pause long enough to recognize the possibility of choice. As Rosenberg pointed out, our awareness of choice is compromised by not living in life-enriching structures. "Until we can create them worldwide . . . we've got to learn how when we're in these other structures never to give others the power to make you submit or rebel. . . . Then even when you're in the domination structure you still live with this other story."[6] He recognized that it takes tremendous energy to experience choice within domination systems.

When fully aware of our choices, we fight *for* what is important to us, not *against* perceived enemies. We stay connected to our personal power, with an awareness of the needs we are responding to. In fact, Rosenberg distinguished violent from nonviolent actions with two variables—not seeing an enemy, and not intending to cause suffering. We take action toward a vision instead of reacting from fear and self-protection.

Nobel Peace Prize winner and antiapartheid revolutionary Nelson Mandela spent twenty-seven years in prison before being elected president of South Africa.[7] Mandela writes about his inauguration: "The day was symbolised for me by the playing of our two national anthems, and the vision

> We may in fact choose to hear a demand as a "please," and move to contribute to the person/group—according to their very strategy—with a peaceful heart, as we connect to needs.

of whites singing 'Nkosi Sikelel' iAfrika' and blacks singing 'Die Stem,' the old anthem of the republic. Although that day, neither group knew the lyrics of the anthem they once despised, they would soon know the words by heart."[8] Mandela rejoiced that his people, neither submitting nor rebelling, had come together in choice. We may in fact choose to hear a demand as a "please," and move to contribute to the person/group—according to their very strategy—with a peaceful heart, as we connect to needs.

Awareness

Recognizing that we are always ultimately in a position of choice (even if we do not enjoy the options and/or consequences) presupposes that we are aware of ourselves enough to acknowledge the signs of reactivity. Studies in the field of human consciousness suggest that we have less choice than we would want to believe. For example, clinical psychologist Christopher Germer writes about the important role awareness plays in relation to choice. "From a neurological perspective, free will is an illusion, but we still have 'veto power' over an impending action if we become aware of it early enough."[9] Our ability to choose a response rather than reacting thus relies on our capacity for self-regulation. By pausing and taking full ownership for our internal processes such as physical sensations, feelings, thoughts, and needs, we can choose a response rather than react by blaming, shaming, or internalizing. From such self-regulation and self-responsibility, we can make choices that engage personal and/or collective power.

Our ability to choose in a moment of crisis is largely dependent on our willingness to cultivate awareness of ourselves and the recognition that we always have some degree of choice. The more we have cultivated our awareness of interdependence, the more likely we are to reach out, ask for support with what matters to us, and share resources.

When we are stimulated and/or in a heightened state of stress, our body constricts and our thinking becomes distorted and confused. We may not experience ourselves as having choices. If we practice embracing freedom of choice in unstressful situations, we enhance our awareness and capacity for conscious choice in more stressful moments. Over time, we learn to gently drop the principle of choice into our mind in instances of distress, even if specific options are beyond our reach in the moment. Proactively reconnecting with ourselves and our intentions through mindful breathing and self-empathy, we bring the prefrontal cortex back online, empowering ourselves to regain homeostasis. This allows for the mind to envision options that were unreachable before.

Our ability to recognize and take responsibility for our inner experience will support a sense of personal empowerment as part of us compassionately witnesses with clarity how another part reacts. With such awareness, we are not fully lost in our emotions and can ask ourselves some crucial questions: What is leading me toward a yes? Is it duty, obligation, a sense of "having to," or being unable to do it differently? What about toward a no? Am I telling myself I should react? That I deserve something else?

The degree to which we are self-aware and self-regulated will determine whether we are operating from submission/rebellion or from choice, even if the same decision would be made either way. When we connect with ourselves to freely choose, our willingness is linked to awareness of needs. Our decision is empowered and connected to life.

From Stimulus to Response

At the core of the NVC process is our willingness to pause and open the door to choosing. This can take effort and discipline. "To practice NVC, it's critical for me to slow down, take my time, to come from an energy I choose, the one I believe that we were meant to come from, not the one I was programmed into," Rosenberg said.[10] In doing so, we step away from societal conditioning related to scarcity, separation, and powerlessness, toward a consciousness of having enough, and experiencing interdependence and "power-with."

"I am the master of my fate; I am the captain of my soul," wrote William E. Henley in his poem "Invictus."[11] Steering our minds can start with awareness of the breath, which activates the parasympathetic nervous system[12] to put the "brakes" on our reaction. Intentionally breathing to elongate, even double, the exhalation to the inhalation when dysregulated can relax the body and allow the mind to remember that we have choice. When we are connected to the breath, we release our grip on specific strategies. Simply pausing to be present to the physiological sensations of inhale and exhale increases our awareness of choice.

Connecting Needs to Actions

When we respond by making choices that arise from needs, we find greater flexibility around strategies. We reduce the likelihood of perceiving ourselves as the "victim." At the same time, we increase the possibility of acting from a more integrated state of consciousness. In choosing, we act with a clear sense of agency.

Often our understanding of "meeting" a need is still intertwined with the implicit expectation to have needs fulfilled. We can instead seek to "meet" a need by encountering and being present with it.[13] For example, if we experience our need for harmony as not being met in a particular situation, we might choose to encounter the energy of that need internally, noticing the sensations in the body and how that energy lives in us. In that way we satisfy our sense of connection to needs while mourning that a need is not fulfilled externally. This practice empowers us to live in peace with unmet needs.[14]

Acknowledging our needs, whether met or unmet, empowers us to tap into sweet mourning when we do not recognize the manifestation of what we cherish in our outer world. From that place of quiet acceptance and embrace, we can act to manifest what we value. If we long to experience the joy of looking into the eyes of a beloved pet who is not present, we can hold space to mourn as we feel moved to. We can then root ourselves in the qualities of joy, connection, and love, awakening them in our body-mind. Rooted in needs awareness, we stay grounded in our personal/collective power, even when the winds of life stir everything and everyone around us. We are rooted in our personal power, the captains of our souls.

When in full awareness of choice, we respond without urgency or attachment to the outcome. Resolving the inner tug-of-war between submission and rebellion, we are free to choose cooperation or non-cooperation. Either choice, rooted in the power of self-connection, is a nonviolent way to manifest a life-giving vision. Recognizing our inner and outer resources in the moment, we access them to the best of our ability. Choice is the ultimate inner resource.

Choice on the Systemic Level

Mahatma K. Gandhi writes: "Just as one must learn the art of killing in the training for violence, so one must learn the art of dying in the training for non-violence. . . . He who has not overcome all fear cannot practice ahimsa."[15] Full choice is grounded in the courage to be truthful. By supporting one another to name and befriend our fears, we can gently hold our shame, often rooted in the fear of not belonging, and connect with our collective truth. We choose to operate from our hearts and are not driven by unresolved pain. At the systemic level, full choice entails staying grounded in collective power even when in a low-power position. Together, we can pause. Co-regulation (regulating our brains with the supportive presence of others' regulated brains) enhances self-regulation.

We can build on the ability to brainstorm together for possible strategies to respond rather than react. When we share a commitment to seeing the humanity in all people, we support one another in dissolving enemy images.[16] We can name our fears, recognizing

> At the systemic level, full choice entails staying grounded in collective power even when in a low-power position.

that we do not need to submit to them. And by acknowledging the myriad ways in which the culture of violence has conditioned us to internalize its voice, we can remind one another of our common humanity.

This key distinction supports us in understanding our reactions and tapping into the power of choice. Individually and collectively, this awareness and awakening acts as an antidote to our conditioning toward powerlessness. Empowering our communities to brainstorm strategies counterbalances the conditioning toward scarcity-based pathways. Personal liberation and systemic liberation work hand in hand.

SUMMARY

- ➷ Examining the distinction between choice and submission or rebellion, we focus our awareness on ourselves, our resources, and our surroundings. Self-awareness frees us to cultivate our ability to choose.

- ➷ Our reactions of submission or rebellion are often born of unresolved pain and trauma. Choice can slowly be restored as we consciously connect with our needs.

- ➷ A commitment to pause can reconnect us to our own power and sense of choice.

- ➷ Rooted in the awareness of interdependence, an empowered choice aims to share resources.

- ➷ This key supports our understanding that collective choice leads to systemic liberation.

WALKING THE TALK:
A LIFE EXAMPLE FROM THE UNITED STATES

BY KRISTIN COLLIER

At the acupuncturist's office, I was told that I'd been "doing too much" by gardening and taking care of my household. The acupuncturist hinted that if I didn't scale back my efforts, she couldn't help me. I have been told this before, and confusion, shame, and anger welled up inside. I touched needs for health and responsibility, thinking of my role in the family. According to this provider, the strategies I'd chosen to address these needs conflicted. Rankled, I did not want to submit to or rebel against what I perceived as her demand. At home, I sat with feelings of anger and loneliness. I breathed into these, creating space. After a time, I realized that I had a choice in how to respond.

I wanted understanding for the way I see myself and my domestic and parenting work. I thought of a chart in my acupuncturist's office that cited examples on a pain scale from one (chilling and enjoying life) to ten (mauled by a bear). Number 4 read, "It hurts, but I'm still working, so it's ok." Part of my "work" is domestic, parenting and gardening for food and for the planet.

I felt the back of my heart and rib cage warm, and the sensation grew uncomfortably as it crept up my neck. Tears sprang to my eyes. What I was hearing in "you're doing too much" is "your 'work' is not important, because you *choose* it rather than *having* to do it. Avoiding such 'extras' will help you." I breathed in and out slowly, holding my tense reaction with care. After a few more deep breaths, I invited my body to relax.

My anger related to a thought that others—and even I!—could not trust that *I* would best manage my needs for personal and communal wellness and sustainability. I also longed for unpaid work caring for the home, community, and planet to be communally held as valuable.

I realized my initial shame stemmed from "going against" the advice of the authority—a conditioned response. I sat with my own precious values for integrity, interdependence, and trust until I was filled with a comfortable warmth. I felt compassion for my initial response of shame. I also felt compassion for my practitioner, understanding that our reactions to one another sprang from internalized systemic conditioning that places her authority and knowledge in a hierarchy above my own. I connected with a deeper trust in myself that I would find a balance that worked best for me and remembered that what I do to contribute to others with presence and choice typically benefits us all. I knew I had the support of my family to help me navigate this and felt empowered to express what was important to me at my next appointment.

PRACTICE

Making Choices With Awareness of Needs

Our bodies can help us to notice when we move between the options of choice, submission, and rebellion. This practice supports needs awareness in the body as we explore these options. This is a kinesthetic mind-body experience with self-reflection. Please, find a quiet space where you can stand or sit in a relaxed and alert manner. We imagine that this practice will take twenty to thirty minutes.

Bending the elbows, bring each hand out to the side at chest level, palms turned upward. Imagine that the left hand holds the *yes* and the right hand holds the *no* related to a specific choice.

In the hand holding the *yes*, determine which needs would be met by this choice and which needs would not be met. And now, inquire with curiosity, "What is leading me to say yes? Is there a sense of duty? Obligation? A sense that I can't say no? I have to?" Slowly transform any life-alienating thoughts by feeling into what matters most. Allow space and time to really connect with the needs and your experience of them. Imagine holding those needs in your hand with care, notice how those needs feel resting on your hand. Give yourself time to savor them.

When ready, move awareness to the hand that holds the *no*. Consider which needs would be met and which would go unmet if you choose to decline. Ask yourself with compassion questions like, "What is leading me to say no? The thought that I 'deserve' otherwise? That I have to affirm myself?" Slowly unearth the needs that are present underneath your thoughts. Again, allow yourself to slowly connect with how precious these needs are. How do these needs feel in the hand that holds them?

Cultivating needs awareness, offer yourself the spaciousness to honor and assess both possible avenues—the *yes* and the *no*—around this choice.

Once you have reached some clarity around what you value underneath the *yes* and the *no*, ask yourself:

- ∾ How can I respond to the needs in the left hand while trying to meet the needs in the right?
- ∾ How can I respond to the needs in the right hand while trying to meet the needs in the left?

We can rest in our breath as we make time and space for this integration of needs. We may mourn any needs that we imagine would not be met and allow for some sense of inner peace to emerge, if possible. Observe whether the emotional tide settles. See if your heart can find solace in the mourning and be at peace with some needs not being as fully met as you would like. (The distinction of meeting as "encountering/being present to" needs rather than "fulfilling" them is critical here to tap into the life-giving qualities of mourning.)

When you sense yourself fully connected with both sets of needs, equally at ease with each option (not defaulting to one, nor resisting the other), let the two hands slowly join together. Remain open to what emerges. How does this slow integration feel as your hands come closer together? Do they unite? If not, what keeps them apart and what might be needed to foster a meeting between the two?

PART II
COMPONENTS

In this section we have clustered the key distinctions relating to the components of the NVC model—observations, feelings, needs, and requests—which we can use to train our minds. Brain science has confirmed that we can use the mind to change the brain in support of well-being and choice. Intentionally training the mind involves clearly directing our attention.

Rosenberg offers four anchors for our attention in order to explore our inner experience and to share it with others. As a precursor to attuning to feelings, we might notice sensations in parts of the body. As we learn to focus on observations, feelings, needs, and requests, we stabilize the mind and restore emotional balance. Please see page 458 for a List of Physical Sensations and for Some Basic Feelings and Needs We All Have, see page 460.

6

OBSERVATION AND OBSERVATION MIXED WITH EVALUATION

*Attitudes, actions, and the way you see the world are
the result of the autonomic nervous system moving
between states of connection and protection.*

—DEB DANA

The key distinction that considers observations alongside observations mixed with evaluation can support us in understanding how we witness the world around us and our reactions to it. We have likely all experienced the dawning of awareness when what we thought was a description of sensory information turned out to be an observation mixed with judgment. Exploring this key gives us the space for greater self-understanding, as well as for choice about where to place our attention.

The brain, an organ shaped by our history, aims to protect us. It quickly and subconsciously interprets sensory information and organizes it: safety or danger? Connection or protection? When integrating the NVC process, we are invited to focus awareness and curiosity on this biological reaction, bringing compassion to it. Taking a step back, we can reflect on the cues (observation) that ignited our assessment (evaluation) and explore whether our behavior stems from an impulsive reaction or from a mindful response. As we pause to observe, we create space for self-awareness. By recognizing what stimulates us, we can choose how to act. With practice, we can also learn to discern whether we are reacting to something happening in the present moment or to cues from the past that have resurfaced.

Marshall Rosenberg frequently credited the philosopher J. Krishnamurti with saying that the ability to observe without evaluating is the highest form of intelligence.[1] Yet that in itself is an evaluation! Judgments and evaluations have a purpose; Rosenberg did not ask us to avoid them entirely. He encouraged us to be aware of and sort them from the sensory experience so that we can increase the likelihood of responding from conscious choice. Observing our thoughts without believing or acting upon them involves "metacognition"—the act of reflecting on our cognition (thinking process). In so doing, we tap into structures and functions of the brain that have evolved more recently. Cultivating a willingness and ability to observe with awareness, we can better understand ourselves, clarify our reactions, and when ready, direct our compassion to more effectively connect with others.

The Power and Limits of Evaluation

The capacity to quickly evaluate stimuli is a survival strategy of the brain. But the value of appraisal extends far beyond that. Evaluating what is safe and what is a threat contributes to the survival of our species. Our ability to assess can also be immensely valuable. Evaluations can help us to determine whether what we are experiencing aligns with needs. For example, if we are sharing a meal with friends, we may assess the situation and count joy, connection, and food among the needs being met. If we are hosting, we may also be meeting our need for contribution. In alignment with this need, we look for anything missing and discover the drinks are not on the table. We swiftly assess strategies to bring these to the table before acting.

As humans, we are also meaning-making creatures. Needs for understanding, an internalized sense of order, creativity, and purpose drive us to assign meaning to our world.

Evaluations, though, often incorporate thoughts, moralistic judgments, assumptions, and internalized norms. Our interpretations are narratives we have absorbed often without realizing it. When an observation is mixed with evaluation, we confuse thoughts, judgments, and overarching narratives with our sensory experience. We may state our evaluations as if they were facts. Mixing observations with evaluations in interpersonal relationships may be perceived as an attack or blame, activating defensiveness and emotional shutdown. When we mix observations with evaluations, we tend to react primarily from our internalized story rather than from the sensory experience. It is important to say that Rosenberg did not imply with this key differentiation that we should let go of our capacity to evaluate, but encouraged us to bring awareness to the process of mixing observations with evaluations.

> Evaluating what is safe and what is a threat contributes to the survival of our species. Yet our evaluations often also incorporate thoughts, moralistic judgments, assumptions, and internalized norms.

Whenever we notice some intensity within, we might pause to witness our habitual thinking.[2] As we do so, we may discover old interpretations and beliefs stemming from past experiences. As long as these unexamined associations continue to be recycled, they will continue to stimulate reactions. Bringing awareness to evaluative thoughts enables us to choose a different response and step into our power.

Observation

When we intentionally shift our attention to an observation, the first of four components in NVC expression (observation, feeling, need, request), we aim to identify to the best of our abilities the sensory input only.

What do we see, hear, touch, taste, and smell that affects our experience? We might also observe thoughts, memories, and imagination, whether they arise as words or images. Concretely this may sound like: "When I hear/see..." or "When I remember (or imagine) seeing/hearing...." The intention in sharing an observation is to create a shared reality on which to build connection.

> The intention in sharing an observation is to create a shared reality on which to build connection.

What we observe is contingent upon a constellation of factors, such as specific time and context. When irritated, for example, chemicals in our brain change our perceptual processing, narrowing our focus on different stimuli. As the saying goes, focused on the trees, we miss the forest.

The NVC observation aims to sort our sensory experience from opinions, beliefs, and any framework or language that implies moralistic judgments. Pausing to observe, we take a step back and identify the sensory stimuli we are responding to. We can notice that our meaning-making mind is adding its preferred interpretations.

Language allows us to communicate our thoughts, and is a primary aspect of thinking. As a social construct, language per se is not observational. Words that refer to objects—"table" for example—seem observational. However, deeper inquiry suggests this view points to a social agreement of labeling crucial coexisting qualities—a piece of furniture with a flat top that provides a level surface on which objects may be placed. A table may be round or square, have multiple legs, and be made of wood or plastic. "Privilege" is an abstract noun that aims to cluster many observational experiences. But it, too, is not observational. The point is that within our cultures, we are socialized to agree upon what we define as "table," or "respect," or "privilege." The more conceptual agreement there is, the less we question our "observations." The more emotional charge there is around an "observation," the less agreement we experience. Ultimately, our growing awareness of the cultural lens allows us to decide how we want to see the world. A seed of choice lies in what meaning we assign to our "observations."

As a social construct, language per se is not observational.

It can be helpful to think of an observation as something a video camera might record—what we see or hear can be captured in a recording of the event. Staying with that metaphor, an observation mixed with evaluation is how the person behind the camera interprets what they see. This metaphor can be expanded. As we hold an observation with care and awareness, there is another crucial point to consider: Whoever is behind the video camera will direct it toward certain aspects of an event. The brain learns to register which details in an event are relevant to notice, particularly details perceived to relate to safety. For example, due to personal, cultural, and historical experiences regarding police, Black people generally are much more likely to notice the presence of police and place it in the foreground in relation to many other elements that may be present in the situation.

As we learn to identify an observation, we are called to consider that our attention is, both consciously and unconsciously, focused on one aspect of an experience. The lens through which we observe is shaped by prior knowledge, expectations, past experiences, beliefs, and our quality of attention.[3]

This preprogrammed selectivity of stimuli explains significant differences in perceptions, feelings, and needs. For example, an Islamic person living in the United States is conditioned to place attention on different stimuli than an Islamic person living in Saudi Arabia.

The lens through which we observe is shaped by prior knowledge, expectations, past experiences, beliefs, and our quality of attention.

These variances in perception can be noted in personal and social identity groupings across the board. Our gender identity, sexual orientation, race and ethnicity, and mental and physical abilities all influence our perceptions of reality, which are often amplified and compounded by intersectionality. A transwoman of color is likely to observe movement on a dark city street differently than a White cisgender woman, all other variables being equal. All our observations, influenced by personal, family, cultural, and systemic conditioning, are the result of filtering things out and including only what the brain registers as relevant. As much as we would like to think otherwise, the observation is still a subjective experience.

Holding these filters with care, we can acknowledge that the appraisal process varies, person to person. Any reaction we have is, in part, the result of the brain filtering for certain stimuli and interpreting it in a way that is unique to our experience. Trauma adds another layer of complexity. With such understanding and self-compassion, we can hold our entire experience—including ongoing reactivity—as sacred.

Rather than seeing these differences in observations and their appraisal as obstacles to connection, this diversity offers us an invaluable opportunity to appreciate the subtleties of being human. The more we can appreciate that multiple observations are possible, both internal and external, the more we can grow in compassion and love. The path from evaluation to observation can be a rich territory of self-discovery, empowering us both intra- and interpersonally, as well as collectively.

STEPHANIE: I enter my daughter's room and feel shocked. The room is a total mess, I think. Asking myself what it is that I see, I take note of a wet towel on the bed, several pieces of clothing on the floor, paper, glue, and scissors on a bookshelf. This awareness helps me to understand the subconscious mental process that got stimulated by sensory information, what we call an "observation" in the NVC process.

I pause and see myself thinking (observing thoughts), "She is so messy!" And then I become aware of and observe a memory. As a child, my parents would never have allowed me to keep my room like that. This is part of why I feel overwhelmed as the need for order emerges in me.

When I walked into the room, I was not just reacting to the present moment. My primary reaction stemmed from past conditioning that I subconsciously carry within; I felt flooded by fear because my brain associated "disorder" with getting scolded, and my body remembered the feeling. In fact, my muscles constrict as I think of this. I observe my explicit memories, implicit associations, and body sensations. Breathing into this awareness, I feel empowered to understand where my reaction and evaluation came from. And owning my perceptions, I can dialogue with my family more skillfully.

Understanding Why We React

Understanding why we react can help us hold it with care. The subcortical regions of the brain appraise stimuli as safe, dangerous, or life-threatening. Based on previous similar experiences, the brain assesses a situation and directs us to safety, either through social engagement or through self-protection that mobilizes or immobilizes (fight, flight, or freeze). This survival-based biological system is so basic and ubiquitous that we share it with many other living beings, including invertebrates. The practice of redirecting the mind to observation empowers us to find our center and monitor sensory information, physical sensations, emotions, and mental activity. The autonomic nervous system, in particular, attends to cues from inside the body, the outside environment, and our relationship with people. This is called neuroception.[4] Awareness of neuroception can support self-understanding and healing from trauma. With self-compassion, we can observe our inner state and the ways it has been shaped by the past. Author and licensed clinical social worker Deb Dana writes, "Neuroception launches a cascade of embodied events that become a story. . . . The physiological state creates a psychological story."[5] Thus, the stories we tell ourselves to make sense of experiences do not begin in the thinking brain, but rather in the autonomic nervous system. Pausing helps us interrupt habitual patterns of reacting based on past experiences (and the meaning our brain has made of them). It allows us to make new choices and thus reshape our autonomic, automatic, patterns of mobilization and immobilization.

The more we understand this process, the more we can step out of identifying with what is stirred in us. We may begin to observe how the mind attaches pleasant/unpleasant qualities to external or internal events. Self-observation also supports us in learning to see how raw sensory input gets quickly intertwined with evaluations. Gradually, we become more aware of how the focus and interpretation of our experiences are affected by our history and conditioning.

It is worth noting that how we perceive and interpret stimuli is biased in such a way that we only take in what supports our particular worldview and the emotion/mood we are feeling at the moment. We are affected by our emotions, our overarching emotional storage system, and the body which stores this energy in motion. This is one more way that our physiological state connects with the story and lens that we filter information from. As the old adage goes, "We see things not as they are, but as we are."[6]

Our emotions anchor themselves in our body around core beliefs we internalized from moments of intense stress or trauma, especially during early childhood when we did not have easy access to resources and/or the capacity to protect ourselves. Perhaps we heard the messages that formed these core beliefs from parents or other adults. Then, in an attempt to guide and shield us from future pain, our minds recorded or crafted them. Core beliefs can be about ourselves: "I always mess things up in relationships," or "there's something basically wrong with me." We may have core beliefs about other people: "I've got to look out for myself because no one else is," or "People of a different ethnic group, religion, or gender are threats to people like me." And they might be about the world: "It's dangerous out there!"

We might harbor such subterranean limiting beliefs for decades. Yet, if we become aware of them and decide they no longer serve us, we can (with empathy, and compassion from others, and sometimes through trauma-release support) loosen their grip and learn to embrace our history with compassion. We might ask ourselves which thoughts come up regularly when we find ourselves in challenging situations. What have we learned in the past that now limits us?

In discovering that a core belief we no longer wish to subscribe to has touched our present reality, we can root ourselves in the power of the observational mind. We might review our actions, reactions, and inactions. Mindfully observing the emotions that arise, we make space for our feelings without fully identifying with them. We can pause and ask ourselves whether there are connections between a memory and how we think, feel, and behave today. As we separate what we actually see, hear, or otherwise sense from the stories or beliefs we have developed about similar situations, a path for new interpretations and responses opens. Beginning to connect with the inner and outer resources that can help us interrupt the thoroughfares of habit, we may cultivate more personal power, day by day.

Clarifying What Is Ours

Observation is a practice that can help us connect the dots between our reactivity and the stories we tell ourselves. The more we become aware of the train of spiraling thoughts, the more we can redirect our attention. In so doing, we empower ourselves to connect to a broader perspective of what is observable. With practice we may be able to do so also in moments of dysregulation. We can learn to observe and appreciate our thoughts,[7] realizing that they are our *thoughts* and not our direct experience. By differentiating between external cues and our brain/body's reactions, we avoid getting sucked into automatically believing they are the truth. That space allows us to distinguish between habitual, repetitive thoughts and interpretations, and what is actually happening now.

Evidence shows that when the brain is processing a stimulus, there is a time frame during which additional or new information cannot be addressed. The technical term for this is the "psychological refractory period." A pause is crucial to allow the brain to let in more information and choose a response. Without that pause, we will mindlessly react to what we take in through our macro lens (magnifying one object) rather than a wide-angle lens (allowing for many objects to be included in the picture). Our pause calls us to awareness so as to nurture a broader perspective.

Being fully present can also be a gift when we find ourselves in boundless joy. Then, too, we can ground ourselves in observation of the sensory input, fully savoring what exactly contributes to our delight. Attunement to the observation may amplify a cascade of nurturing emotions. In this unfolding, our presence frees us to open as the moment calls, expanding our awareness within and without.

The Power of Observation in Social Change

Deepening our self-connection naturally opens the door to our sense of connection with others. Nurturing curiosity grows our capacity to observe our own body language and that of others—eye contact, facial expression, tone of voice, posture, gestures, timing, and intensity of response. Observing is a step toward determining the needs in play, and this information will contribute to our connection with others in the energy of life.

An observation, despite the variety of angles it can be made from, is typically less arguable than a judgment and less emotionally charged. So observations can de-escalate conflict based on different interpretations. Observations create more space for sharing context and increase the possibility of a shared reality on which to base the conversation.

Even so, sensory input—an observation—can be processed, or perceived, differently. Bringing attention to the host of internal and external stimuli and how differently they can be processed, contributes to holding with loving awareness the complexity of both our and other people's experiences. Acknowledging these differences empowers us to connect with one another's humanity, rather than trying to convince others to see things our way.

Humbly, we can recognize that we are limited by our viewpoint and do not have observational access to others' feelings, needs, and intentions. While we do not really know all that goes on, we can choose to stay grounded in the information that reaches us through the senses.

It is our understanding that the distinction which Rosenberg offered between an external stimulus and an internal stimulus offers the foundation for growing an awareness of systemic patterns beyond single instances of experience. Those patterns transcend individual past experiences that still inform perceptions in the present, such as thoughts, beliefs, trauma reactions, and implicit associations. Those patterns encompass recurring and sometimes harmful stimulations at the systemic level and can therefore be understood as included in a deeper level of internal processing of external stimuli.

Expanding our awareness so as to include the systemic patterns related to the observation will offer us important clues that can contribute to connecting with someone else's experience. Sometimes, an observation standing alone does not convey a larger, systemic reality. To take in the wholeness of a picture from a broader perspective, we can take several steps back, as if observing a mural. We may notice aspects we were previously oblivious to.

STEPHANIE: Yesterday I approached an unhoused, dark-skinned woman, wearing a hijab. I held a bag with a comforter in my hand. As I approached her, I said, "Good morning." She glanced at me and then bent into her tent, reemerging with her phone. She kept her phone in what seemed to me a tight hand, her elbow bent at mid-chest, while I asked if she wanted the comforter.

This is the external observation that I can report. If I stay with that visual observation, I feel confused, and connect with my need for understanding. It is only when I take into consideration the systemic aspects related to the visual observation that her behavior starts to make more sense to me. Hate crimes against Muslim people have been on the rise,[8] as well as violence toward unhoused people by housed people.[9] When I observe myself considering those frightening statistics in conjunction with my visual observation, I experience feelings of angst and sorrow. I want all people to be safe and have their basic survival needs met.

Depending on what aspects related to the observation I am holding in my awareness, my response to the woman will take a very different shape. If I only attended to my sensory observation, I might connect with needs for care and connection that I would perceive as unmet. However, if I held in my awareness these systemic patterns, I would connect with needs for compassion and care. I would then have a framework to understand how my approach likely stimulated feelings and needs in her that would not have been stimulated had she been a housed, non-Muslim, light-skinned passerby.

The observation related to our natural sensory experience does not integrate our constructed reality which is based on domination and power differentials. With awareness of the lens through which we see the world, we can devote our energies to gradually "correcting" our myopia, or shortsightedness. We can mourn the gap between our sensory processing and a wider awareness of the inequities among human beings linked to their social location.

While some of us may have a very attuned awareness of certain patterns, we may be completely oblivious of others.

STEPHANIE: I have never been unhoused, so it takes some intentionality for me to acquire a systemic lens in that regard. The more I develop a systemic lens, the more I can connect at a deeper level with people whose social location is very different from my own. This wide-angle view allows me to include aspects beyond external sensory stimuli and individual internal observations. I am empowered to see themes arising from collective persistent attitudes, and the chronic stress-inducing patterns that influence how I see the world.

Each instance in isolation carries one message; compounded, they can deliver quite another. As author and activist Steven Wineman reminds us: "To be a member of a disenfranchised race or ethnic group or gender or class or sexual orientation, or to be a child confronted at every turn with an overwhelming system of adult power, is to be bombarded on a daily basis with messages that who you are as a person does not matter in the larger scheme of things; that you are not as good, not as smart, not as powerful, not as valid in the core of your being as the enfranchised others. Those messages are conveyed through acts of violence and gross brutality, such as sexual violence and gay bashing; they are manifested in material conditions such as severe poverty; and they are also encoded in countless mundane events which are invisible to the dominant group. The totality of these messages can be chronically traumatizing to the extent that they repeatedly create experiences of violation and powerlessness among oppressed people."[10]

The practice of Nonviolent Communication aims to foster compassionate, heart-to-heart connection and to care for the needs of all people.[11] We are aware that including a systemic perspective when discussing this first NVC component may be controversial. We understand the observation component to be a strategy for connection and shared reality: Including a systemic perspective may support those needs.

According to Rosenberg, an observation is "specific to time and context"[12] rather than a tool to reach some "objective truth" around the human experience. The systemic context of Chinese people living in China, for example, is different from the context of Chinese people living in the United States. And the context of Chinese people living in the United States is different from the context of White people living in that same country.

When we refine an observation, we tease out opinions from observations. Nevertheless, recurring patterns of systemic oppression are not opinions. These patterns are often measurable. That many people find the data difficult to really take in is, in and of itself, one such pattern. If we make observations without taking into account these systemic patterns that deeply condition our experiences, our observations will lead us to different feelings and needs. Connecting with a wider frame informs what we will observe and how we will make sense of it.

Patterns of systemic oppression stimulate internal psychological effects not readily observable to the person with systemic power, privilege, or social status within the dominant culture. But those psychological effects do have observable symptoms. Here are some examples: In the United States, Black men are 30 percent more likely and Black women 60 percent more likely to be diagnosed with high blood pressure than White men and women respectively. Black infants have a 2.2 times higher infant mortality rate than White infants, regardless of the socioeconomic status of the mother. Black children are 61 percent more likely than White children to attempt suicide as high schoolers as a result of depression.[13]

For those of us who are not affected by those systemic recurring patterns, the "observation" of systemic realities may just seem a cognitive exercise more closely linked to an evaluation. As such, it may be perceived as more disconnecting than connecting. Yet for those of us who live or witness day after day those dynamics, the systems that define power and privilege are omnipresent and shape our moment-to-moment inner experience.

Privilege has sometimes been described as whatever it is you do not have to think about. Understanding privilege at the personal and interpersonal level, we can easily hear blame. But the concept of privilege is connected to a cluster of concrete, measurable life experiences tied to the domination structures we continue to maintain. It is structural and unrelated to our attitude, and yet understanding privilege gives us greater choice in responding to life and people around us. When we realize we have greater access to power and resources, even if just in certain areas of life, we might wake up to realities that we are not accustomed to seeing, mourn the disparities in life that are linked to the systems of domination that are in place, and humbly use whatever privilege we do have to support more equity in the world.

We believe Rosenberg is addressing the systemic level when he talks about "gangs" in order to refer to "school systems, governments, police, corporations."[14] Learning to track the "invisible" patterns that lead to the staggering statistics we touched on and many other such data points is a challenging journey for White people. It requires tremendous courage and tenderness. This journey is, in our understanding, a key to connecting with the life context of another person's core subjective experience, and thus is essential to the possibility of truly meeting each other. Certified trainer and assessor Roxy Manning has coined the term "systemic observation" as a way to take into account the repeating patterns that reinforce separation and choicelessness.[15] This wide-angle lens offers a broader scope with which to witness chronic internal reactivation by stimuli linked to the structures and systems we are all immersed in and by which we are all affected differently.

While bringing attention to these patterns can support us in growing greater awareness, there are also potential pitfalls. Attending to a wider picture, we may risk losing the specificity of the NVC observation. That specificity often supports heart-to-heart connection. The question then is how to remain attentive to systemic patterns while also offering enough specificity to move hearts. There is no either/or here.

Another potential risk is that in our desire to bring attention to systemic patterns, we may unwittingly cast people into categories. For example, clustering all Muslims as one group leads us to believe that each and every one experiences life in the same way. We then easily assume that all of them are fearful of living in the United States. When our "systemic observations" are still based on narratives of separation, we can unwittingly continue to reinforce a mentality of "us" vs. "them." While growing an awareness of systemic patterns can support understanding, connection, and a shared reality, we also want to maintain awareness of the power to choose. Others are not bound by our interpretations, even if based on systemic facts.

STEPHANIE: While I found it supportive to uphold a systemic awareness around the unhoused Muslim person, I still want to stay curious and not jump to conclusions around her unique experience with me. Otherwise, I risk losing the opportunity to connect with her, based on a systemic narrative that I paradoxically hold onto in order to connect.

Systemic awareness can support a shared understanding of the depth and intensity of the needs stimulated by an external stimulus. As Manning writes, "If the intention of naming the observation is to create a shared reality . . . we often cannot have a shared reality without understanding the internal and systemic observations from the perspective of the person stimulated."[16] The question then is: how can we grow a systemic awareness, rooted in interdependence, as a humble integrating act of the collective and the individual? Any little step we can take in the direction of such integration supports us in creatively attuning to strategies that address the individual and also reshape systemic layers to better serve all beings and the earth. Attending to our observations can become a spiritual practice that invites us to be present with what is, rather than believing our stories, assumptions, or interpretations about what is. And it can become a practice that contributes to shifting the social landscape we live in.

This key distinction supports us in cultivating mindfulness in the present moment. With it, we can differentiate a witnessing awareness from mental activity that interprets and classifies experiences, both in the moment and systemically. In that sense, the observation can help us identify and frame stimuli in new ways, so we can release fixed views related to shared social constructs. The observation can become a fulcrum that supports us in reaching deep within ourselves and reaching out to all life with greater compassion.

SUMMARY

- ↢ This key distinction hinges on the understanding that an observation can be of external sensory stimuli and internal thoughts, beliefs, trauma reactions, and implicit associations.

- ↢ The evaluation consists of thoughts, judgments, assumptions, and internalized norms due to socialization and our personal history.

- ↢ Acknowledging how observations can be mixed up with evaluations can prompt us to learn about the lenses of others, especially those with less privilege, so as to expand our understanding and support deeper connection.

- ↢ Redirecting the mind to sensory stimuli, we can become increasingly aware of the ways our "emotional storage" influences what we see, then intentionally expand our view with a wide-angle lens.

WALKING THE TALK:
A LIFE EXAMPLE FROM BRAZIL

BY YURI HAASZ, CNVC CERTIFIED TRAINER

In my earliest memory, I huddled with many people in a dark place, fear and tension heavy in the air. Our Jewish family and community drew together in the bomb shelter; Israel was at war in 1973. Throughout my life, this event and others like it were woven together in a narrative of the "others" who wanted me and my family dead. They wanted all of us Jews dead. We had to defend ourselves to survive. This ubiquitous story was reaffirmed in school history books, in public commemorations, and in the names of streets and squares.

Decades later, I dove into academic research on the Palestine question during my master's degree, only to have my world undone. Researching in the field, doing human rights work, and most importantly, discovering the Israeli new historians and like sources, I learned that a host of facts had been withheld from the narrative I had been fed growing up. To my shock, these facts around the events of 1948 and beyond, registered in the Israeli government archives, had been legally kept secret for decades. And even after coming to light, they were—and still are—denied by official institutions. These facts, continuously culled for the construction of a contemporary collective narrative, can be confirmed by eyewitnesses to this day. They are also supported by the evidence of destroyed Palestinian villages.

When Israel was created in 1948, nationalist Jewish (Zionist) militias crafted the "Plan Dalet," a systematic expulsion of the Palestinian people from lands where Palestinians composed 95 percent of the population at that time. These Zionist militias planned strategic massacres to shock and scare the people so they would flee. I have replaced my narrative of "fighting to defend ourselves" with a new narrative that I now believe to be true, however painful it is: "It was an ethnic cleansing."

This is how my family "inherited" Israel and how my world came to be. It is also the history and origin of Palestinian anger and frustration. Falling upon this new perception, my world collapsed; my identity was displaced. I began to rethink my life and what I wanted for myself and others in this world. I started to speak out, to create human rights projects, to engage in difficult dialogues for change. I found myself wanting justice and reparations for Palestinians, wanting new and different strategies for Jewish autonomy that didn't inflict domination over another people.

My former understanding of the world had been wholly shaped by the lens of a single story. Evaluations, judgments, theories, thoughts, and assumptions filled the gaps between real-world events to create the dominant narrative of my people. I began to focus my personal lens on the observable facts, a shared reality gleaned from sources on both sides. Critical Jewish academics who dare to challenge the national narrative cite evidence from Israeli archives. The documented reality of Palestinian survivors is further confirmed by evidence in the field. My understanding of the world at once was completely transformed, and my perception of my own needs and strategies along with it.

PRACTICE

Expanding Observational Awareness

We cannot sense another person or ourselves when we are distracted by our unbridled thoughts. This exercise is intended to support the integration of both brain hemispheres when practicing being present, also called "presence." While the left hemisphere picks up on language, the right hemisphere interprets nonverbal communication. Please find a quiet space and a partner. A human partner ensures verbal dialogue, yet this practice may be adapted to experience sensing with any being you choose to become present with. Begin by just reading through the practice together, for greater ease and flow in the moment. Then, decide together who will speak first. We imagine this exercise will take no more than thirty minutes, counting transition time between speaking and listening.

INSTRUCTIONS FOR THE SPEAKER

Share what is on your mind/heart with an approximate intensity level of a maximum of five on a scale of one to ten, so there is enough emotional "charge" to give it life, without being so much that the charge could distract from learning.

INSTRUCTIONS FOR THE LISTENER

While the speaker shares, bring your attention to their body language—movement of the eyes, facial expressions, pauses, postures, gestures. Also attend to their speech patterns—tone of voice, intensity of voice, rhythm of speech. Make a mental note of the ways their nonverbal communication is connected with the content of the sharing. If you feel inclined to mirror the speaker's body language, physically or mentally, we invite you to do so if it feels natural and easy, not exaggerated. Sensing into your own body, notice: How does that feel? Do any particular sensations come up? Any specific emotions?

Take a moment for both of you to center yourselves. Recalling the awareness practices you may have done individually from the beginning of this book, sink into the present moment, perhaps by sensing places in the body where tension may be held and then relaxing them. Acknowledge any thoughts that arise and allow them to pass, if they will. You may return to give these thoughts focused attention later. Invite your awareness to open to mutuality. When ready, convey this to your partner with a gentle nod of the head.

- Set a timer for five minutes and begin. The speaker shares about what is on their mind or heart.

- Once the five minutes are over, pause together, then set a timer for three minutes. Regain a sense of presence as needed. The listener now reflects back, in observational language, the body communication witnessed during specific moments of the sharing. For example, "When you were talking about your son's birthday, you paused, then the pitch of your voice rose. Your hands that had been resting on your lap until then moved up to your heart. And then you laughed."

- Reverse roles.

- At the end, set a timer for four minutes. Speaker and listener exchange their feelings, needs, and insights about what just happened.

- When the practice is complete, gratitude may be offered between partners.

7

FEELINGS AND FEELINGS MIXED WITH THOUGHTS

Don't allow your mind to tell
your heart what to do.

—PAULO COELHO

The key distinction between feelings and feelings mixed with thoughts aims to help us discern how thoughts and perceptions relate to our feelings, consciously or unconsciously, so as to increase our sense of agency.[1] Our emotions help us to survive, to communicate in social situations,[2] and to move into action.

There is a sense of empowerment in understanding that our feelings arise because we assess needs as being met or not met. This cognitive assessment is often not as conscious as we imagine it to be. How we feel also influences our thoughts and how we experience the world. Coming to terms with this incredibly complex feedback loop supports us in cultivating compassion for ourselves and others. Building awareness around our thinking and perception can allow us to question them. Taking ownership of our feelings, we cultivate other perspectives and can communicate in more effective and connecting ways. The practice of NVC becomes a way to mindfully navigate our human experience.

Emotions are considered by many neuroscientists to be adaptive responses orchestrated by the brain in order to alert us to crucial stimuli, allowing for a rapid survival response to the environment. As such, their function differs from thoughts, which allow us to assign meaning to our experiences. The complex and multifaceted process that gives rise to feelings starts with interoception (how the brain reads internal sensations and the physiological state of the entire body). "The term *feelings* emphasizes conscious experiences of something happening in one's own body, and these kinds of interoceptive conscious experiences are often distinguished from other perceptual experiences, or from 'cognitive' experiences (what we might typically call *thinking*)," write neuroscientists Ralph Adolphs and David Anderson.[3] We have included some basic neuroscience around emotions, feelings, and thoughts, as we hope it can contribute to greater awareness and understanding of this key distinction, so as to support greater compassion for ourselves and others.

We also want to acknowledge that among neuroscientists and psychologists, there are different understandings of the nature of emotions and how emotions emerge at the somatic, perceptive, and cognitive levels. There are different models of "basic emotions," or universal ingredients of our emotional life that include a specific neural activation and commonly shared physiological expression, while some scientists do not believe in "basic emotions" at all. New neuroscience data on emotions continues to emerge, and we find value in investigating different approaches as they shed light on different aspects that influence our emotional experiences. This exploration is an attempt to step out of the "either/or" mentality and entertain the possibility of embracing more of the "transcend and include" principle philosopher Ken Wilber speaks of.[4]

Consciously attending to our feelings and uncoupling them from the thinking process, we can learn to harness the energy of our emotions.

Feelings offer us information that helps us to understand our inner life and the value we have assigned to stimuli.[5] Appraisal theory postulates that an emotion emerges within milliseconds "as we progress from detecting the relevance of an event, to evaluating its implication, our ability to cope with it, and its normative significance."[6] Charles Darwin first posited that emotions move us to approach or withdraw from a stimulus depending on how safe/rewarding or unsafe/punishing we assess it to be. As we integrate this key distinction, we identify and relate to our feelings rather than reacting to or rejecting them.[7] Consciously attending to our feelings and uncoupling them from the thinking process, we can learn to harness the energy of our emotions.

Emotion and Feelings

Many neuroscientists describe *emotions* as functional internal states outside of our conscious awareness and *feelings* as the conscious awareness of emotions or the bodily sensations that arise in response to a need that calls for our attention.

Neuroscientist Joseph E. LeDoux first posited the distinction between emotions and feelings in the 1980s. "I treated *emotions*," he writes "in terms of essentially non-conscious brain states that connect significant stimuli with response mechanisms, and *feelings* as conscious experiences arising from these non-conscious brain states."[8]

Rosenberg uses the terms *emotions* and *feelings* interchangeably, as we all do in everyday speech, to point to the brain states that we experience when faced with situations that either threaten or enhance our survival.

Yet we want to bring attention to how this distinction between emotions and feelings can contribute to the relationship with our emotional life. Emotions and feelings are mediated by different brain mechanisms. In LeDoux's words: "feelings are states of consciousness about emotional situations."[9] In other words, consciousness is what makes feelings possible. It is our understanding that the practice of NVC aims to support greater consciousness by bringing attention to our experience. As such, this distinction can support our practice. NVC supports us to take ownership of our internal experience. We experience emotions, but step into agency when connecting to our feelings. For example, one child experiencing intense emotions may punch another child. As they learn to recognize and name their feelings, children are empowered to modulate behavior and express their anger through words rather than their fists. Regulation is linked to conscious awareness of feelings.

As feelings are linked to conscious appraisal of brain states, and appraisal is linked to experience-dependent associations, feelings are susceptible to conditioning based on our social and physical contexts. This fascinating insight can support us in understanding how people of different cultures and who speak different languages express feelings differently.

Personal power and choice lie in this distinction between emotions and feelings.

As personal healing and social transformation rely on transforming conditioning, the differentiation of emotions from feelings carries significance. Personal power and choice lie in this distinction between emotions and feelings.

Emotions as Social Constructs: Feelings Mixed With Thought

Emotions are considered by some neuroscientists as social constructs insofar as emotions are linked not only to attention, perception, and memory, but also to beliefs, roles, and power dynamics. In other words, there are personal and contextual factors that play a role in our emotional experiences. This is not to say that emotions do not have a body-based component or that we can simply talk ourselves out of emotions. The concept of emotions as social constructs seems supportive in discerning how our thoughts, influenced by social conditioning, affect our moment-to-moment experience and in finding our way back to a more direct, life-giving relationship to ourselves.

We may innately[10] respond to certain stimuli with specific emotions, and certain circumstances are likely to elicit specific emotions in most of us (grief, for example, in the case of the loss of a loved one). And, our emotional experience seems also largely influenced by enculturation. Neuroscientist Lisa Feldman Barrett writes, "[Emotions] are not universal but vary from culture to culture. They are not triggered; you create them. They emerge as a combination of the physical properties of your body, a flexible brain that wires itself to whatever environment it develops in, and your culture and upbringing, which provide that environment."[11] While Barrett's approach with all its implications may have points of alignment with the practice of NVC and also clear points of discrepancies, such a statement seems to line up with Rosenberg's guidance to recognize the internal/external factors linked to our emotions and to take full ownership of and responsibility for our feelings as they emerge from our personal, family, and cultural history and experience. Barrett's quote may support us in teasing out the event/stimulus for our emotions from the cause or the meaning we give to our interoceptive experiences. Her body of work can also invite us to question our default assumption about the "undeniable truth" or solid nature of our emotions, without denying the real effects that situations have on us.

The culture we live in influences how much awareness we have of physical sensations, how we experience different emotions, and how we understand the relationship between emotions, physical sensations, and thoughts.

Socialization based on gender stereotypes such as "men are tough and women are weak" rely on feelings to reinforce patriarchal culture. Such a narrative programs men to control their emotions. And just as men are ranked higher than women, so thoughts are prioritized over feelings. The expression "don't be a sissy" links specific feelings with women and children; in fact, the term equates a woman's status with that of a child, as denoted by the "baby talk" word "sissy." Such a stereotypical gibe toward a man threatens his gender identity and social status. Thus sexism and its consequent power inequality get reinforced by unwritten codes related to our feelings. That same dynamic can emerge in the relationship between the broader culture and its subcultures. Ethnic groups and subcultures that are more emotionally expressive may be dismissed, seen as "less than," or even punished because patriarchy glorifies control.

Most emotional responses and the behaviors that accompany them occur immediately after a stimulus and with little or no conscious effort. Adolphs and Anderson write that "you typically have to exert effort for the emotion *not* to cause the behavioral response."[12]

"Even when you feel no sense of agency when experiencing emotion, which is most of the time, you are an active participant in that experience,"[13] writes Barrett. Understanding cognitively that we play an active role in the arising of an emotion does not mean that we invalidate, deny, or avoid that emotion. Quite the contrary, part of our participation also lies in our ability to step back and to bear witness to our emotional experience with compassion. Such witnessing allows us an adequate distance to explore our experience with curiosity and tenderness. The value of this key distinction is most effectively apprehended in practice when we are not activated so that we may find ourselves more aware of that "participant" role when we are. Cultivating such awareness allows us to take responsibility for our feelings as interacting with our thinking patterns and underlying needs.

Since 1987 there has been an ongoing dialogue between neuroscientists and Buddhist scholars, including His Holiness the Dalai Lama. These exchanges also bring meaningful contributions to the understanding of emotions as mental construct. Buddhist psychology labels the "feeling tones" (*vedana*) as "pleasant, unpleasant, and neutral." While there are debates among Buddhist schools, "vedana" is generally understood as the link between the body and the mind. These bare affective qualities (attractiveness/averseness) are the valence the brain assigns to sensory stimuli and their impact on the body-mind system. They color our perceptions and mental activity, and can be seen as correlating with the foundation of feelings, recognized in their pervasive influence on our emotional experience. These subjective, filtered reactions, whether physical or mental, are considered part of our survival strategies and start immediately after sensory information enters the brain. As such, they are considered constructions of the mind, not inherent to the object of experience, but pointing to how the object is known.

As soon as sound enters the brain, it gets labeled as "sound" (birds chirping: pleasant) or "noise" (the siren of an ambulance: unpleasant). Yet all sound waves are a form of energy linked to air molecules vibrating in a pattern. The body-mind system is impacted (feeling tones are triggered), and the brain determines the tonality of the experience (feelings are constructed). From this interpretative range of hedonic tones linked to body sensations, the many emotions we feel emerge.

The practice of NVC supports us in cultivating awareness of stimuli (observation vs. evaluation) and how the mind quickly interprets and judges those stimuli. Noticing this initial approach/withdrawal, pleasant/unpleasant response and naming our emotions empower us not to get completely caught up in their arising and passing, while deeply honoring them as part of our experience in the moment.

Anger: An Example of a Feeling Mixed With Thought

If we identify with our emotions—"*I am* angry"—we might feel utterly helpless. "Whenever you don't own your feelings, your feelings own you," writes leadership consultant Julie Diamond.[14] The practice of self-awareness and self-connection inspired by this key may provide a lifeline, when we would otherwise struggle with a sense of drowning in our indiscriminate experience of feelings mixed with thoughts.

Anger is included in both neuroscientist Jaak Panksepp's and psychologist Paul Ekman's theoretical models of basic emotions. Rosenberg invites us to inquire more deeply and realize that the emotion of anger is a combination of thoughts, feelings, biochemical reactions, and physiological arousal. Rosenberg highlighted that anger is indeed life-serving, as it alerts us that our needs are unmet. Yet he pointed out that anger is also a signal that we have been distracted by judgmental thinking, which implies wrongness, badness, or punitive thinking (the "deserve" mentality).[15] By recognizing how our thinking constructs our experience of anger and by unearthing the needs present in us, we can reclaim our true personal power in ways that blaming self or others does not.

The stimulus of our anger is not the cause of our anger.[16] Our evaluation, the narrative we attach to the stimulus, and the judgments we apply to the situation, contribute to our experience of anger. Unexamined thoughts mixed with our feelings contribute to disconnection from our needs. One way to take ownership of our feelings and bring awareness to our thinking is to specifically name the thoughts that accompany the feeling, "I feel angry because I am telling myself that. . . ."[17] Rather than recycling our violence-provoking conditioning to blame others for our feelings, we can take responsibility for our experience and redirect the energy of our feelings to fulfill our needs. Whenever we uncouple feelings from life-alienating thoughts, we can discover that, as Rosenberg says, "The basic function of feelings is to serve our needs."[18]

Some scientists, including Lisa Feldman Barrett, question whether we ever have an emotion that is separate from thought. According to Barrett, emotions are not caused or triggered by stimuli, otherwise emotions would be reflexes. Our memory and expectations largely "construct" our emotional response to a stimulus, according to the context. "Emotions are not reactions to the world. You are not a passive receiver of sensory input but an active constructor of your emotions. From sensory input and past experience, your brain constructs meaning and prescribes action."[19] In her theory, emotions consist of many components relating to our individual differences and the cultural effects linked to our life experiences. We find her understanding of emotions quite fascinating as it clearly points to a link between the individual experience of emotions and a wider systemic awareness of how our social programming affects us.

Much of this research was not available when Rosenberg's foresight invited us to distinguish feelings from thought. From a scientific standpoint, the complex interplays between the two are still being investigated.[20]

Thoughts Over Emotions?

In the Western world, our conditioned distrust of emotions deems them inferior to the human capacity for reason.[21] While brain science seems to offer anatomical confirmation that emotion and reason evolved distinctly, it also advocates for the integration of emotion and cognition rather than their persistent dichotomization in our lives.[22]

We may avoid experiencing emotions or dodge responsibility for our feelings by using a number of costly strategies. These strategies often use thought to direct emotions. We might attempt to numb or suppress our emotions,[23] squelching tears and bottling up our feelings. This could result in an unexplained "bad mood" or unexpected explosions as we mindlessly discharge that energy in other situations, behavior which could be assessed as acting out of proportion. We might employ avoidance strategies; consumerism thrives on that. Or we might "swap" one set of emotions for another that we deem "safer"—perhaps exchanging the intensity of anger for the relative calm of sadness. In this way, we attend only to those emotions we have learned are socially acceptable.

Enculturation affects our ability to feel our feelings and distinguish them from thoughts. The less we distinguish thoughts from feelings, the more we may spiral into alienation from our bodies and our emotions. This inability to relate to our emotional life can lead to health problems. We may spiral into anxiety or depression, and/or anesthetize our unbearable discomfort with drugs or alcohol.

The less we distinguish thoughts from feelings, the more we may spiral into alienation from our bodies and our emotions.

On a systemic level, avoidance of uncomfortable feelings related to power differentials can have serious consequences in terms of perpetuating systems of inequality and violence. When we are in a position of privilege, we very likely resist taking in the impacts related to it because uncomfortable emotions are activated—the very emotions we are socialized to avoid. We can proactively endeavor to shift this reaction. As White people, for example, we can learn to approach discomfort rather than withdraw from it, if we want to fully take in the many ways in which we benefit from structures and systems that have been created and still operate to prioritize the needs of White people.

The discomfort is part of an internal feedback system that points to universal needs for care and equity, yet we avoid feeling this discomfort at all costs as it often triggers shame. Accountability around this cycle of inequality is hard-won, as it must crack the cast of socialization. Yet placing the onus of awareness and empathy on those in harm's way is unsustainable and risky at best. Meenadchi, who shares their trauma-informed NVC practice, writes, "Because violence exists in context and because hurt people hurt people, many NVC practitioners place the onus of compassion upon people who have experienced harm. The implication is that if survivors of interpersonal and systemic abuse could only sufficiently empathize with their abusers, the violence would de-escalate and ultimately cease. It's bizarre to me."[24] More people are speaking out about the expectations placed on the oppressed to shift this dynamic.

Poet, novelist, and activist Audre Lorde writes, "Black and Third World people are expected to educate white people as to our humanity. Women are expected to educate men. Lesbians and gay men are expected to educate the heterosexual world. The oppressors maintain their position and evade their responsibility for their own actions."[25] We may indeed feel brokenhearted at the realization that our well-being has come at a cost for others. Teasing out thoughts from feelings, we may learn to uncouple our grief from the deep-seated shame that is attached to a thought that there is something fundamentally wrong with us. This discernment empowers us to realize the impact of enculturation so we can make conscious shifts toward a culture of peace.

Thoughts Disguised as Feelings

Our emotions interact with our thoughts, needs, and internal and external environments. These elements continuously interact with one other.

We interpret sensory data through a wide-angle lens of conditioning and past experience as we come to acknowledge what feelings and needs are alive.

To complicate matters further, our language allows for thoughts to be confused with feelings in conventional expression. When we begin a sentence with "I feel like/that/as if," a thought, not a feeling, invariably follows. We might say, "I feel like going to the beach." We might also follow "I feel . . ." with a judgment about ourselves, like "I feel clumsy." Some words are known as feelings in the English language, yet through the NVC lens they are seen as feelings mixed with thoughts because they explicitly include the interpretations of someone else's behavior rather than describing our inner emotional state. When we say that we feel disrespected, framed, manipulated, rejected, or cheated (passive voice), these expressions do not represent our actual emotional state so much as they reveal what we think others are doing to us.

Describing our "feelings" in these ways gives us a sense that we are speaking in "I" statements about our genuine experience . . . and yet, we are not actually sensing or taking responsibility for our feelings mixed with thoughts. Sidestepping responsibility, we give our power away and often inadvertently blame or shame others, perceiving them as the cause of our feelings. We might also direct our feelings violently at others by consciously stating or unconsciously implying that they are at fault—"I feel . . . because you . . ." Or, "You make me feel . . ." Both convey that we are not responsible for our own feelings and someone else is, leaving us powerless.

The NVC Process as Emotional Regulation

The practice of NVC helps us to cultivate a conscious relationship with our physical sensations and to name feelings.[26] Instead of dismissing them as "irrational," we engage with feelings as a key to our personal power. We shift from the right/wrong mindset that can further fuel our feelings to experiencing this emotional energy as an entry point to connecting with needs. Rather than interpreting sensory input as objective information about the world, we pause to acknowledge that this is our subjective experience. Developing NVC skills and emotional intelligence involves growing our capacity to consciously feel our emotions and name them, choose when and how to act on them, attune to the feelings of others, and be able to differentiate our own feelings from those of other people.

Connecting with our bodies, we can learn to listen to our inner experience, trusting that it has a valuable message for us. The more we integrate the practice of NVC, the more we are able to discern how our thoughts and feelings affect each other so that we may act in alignment with our values rather than solely out of social conditioning. Understanding that thoughts shape our reactions can help us realize that our feelings are not a "natural" response to the external world. The practice of self-empathy, when exploring feelings and thoughts, helps us to regulate our emotions so we can exercise greater agency based on needs awareness.[27]

According to Stanford psychologist James J. Gross, emotional regulation is the ability to intentionally influence the experience and expression of our emotions.[28] As humans, we do have the power to relate to our emotions in ways that can influence which emotion we choose to feel, when we want to connect with it more fully, and how to express it. One of the functions of the prefrontal cortex is to modulate emotions. Yet that capacity is built within human relationships. As author and CNVC certified trainer Sarah Peyton writes, "Self-regulation is always internalized coregulation."[29]

Emotional regulation is the process through which humans develop the ability to soothe and modulate distressing sensations and emotions. This process begins early in life through connection with nurturing and reliable primary caregivers. Interdependence, foundational to the practice of NVC, is in play once again. Emotional modulation can occur in a variety of ways at the moment the emotion is arising or once it has fully emerged. Gross identified five major strategies to utilize the power of our thinking mind to regulate emotions depending on the stage of the emotion:

- *Situation selection*—choosing situations that contribute to the emotions we prefer to experience.
- *Situation modification*—changing an unavoidable situation to modify its emotional impact.
- *Attention deployment*—choosing to focus our attention in a different direction.
- *Reappraisal*—cognitively reframing a situation/relationship/ self-image to assign it a different meaning.
- *Response modulation*—shifting nonverbal communication such as intentionally changing body posture or tone of voice, establishing mindfulness, visualization, and/or generating the opposite emotion.

As a relational approach, NVC offers self-regulation strategies in all five areas, contributing to our awareness and agency in regard to feelings mixed with thoughts. Awareness of feelings, the pinpointing of observations (vs. evaluative thoughts), and requests (vs. demands based on rigid thinking) can help us navigate situation selection and modification. Empathy, as a practice of co-regulation, and self-empathy as internalized co-regulation uniquely contribute to attention deployment by helping us identify stimuli that have an emotional impact on us. These practices bring attention to body sensations, feelings, and needs rather than the proliferation of thoughts. Reappraisal commences when we notice right/wrong thinking, then alchemize that dichotomous thinking into needs awareness. One way of modulating our response is to connect with the evaluation of a need (one that is not survival-based[30]) as "unmet," honing in on the feelings and the feelings mixed with thoughts. This discernment can support our ability to move beyond the cognitive assessment and open up to the fuller qualities of that need, regardless of whether or not it is "met."

Our mental representations shape our feelings and perceptions. Thoughts lead us to filter our experiences, including at times to catastrophize and overgeneralize. "We will never learn to live compassionately as a human family! Why even try?!" we might say. When we tell ourselves that we are stupid or not good enough, we may experience a sense of shame. And when we look deeper into that shame, we may recognize heaviness or hollowness in the body, feelings of overwhelming sadness or discomfort, and a longing for connection, love, and belonging. Honoring those sensations, emotions, and needs can support a sense of calm.

Conversely, we can tap into the power of thoughts, using them intentionally to support emotional regulation. Neuroscientists Elizabeth Johnston and Leah Olson write, "Although we tend to think of distraction as negative when it prevents us from focusing on the task at hand, when it is deliberately used to take our attention off an upsetting or distressing problem, it is an effective regulation strategy."[31] The authors continue to explain that sometimes emotions are too powerful to be reappraised on the spot and attention deployment may be the most effective strategy in high-intensity moments. We can develop this competence that enables us to separate feelings from thoughts and tap into the power of one or the other with intentionality so as to exercise choice.

Feelings Moving Us Toward Needs

Stephanie learned from a conversation with certified trainer Lucy Leu, who collaborated closely with Rosenberg, that untangling thoughts from feelings to the degree that we are consciously capable is so important to self-awareness and compassion that Rosenberg initially included thoughts as an additional component in what later became the four components of OFNR (observations, feelings, needs, requests). While he did explore how thoughts influence our experience, he chose to focus on feelings and needs.

As part of the NVC practice, Rosenberg encouraged distinguishing thoughts from observations as well as thoughts from feelings. He cautioned that mixing these seems to interfere with connection. In an exchange with Stephanie, CNVC certified trainer Marion Little reiterated that Rosenberg did not altogether discourage judgments, labels, evaluation, and analysis. In fact, he recognized these ways of thinking as useful for many purposes related to cognitive understanding. However, he repeatedly emphasized that when there is distress or distrust between people, these approaches tend to objectify others and interfere with connection.

Rosenberg realized that even when we own our thoughts, others tend to react to those thoughts when we share them. For example, saying "When I see you offering a hundred dollars to the homeless person, I think you are too generous," we are not mixing the observation with the evaluation and clearly are taking ownership of our thoughts. Yet others may still suffer a negative impact from our words, as if we did not observe our thoughts but rather fully believed them. That is why Rosenberg encourages us not only to move away from identifying with our thoughts but also to directly connect with needs. In a sense, Rosenberg's approach invites us to take the most direct route to what is life-serving.

Assessing whether needs that are not essential to survival have been met almost invariably involves thoughts, interpretations. and beliefs. The feedback loop among thoughts, physical sensations, and feelings undoubtedly affects our experience.[32]

We can use our feelings to root us in the body, tapping into a more expansive awareness of the need . . . the universal flow of life beyond the thinking mind. The power of a feeling is in its connection to needs, as it directs us toward what we desire. When our attention is on what matters to us, the energy of our feelings moves us toward requests that are clearly connected with our needs. Without this focus, we may be chaotically flooded with emotion or contract into psycho-emotional rigidity.

Anger, for example, can be directed to mobilize resources toward action as we stand up for our needs or use our influence to amplify others' voices. This energy can also be used to clarify our limits connected to

> **The power of a feeling is in its connection to needs, as it directs us toward what we desire. . . . Emotions are only destructive when suppressed or acted out without choice.**

what is important. Emotions are only destructive when suppressed or acted out without choice. Rosenberg classified anger, depression, guilt, and shame as feelings that are particularly entangled with the thinking process, as they often breed life-alienating thoughts.

The emotional brain does not distinguish between an internal and an external stimulus. A thought in the form of images or words such as, "I am a mess," triggers a similar response to that when we hear someone say to us, "You are a mess!" Both external and internal events trigger a cascade of biochemical reactions. Indeed, there is evidence that physical and emotional pain are registered by the same brain system.[33] Because an emotional state can be activated by an internal stimulus alone, we can to some degree consciously choose to direct our attention in life-giving ways.

Emotions may have evolved out of reflexes, yet we can consciously channel the momentum of their energy to carry us toward what matters to us most. Emotions and moods are also contagious. When we feel connected with our aliveness, others around us will benefit too. We might express what we want from this place of wholeness rather than lack to cultivate vulnerability and connection.

Between a stimulus and a behavioral response there is an emotion. Supporting us in deconstructing stimuli from interpretations and feelings from thoughts, the practice of NVC offers us a path toward liberation as we explore how to direct the power of feelings in ways that contribute to what matters most.

SUMMARY

- ✎ As we learn to observe, relate to, and uncouple feelings from thoughts, we increase inner spaciousness and choice, and decrease the likelihood of reacting from or rejecting our feelings.

- ✎ When we uncouple feelings from feelings mixed with thoughts, we can seek the precious needs beneath.

↵ Consciously differentiating feelings from thoughts, we can enhance our ability to self-regulate by skillfully choosing strategies—situation selection/modification, attention deployment, reappraisal, and response modulation.

↵ When we differentiate feelings from feelings mixed with thoughts, we may empower ourselves to approach anger or shame, accepting our experience and even our thoughts, with greater understanding and compassion.

WALKING THE TALK:
A LIFE EXAMPLE FROM KENYA

BY SAM ODHIAMBO, CNVC CERTIFIED TRAINER

I remember my first love twenty years ago, just after high school. My family and friends guessed it was only a matter of time before we would be married. I loved her, and back then, this was the only feeling I recognized myself capable of. But, growing up male in Nairobi, I neither talked of nor expressed my emotions. A man was supposed to be strong. Emotions were reserved for women.

One day, a friend told me that my committed girlfriend had been invited by a close male friend of mine to his house, and that she was even preparing lunch for him. I could not take it. She had betrayed our love and the plans we had together. It seemed as if my life and dreams had been shattered. This information destroyed me. I did not at the time understand that I even had feelings about what I'd heard, or that they were affected by my thoughts.

I didn't know what to do. In an effort to man up, I chose to remain silent. In the weeks that followed, I lost weight and couldn't concentrate on my responsibilities. I never checked in with my girlfriend on the matter. I just cut the ties. Friends and family asked me what happened, as she no longer visited. I said I didn't want to talk about it, and indeed I never did. Thus, our relationship ended.

When I reflect back, I am so sad that I never experienced the choice to express myself about what I had heard, nor to invite her perspective. I mourn that I lost my chance to get clarity and the opportunity to rebuild the relationship or find closure. The man in me had wanted to cry and let out the pain, to be held and cared for. I had longed to be supported and to reconnect with my girlfriend, as I indeed loved her.

NVC helped me to realize the depth of my feelings as well as the thoughts attached, and my gratitude for that is bittersweet. I am now in awe at how powerfully emotions move us and at their long-lasting impacts on our lives. Equally powerful, it seems, is the impact of our ability and/or willingness to notice how our thoughts affect our feelings; the impetus of our action today has a ripple effect on those around us and on the shape of our tomorrow.

PRACTICE

Discerning Thoughts and Feelings

It can be surprising to discover how much our thoughts affect our feelings and vice versa. This practice is designed to support you in expanding your awareness of how thoughts affect feelings around foods you eat. This is a meditative self-reflection practice which could contain a journaling component. We invite you to find a quiet space for reflection, and a pen and paper if you want to capture your experience in a journal entry. We imagine that this practice will take about twenty to thirty minutes.

If you could have any food at this moment, what would it be?

- How do you feel as you think about this food?
  - Take some time to enjoy the feeling. Breathing into it, notice any sensations in the body.

- Do you have memories of people related to this food?
  - What sensations arise in the body as you recall these memories? Take your time to get familiar with these sensations.
  - Can you consciously name a feeling associated with these sensations?
  - Is the feeling similar to or different from the feeling you have about the food?

- What do you know about this food?
  - Is it a food familiar to your family culture? Is it from a subculture? Mainstream culture?
  - Do you imagine your feelings about this food would be different if you came from another culture?

~ Do you believe the food is healthy?

○ Does this perception affect how you feel about the food?

Reflecting on this exploration, would you guess that thoughts affect your feelings more or less than you had previously supposed?

Now that you are more aware of some thoughts that may be connected to the food, have your feelings shifted?

How might what you learned or experienced in this practice be applied to other areas of your life?

8

NEEDS AND STRATEGIES

The object of life is life; the object of well-being is to
encourage that which produces the sense of well-being.

—JEAN LIEDLOFF

The key distinction that juxtaposes needs and strategies directs our attention to the relationship between needs and the strategies we use to meet those needs. Universally shared, our needs aim to sustain us in living a physically, psycho-emotionally, socially, and spiritually fulfilling life. Their energy is manifested moment by moment. This life force binds us in a myriad of ways and is as diverse in expression as the rocks, flora, and fauna of our planet. With practice, we can expand our needs awareness [1] and discern them from strategies linked to our personal and societal conditioning.

Needs are the cornerstone around which human experience is organized and understood within the framework of NVC. On the NVC path, we are called to acknowledge, befriend, and

Universally shared, our needs aim to sustain us in living a physically, psycho-emotionally, socially, and spiritually fulfilling life.

engage with these needs. They are intrinsic energies that motivate us to action. Food, shelter, and water are some of our biological needs for survival that can be met in a limited number of ways. An infant, for example, needs human milk or, when not available, well-balanced formula. But for our psycho-emotional, relational, and spiritual needs, there are usually more possible strategies. People from different cultures and different systems have diverse ways of addressing needs and of prioritizing personal needs over collective needs or vice versa. Given how much of the world has been impacted by colonialism, each and every community is called to reconnect with its own authenticity in finding strategies to meet needs rather than defaulting to Western conditioning.

Thoughtfully, we can engage strategies to satisfy needs within an awareness of interdependence. Inquiring into our experience, we can explore how we perceive dichotomies of needs—met/unmet, mine/yours, personal/communal. We can learn to touch this energy of needs in ways that effectively sustain life within us individually and in community. With practice, we begin to recognize our common humanity and realize that our well-being is inextricably linked to that of others.

Needs: Our Intrinsic Motivation

Needs are the core organizing principle of the NVC framework for making sense of life and human behavior. Needs are central to the awareness we aim at cultivating in the NVC practice. These universal aspects of being alive offer a sense of guidance and can bring us home to wholeness and well-being. They are essential to our nature. In the Western world, we have been socialized to live disconnected from our feelings and needs while exalting the power of the thinking mind.[2] And when we learn to identify and relate to the power of needs, we tend to limit our focus to personal/interpersonal rather than communal needs.

Needs, as a life force, remain an ever-present motivator independent of any particular person, location, action, time, or object.[3] Attending to this universal energy, we open our heart-mind and witness our common humanity. Our subjective experience in the moment becomes a gateway to a wider perspective beyond the boundaries of our skin. Needs are the life impulse that sends a lotus seedling from muddy waters to find the sun and, in blossom, sets a child jumping for joy.

To fully comprehend this energy internally and externally, we are called to experience it directly and intuitively. The thinking mind is our ally in bringing us to the threshold of apprehending such life force. Yet to develop this awareness of needs, we are called to go beyond the mind of dichotomies, beyond language itself.

Needs are the core organizing principle of the NVC framework for making sense of life and human behavior.

Uncoupling Needs From Strategies

This key distinction invites us to shift from a scarcity mindset, imbued with patriarchal conditioning, to the simple awareness that there are countless strategies, or ways, to meet or satisfy our needs. Our inner and outer worlds are abundant with resources that can respond to needs. The narratives and beliefs we unconsciously hold around the ways we can or cannot meet needs are among the limiting factors for creatively doing so. Uncoupling needs from strategies is in itself a strategy to recognize and undo the paradigm we have been conditioned into, shifting collectively toward new visions and ideas.

When we focus our attention primarily on the strategies that we think will satisfy us, our imagination is limited by the finite nature of what, who, where, and how we want to meet needs. Unintentionally, we narrow the world of possibilities, seeing our preference as the only option.

In our phrasing, we tend to attach "needs" to people, locations, actions, time frames, and objects, and this extends beyond English.

I need you to help, because I need to be at work.

I need to go to that meeting.

I need the car to get there, and I need to go now!

Yet when we say "I need to . . ." or "I need you to . . . ," what follows is a strategy. While this type of language communicates clearly what it is we aim to do, with whom, and possibly where, it does not reveal the deeper needs that drive these intentions.

Maintaining an awareness of needs irrespective of strategies, by contrast, contributes to greater understanding, freedom, and choice. We may savor internally the quality of the energy of peace by letting it resonate within our hearts. Or we may attempt to satisfy our need for peace with the support of an external strategy such as listening to music, strolling on the beach, or engaging in nonviolent social action.

When we embrace NVC as a life practice, we cultivate the awareness of needs beneath particular strategies. We can express what truly matters to us in a fiercely intimate self-revelation. We might share what we need directly, such as "a need for collaboration." Or we may embed it in a sentence more casually, saying something like, "teamwork is really important to me."[4] What is most important in both intra- and interpersonal communication is not our words, but our consciousness—the focus of our attention is on connecting with needs rather than strategies.

Uncoupling needs from strategies allows us to find the spaciousness to own our experience and step into our power. By sorting our needs from strategies, we stay in touch with what moves us to action, rather than focusing on a specific procedure.

A whole new vista opens up to us when we connect with the life energy of others in this way. We can then touch our collective power and savor the interrelation between personal and communal power.

While we are conditioned to equate experiencing needs with "being needy," over time we release any shame around having needs. We can then progressively awaken to the secret hierarchies we have learned, prioritizing certain needs over others. As we liberate our heart/minds from this socialization, our collective capacity to attend to needs—our own and those of others and of life as a whole—increases. We begin to imagine strategies that work for all.

Conflicting Needs?

We may *perceive* needs as conflicting in our consciousness, perhaps because we are socialized to see them within a framework of either/or, win or lose, or because we value certain needs more than others. Or we might experience attachment to a specific view of a need and/or confuse it with a strategy. Our discomfort intensifies in the context of a power differential.

Conflict arises at the level of strategy. Our chosen strategies often relate unconsciously to the narratives we have been exposed to. While we envision one solution to meet a need, another person or group of people may envision a strategy that is quite different. Different countries have very different economic and political strategies to respond to human needs. Capitalism and socialism, for example, propose two very different ways to allocate resources, based on different priorities. One aims toward fairness, prioritizing needs based on perceived contribution—"meritocracy"—while the other purports to base resource allocation on a notion of equality. Neither achieves its stated goal.

Intense conflict related to ideological differences speaks of the attachment we have to our own view and desired outcome, whether we are aware of it or not. The more we open ourselves to life's inherent unpredictability, the more we may connect with a variety of strategies. As we humbly invite the mind to expand, we begin to release our fixation on a specific outcome.

It is an undertaking for most of us in the Western world to move our perspective of universal needs from the individual to the collective. If more than fourteen million children under the age of five suffer from severe acute malnutrition,[5] then the entire world population is insecure. Interdependence means the well-being of a part affects the well-being of the whole. Sometimes there does not seem to be an immediate strategy that cares fully for everyone. In those instances, a collective orientation toward needs invites us to prioritize the needs of those whose access to resources has been systemically prevented. This strategy might be kept in place until all have a sense that equity and balance have been restored. Holding needs "equally" includes this broader scope of time. We do share responsibility when some—even intergenerationally—are benefiting from the suffering, enslavement and/or exploitation of others. Equality and equity are not interchangeable, given the realities of the world we have created.

We are more likely to connect with others when we are aware of and focus on what is important to them. Whenever we do not consider their needs, we risk seeing their strategies as obstacles to our own happiness and well-being. That attitude will reinforce power differentials. Flexibility around outcome frees us to attune to the life energy emerging between us in the moment, as we seek to connect with what matters to us and others.

Needs: Mine/Yours, Personal/Collective, Met/Unmet

The brain aims to ensure our survival, tirelessly determining what is safe and what is dangerous. Since the patriarchal turn, the right/wrong, good/bad framework has been superimposed on the basic safe/unsafe dichotomy through social conditioning, leading to ever more polarities.

Yet as long as we approach our experience of needs with a dichotomous mindset of my needs/your needs or our needs/their needs, we unwittingly reinforce a mentality of separation. We hamper our ability to experience the universality of needs. A "line" between mine and yours, personal and collective, emerges. But such lines are like boundary markers on a map. They leave no imprint on the actual territory of interdependence. The map can be a valuable support in navigating the territory, yet the territory is far more than the map itself. By exploring how I/me/

> As long as we approach our experience of needs with a dichotomous mindset of my needs/your needs or our needs/their needs, we unwittingly reinforce a mentality of separation.

mine affects awareness of you/your/yours and vice versa, we awaken in a tangible way to the web of inter-being, the universal vital force.

We often assess our needs as met or unmet with an unexamined expectation that needs be fulfilled by others. We may use the language of needs while subtly blaming others for our unmet needs. Indeed, needs are met through interdependent relationships. Then again, when we take the stance that others "should" meet our needs, we disconnect from our personal/collective power. Taking responsibility for the needs we connect to in the moment empowers us to move into action.

Here is where NVC as a spiritual practice and NVC as an approach to social change merge together, beyond an either/or mindset. Of course, we can "meet" needs, as in "relate to." Approaching our hearts with acceptance and care, we may give ourselves empathy or receive empathy from others. We can mourn the needs we perceive as unmet while touching, if only for a moment, the foundational life force that unites us all. The late CNVC certified trainer Inbal Kashtan used to call this "a heart broken open." We can learn to mourn and hold our pain with love to such a degree that we humbly touch peace within our heartbreak. We can learn to live in peace with unmet needs. Yet we want to be careful not to use NVC as an easy-way-out "apolitical" approach that does not acknowledge the magnitude of suffering in our world and our responsibility in regard to it. By solely focusing on personal and interpersonal experiences without connecting the dots to the bigger picture of larger social and political structures, we end up using NVC to maintain the status quo.

Much suffering worldwide is material, and no amount of self-connection will shift the effects of a lack of safe water, adequate food, and dignified shelter. It is true that we can touch the life energy within, and it is essential to do so to stay in our power. At the same time, this inner connection to needs is not a substitute for bringing about healing justice in an inequitable world. It is the foundation.

"A need is life seeking expression within us," Rosenberg used to say.[6] Any need that goes chronically unmet will end up killing us. It is only a matter of time. We can survive without air for three minutes, three days without water, and a few weeks to a couple of months at the most without food. Babies who are fed and changed, but do not have a primary figure that meets their need for life-giving touch, attachment, and love will not thrive and may actually die. For other children, the excruciating pain of a chronic unmet need for love will likely come to the surface in ways that stimulate more pain for themselves and others.[7] Unmet needs for connection in elderly people often also contribute to earlier death. So, if needs are life seeking expression, needs are not interchangeable. A need for food cannot be fulfilled by spiritually connecting with the universality of that need, for example.

The mind is conditioned to think in dichotomies, yet we can harness its capacities. As the mind allows us to connect with our subjective experience, it can bring us to the threshold of the life force beyond the dualities we currently live in. It can take us beyond even language itself. When fully owning such polarities, we can assess whether we have the spaciousness to let go of the dichotomy of needs met/unmet or mine/yours. Whenever we do, we open to the potential of resting with our undivided attention on needs. Cultivating needs awareness grounded in the body, beyond the cognitive level, leads us to a deeper intuitive understanding of the life force. We can experience a direct apprehension of this energy within and without. That is the transformative spiritual energy that moves us toward wanting to serve life and create life-giving systems for all life-forms.

> NVC as a spiritual practice and NVC as an approach to social change merge together, beyond an either/or mindset.

Needs: Expressions of Our Shared Humanity

Growing our awareness of interconnection helps us deconstruct the dualistic notions of our societies. As a starting point, the NVC practice of self-empathy encourages us to befriend our internal subjective experience, especially our feelings and needs. Self-empathy supports us to tap into our capacity to be in relationship with others and to acknowledge their subjective, needs-based experience.

The more an awareness of inter-being colors all our relationships, the more our sense of separateness dissolves. We touch our oneness, understanding that our well-being is directly linked to the well-being of others. Then we balance our intentions with awareness of impacts. Needs awareness becomes a unifying principle beyond the duality of met/not met, mine/yours, individual/collective and opens us to a reality of interconnectedness. And we empower ourselves to experience the inner freedom and clarity that emerges from this awareness of inter-dependence. In the words of author Jean Liedloff, "Consistent with the economical character of nature, he wants no more than he needs."[8]

Even when we filter our human experience through an investigation of observations, feelings, and needs, this process is mediated by our conditioned thinking mind. Once our thoughts and perspectives are unveiled and witnessed, their power begins to dissipate. Each of our experiences, whether pleasant or unpleasant, can be met with presence and awareness of needs. To befriend our experience, honor it, and live more authentically, we are called to welcome emotions and thoughts without judgment.

Zen master and global spiritual leader Thích Nhất Hạnh points out that the lotus flower floats above the still waters of a lake while sending its roots deeper and deeper into the mud below. Its blossoms open, petal by petal, touched by the rays of the sun. The lotus is appreciated by sundry beings for the beauty, food, and shelter it offers. Drawing warmth and sustenance from the murky depths, the lotus withstands the freezing temperatures of winter. The lotus plant models the value of honoring our personal, historical, and spiritual being. "No mud, no lotus,"[9] Thích Nhất Hạnh reminds us.

Our individual perception of "unmet" nonmaterial needs offers a paradox. This perception can both keep us from touching a deeper truth within and invite us to a more spacious sense of peace. When we are attached to the storyline of our perception of unmet needs, we are more likely to "wallow" in feelings.[10] This can begin a downward spiral of thoughts to match the feelings, freezing the mind in a state of rumination on all that reinforces our story. Unable to open our minds to alternative perspectives, we fall deeper into the trench of "unmet" needs, or despair that things will "never get better."

In this situation, our perception of needs is often linked to strategies. If we hold an unexamined view that love means having no conflicts, for example, we may approach our children arguing over a toy and quickly encourage them to share the toy. We long for them to reconnect with the love they have for one another. Unable to suspend our views, even temporarily, we instead are likely also to suspend curiosity about what is going on for them, and miss their needs.

In the heat of the moment, we are often captivated by the thoughts and beliefs attached to our vantage point. Later, at a time when we have more spaciousness, we can explore the ways we have linked needs to strategies and stories, as "love" was linked to sharing in the example above. By discerning how we relate to needs and what thoughts, words, and images we attach to them, we can bring greater understanding to our experiences.

We may at times find ourselves inclined to seek security in a spiritual bypass by denying rather than accepting our very human reactions within this world of dichotomies. Experiencing emotional reactions to pleasure and pain, success and failure, gain and loss, fame and shame is part of our experience. Given the systemic inequalities in the world we have created, our reactions are intensified as many of us are chronically searching for pathways to attend to our needs. We approach what we find pleasurable and resist what we perceive as unpleasurable. Our choice point is in how to hold these reactions . . . will we respond with compassion or resistance? As one of Rosenberg's teachers, psychologist Carl Rogers, said, "The curious paradox is that when I accept myself just as I am, then I change."[11] Alternately, we might find ourselves seeking refuge in a psychological bypass, denying that there is more to this human life than these dichotomies. In the first case we deny our human fallibility, in the latter our freedom.

Our individual practice may also grow our willingness to examine widespread beliefs that suggest that our needs do not matter, will not be met, and, in fact, are a sign of a selfishness we should be ashamed of. Many of our beliefs, born from a mindset of domination, also limit our perceptions of ourselves or others. Examining our limiting beliefs may lead to acceptance and compassion for the impact they have on our connection to needs.

With the support of our communities, we may find the resources within us to step away from such life-alienating beliefs. Together, and with their support, we can touch deeper layers below conditioning. Collectively we can take actions, however small, in the direction of personal and communal power. Together, we begin to break these patterns of self-deprecation and/or "learned helplessness." Such personal and cultural transformation chips away at the dynamic that benefits the few who control most of the resources in economic systems of domination.

Social conditioning can also lead us to prioritize certain needs and even strategies. We might examine how these internalized hierarchies manifest in our individual lives. And once again, with the support of a community, we are empowered to investigate how they manifest socially and culturally. We can support change in these systems by observing and stating that prioritizing some needs over other needs or glorifying certain strategies can become a means to maintain domination systems.

Marriage, for example, is considered in most cultures as an end women should aspire to. This outlook on marriage may relate to social and economic inequalities between the genders. We generally socialize girls in that direction, but not boys, creating a power imbalance in the marital relationship. "The institution [of marriage] matters to one more than the other. Is it any wonder that, in so many marriages, women sacrifice more, at a loss to themselves, because they have to constantly maintain an uneven exchange?"[12] writer Chimamanda Ngozi Adichie queries. She notes that when Hillary Clinton ran for president of the

United States, she described herself as a "wife" first, while Bill Clinton's description began with "founder."

Acknowledging how socialization informs the way we connect to needs and strategies can help us deconstruct together their imprint on our experience. Ultimately, liberation—for all—from such systems of domination can only be achieved collectively.

Examining our thoughts, words, and actions on an individual level, we can touch deeper levels of awareness of feelings and needs. That allows us to open this exploration to a wider systemic scope. Those of us whose basic needs are met have a responsibility to raise awareness around the layers of needs that are unmet by systems of domination. We view it as our privilege and communal responsibility to listen deeply to those who are willing to share their experience of systemic hardship, however painful it is to take in their experiences. We can then take action to contribute to a world where more needs are attended to. In community, we touch more needs than we can as individuals, contributing to interdependence and expanding access to resources.

SUMMARY

- ↶ As we learn to discern needs from strategies, we slowly create spaciousness between our strategic preferences and our needs. With that clarity, we are better equipped to evaluate strategies.

- ↶ Differentiating needs from strategies allows us to be creative, finding ways to satisfy needs collectively.

- ↶ When we touch the energy of needs within us, we touch our shared humanity.

- ↶ Awareness of our shared humanity can support us in opening our hearts and minds to strategies that embrace needs beyond the dichotomy of mine and yours, ours and theirs.

WALKING THE TALK:
A LIFE EXAMPLE FROM COLOMBIA

BY CAMILA REYES, CNVC CERTIFIED TRAINER

Like so many other women in Latin America, I was shaped by a patriarchal culture. I grew up hearing the message that my value as a human being and as a woman depended on whether a man desired and valued me.

My culture delivered a key message: Being close to a man would increase the chances that I'd achieve my dreams. I grew up believing that being seen depended on my physical beauty or ability to attract male interest. This reinforced my belief that I did not matter intrinsically; rather, I was valued based on how others perceived and found use in me. I thought I "needed" a partner and opened up every time a man valued me or told me I was special. After twelve uninterrupted years of romantic relationships, a small voice inside told me that I was lost and disconnected from my power. I came across NVC and learned that having a partner was not a need but a strategy; my needs did not depend on anyone outside of me. This helped me understand why, even if I had a man next to me, I couldn't necessarily meet my needs.

Clarifying the difference between needs and strategies helped me see myself for the first time! I came to realize that my worth does not depend on the strategy of turning my power over to someone, but rather on my capacity to stay present around my own needs.

Recognizing and connecting with my needs helped me to start living for myself. I saw that my deeply felt needs for love, connection, mattering, and purpose were my responsibility. I started looking for other strategies to meet these needs. I am now getting to know myself and heartfully pursuing my dreams. I'm letting go of having a partner for a while to create space for me.

This personal shift has been a source of freedom and inner power that has helped me find the strength to cross many of the boundaries that patriarchy imposes. Restrictions are still there, but I no longer internalize or normalize them. I know that the value of my existence is determined by me alone and never relies on the perception of others.

PRACTICE

Discovering Core Needs

Sometimes we discover what matters to us the most in ways that we least expect. This imaginative practice is intended to support you in getting in touch with the needs you most cherish. It is a meditative and journaling practice. We invite you to find a spot with paper and pen where you can write for twenty to thirty minutes undisturbed.

Find a comfortable posture, straightening your spine, and bringing your attention inward, perhaps closing your eyes or lowering your gaze. Focus attention on your breathing, just following the ebb and flow of the breath, allowing the body-mind to settle.

The body is sitting still. The mind rests on the natural flow of the breath.

And then, whenever ready, pick up the paper and pen in front of you. Notice how the pen feels in your fingers. Set a timer for ten minutes. When you are ready, imagine yourself at the end of life. Then, "looking back," reflect about the choices you have made and what you have accomplished. What stands out for you?

Write without lifting the pen from the paper for about ten minutes. Allow whatever comes to find its way into words. Let go of all worry about grammar and punctuation, and let the stream of consciousness emerge and manifest on the paper.

After ten minutes, pause and place the pen at your side. Reconnect with your body, breathing in and out.

Then, at your own pace, read with an attitude of genuine curiosity what you just wrote. Read it once more, aloud if you like, and notice what the words tell you about what you value.

~ What are some core values that you notice in your writing?

~ Consider some of the choices you are making now. What might you want more or less of to experience greater alignment?

~ Do you recognize some strategies in what you wrote?

~ What do they tell you about the values you connected to while writing?

9

REQUESTS AND DEMANDS

Let's think of using requests in NVC to continue the dance,
not as a test of our success in getting what we want.

—LUCY LEU

The key distinction juxtaposing requests and demands shows us how our energy, attitude, and communication affect relationships when we ask for something. How we ask has long-term repercussions for ourselves, others, and the planet.

When demanding, we tell someone to do something without mindful consideration of impact and without openness to hearing no for an answer. Requests, however, are rooted in power-with. When we make a request, we ask for what we want with the intention to meet needs. We stay in our power and invite others to stay in theirs, seeking solutions that work for all. When we enter a dialogue and make a request, we are committed to considering the needs of all who are affected. We receive a no with openness to hear about the needs behind it; we consider it an invitation to further dialogue, not the end of the conversation. The purpose of the dialogue is to reach a strategy that will work for both parties, not to simply get what we want.

It is important to note that we can use the language of a request (for example, "Would you be willing to please . . . ?") and still be making a demand. If we are not actually willing to receive a no, or if we think the other person "should" do what we ask them to do, then we are probably in demand territory. Conversely, using language that might resemble a demand could still be a request if there is enough trust and connection that the receivers know they can say no or suggest something else without being punished. The key distinction between a request and a demand is not so much in the phrasing as in whether connection and power-with are prioritized.

In order to formulate a request, we listen deeply to needs while cultivating an openhearted awareness that honors the self-determination of the person or people we are asking. We ask for what we want, not for what we do not want. The request is doable and includes a time frame to maximize clarity. If the response to our request is no, we look with curiosity to what prevents the person or group from saying yes. Grounded in interdependence, we desire to get what we want only if it works for others too. We make requests also to sense how getting what we want could impact others. Investigating this, we can shift strategies as needed to care for all present.

> **The key distinction between a request and a demand is not so much in the phrasing as in whether connection and power-with are prioritized.**

As we will explore later, saying no to another's request will require some courage if we are in a down-power role or position.[1] When we are in an up-power role and the response to our request is a yes, we might still want to reexamine our request, tuning into the needs that may prevent others from saying no. Empowered with this clarity, we can seek strategies that reflect interdependence in action.

Demands

Whether intentionally or not, demands try to leverage a sort of power over others as we pursue what we want. Demands emerge from a sense of scarcity and separation. Paradoxically, we often experience fear that if we do not make a demand, our needs will not be met. In an attempt to force compliance, we tragically utilize fear of punishment, desire for rewards, and words that induce guilt or shame. Demands typically weaken one's connection to personal power, moving one toward submission or rebellion.

We also make demands of ourselves. One part of our mind reigns in dominion over another, telling us what we "should" or "shouldn't" do, experiencing an inner conflict. We might have demands of ourselves even around using the NVC process, thinking we "should" always empathize or share our needs. People who practice NVC sometimes even have implicit or explicit demands of others around using the NVC components of observations, feelings, needs, and requests.

In the Western world, we are conditioned to prize self-sufficiency and individualism. This orientation can leave us feeling anxious and alone, reducing our capacity to empathize with others, and limiting our creativity. In a mindset that others "have to" do what we want or our needs will not be met, we will likely lose sight of our demands' impact. In seeking to rely on our own resources, we slip from one extreme of the continuum to its opposite: we either do not even ask for what we need, or we give orders. Either way, we contribute to the shortage of functional collaborative communities. Our ability to give and receive support is diminished.

Underlying demands is a deep conditioning that pushes us to equate noncompliance with personal rejection. Both receiving or giving a no may activate shame, if we perceive it as a threat to core needs for mattering and belonging. After all, most of us have been socialized to believe that those needs will be met on the condition that we are "good."

Our fear of hearing a no also stems from personal trauma history or collective trauma due to systematic oppression. Demands give us a semblance of being in control when inside we have internalized a sense of powerlessness that prevents us from tapping into personal/collective power. For example, children who are adopted and therefore traumatized by separation from the biological mother, tend to rely on themselves and not ask for help. Their demands are a request for support in disguise.

While the human brain is wired for connection, trauma rewires it for self-preservation. Yet, because these kids make a lot of demands, they are labeled on a continuum from "bossy" to a diagnosis of "Oppositional Defiant Disorder."

Whatever the circumstances, when we notice ourselves making or receiving demands, we can pause and, with compassion for ourselves and others, remind ourselves that these demands largely arise from trauma and conditioning.

Requests

Unlike demands, requests are based on relational awareness, mutuality, and interdependence. Requests are the fourth component of the NVC process of expression. With requests, we move our attention from inside ourselves to the outside world as we take action. Having touched the depth of our experience—feelings and needs—we funnel personal and collective power toward mobilizing resources. Perhaps the greatest gift we can give ourselves is to discern what matters to us most and then cultivate the courage and ability to make effective requests. Rosenberg reminds us, "The number one reason that we don't get our needs met [is that] we don't express them."[2]

And yet, expressing needs alone is not enough. If we are not making a conscious request then, as Rosenberg says, "We talk *to* others or *at* them without knowing how to engage in a dialogue *with* them."[3] Because requests are always linked to needs, discerning our needs and explicitly naming them before making a request contribute to power-with, understanding, and goodwill. Making requests in order to meet needs invites responsiveness.

> Unlike demands, requests are based on relational awareness, mutuality, and interdependence.

Requests arise from trust that, as human beings, we enjoy contributing to one another when free to do so. The phrase, "Would you be willing to . . . ?" upholds and conveys our intention to engage with the person in a way that safeguards their autonomy. If they choose to say yes to our request, we want to make sure that they do so from wholehearted willingness as it meets their need for contribution. Our conditioned habit of saying yes even if we are not really behind it tends to drain our life energy. While any given strategy may not be our preference, there is a deep and quiet joy of interconnection when we are asked and feel free to decide whether and how to contribute. Supporting one another's freedom, we give and receive from the flow of mutuality.

The vulnerability of our request may be met with a no. Our response to that no is the litmus test of whether we are energetically aligned with a request or a demand. Reactivity in the face of a no points to demand energy. Being socialized to hearing no as the end of a conversation, the brain can easily perceive that no as a threat and shift into survival mode.

By increasing our ability to self-connect and self-regulate, we can learn to meet a no with empathy, as an opportunity to connect with the other person's feelings and needs. We might discover what needs they are saying yes to by declining. The conversation can offer clarity about the possible impacts of our choices and help identify strategies that will better address everyone's needs. Requests are a commitment to the awareness of interdependence and power-with, harnessing the tools of honesty and empathy.

Systemic Conditioning and Requests

Our capacity to envision ways to meet needs has been limited by socialization. Cultivating a systemic awareness of how we and others have been conditioned is essential to applying the NVC process in life-giving ways. Otherwise, we risk potentially tragic consequences as we unwittingly maintain the power dynamics of domination even while practicing NVC. Later in this chapter we will explore how using requests without awareness of power differential can actually perpetrate patterns of domination and submission. Misunderstanding power-with as an abdication of the power invested in our role is an example of contributing to an unhealthy relationship with power.

Attachment to a specific strategy is a quick way to spiral toward a demand. For example, eye contact is a sign of respect and connection in mainstream Western culture. In cultures rooted in their ancestral lands and traditional teachings,

Cultivating a systemic awareness of how we and others have been conditioned is essential to applying the NVC process in life-giving ways. Otherwise, we risk potentially tragic consequences as we unwittingly maintain the power dynamics of domination even while practicing NVC.

however, eye contact within a relationship with a clear power differential is considered a lack of respect. Hence, an adult Westerner's request for eye contact with an Indigenous child does not consider the needs and cultural lens of the child or how the child may actually be attempting to meet the very need—respect—that the Western adult experiences as not being met. Because of the power dynamic, children in this situation are often punished and uprooted from their culture.

It takes energy to separate needs from our social conditioning. The heart of requests lies in power-with as we uphold self-determination. When we are aware of our needs and open to further conversation, our capacity to be authentic, mutual, and flexible is increased, inviting interdependence.

Connection and Solution Requests

It is important to distinguish between connection and solution requests. The purpose of connection requests is to establish sufficient trust that all parties understand and care about one another's needs. The focus is on the relationship, before moving to solutions. A solution request proposes a specific action to meet needs. In both cases, we know that dialogue may reveal a different solution, acknowledging everyone's needs.

Often, connection requests take two basic forms: We can ask for a reflection back from the listener, to make sure our message was received the way we intended. Or we can request the listener's honest expression. Our intention is to create understanding. We might ask for honesty with,

"Would you be willing to tell me what comes up for you when you hear me say that?" Or, we might seek a reflection by asking, "Would you tell me what you heard me share so far, so I am sure I was clear enough?"

When trust is low, we may instead ask a specific question that calls for a yes or no response. This can help establish the shared understanding and care that are essential before a solution is likely to work. Here are some examples:

The question "Did you hear anything in what I said as a criticism?" can help us understand the impact of our words without requiring the other person to do the hard work of reflecting what they heard. Similarly, we can ask, "Is there anything in what I said that leaves you doubting that your needs can be met here?"

"Is there any relief for you in hearing what I said?" can be a helpful request when we are aiming to de-escalate a conflict. "Was this more than you could take in?" can smooth out an impending overwhelm. Overall, yes and no questions are often easier for people to respond to, especially those not familiar with NVC.

Solution requests, on the other hand, focus on concrete, doable actions. We might ask, "Would you be willing to call me back between eight and nine o'clock tonight?" Our solution request rests on trust and upholds flexibility without attachment to outcomes.

Underlying all requests lies this question: Do I matter? We can cultivate tenderness toward our inclination to look outside for confirmation of our worth. This yearning is yet another effect of our domination-based conditioning. Cultivating self-connection also supports the brain in experiencing enough internal safety to stimulate the social engagement system. Mattering to ourselves is foundational in navigating the complexities of honesty and empathy. Self-connection also reduces the likelihood that we will be blown around by the winds of submission and rebellion, or self-doubt.

At the same time, we can open ourselves to the vibration of universal needs within us. Given enough space and warmth, the line between met and not met blurs, and the universal energy that nourishes creativity expands. Held in our own embrace of deeply mattering to ourselves, we more easily release fear-based, scarcity-driven attachment to strategies.

Depending on the level of trust in the relationship, connection requests may nurture the dialogue. In fact, willingness to contribute only springs forth when we trust that we matter. As psychiatry professor Stephen W. Porges reminds us, "Prosocial behavior will not occur when our neuroception misreads the environmental cues and triggers physiological states that support defensive strategies."[4] Making connection requests that elicit honesty or empathy are specific skills that support the prosocial behavior Porges refers to.

Listening Deeply to Needs

Self-empathy and empathy help us clarify which needs are most alive in the moment. While needs are rarely if ever in conflict,[5] strategies often are. Fully connecting to all the needs perceived as being in conflict helps us gain clarity around possible strategies to meet both sets of needs. If a solution does not arise, our efforts to hold the needs with care allows us to fully mourn those not addressed, accepting what is, without resistance or clinging.

Being compassionate with ourselves and empathetic toward others, we cultivate curiosity about what is alive for them. Tending to any beliefs from personal experience or socialization that might distort our view is also valuable. When we notice that we are attached to our views and desired outcomes, we can meet ourselves with compassion.

Brain-Wise Skills for Requests

Requests that are doable—clear, concrete, and action-oriented—have a far greater chance of fulfilling our needs. Specificity is important. "Would you be willing to show a little more consideration to your brother?" does not convey what it is we want. "Would you be willing to ask your brother what he would enjoy doing too, so we can make a decision together?" suggests a doable action while also mentioning the needs behind the request—in that case, partnership and inclusion. A clear request reduces uncertainty, allowing the brain to rest in safety.

If we cannot imagine how to make a doable, solution-oriented request, sharing our challenge and asking for help initiates power-sharing. For example, "Would you be willing to work together to find a solution to this dilemma?"

As we only have power in this moment, requests are formulated in the present-tense and are time-specific. For example, "Would you be willing to set an alarm now that will remind you to feed the dog tonight at six?" asks for willingness in the moment to take an action to support a future action. We can only ask for and give a commitment in the present; the future is not in our hands. If our request is projected into the future, such as, "Are you willing to pick me up at nine tomorrow?" we can humbly remind ourselves that this request may end up not being doable, given the inherent uncertainty of life.

Finally, requests stated in positive rather than negative terms support understanding. Saying what we do not want does not convey clarity about what we do want. Posing requests in the negative tends to provoke resistance, interfering with the listener's experience of freedom and choice. Additionally, the brain processes nonthreatening information—requests structured in the positive—more swiftly and accurately. If we say to children, "Would you be willing to stop jumping on the bed?" their brains struggle to register what we are asking them to do. Instead, we could ask, "Would you be willing to jump on the trampoline outside?" This request provides necessary clarity to support the children in making a choice while considering needs for fun and exercise.

Requests Not Attached to Outcomes

An effective request can inspire creativity and bring forth a broader scope of resources from the other person or the group. When we set forth our request without attachment to a specific outcome, we nurture freedom and partnership. One way to tap into the creativity and expansiveness of requests, rather than the urgency and constriction of demands, is to imagine several other requests that could also contribute to the needs we want to address.

Power Differentials and Requests

Power differentials and cultural conditioning play a significant role in our ability, or inability, to make and respond to requests. Cultivating awareness of power imbalances enables us to align our requests with our intentions of compassion and mutuality. For those with a less powerful role, lower status, or less systemic power, it is more difficult both to make requests and to say no. In a low-power position, we may give in and say yes, even if that means not addressing some needs. Saying a less than full-hearted yes is still an attempt to meet needs—perhaps for security, ease, well-being, or safety.

Requests When in an Up-Power Role

When we have more structural power, we have greater capacity and perhaps also willingness to make and respond to requests. Yet we often have less capacity or willingness to hear how our requests affect others. The growing edge—the area of new learning—will lie in recognizing the power imbalance and its impact on others. When we make requests from a high-power position, it is unlikely that the other person will be able to enter a fully empowered dialogue with us. If we truly want a power-with relationship with the other person, we may choose to be considerably more mindful of how we engage. We may ask ourselves to take 150 percent of the responsibility in the relationship, as a reminder of the power differential that is in play. By asking ourselves what this 150 percent may look like in this situation, we empower ourselves to manifest our intention to connect.

Rooted in self-responsibility, we may inquire into our relationship

If we want a power-with relationship with someone in a lower power position, we may put considerably more mindful attention on how we engage.

with our greater access to power. In fact, according to author and psychologist Dacher Keltner, the very skills that may have led to our up-power position are the ones that most easily deteriorate once we experience increased access to power. "Power is a dopamine high," Keltner writes.[6] A mix of more testosterone, less cortisol, and unregulated dopamine all too easily leads to an empathy deficit, self-serving impulsivity, and unethical action.

In the up-power role, therefore, we might lower concern around saying no by explicitly naming our intention to seek strategies that work[7] for everyone. Two core approaches help establish a safe environment within power differentials in our families, work, organizations, and beyond. First, we can proactively nourish a culture that embraces multidirectional feedback. Second, structures for cooperative decision-making can be created. Sharing our intention and balancing it with an expression of curiosity about possible impacts also conveys a sense of care. We might say, "I would like to know how saying yes to this request would affect you, because it is in my best interest and the interest of this company to have your feedback." Our sincere openness to feedback could also give rise to brainstorming more strategies.

Whenever the answer to our request is a yes, yet we pick up on some incongruence between words and body language, or we feel in our guts that it may be a mixed yes, that is a time to slow down the conversation and check in. Body posture, tone of voice, and intensity of response are some of the nonverbal cues that can alert us to discomfort in the other person. It is essential to attend to any discomfort prior to reaching agreement, or the agreement either will not be honored, or will come at a cost to the relationship.

Connection requests may contribute to trust as we inquire about needs that incline them to agree and what needs could go unmet. Life-connected choices stem from a clear understanding of needs. Knowing how challenging it is to take a stand that is different from the majority, we can invite dissent. Exploring together the needs that would not be met if they agreed, we increase the likelihood of reaching a truly collaborative agreement that works for all. Empathizing, we can imagine what needs may prevent them from saying no. Eliciting and sharing ideas for how to reduce the power differential also supports partnership and reduces the impact of social conditioning.

Whenever we are in an up-power position and receive a no, we might actively celebrate the trust that allowed for a no to be expressed. Sharing gratitude for the clarity and honesty of the answer is one step toward rebalancing the power differential. Conversely, when we are the ones saying no to a request from someone in a down-power position, it is important to name what is preventing us from saying yes, to extend care toward those who stretched into power-with.

Requests When in a Down-Power Role

When we are in a down-power position, our growing edge will be to remain self-aware and rooted in our personal power. Being grounded will help us determine our course of action. Severely challenging consequences may await us, depending on the action we choose. Saying yes with awareness of the needs we are choosing to meet (for example, our livelihood) contributes to reclaiming our power in ways that a habitual yes does not. Knowing that our lower-power role has nothing to do with our inherent dignity will support us in tapping into our capacity for influence.

When habituated out of fear to tend to the needs of those in higher rank, it is vital that we discern between care—the heartfelt desire to contribute—and caretaking—taking responsibility for the feelings and needs of the other person. This differentiation will support us in navigating our threshold of willingness. As trauma specialist and author Resmaa Menakem writes, "Just as many white bodies go on alert when they sense a Black body nearby, many Black bodies also go on alert when they sense a white one in the vicinity. But there is a crucial difference here: The white body

> **When we are in a down-power position, our growing edge will be to remain self-aware and rooted in our personal power.**

tends to shift into immediate self-protection; but the Black body is habituated to shift into soothing the white body as a self-protective strategy."[8]

Whether making or responding to a request, cultivating an inner clarity about the needs in play will empower us to find a sense of choice. Tapping into collective power by connecting with others can also help transform learned helplessness into freedom of choice. From the experience of power-with, we can slowly expand our sphere of influence to serve life.

SUMMARY

- ↤ Differentiating requests from demands, we find that both are attempts to meet needs.

- ↤ Requests stem from trust that human beings enjoy contributing to one another when free to do so.

- ↤ As we learn to tell requests from demands, we harness the tools of self-connection, honesty, and empathy. We come to see that requests are a commitment to awareness of interdependence and power-with.

- ↤ Discerning demands from requests, we can cultivate awareness of power imbalances.

  - ○ If someone with less structural power agrees to our request, we can inquire into what needs lead them to express agreement and which may prevent them from saying no.
  - ○ When we are in a down-power position, we can practice self-empathy and self-reflection. Being grounded in our needs and honoring them with the utmost care, we empower ourselves to make conscious choices, with awareness of consequences and our willingness to face them or not.
  - ○ We can fine-tune our ability to discern care from caretaking, which will help us stay rooted in our personal and collective power.

WALKING THE TALK: A LIFE EXAMPLE FROM THE UNITED STATES

BY BETH MORGAN, CNVC TRAINER CANDIDATE

One sunny morning, I realized I needed to take my cat to the vet. I asked my daughter who lives with me if she could give us a ride. I planned to find another way home, as my daughter would be working. Because of extreme visual impairment, I don't drive.

The vet checked us in quickly, and I agreed to leave my cat for observation. My daughter had already returned home. I decided to try walking. The veterinary clinic is separated from our neighborhood by one busy street. I stood at the curb with my cane, listening for the traffic to clear. After several minutes, I called my daughter to pick me up. I knew she would be getting ready for work but thought a three-minute drive wouldn't be too much trouble.

My daughter answered the phone and responded that she didn't want to pick me up, because she needed time to finish getting ready. "Okay," I said, and hung up. I stood there as cars whizzed by and tried to focus on my options, but it was too early to call others. If it wasn't for this busy street, I could walk home in less than ten minutes. Then all my judgments arose . . .

"It would not have been that big of a deal for her to come pick me up. After all the things I've done for her! She's just thinking of herself."

My reaction told me that I had made a demand, not a request. And yet I knew that I wanted my daughter to respond authentically and not just to comply with resentment, regardless of the convenience for me. I began to celebrate that she felt free enough to say no, to trust that she could be real with me. I guessed that she'd said yes to her needs for integrity and ease around getting to work on time, and this I celebrated too. She had taken responsibility for her needs. It reminded me that I could do the same.

Right then, a man approached and asked if I wanted to cross the street. He had a blind friend, understood what support might be needed, and seemed happy to help. I thanked him, headed home to tell my daughter about the experience, and realized that she had already gone to work. My judgements returned.

"She left without even calling to see if I needed her . . . She doesn't care about my safety!"

Immediately, I knew this was not true. She has demonstrated her love and care in so many ways! But why hadn't she checked in on me?

Instantly I knew: she had trusted I would find a way to meet my needs! She had faith in my creativity, resourcefulness, and common sense. As someone who is considered "handicapped," I am used to people worrying and often offering assistance when it is not needed. I am accustomed to people being unaware of my capability and lovingly trying to watch out for me and be supportive. The gift of my daughter's trust in my inner resources filled my heart with love and gratitude and proved the biggest celebration of all.

PRACTICE

Making Requests in a Power Imbalance

Sometimes we make requests without realizing that power dynamics are in place that affect others' ability to freely make and receive requests, staying aware of choice. This practice offers an opportunity to integrate an understanding of power dynamics into the NVC requests skill set. This is a self-reflection and possibly journaling practice. We invite you to find a quiet place, and pen and paper if you would enjoy writing your responses. We imagine this exercise will take twenty to thirty minutes.

Bring to mind a situation where you have some sense of disconnect linked to power differential. Determine where you stand within the power imbalance. Seek clarity about which skills and actions might be most relevant.

WHEN IN AN UP-POWER POSITION

- What support do you need to willingly accept taking 150 percent responsibility for fostering a power-with relationship? What would such a choice look like?

- If in a relationship that is still building trust, what comes up for you when you consider the discomfort of not accepting a yes at face value?

- Are you open to examining the possible discrepancies between your intention and the impact of your actions when making requests?

- Given these considerations, what kind of request do you have of yourself?

∿ What kind of request do you want to make of the person in a down-power role?

WHEN IN A DOWN-POWER POSITION

∿ What are some ways for you to stay connected to your personal dignity and power?

∿ If you feel inclined to respond quickly in ways that meet needs for those in up-power roles—perhaps needing safety, security, and harmony for yourself and others in down-power roles—how do you differentiate between caring and caretaking?

∿ What other needs might lead you to choose to say yes, even when you are not fully willing? We invite you to bring tenderness to those needs. Are there any ways for you to stretch into an inquiry about whether the risk may be smaller than you have been conditioned to imagine? How much risk are you willing to take?

∿ What are some ways in which you can channel collective power?

∿ Given these considerations, do you have a request of yourself?

∿ Do you have a request of the person in the up-power role?

10

IDIOMATIC LANGUAGE AND CLASSICAL (FORMAL) LANGUAGE

Love and kindness are the
universal language of all creation.

—DEBASISH MRIDHA

The key distinction that examines the strategies of idiomatic (informal) and classical (formal) language of NVC helps us choose words that are likely to create attunement in different contexts. Connection is a primary value in Nonviolent Communication. Choosing words with awareness of the social location of our conversation partner contributes to flow and understanding.

The NVC process of communication includes countless strategies for nurturing relationships. In one of these strategies, classical NVC language, we specifically engage NVC's four-step template for expression. Sharing an observation, feeling, need, and request, we might say, "When I hear you say you appreciate my cleaning out the car (observation), I feel so happy (feeling) because I value contribution (need). Would you be willing to share some other ways I might support you (request)?" We might also use the two-step template for empathy and guess at someone's feelings and needs: "Are you feeling elated because you value creativity?"

Conversely, we could choose idiomatic language, in which the spirit of connection is captured in a more familiar, everyday manner. We might say, "I'm so glad that my cleaning out the car was sweet for you. Anything else I can do to help?" Our idiomatic empathy may reflect back in ways that include words beyond feelings and needs. "You feel on top of the moon, don't you?" We might later add, "Yes to creativity!"

Classical language, sometimes called "classical giraffe,"[1] relies explicitly on the components to give empathy and express with care our truth in the moment. Idiomatic language, also called street giraffe or colloquial NVC language, relies on the same spirit, while welcoming all verbal expressions that emerge from a consciousness rooted in compassion and interrelationship. We limit ourselves neither to words on the feelings and needs list, nor to the order or totality of components. With idiomatic language we are flexible, enabling connection in a casual manner. Aiming to build a bridge between our own and someone else's world, we mindfully choose our words in consideration of the culture, environment, lifestyle, age, and any other element that will support those we are talking with. Connecting with an open heart and choosing words that match the social environment, we increase the likelihood that our communication will resonate.[2]

Both idiomatic and classical NVC language intend to prioritize relationship and nurture connection. Holding this intention, the essence of idiomatic and classical language is the same, whether in empathy or self-expression; the form alone is what differs. Colloquial NVC flows more easily over time, out of a practice of classical language. Our formal practice allows us to stay grounded in the principles and intentions of the consciousness underlying the practice of NVC. As we gain experience with the intention of NVC, and as we integrate the deep shifts in awareness that the practice entails, we have more consistent access to the consciousness of compassion. We simultaneously gain more fluency in translating from one form to the other.

Classical Language

Rosenberg created a communication process that aims to support connection with the divine energy in ourselves and in others. He writes, "Even if they practice NVC as a mechanical technique, they start to experience things between themselves and other people they weren't able to experience before. So eventually they come to the spirituality of the process."[3]

The classical NVC language's gift is clarity. Its four components are a map with which the mind can orient itself. When making our way into this territory as beginners, practice and repetition will be our guides. The structure and order of words direct our path into a world where we can connect with one another's humanity. Language centered around universal needs serves an awareness of interdependence. The more we integrate the four components, the more we also support the transformation of the mind toward compassion. When we can authentically speak from our heart, with clarity about our own experience and care for the impact of our words on others, what we say can be a welcome change from habitual speech that is based on judgments and assumptions.

The four components of classical language are a boon, too, for seasoned practitioners who have been stimulated or have lost touch with their hearts. Whenever the brain experiences stress and con-

Taking a breath and coming back to the anchors of observations, feelings, needs, and requests can support the self-regulation, empowering us to engage again.

flict, it loses access to the higher functions of the prefrontal cortex, such as insight, empathy, and attuned communication. In those moments, taking a breath and coming back to the anchors of observations, feelings, needs, and requests can support self-regulation, empowering us to engage again.

Formal Language as a Roadblock

At the same time, classical language can also present challenges. Despite our goodwill and attempts to connect, the conversation may not have enough color and texture to weave interconnection with the other person. The four components themselves may be flagged by the listener's brain as unfamiliar or insincere, and therefore potentially unsafe. Consequently, they might find themselves uncomfortable or even on the alert. The flow of trust and connection may suffer.

> STEPHANIE: I can recall when I eagerly set off to practice NVC, only to receive in response, "Stop it with this flowery language!" Much to my chagrin as a new practitioner, my classical giraffe empathy guesses and expression contributed to confusion and resistance in the listener who found the words awkward and formulaic.

Classical language, in its most formal state, differs from the way many of us have been taught to speak,[4] and this difference can call more attention to itself than to the message it tries to convey. Shifting to street language at this time can contribute to greater connection and flow.

The vulnerability of feelings and needs touched on by classical language may also be more than what the listener is seeking. Such expression might be perceived as an open invitation for the listener to experience their own feelings and needs. This is deeply personal territory for many. It is important when choosing classical expression to be mindful of the nonverbal communication we receive and the energy between speaker and listener(s), so as to honor personal choice around emotional vulnerability.

Whenever we are relying on the practice template outside of a practice session, we run the risk of inadvertently "using" others for our own learning and integration. If, in addition, and as often happens early in the practice, we use the language of feelings and needs on top of rather than instead of the language of judgments and reaction, that gap is very likely to be perceived and the whole expression received as inauthentic.

Yet when we are connected to an observation, expanding our feeling vocabulary, identifying needs, and coming up with clear requests, we empower ourselves to slowly integrate "giraffe consciousness" with "giraffe language." How, then, do we manage the transition?

One strategy is to gain a lot of practice, either through individual practice or within the NVC community, before we use our new skills with those who are not trained in NVC. Another strategy is to let the other person know what we are doing and why, and get their agreement in order to have a conversation that is different from habitual patterns, even if it feels out of flow. For example: "We've had this conversation dozens of times unsuccessfully. I'd like to try using some communication skills I've been learning recently. It may sound clunky, but I feel hopeful that it may lead us somewhere new. Are you open to trying it for maybe fifteen minutes?"

Idiomatic Language

Whenever classical language does not contribute to connection in the moment, this dilemma can be sidestepped by understanding that NVC can be spoken with chameleon grace in any setting, with any words. The fluency of idiomatic language is only limited by the skills and willingness of the speaker to stay attuned or reattune in the moment to an awareness of needs. Being mindful of a person's social location,[5] we can choose the words we deem most likely to connect.

> KRISTIN: When I celebrate with my one-year-old niece, I sometimes exclaim, "Yay!" while clapping my hands. When helping my seventy-year-old neighbor who is unfamiliar with the NVC process, I often reflect back strategies as well as or instead of feelings and needs: "You'd love it if people were warmer down at the VA, is that it?" When he knows I am "with" him, I continue to nourish the connection by reflecting back what I imagine is precious to us both, "Care and understanding are so important, aren't they?"

Our language is grounded in the intention to cultivate the relationship and find a path forward that works for all. Aligning ourselves with the vibration of feelings and needs that we perceive or express, we also stay closely attuned to others' verbal and nonverbal cues that indicate the impact of our words. Our static NVC map—observations, feelings, needs, requests—transforms into a dynamic compass always pointing to connection. We look for the needs that every action is attempting to meet. Charting our progress, step by step, we walk with compassion.

> **Our language is grounded in the intention to cultivate the relationship and find a path forward that works for all.**

With idiomatic language, our expression can sound more natural even as we continue to honestly express what is in our hearts. We may express all or none of the components of classical language, in whatever order contributes to connection. How the components relate to one another—our feelings are linked to observations and point to needs, for example—is inherently understood yet not necessarily expressed.

> STEPHANIE: "I hate physics," my teenage daughter snaps. While a full empathy guess may sound like, "Are you feeling outraged because you really value ease while learning?" a more direct "street language" approach could sound like, "You sound furious!" Meanwhile, I mentally connect that feeling to a possible need for ease. Or I might say, "Studying physics seems really dumb to you, is that it?"

Meeting People on Their Terms

Using idiomatic language, we meet people where they are. Our awareness might include worldview, gender, culture, age, mood, and common language. If we notice we want them to be somewhere else, we may want to give ourselves empathy. We might enjoy our self-empathy in the form of classical language yet understand that this style may not be a gift to those unfamiliar with the practice of NVC. Gifts are best received if they take the shape of what we guess the receiver would enjoy, rather than what we, as the giver, would want. We might also be wary of "gifting" them with NVC because we believe they need it!

The spirit of the NVC process, grounded in compassion and mutuality, is about deepening our experience without ever requesting, let alone demanding, the same from others. Our words matter less than the intention to connect. Also vital is our inner clarity in touching some or all of the four components. Some examples follow in the table below:

	Classical/Formal Language	Idiomatic/Street Language
EXPRESSION	When I see you grinning from ear to ear after opening that gift (O), I'm so happy (F) as I value contributing (N) to your well-being. Would you be willing to share how it is for you to hear that (R)?	(Big smile in response to a smile.) Did I nail it?
	When I see you sitting on the couch while the rest of us are doing dishes, I feel annoyed and want more teamwork. Would you be willing to share what's keeping you from joining us?	Hey! Dishes happening in the kitchen, team effort. What's shakin' with you in the living room?
EMPATHY	Are you feeling frustrated and needing clarity?	(With vocal tone to match frustration.) It doesn't make sense to you, does it?
	Are you feeling tender, touching your need for mattering?	(With warmth and a smile.) You *know* you matter, don't you?

Note: Because idiomatic expressions of NVC use fewer words, we have added some notes on tone and body language to help convey the full meaning. A match of tone of voice and body language to words is vitally important in both types of expression.

The primary goal of the practice of NVC is, as Rosenberg says, "communicating—both speaking and listening—that leads us to give from the heart, connecting us with ourselves and with each other in a way that allows our natural compassion to flourish."[26] This quality of connection allows us to give and receive fully. Whenever the language of NVC becomes a barrier to connection, we may take a step back, breathe, and appreciate the principles of NVC rather than focusing on any particular component of the practice.

Idiomatic Language and Interdependence

Embracing the intention to connect, we ground ourselves in a consciousness of compassion for self and others as well as interdependence. Our willingness to adapt and choose the words we imagine best fit the situation and people involved reflects an awareness that their well-being and connection is also our own. Attentiveness to verbal and nonverbal feedback will help us discern whether we are contributing to connection or not. We create connection by "visiting" others' worlds instead of subtly requiring them to come into ours. In meeting them where they are, we meet ourselves where we are *with them*. The power of presence guides us. When we initiate this internal shift and manifest it from the inside out with idiomatic empathy or self-expression, our authenticity and care become more accessible to the listener.

As our experience grows, we integrate the intention of the NVC practice into our being, so that we come from compassion and interdependence more reliably. Then we can expand the range of our verbal expression while remaining true to the principles of NVC; our language authentically comes from our heart even as our words may not mirror the formal practice of NVC. This authenticity gives us a more powerful capacity to connect, whereas using classical language is often wrapped in some residual desire to "get it right" on a mental level.

Our practice of the four components of NVC expression enables us to translate to idiomatic language. Whether we choose to lean on pieces of classical language or abandon the words altogether, our consciousness has been and continues to be supported by our needs-based awareness. We maintain clarity that our perspective, rooted in observations, is our own. When we realize that our feelings are connected to needs rather than anything someone else is doing, we take ownership of our experience.

Being present with another person, whether in silence or spoken word, our minds can rely on the regular, formal practice of these components, shaping our ability to respond with compassion. We slowly grow our capacity to translate these components into the words, gestures, and silence that connect best in various settings. And with practice, our clarity and authenticity expand and set the tone, as we choose what we imagine will serve best in the spirit of interdependence—idiomatic or classical language.

SUMMARY

↪ When discerning whether and how to use classical NVC or idiomatic language, we strengthen our intention to connect. This intention motivates us to nurture the spirit of NVC.

↪ Practicing the four components—observations, feelings, needs, and requests—we simultaneously deepen this foundational consciousness and gain more fluency in translating from classical to idiomatic language.

↪ Idiomatic language allows for the components of NVC to be used in any environment, supporting the effective listening and expression crucial for social change.

WALKING THE TALK:
A LIFE EXAMPLE FROM THE UNITED STATES

BY MICHAEL CHRISTIE, CNVC TRAINER CANDIDATE

Early in my experience of teaching NVC to the incarcerated, I taught an NVC and mindfulness class at the local prison. Each week, eight to ten men gathered with me for these practices and discussions. These men looked forward to the calming practice of mindfulness and expressed excitement about learning NVC. Because of the inevitable issues of trust and safety they had with authority figures, I felt grateful to have built some equity with them previously, in my role as chaplain.

I first stepped away from formal NVC and toward street giraffe when deciding how to name the practice of Nonviolent Communication. When I started to recruit for the "Nonviolent Communication Class," one inmate asked, "Hey, Chap, is this class for domestic violence or violent people? Because I ain't violent."

"Absolutely not," I said. "Think of it as a class on advanced communication skills that will help you get what you want." That description appealed to the men. It was a step toward creating trust and safety.

We started the series by discussing observations, feelings, and needs. Easy enough. Then came the request. Would the formal language structure of NVC work in the prison setting? As an African American male, I felt uneasy with the formulaic approach of classical giraffe and concerned about whether it was doable for these men to make requests using classical NVC. First, I dealt with my own discomfort, so I could feel free to share the tool of requests as a concept.

In our circle time that week, one offered to practice with a situation in which he felt frustrated with another inmate. One of the men suggested a classical OFNR (observations, feelings, needs, requests) response. "Why don't you tell him, 'I feel irritated or disrespected when you talk while I am talking, and I am requesting that you listen when we have a conversation.'"

The inmate looked at me with a puzzled expression and said, "I can't say that, man. You want me to look like a punk around here?"

Some of the other men quickly agreed with him and said that wouldn't work in prison. People would think you were soft if you talked like that. I understood and wrestled with how I could make this easier.

I suggested he try to express his needs in a way that would make sense in prison culture. Maybe he could say something like, "Man, when you start talking while I'm talking, it annoys me. I just want some respect. Can you listen a minute?"

That offering seemed to resonate more and gave us all some hope that the concepts of NVC could be applied in this social context.

PRACTICE

Translating Classical to Idiomatic Language

Consciously choosing when to engage with classical and when with idiomatic giraffe supports us in living in alignment with awareness and connection. This journaling practice offers a point of reflection to aid the transition from classical to street giraffe. We encourage you to find a quiet place to write with a keyboard or pen and paper for twenty to thirty minutes.

We invite you to think of a time when your classical giraffe did not have the impact you had hoped it would. Choose an instance of moderate challenge for you, a five at the most on a scale of one to ten.

Thinking of that time, what exactly did you say, and what was the exact response, to the best of your recollection? This observation includes verbal, nonverbal, and possible energetic components.

Did you have a sense of openhearted compassion when you spoke and an awareness of interconnection? If not, what might you have done differently to support yourself in reconnecting?

Pause and reflect on what language might have connected you with this person at that time. Is there a way that you might use phrases that are familiar to this person while holding with care what you imagine could be their needs and/or your own? Write down the needs on one side of the page and the words you would use in street giraffe on the other.

Checking in with yourself now . . . how are you feeling and what needs are alive in you?

PART III

OPTIONS FOR CONNECTION

I n the following cluster, we explore the three main practices of Nonviolent Communication: self-empathy, empathy, and self-expression. These are ways in which we can grow and nourish a compassionate and honest relationship with ourselves and others. These strategies for being in relationship with awareness and choice are interrelated. They support an integration of authenticity and belonging, beyond the conditioned assumption that those needs are mutually exclusive.

The NVC Tree of Life is a visual representation of the three different NVC options for connection. We invite you to refer to the diagram before engaging with the chapters in this cluster. Notice how it speaks to you. We invite you to return to it after reading these chapters to check whether or how your understanding has shifted. The visual diagram is available at https://thefearlessheart.org/nvc-reference-materials/the-nvc-tree-of-life/.[1]

ON JACKALS AND GIRAFFES

In this section, you will find many references to jackals and giraffes. The giraffe, known for its exceptionally long neck, sees the world with a panoramic view. A gentle herbivore capable of chewing and digesting thorns, the giraffe has a powerful heart and fiercely protects the life of its young. Rosenberg chose the giraffe as a symbol of the life-affirming qualities we aim to foster in the practice of NVC. As Miki Kashtan often says, "If you are going to stick your neck out, you better have a big heart!"

The jackal's shorter stature, by contrast, only allows for a limited view. Carnivorous by nature, the jackal is equipped with sharp teeth and is perhaps best known for its ululating sounds. When one starts howling, the others follow. In NVC, the jackal metaphorically represents a disconnection to life.

In various cultures around the world, jackals and giraffes have entirely different sets of qualities connected to them. In some places, the jackal is revered. We refer to jackals and giraffes only in relationship to the symbolism Rosenberg bestowed upon them. And, when using these metaphors, Rosenberg would quickly add, "There is no such thing as a jackal; only a giraffe with a language problem."

11

BEING GIRAFFE AND DOING GIRAFFE

Doing is never enough if you neglect Being.

—ECKHART TOLLE

The key distinction between "being" and "doing" giraffe invites us to carefully distinguish doing—taking an action with or without awareness of needs—from being—cultivating a way of life that contributes to needs for all involved. Awareness and presence allow us to notice our relationship with the continuum of being and doing.

When we "do giraffe," we use the components of NVC (OFNR—observations, feelings, needs, requests) to communicate; however, we are not as attuned as we would like to authenticity and mutuality. Without fully aligning to core needs and intentions, our words scarcely capture the rich complexity of our inner experience. When we are "being giraffe," our words—whether in classical NVC language or not—express our truth in the moment with an awareness of interdependence. We are connected to the life energy in us as it seeks to flow with the life energy in others—"Life calling for life," in the words of the late certified trainer and author Robert Gonzales.[1] *Being giraffe* means the head and the heart are integrated, rational and emotional intelligence stream together, and an empathic space emerges where there is no perceived separation between you and me. Being giraffe, we cultivate short-term and overarching intentions that support connection. Intention is balanced with awareness of potential or actual impact. We rely on self-empathy to support being fully aware and present in the moment. In differentiating *doing giraffe* from *being giraffe*, we hone our skills in discernment, and exercise humility. Our willingness and abilities around self-awareness expand, manifesting our commitment to live our values.

Doing Giraffe: Choice or Habit?

"Doing giraffe" can be an active choice, a practice for when we are learning NVC, whether for the first time or expanding in a new area of challenge. Seeking to integrate a feelings-and-needs vocabulary as well as the skills of empathy and self-expression, we persistently and courageously "do giraffe." The formula (OFNR) can serve as an anchor to support even seasoned practitioners in times of distress, fostering an intention to connect and upholding an awareness of interrelationship.

> "Doing giraffe" can be an active choice, a practice for when we are learning NVC, whether for the first time or expanding in a new area of challenge.

Yet "doing giraffe" can all too easily arise from a state of disconnection and mindlessness, even if the language appears to be fully in alignment with the consciousness we are aiming for. When our intention for choosing empathy or self-expression is unclear to us, we may be operating from a state of inner ambiguity. Our commitment to prioritizing the relationship and seeking authentic, heart-to-heart connection can get foggy if we become attached to form over essence.

If our expression—whether empathy or honesty—is a mechanical application of "rules" rather than arising from an integrated state of mind and heart, we will not be enlivening our words with our full presence. In those instances, our words could unwittingly contribute to disconnection and incongruence. Internal dissonance leaks into tone of voice, posture, and facial expressions, no matter how skillfully we employ the formula.

"Doing giraffe" may signal that we are operating from the life-disconnected paradigm that we have been socialized to. We might tell ourselves that we "should" practice NVC. We may hold unconscious intentions within that mindset, such as to fix people or situations, get our way at all costs, or "do" the right thing.

When we operate from these states, we may be denying our personal responsibility or coming from blame (self-blame included), guilt, or shame. Sadly, pairing these life-disconnecting mindsets with the technical skill set of the NVC process can contribute to confusion for all involved.

Understanding Why We "Do Giraffe"

There are many reasons why we find ourselves "doing giraffe." Conditioning, past trauma, and unconscious core beliefs about ourselves, others, and life itself, can prevent us from fully connecting to our own inner feelings and needs. At other times, disconnection may be due to resistance to the pain we experience in the moment. We would rather change another person's behavior or soothe their pain, seeking refuge in the habitual patterns of trying to get what we want in an outcome-oriented way rather than approach our own discomfort.

"Doing giraffe" might also be a subconscious endeavor to protect ourselves from the uneasiness of vulnerability, preserving a comfort zone. When urgently self-concerned, we inadvertently unplug our consciousness of interdependence. We then might numb out and give up on what we want altogether, engaging in "knee-jerk" empathy instead of courageous vulnerability.

"Doing giraffe" can also be a stage for those of us who are newer to the practice of NVC. The integration of NVC language with our heart experience and the awareness of interconnection is a process that takes practice and time. The effort to learn may prevent us from

> **"Doing giraffe" might also be a subconscious endeavor to protect ourselves from the uneasiness of vulnerability, preserving a comfort zone.**

relaxing and trusting that presence is enough. The four components of OFNR become anchors for our attention while we train the mind to experience mutuality and power-with. As former CNVC board president Kit Miller said, "NVC is an awareness discipline masquerading as a communication process."[2] Even when we have been practicing NVC for decades, relying on the four components in a moment of reactivity can help us show up the way we hope to. With attention regulation, emotional regulation follows.

All relationships reveal some power differential. Many of us have had the experience of seeing the person we want to connect with as an authority, someone more skillful or knowledgeable than ourselves. Experiencing them as separate and more powerful, we might fear being judged and want to "do it right." This perspective has been ingrained by the power-over dynamics within our educational systems that equate learning with "doing it right," which leads to praise, while "doing it wrong" leads to punishment. "Doing" NVC then becomes a performance of our competency rather than a practice to touch our own humanity and that of others.

Our unconscious desire to rescue children from unpleasant situations, linked to our own needs for protection and contribution, can also lead us to "do giraffe." Observing that another child has taken their toys elsewhere, we see our daughter crying alone. We might empathize in hopes of soothing her, or engage with the other child, requesting he return with the toys for peaceful and playful sharing. The stress we experience, often a driving force behind "doing giraffe," may lead us to jump to strategies of empathy and expression, with a specific outcome in mind. We might offer empathy to change a child's mind, or make a demand sound like a request. This is one of the main reasons why so many children, especially older ones, develop what some of us call an "allergy to NVC." In addition, our "doing" could outweigh our ability to see the children as competent in their own right. We miss the opportunity to be fully present, acknowledging that they, too, can learn from uncomfortable situations.

Children are very attuned to authenticity. When they sense dissonance between words and presence, they react in ways that can alert us to the incongruence. If we are not receptive to the feedback implicit in the child's behavior, we may think the process of NVC "doesn't work," which, ironically, is another red flag of the "doing" mentality. We discover that the form of NVC, separate from the intention, may not lead to the connection we long for. The overarching intention of the practice of NVC is about connection and not about getting our way at a cost to others.

Being Giraffe: Growing Your Heart

When we commit to cultivating the consciousness implicit in "being giraffe," we choose to see all actions, both our own and others', as attempts to meet needs. We come to relate to this universal energy with awareness and intention. The language of NVC supports us in cultivating and manifesting this consciousness, though we can connect with this life force regardless of whether we speak or even think in terms of needs. We have likely all known people who, even without having heard of NVC, live from and with a sense of interconnectedness, love, and mutuality. This state of heart and mind exists within and outside the practice of NVC.

"Being giraffe," we align with the qualities we want to embody in relationship to ourselves and others. We develop greater awareness of our state of mind so as to live our values and attune to our inner experience. "Being giraffe" is an ongoing practice of returning to our universal human needs, over and over, even as our mind seems to have a mind of its own. Our habits pull us toward deeply grooved patriarchal patterns, yet the mind may be trained otherwise.

> "Being giraffe," we align with the qualities we want to embody in relationship to ourselves and others.

The Gift of Intention

To cultivate "giraffe consciousness," we prioritize connection with ourselves and others as our overarching intention. "The spirituality embodied in NVC exists not so much to help people connect with the divine as to come from the divine energy we're created out of, our natural life-serving energy,"[3] writes Rosenberg. We increase the likelihood of coming from this life-serving energy whenever we hold the intention to welcome each encounter, conflicts included, as an opportunity to bring ourselves gently into a state of awareness.

Intentions—a guiding principle and commitment to a way of being and acting—call for ongoing attention. The skill of self-inquiry and recommitment to our intentions grows with practice. Over time, as we steer the mind to reflect and renew, through journaling, empathy, and self-empathy, it takes less effort to stay the course we have chosen. Mind states, with practice and repetition, become mind traits.

We may have moment-to-moment, short-term, and overarching intentions, all of which can align with a commitment to live nonviolently. While our short-term intentions relate to a specific time period, our moment-to-moment intentions are set around the event at hand.[4] For example, we may have an overarching intention to remember that everyone's needs matter, a short-term intention to cultivate gratitude by focusing every day on three aspects we love about our work, and an intention in the moment to connect with a sense of groundedness while meeting with our boss. These intentions are in alignment, so we feel content.

Typically, conscious intentions are aligned. If we notice a sense of constriction or discomfort, it may arise from inner misalignment, signaling us that an unconscious motivation has slipped in. Checking in with our intentions when we transition from one activity to the next can help us maintain a course that is as attuned as possible with our values. Creating a habit to pause and ask ourselves: "What is my intention?" empowers us to "wake up" and observe whether our intention in the moment is fully in alignment with our overarching intention to "be giraffe."

Another powerful opportunity for awakening to interdependence is granted when we learn about the impact of our actions. When we discover that our behavior has negatively affected others, we can focus our attention on listening to how our actions have affected others without expressing what our intentions were, unless specifically asked. Especially when feedback from nondominant groups is offered, prioritizing listening gives us an opportunity to understand a different viewpoint. Thus the emotional focus then remains with the person who was impacted and we are gifted with an opportunity to learn and grow. We take responsibility for our need to be seen for our intentions rather than demanding that people of nondominant groups to see and value our intentions, rather than our effects. We can get empathy around this elsewhere. (If we sense that hearing our intentions may contribute to healing, we might ask if they want to hear them.)

Intentions and impacts are the linchpin of interdependence. A paradigm of dependence leads me to think that you are responsible for my pain, while with independence, I may think that I am responsible for myself and you for yourself. We forget that interdependence is a net spread wide across space and time. And there is little awareness or sometimes even care for how our actions or inactions impact one another. In the paradigm of interdependence, by contrast, awareness is expanded to hold both intention and impact. Being giraffe, the heart is big enough to hold those two variables as we seek to bring intentions and impacts closer together. Acknowledging goodwill and humbly staying open to recognizing often unintended and unforeseen impacts will help us gradually orient toward interdependence and care.

Self-Awareness and Returning to Our Values

When we consciously practice "doing giraffe," we gradually expand our capacity to "be giraffe." We grow a heartfelt presence that honors openness toward self and other. We also develop an ear for the inner noise of the mind. Simply noticing the cacophony of thoughts may help quiet the mind. Such self-awareness may call us to find a path into silence, pausing our habitual thinking so as to empower us to touch what emerges in the moment.

Bringing our awareness to physical sensations and intentionally scanning for areas of tightness, we offer the body an opportunity to relax, for specific areas of tension to soften. Silently, we may then investigate our feelings with curiosity. Feelings and needs can center our attention as we train the mind toward compassion. Inviting the mind to rest on needs, we align ourselves with what we value deeply. When we find our center, we may discover ourselves in a state of emptiness which is paradoxically full. Aligning and realigning with this consciousness, we can choose to live from this place, moment by moment.

Regular and consistent awareness of and focus on needs awakens our potential to recognize the sacredness of every interaction. Each encounter is welcomed as an opportunity to bring ourselves gently into being rather than doing. This kind of relational approach can become a spiritual practice in its own right. Presence, partnership, and interconnectedness are qualities that reside within us and can be awakened and nurtured. As Rosenberg said: "We are this divine energy. It's not something we have to attain. We just have to realize it, to be present to it."[5]

"Being giraffe" also invites us to attend to our inner motivation when we choose to express ourselves or give empathy, whether verbal or not. Are we in a default mode of habitually choosing empathy, as if it were always the most skillful approach to nurture relationships? Are we expressing ourselves out of clear connection with our needs and care for all, ourselves included, or out of fear that we don't matter? Becoming clear about our motivation and returning to our underlying needs is a form of self-empathy. When we practice this level of awareness, we are more likely to reach out from a state of being, rather than doing, giraffe.

For all its value, "being giraffe" makes no guarantees for interpersonal peace. We accept that we cannot force peace. In times of conflict, "being giraffe" can offer a sense of restful knowing that we have spoken our truth from the heart with intentions for care. If we find we have not done that, "being giraffe" may connect us with a sense of compassion and mourning.

From Doing to Being: Expanding Toward Systemic Awareness

When we shift from a habit of "doing giraffe" to embracing the consciousness of "being giraffe," we make a commitment to honor life in every interaction. We might catch ourselves "doing giraffe" and choose to pause and reconnect before continuing, not because "doing giraffe" is wrong, but because we are not fully connected to what it means to be ourselves at this moment. We might notice that we are focused on the form ("doing") without a clear sense of connection to our intention, ourselves, or others. We might pause to shift and reconnect, because we cherish that connection, and want to live our values. While "being giraffe," we sit with what is alive in each moment, grounding ourselves in compassion, regulating our emotions, accepting everyone (including ourselves) unconditionally, and open to receiving feedback about the impact of our words and behaviors.

"Being giraffe" is not a once and for all "accomplishment." It entails humbly recognizing that we sometimes forget our intentions, that we slip into habitual patterns of reacting, that shedding life-disconnecting

> "Being giraffe" with a systemic perspective invites us to discern whether our attitudes and choices encompass collective liberation beyond our personal freedom.

conditioning and cultivating life-giving awareness is a lifelong endeavor. Firmly and gently, we bring ourselves back to the needs of everyone with compassion. We rekindle the trust that there is no conflict between needs, though there may be a clash between strategies and the narratives attached to them. We continually recommit to honoring the dignity of all. Recognizing our interdependence and partnership, we move one more step away from treating others as objects to be acted upon (power-over) or as authorities to submit to or rebel against.

"Being giraffe" with a systemic perspective invites us to discern whether our attitudes and choices encompass collective liberation beyond our personal freedom. Developing an awareness of patriarchal conditioning and power imbalances helps us learn to distinguish our intentions, which place the focus on ourselves, from the impact of our actions on others.

"Being giraffe," we give and receive from the heart, counterbalancing our conditioning toward accumulation and consequent scarcity. Martin Luther King Jr. is said to have expressed such a shift clearly: "Capitalism does not permit an even flow of economic resources. With this system, a small privileged few are rich beyond conscience and almost all others are doomed to be poor at some level. . . . That's the way the system works. And since we know that the system will not change the rules, we're going to have to change the system."[6] Our practice of "being giraffe" moves us toward this change from the inside out: our personal focus on needs encompasses awareness of the flow of resources in larger systems around us.

A commitment to "being giraffe" guides us toward decision-making processes that take into consideration all needs, being aware of power imbalances so as to foster dignity for all. We align our choices with systems that attend to everyone's needs, rather than sustaining systems of domination. At the same time, we grow in compassion for all the people within these structures.

As we address these complex topics within every key differentiation, it is our hope that this book as a whole is a step toward unraveling millennia of patriarchy, choosing a life-giving awareness. "Being giraffe" entails renewing our present-moment commitment to live with compassionate awareness, even when we shift back into "doing giraffe."

SUMMARY

- In differentiating between "doing" and "being" giraffe, we cultivate intentions that support connection. The head and the heart can be integrated as our short-term and moment-to-moment intentions align with our overarching intention.

- As we check in with ourselves to discern elements of "doing" or "being," we develop self-awareness and recommit to our values.

- In "being giraffe," we listen with curiosity to our deeper motivations and give ourselves empathy as needed.

- Recognizing the potential and/or actual impact of our actions helps us gradually close the gap between beneficial intentions and painful impacts.

WALKING THE TALK:
A LIFE EXAMPLE FROM THE UNITED STATES

BY STEPHANIE BACHMANN MATTEI

Once I experienced a conflict with my close friend Josephine. I requested a phone conversation with the hope that we could find each other's hearts again. Josephine expressed that she was extremely angry with me and asked me several direct "why" questions. I began to believe I'd done something wrong and thought I had to explain myself.[7] I took a breath and reconnected with my intentions for our relationship. I entered the "being giraffe" space.

I deeply love this person, and our friendship has contributed to my life and growth in so many ways. I realized then that I longed to continue to manifest that love (overarching intention) and calmly express myself (moment-to-moment intention). I cherished the care that I trust we have deep down for each other. I sat with my awareness that this period was painful for both of us. I invited my mind to allow this moment to be, just as it was.

I paused to give myself a chance to breathe while I focused on the intensity I perceived in Josephine's voice. Noticing my shoulders tightening and my throat constricting, I held myself with empathy. I softened those parts of my body while taking a few deep breaths and silently acknowledging deep sadness and fear for our relationship. I moved my shoulders slightly backward to open my heart. I visualized my disarmed heart opening up to her and grounded myself in the love that was there.

To muster as much presence and awareness of interconnection as possible, I breathed in for me and breathed out for her. "One for me," I said to myself while I breathed in, and "One for you," while breathing out.[8]

As I sensed my body-mind system relax, I took refuge in the components of my NVC practice. I recommitted to my awareness of interdependence. I set my intention to connect and to be open to hearing of any impact, whether I chose to speak or not, to empathize, or to share my own experience. The conflict did not miraculously disappear, and still, I am at peace knowing that I was able to offer to both of us the best version of myself at that moment.

PRACTICE

Exploring Intention

There is a conscious or unconscious intention behind everything we choose to say or not to say. This practice is designed to deepen our awareness of intentions and support conscious choice regarding if, when, and how to offer nonverbal or verbal empathy.[9] Conscious intentions align us with "being giraffe" rather than only "doing giraffe." This is a self-reflection exercise that we can do multiple times throughout the day as we interact with others. An alarm could be set as a reminder to check in with our intention to do the practice if we have forgotten. We imagine that the practice itself might take about five minutes per section.

As a reminder, in our understanding, there are three layers of intention: moment-to-moment intention (what motivates me in the moment), a short-term intention (perhaps I am holding a request of myself for the next month to practice primarily nonverbal empathy), and an overarching intention or theme to come back to again and again over the course of my life.

Once we clarify our overarching intention and short-term intentions, we are free to set our moment-to-moment intentions, adapting them as we go. Several times throughout the day, we can . . .

~ Pause before empathizing with another person and ask ourselves, "What is my intention in choosing empathy right now? Is this intention in alignment with my overarching intentions? Knowing this, do I want to make any changes in my intention? Will these changes affect what I say or do?"

~ Pause while we are empathizing with someone and asking ourselves, "What is my intention in empathizing right now? Do I want to continue using words or would I rather reestablish presence nonverbally?"

~ Pause and ask ourselves after empathizing, "What was my moment-to-moment intention when I empathized with that person?" With curiosity and compassion, we can check in with ourselves: Are there deeper layers of intention beneath the one I just acknowledged to myself? Was my in-the-moment intention congruent with my overarching intention?

12

EMPATHY AND SYMPATHY/OTHER RESPONSES

Without a word, . . . the speaker
felt that the ferryman took in his words, silent,
open, waiting, missing none, impatient for none,
neither praising nor blaming, but only listening.

—HERMANN HESSE, *SIDDHARTHA*

The key differentiation regarding empathy, sympathy, and other forms of response considers their difference and asks us to discern where our attention lies as we interact with others. Are we focused on our own experience, stimulated by another's sharing (sympathy)? Or is our attention on the experience of the other person, deeply honoring their unique perspective and emotional response while holding them without judgment (empathy)?

Understanding and feeling how empathy and sympathy are distinctly different[1] is one of the first steps toward a mindful practice of relating to the emotions and needs of others.[2] Exploring what empathy is and is not helps us stay present and attune more deeply with our experience and that of others. Our grounded presence, clarity of intention, genuine curiosity, and focus on the empathic space all expand our capacity to connect and create peace within ourselves and in the world. This key distinction allows us to appreciate the many ways of engaging in relationships—empathy, sympathy, and other responses too. There are gifts and challenges in each. Understanding our options helps us choose.

Empathy

NVC, as a relational practice, includes two primary interpersonal components—listening empathically and expressing honestly. Both of these rely on our quality of consciousness. In this chapter, we will share our best understanding of empathic presence in the practice of NVC.

"Empathic connection," writes Rosenberg, "is an understanding of the heart in which we see the beauty in the other person, the divine energy in the other person, the life that's alive in them. We connect with it. The goal isn't intellectually understanding it, the goal is empathically connecting with it."[3]

As a universal quality, empathy here refers to receptivity and connection that contribute to many needs, such as mattering and belonging, trust and compassion, understanding and choice. "Empathy," write Miki and Inbal Kashtan, "is the experience of presence and heart opening to the other person's humanity."[4] As such, empathy is one way to manifest interdependence in action.

Accompanying a person in empathy can offer relief when there is distress, especially if coupled with a sense of aloneness. Empathy can promote emotional healing by supporting our capacity to metabolize painful experiences and create deeper self-understanding and self-connection. Finally, empathy can contribute to inner shifts and transformation by providing support in cognitive perspective-taking. In Rosenberg's words, "empathy allows us to re-perceive our world in a new way and move forward."[5] Seeing with new eyes beyond judgments and enemy images empowers us to reframe, with greater understanding and compassion, how we view ourselves and others. By approaching our pain with the support of another and humanizing whoever's actions may have contributed to our affliction, we empower ourselves to touch peace in the midst of unmet needs.

Reflective inquiry around feelings and needs is one of the NVC strategies for empathic connection. When we imagine it would be beneficial, we may offer a guess by asking, "Are you feeling . . . because you are needing . . .?"[6] This verbal reflection of feelings and needs based on genuine inquiry may benefit the person "receiving empathy"[7] in clarifying or connecting with their own life energy. Guessing may also help us to stay connected if we are uncertain that we understand the essence of what is being said.

Choosing to respond with empathy can give us the necessary pause to find our own heart instead of just reacting. Listening for and paraphrasing feelings and needs is not an inborn talent, but a learned capacity that grows as we practice.

Because the consciousness behind the formula of guessing feelings and needs is paramount, we will describe it in more detail here. After decades of integrating the teachings of the consciousness embedded in the NVC practice from a variety of profoundly gifted mentors, we have identified four factors of empathic consciousness: presence, curiosity, intention, and focus. These factors are interrelated and together they comprise a consciousness greater than the sum of its parts.

Presence

Presence is the fertile ground on which curiosity and the intention to connect can flourish, enhancing our ability to focus on the other person during an interpersonal exchange. Rosenberg enjoys how the Chinese philosopher Chuang-Tzu viewed

> Presence is the fertile ground on which curiosity and the intention to connect can flourish.

presence as "the emptiness of all the faculties. And when the faculties are empty, then the whole being listens."[8] We like this idea of listening from a place that is both empty and whole. Hermann Hesse describes the same quality of presence in his book, *Siddhartha*: "Vasudeva listened very attentively. Listening, he absorbed everything, origin and childhood, all the learning, all the seeking, all joy, all woe."[9] By opening our minds to the truth that is shared by another and keeping our hearts receptive to the felt sense of the other, we grasp what is beyond the understanding of the thinking mind.

Presence empowers us to recognize reactivity as it arises and care for it with compassion. We can then return to empathy and offer our spacious, welcoming presence. In stillness, we can observe and set aside our stories, judgments, and strategies. We relax into an unhurried attitude and let go of any personal agenda. As Zen master Thích Nhất Hạnh says, "Nothing to do, nowhere to go."[10] We sense into what is unfolding in the moment, each unfolding cherished.

Remaining present, we attune to every new piece of information shared. We empathically guess, with or without words, the needs related to the last part that we heard. Connection is only available to us in the present moment—not in the past, not in the future. Empathic awareness calls forth a quality of mind that is on the cusp of the moment as it manifests.

Presence entails awareness of nonverbal as well as verbal communication, both in ourselves and in the other person, while speaking and while listening. Our capacity to be in nonverbal empathy reflects our ability to befriend silence. Eye contact (or lack thereof), facial expressions, tone of voice, gestures, posture, intensity, and timing of response tell us so much more than words alone. Whether or not we are speaking, we are always communicating. Presence also supports us in discerning whether verbal empathy may be distracting rather than connecting. Sometimes a friendly ear in silence is invaluable.

Intention

Rosenberg writes that "NVC is a combination of thinking and language, as well as a means of using power designed to serve a specific intention. This intention is to create the quality of connection with other people and oneself that allows compassionate giving to take place."[11] Rosenberg also says that "out of compassion, out of connection to Divine Energy, [we] serve life."[12] So, in a way, we could say that the intention in NVC is to serve life by attending to the planet and its creatures' needs. Connection to the divine energy is what moves us to this flow of giving and receiving from the heart.

When we choose empathy as a pathway to connection, we do so to relate to our own life energy and that in another being. We seek only to connect in a balance of power. The act of "giving empathy" may indeed contribute, yet this is not our overarching intention. When we perceive ourselves as the "giver," we may unintentionally operate from a mindset of separation. We risk stepping into a power differential as we see the "receiver" as somehow lacking something we have.

If we remain focused on the intention to connect, we are less likely to follow our own stories or get lost in judgments. As our practice deepens over time, we may even be able to stay grounded in hearing judgments someone shares about us. We empower ourselves to hear the feelings and needs contained within the core of these judgments instead of getting lost in the evaluations themselves or forming judgments in response. Attuning our heart to that of another, we are more likely to see that it is not our responsibility to evaluate their experience or reflect upon how it relates to our own. Nor is it our intention to calm them down when emotions intensify.

It is also important to distinguish empathy from agreement. Although we are conditioned to perceive agreement as connection, when we empathize, we are not expressing agreement with someone's perspective or opinions. Rather, we provide a mindful and nonjudgmental presence, creating a safe container for them to express themselves.

Entering the sacred space of relationship takes preparation, even if we decide on the spot to be present with a friend as they begin to share intense feelings. Pausing, we may choose to align with the intention to connect, setting aside any other agenda. It is very challenging to dwell in empathic presence when we are driven by the urge to pursue a specific outcome, such as listening so we may then be heard, or "giving empathy" in hopes that we can peacefully get our way in the end. When we establish a mindful self-connection, set an intention to share empathic connection, and allow the interaction to unfold without expectations, the empathic experience is mutually beneficial.

Focusing on our intention to connect, deeply grounded in an awareness of inter-being, there is no way to say who is the giver and who is the receiver. When we join in this empathic space, "I" and "you" disappear; we become hollow flutes filled with the music of the heart. This "emptiness" paradoxically reflects a "fullness" of our whole being. The more we liberate ourselves from social conditioning, the more we can be openhearted and grounded within ourselves, willing to be affected and transformed by what we hear.

Curiosity

Present with the energy and freedom of the moment, curiosity naturally awakens. The mind that celebrates not-knowing is less inclined to make guesses that "lead" to a particular outcome, such as harmony or reassurance. We follow the other's lead. This choice is grounded in the trust that, as human beings, we have the capacity for self-connection. We lean into the acknowledgment that healing and liberation happen, in part, by learning to trust ourselves. We fully honor choice in content and the ways and degree to which the others reveal themselves.[13] Intention and curiosity live symbiotically; they nourish each other. Together they also empower us to follow the dynamic process of the dialogue rather than staying tied to the initial static content of the conversation. We stay attuned to what emerges moment by moment.

When we give empathy to someone we have known for years, we might find ourselves surprised by an unprecedented quality of connection if we are willing to let go of our attachment to the belief that we "know" them. Releasing all predictions of what they may say and do, we might then enjoy a fresh view that captures less of us and more of them.

Curiosity rests in an awareness that all actions are attempts to meet needs.

Curiosity rests in an awareness that all actions are attempts to meet needs. In Rosenberg's words, "if you learn how to connect empathically with other people, you will hear that they are *always* singing a beautiful song. They are asking you to see the beautiful needs that are alive in them."[14] Typically expressed in the form of questions rather than statements, curiosity invites the other person to check in and see what resonates or does not. It is an act of imagination, humbly recognizing that we do not know for sure what another is thinking, feeling, and needing; we can only guess. Empathy is a vulnerable offering of our presence while we uphold the other's power to define and claim their own experience. Our vulnerability facilitates connection. Accuracy is not the goal.

Empathy embraces all living beings and nature. The Western anthropocentric view limits us to conceive of empathy as only related to humans, but we can bring curiosity to any animal, plant, or part of nature.

Focus

In the state of empathy, we intentionally focus on and create space for the other, directing our attention, sometimes over and over again, back to the empathic space between us. We may notice thoughts, feelings, and needs arising within ourselves. With compassion, we invite ourselves to set them aside, as we bring attention back to the other person. Alternatively, we may realize that they may provide intuitive material for next guesses. While the focus of attention in empathy is on the other person and we follow their lead, we share the empathic space where we discover together the truth of the moment.

Returning to empathy, we direct our focus toward what matters most to the other. We welcome the fullness of their expression. We cultivate curiosity about their feelings and needs, even if they share stories, memories, and judgments of themselves and others. Our own mind may also wander in its desire to make sense of what is being said, and fill in gaps with assumptions. We can acknowledge the fabrications of the mind and invite it to stay with what is present, returning to the space of living energy between us.

Modes of Empathy

According to Miki Kashtan, there are multiple modes of empathy[15]—empathic presence, empathic reflection, empathic expression, and empathic action. When we begin an interaction with empathy, even momentarily, we gain clarity about the needs that are present. That initial clarity of purpose supports us in aligning to another and in choosing what mode of empathy to embrace. We may choose to be fully present with another (empathic presence) whether using words or not, and intuitively attune to their experience.

We may choose to summarize in our own words our understanding of what is being shared (empathic reflection).

> Empathy can also include taking an action that conveys understanding and care based on awareness of needs.

Empathy can also include taking an action that conveys understanding and care based on needs awareness. Holding a sick person's head up and helping them sip water after surgery is an example of empathic action. In addition to being a universal need in its own right, empathy can shine the light on other needs and support problem-solving. This in turn helps identify strategies that are more likely to serve, enabling empathic action.

One more mode of empathy is empathic expression. Since empathic guessing is only a strategy to support connection, sharing how we are moved by what we are hearing can be a form of self-expression in the service of empathy. "When I hear you talk about your child, I feel so moved. I sense your love for her. I am taking that in. Is there more that you want to share about your connection with her?" Empathic expression may be particularly powerful as a strategy for connection when relational trust is affected by power differences. At such times, empathic guessing may call for a level of vulnerability that actually hinders connection and stirs discomfort in both parties, while empathic expression may nurture trust for all involved. The same applies to someone who is put off by empathic guessing for other reasons, such as discomfort with emotional vulnerability.

Empathy in Celebration

Empathy for celebrations is just as important as empathy in times of grief or frustration.

> STEPHANIE: As I am sitting in front of the computer, my son enters the room. I stop working on this chapter and look up at him.
>
> "The professor just gave me feedback on my last project!" he exclaims. "He really enjoyed my advertising survey and thought my questions were well thought out and to the point!"
>
> I grin widely.
>
> "Wow! I see how excited you are. You put a lot of energy into that survey! I bet you are happy to have this kind of acknowledgment . . . right?"
>
> My son smiles proudly, and I guess that my focused presence and complete curiosity regarding his experience contributed to a sense of mutual celebration. He puts his arm around me and squeezes. Don't we all love getting empathy for our celebrations?

Empathy for celebrations is just as important as empathy in times of grief or frustration.

Empathy as a Choice, Not a Demand

In considering the differences between empathy and sympathy, we do not presuppose that empathy is best in all situations or that we "should" show up empathically at all times. Unfortunately, empathy, as one option for connection, may be internalized as an inner demand rather than a choice.[16] In fact, defaulting to empathy may be a protective strategy in which we avoid revealing our own honesty.

Rote empathy can actually contribute to disconnection and even distrust as people question the authenticity of our empathy. Clarity about the different modes of empathy and how they can serve relationships, with consideration

Rote empathy can actually contribute to disconnection and even distrust as people question the authenticity of our empathy.

for systemic power differences, helps us make conscious, informed choices whether to engage in empathy. Considering the context and the many factors that affect relationships can help us discern how to nurture connection with awareness and choice.

Sympathy

"With empathy, I'm fully with them, and not full of them—that's sympathy,"[17] Rosenberg reminds us. When we experience sympathy for another, we identify with or objectify the speaker. Often we also have feelings of our own that emerge from hearing what they are going through. One way to confirm whether we are in sympathy or empathy is to answer this question: "Whose needs am I attending to?" If the answer is "mine," then we know that what we are offering is sympathy. We want to acknowledge that often there are compassion, care, and tenderness in non-empathic responses that do actually support the heart-to-heart connection. At other times, our need for contribution may actually prevent us from being fully present. Here are some possible points of discernment to guide us in distinguishing empathy and sympathy from each other. Each has value. Flexibility here is essential.

EMPATHY	SYMPATHY
My attention and curiosity are directed toward what is alive for you.	My attention is with my own experience stirred by your self-expression. I may have feelings of concern and needs for care at the forefront.
I am grounded in our shared humanity. I am aware that we are connected in this web of life. Together, we are holding your pain and/or celebration.	The distinction between you and me blurs. I unconsciously identify with you which may lead to self-oriented responses. Sometimes, though, conscious identification can provide me with context to understand you.
I listen with curiosity, and I follow your lead.	I may ask questions to better understand. These questions may be geared to my curiosity and care and may not necessarily be aligned with where you want to go. I might offer unsolicited support, intending to help you navigate your experience.

Sympathy in Action

STEPHANIE: When I realized I was pregnant with our first child, my husband and I were overjoyed and eagerly anticipated nourishing this new life together. I was less than twelve weeks pregnant when, at our first ultrasound, a heartbeat could not be detected. Another ultrasound followed a week later and then another. No heartbeat. Our ob-gyn informed us gently that the baby had stopped living and that I would miscarry. She stepped in close and rested her hands on my shoulders. My tears began to fall.

"Stephanie," she said. "Listen carefully. You have done nothing wrong. It's not your fault. Please remember that. Call me anytime you doubt yourself." It happened twenty-four years ago, and I remember it all as if it happened yesterday.

I did miscarry, and I cried for weeks.

I understood that the people who knew about our loss truly wanted to support me and show their love and care. I recall the first Sunday I sat in church after the miscarriage, sobbing silently through the service. A friend came to sit beside me. "I can't stop crying," I told her. She looked at me.

"You don't have to stop," she said, caressing my tear-stained face. I treasured that moment of healing, savoring her unencumbered, nonjudgmental presence. Her expression conveyed to me, in the fewest and simplest words, understanding and empathy for the intense grief I was experiencing. As we say often in this book, the classical form of NVC is rarely needed outside of a practice context.

Yet that is only one memory. Most of the people in church that day came to me with words like, "You can try again." They said, "Now you have an angel in paradise." One whispered, "It happened to me too. . . . I was actually happy to miscarry because I was not planning on having a baby!"

Their sympathy, reassurance, and various other expressions, while stemming from care and sometimes companionship, revealed a distinct quality of relating to my loss through their own feelings about such bereavement. Few were able to stay present such that we could hold space for my despair together.

Sympathy as a Conditioned Response

One might wonder if we are culturally inclined to offer sympathy. Capitalism reinforces the separation mentality that makes it more difficult for us to empathize with one another.

We could also unwittingly slip into a kind of sympathy in which we feel discomfort, anger, or despair for others who receive treatment that we see as life-alienating. We may be especially inclined to do so when we are the beneficiaries of these systemic structures. Attempting to give people empathy, we may experience such a rush of pain for them (our pain) that we abandon the empathic space without awareness and instead go on to receive empathy from them.

CNVC certified trainer and assessor Roxy Manning writes about such an incident in her article "Cross Privilege Dialogues." Manning says that she shared her feelings with a trusted empathy buddy with greater status power, in passing, about a microaggression her son had experienced the day before. Her friend expressed outrage at what happened, with feelings more intense than Manning's own. In that moment, Manning experienced a dilemma that is familiar to Black women and other BIPOC.[18] She asked herself, "What do I do with this moment?" She goes on to explain, "Often, when a white person reacts much more strongly to some event in my life than I do, I slow down and give them space. I let them have their moment of coming face-to-face with the systemic inequities that I live with daily. I agree with them that it's completely unfair. I empathize with their desire for a world that is better. But as I do all that, there's a small part of me that is frustrated and rolling my eyes. That part is saying, 'Look, don't you see what's happening here? All of a sudden, my minor pain is about you. Instead of the simple nod to shared reality, to my experience being seen, that I was hoping for when I shared, I'm now taking care of you.'"[19]

Manning points out that people in cross-privilege dialogues are impacted differently in fundamental ways when speaking of such incidents. One suggestion she offers is that we ask for permission to shift the focus—which is not, as Manning notes, mutually beneficial. If there is agreement, we may express ourselves without taking for granted the other person's readiness to hear us.

Other Habitual Forms of Response

Sympathy is one of the many conditioned responses that shift attention from the speaker to the listener. Unlike empathy, other forms of response have a common quality of being outcome oriented. For example, the goal of sympathy, advice, or reassurance might be to ease the distress of a listener who has unhealed pain related to a similar situation. By stepping into a role of fixer or advisor, the

> The goal of sympathy, advice, or reassurance might be to ease the distress of a listener who has unhealed pain related to a similar situation.

listener may be unconsciously attempting to meet their own need for efficacy, rather than feeling helpless. Shifting the focus to ourselves this way does not honor the speaker's opportunity to find confidence by navigating difficult circumstances.

Consoling can cloak resistance to someone else's pain. We may imagine they cannot handle such discomfort, when they might be quite capable of it, and we may be the ones who are struggling. Hugging or handing tissues, while intending care, may reveal a desire to stop the discomfort that someone's pain is eliciting in us.

Fixing, storytelling, correcting, explaining, and teaching, among other responses, shift the focus from empathic presence to the listener's thoughts, beliefs, opinions, and/or experiences. Without active discernment about whether these responses address needs, we may continue to apply them without attention to the context.

Typically, when we respond with anything other than empathy, we do so intending support or connection, whether or not it actually contributes. Often, pure presence is what we most need in order to venture into self-inquiry. Such accompaniment may empower us to explore our inner world. As the emotional experience shifts, creative space opens and expands. Then solutions we had no access to before may emerge.

Sadly, if we are quite invested in our strategy and are "certain" it is the best response, we may not be open to hearing feedback stating otherwise. This assumption that we know what is best could in itself be part of an unconscious power-over stance. When we are openhearted, by contrast, we stay open to receiving feedback about the impact of our words.

The Value of Empathy

"Empathy is a respectful understanding of what others are experiencing," Rosenberg tells us.[20] Respect includes awareness of the personal and collective conditioning that impacts our ability to be present with ourselves and others. In order to empathize with those whose experience is culturally and systemically different from our own, it is crucial that we learn to decolonize our minds.[21] By actively seeking to hear the voices that have been silenced for centuries, we heal the wounds of socialization as individuals and as communities. Liberation is catalyzed by changing the stories we tell ourselves and one another.

As a pathway to nonviolence, empathy empowers us to reconnect with the fundamental humanity in every person.

As a pathway to nonviolence, empathy empowers us to reconnect with the fundamental humanity in every person. Touching our essence together, we move toward collective actions and solutions. Rosenberg's legacy invites us to experience empathy as the flow of divine energy moving through our hearts.

SUMMARY

- ⟜ This key distinction supports us in discerning empathy from sympathy, by noticing whether our attention is on our own feelings or on holding space for those of others.

- ⟜ Being present to needs helps us mindfully determine whether empathy, or some other response, will serve in the moment.

- ⟜ Fostering genuine curiosity, moment by moment, we follow rather than lead in an empathic exchange. Experiencing this freedom to respond, we may switch modes of empathy— presence, sensing, reflection, or action—at any time or perhaps shift to a different response altogether.

- ⟜ This key helps us to determine whether we are in empathy, sympathy, or another form of expression by inviting us to consider our intention and attachment to outcome.

- ⟜ Discerning empathy from sympathy supports an inquiry into our personal and collective conditioning.

WALKING THE TALK:
A LIFE EXAMPLE FROM THE UNITED STATES

BY KRISTIN COLLIER

I am called to support a student who has thrown a chair toward a teacher. I am grateful that our school prioritizes empathy; one may wonder how school systems in general obstruct empathic space. Most of our students come to us because many needs were not met in the public school system. When I arrive, seventeen-year-old Steven, diagnosed with autism, paces back and forth through a nearly empty room.

"Hey," I say.

"Hey," he says.

I take a seat and look out the window, opening my heart and mind. Jackal interrogation intervenes: Didn't he know better than to throw the chair? I set this question and my reaction aside for later. For now I want to focus my curiosity on what is alive for Steven.

"I can never remember names," he says. "She told me, but I forgot. I hate that about myself!"

I nod, choosing not to speak. Steven is easily overstimulated and guessing at his feelings aloud often invites a vulnerability he's not ready for. I let him lead.

"She said it was unacceptable that I called her 'Miss.' But I couldn't remember her name!" He grinds his teeth as tears emerge. "I threw a chair! I couldn't think and she kept saying I was disrespectful. I'm sorry," he says.

I nod. "You felt angry, right? I bet you just wanted to focus on your work. Is that it?"

"Yes!" he says, covering his face with his hands. "Now I messed it all up." My mind goes to strategies to calm him. I take a breath, remembering that I have committed to empathic presence with an intention only to connect. "Are you wishing people understood that it's hard for you to remember names?" I ask.

"Yes," he says. Steven takes a deep breath. "Do you think they will let me try again?" he asks.

Steven comes to sit beside me, and we discuss possible strategies for reconnection.

PRACTICE

Building Internal and External Awareness

This practice is offered in the spirit of supporting awareness of our inner and outer worlds at once. We can grow our capacity to hold our personal experience with that of another, discern where we are directing attention, and build skills in making choices that consider the needs of all involved. This practice is a meditation. You can record and play back this meditation or read it through once before referring to it as needed, as you move through the practice. We encourage you to find a comfortable sitting posture that allows for some ease in the body and alertness in the mind. We invite you to set aside ten to fifteen minutes for this practice.

Stabilize awareness by allowing the mind to rest on the natural flow of breath and the movement that breathing produces in the body, wherever you sense it most prominently.

Following your own rhythm, whenever you are ready, invite awareness to expand and encompass the body in its totality . . . the head floating between the shoulders, the trunk steady and straight, the arms and legs resting.

How does it feel to inhabit this body right here, right now?

Inviting awareness into the entire body . . . what are some of its sensations?

And now, slowly shifting your awareness to the external world, focus on sounds coming from close by and far away. . . . At a certain point, letting go of external sounds, you may notice inner sounds such as the heartbeat. Rest your attention inside the body, on its sensations.

Then, according to your own rhythm, redirect awareness again to the world of external sounds.

And now, staying mindful of both the internal experience of the body and the external experience of sounds touching the eardrum, foster an open awareness to encompass what you are sensing both inside and outside.

Breathe into this experience.

REFLECTION

- ∼ What, if anything, did you enjoy about this exercise?

- ∼ Did you find it challenging to experience the world inside and outside of you at once?

- ∼ How do you imagine this exercise might apply to your life?

- ∼ Do you have any specific requests of yourself to grow this practice in the coming week?

13

EMPATHIC SENSING
AND INTELLECTUAL GUESSING

Empathy is the door to wisdom.

—SUZY KASSEM

This key, differentiating empathic sensing from intellectual guessing, acknowledges that we can become more aware of the distinct somatic quality of empathy and cultivate greater sensitivity in our empathic presence. Empathy is rare in Western culture, which prizes intellect over the body and its sensations. Empathy is neither a capacity of the mind alone, nor a quality only of the heart.[1] When we attune to sensing empathically, we become present, integrating our minds with our hearts, our bodies, and our human capacity for imagination, rather than operating only from our heads, disconnected from the rest of our faculties. This embodied experience of empathy nourishes the giver and receiver alike, as we foster a receptive consciousness.

Conversely, when we guess intellectually, we hear what the other person says, while analyzing

> When we attune to sensing empathically, we become present, integrating our minds with our hearts, our bodies, and our human capacity for imagination.

the situation, the feelings expressed, or the manner of speaking. This mental activity, uncoupled from other forms of human intelligence, takes us away from a felt sense of the energetic quality of their feelings and needs. We can learn to notice the signs that we are intellectually guessing and create space for an integrated state of presence, in which the mind, heart, and body are aligned. Activating our imagination, we can then feel into the empathic space, with or without words.

Intellectual Guessing

When we make empathy guesses only from our head, we often hold the intention to connect, yet our faculties are not aligned. We may find ourselves, without being aware of it, removed from the direct experience of felt emotions. We might subconsciously try to control the intensity of the experience out of a desire to protect ourselves.

With a cognitive approach only, we package emotions in static forms which are at odds with their dynamic nature. Emotions, from the Latin root *movere*, meaning "to move," naturally shift and flow from one to another as energy in motion, whether we are aware of this or not. Relying only on intellectual guesses can move us away from the sensations related to a fluid, empathic response.

Brain science tells us that we are hardwired to perceive the mind of another. Mirror neurons in a listener's brain light up in the same regions as they do in the speaker's, allowing the experience of empathy. When we make intellectual guesses only, we place our attention on thinking rather than on the felt sense of the other person. This short-circuits our ability to be receptive, increases the risk that our guesses will come from a detached perspective, and distances us from the heart of the matter.

If we are trained in the process of NVC, our intellectual guesses may revolve around feelings and needs. On the surface, our words may be the same as those that accompany empathic sensing. While using the language of feelings and needs, our guesses may still heavily rely on labeling feelings, based on intellect alone.

When learning the language of feelings and needs, literacy in the mind is built before fluency of the heart. As seasoned practitioners, we still have growing edges. Depending on a myriad of conditions, we can be overwhelmed with sensation or triggered by pain from the past. Momentarily, the limbic system overrides the higher executive functions of the prefrontal cortex, functions which would allow for heart-centered empathy in which mind, body, heart, and imagination are integrated.

Building Awareness of Intellectual Guessing

Learning to recognize the signs that we are intellectually guessing will gradually empower us to track the energetic presence we are offering. Are we aware of our bodily sensations? Is our mind engaged in an act of imagination? Are our hearts open to being moved?

Sometimes, at the end of an exchange, which could include emotional sensing in varying degrees, we realize we do not feel fully satisfied. Looking back at our guesses, we may notice that we were thinking more than attuning to the experience of the other person's feelings and needs. Reflecting on when we shifted away from soft presence, we may have a request of ourselves regarding the next time we give empathy.

> KRISTIN: I noticed that I had shifted into offering only intellectual guesses when I perceived my friend "complaining." Labeling her sharing that way caught my attention, and I offered myself empathy to discern why I interpreted her expression this way. I realized I felt bored and wanted connection. I chose to make a short-term intention to connect with the needs I guessed she was trying to meet. Checking in with her to see if my guess resonated, I primed the neural pathways that bridged my mind and heart, becoming less bored and more connected. I then was able to maintain empathic presence.

Empathic Sensing

As humans we have a lifelong capacity to sense empathically. At the thresholds where beings enter and recede, in birth and death, and often when we fall in love, we may find it effortless to attune this way. We are undeniably present and alive with such transitions, as time melts away around us. Perhaps the magnitude of these events awakens us, and the felt experience emblazons itself in our memory. Recalling the clarity we feel within and between us in these moments, we might compare and contrast the muted sense of presence we typically call forth in our day-to-day lives. The memories of such naturally arising "peaks" of awareness may inspire us to expand more often.

When we attune and resonate empathically, we are present with all our senses to what is alive in the other person at the moment. We foster connection at the heart level with their experience. We seek to understand them from the inside out, trusting our intuition about what they may be feeling or needing.

> We have a lifelong capacity to sense empathically. At the thresholds where beings enter and recede, in birth and death, and often when we fall in love, we may find it effortless to attune to this sensing.

While we may think our way to a guess based on the story they are telling, or imagining how we might feel if that happened to us, we integrate our thoughts with the other faculties for resonant empathy. The four factors within empathic consciousness described in Chapter 12 are alive in empathic sensing: We bring a quality of presence that directs our attention to the felt experience, cultivate curiosity, uphold an intention to connect, and focus on the other person's experience, body language, feelings, and needs. We practice this openhearted sensing regardless of the words that our conversation partner is employing, even if they are unhappily directed at us.

Touching Fullness by Emptying the Vessel

Before holding an empathic space with another, it is important to prepare ourselves. We may pause to self-connect, acknowledge our stream of thoughts, stories, and beliefs, and then invite ourselves to momentarily release it. Acknowledging to ourselves any limitations on our capacity to listen (due, perhaps, to traumatic experiences), we make peace with what we can achieve in this present moment.

The "sensing" begins here, as a body-based awareness. Scanning within, we can observe whether our bodies are unsettled or relaxed, constricted or open. We may consciously sit with whatever we notice, offering it our full attention as its quality shifts and moves. We might also intentionally invite the body to relax. Observing our state of mind, we can discern whether it is focused or scattered, sharp or foggy. With compassionate awareness, the mind gathers and integrates. Curiosity arises. We are present to ourselves, inquire into our feelings and needs, and prepare to offer our undivided attention to another. Empathic sensing is making a gift of one's full presence which, paradoxically, consists of quieting the mind so as to offer a settled body and calm presence. From here, we can then reintegrate the mind. Our listening is born from a state of inner silence.

The "sensing" begins here, as a body-based awareness.

Feeling With Another

When we sense empathically, Rosenberg says that there is a "direct grasp of what is right there before you that can never be heard with the ear or understood with the mind."[2] We attune energetically, intimately, to the person who is expressing. At the same time, we tap into the mind's capacity to fine-tune itself to be receptive to this person's particular life experiences, discounting none. We hold both the individual's predicament and the universal qualities within them at once, bypassing neither. A "witnessing" presence within us observes this merging in the shared energetic space and is mindful not to become enmeshed with the other person's emotions. Paradoxically, this clarity that the other person's world is theirs allows our hearts to stay fully open to be moved. From this viewpoint, we can take in the other person's humanity and let ourselves be affected by this encounter with another human being, experiencing present-moment interdependence.

While at first we may not "sense" much, our efforts to be receptive to sensation expand our awareness of this unknown territory. With practice and repetition, we realize that empathy is not a fill-in-the-blanks exercise. Rather, it may use language to point to something beyond words. Sensing becomes less challenging as we gather more of a felt experience that is unique to us. For many of us, letting go of the secure framework of words is essential if we are to learn to trust our intuition. Empathic sensing, like swimming or walking, is learned with practice.

Focused on feeling within a shared empathic space, we attend to the ever-changing sensations within our body that are accompanied by shifts in emotional energy. We might experience fullness, deep aching, the thrill of excitement, a rush of despair, even tears. Grounding our attention in physiological sensations, we are more likely to be present to ourselves and our partner.

Sensing empathically, we may experience an intuitive or "felt sense" of what another person is experiencing. Our heart contains its own "little brain" with over forty thousand neurons that can sense, feel, and remember. We might also have a "gut feeling"; research shows we have two to six hundred million neurons lining our gastrointestinal tract from esophagus to rectum (enteric nervous system).[3] The cells of the heart and gut are in conversation with our brains and sometimes even direct our bodies. We can develop a relationship with these other "brains" to better understand ourselves and others. Integrating those amazing capacities of our body-mind system can support us in increasing our potential to be fully present.

Checking In

As cathartic as it may be for the speaker to share emotions empathically with another person, as the listener we can never have a complete understanding of what they are feeling. Looking for nonverbal cues, we may get a sense through eye contact or a deep sigh that our presence reverberates within them. This may be enough, especially if the person is in their own inner process of self-connection. A silent accompaniment may be most supportive, words a distraction. At other times, especially when the other person is not in a state of connection with themselves, an empathy guess about feelings and/or needs may support the process of co-regulation. Again, it is our integrated faculties of mind, heart, body, and imagination that empower us to intuitively gauge the situation, make a choice about connection strategies, and stay alert to signs of impact.

In the NVC process, verbal empathy often takes some form of, "Are you feeling ... because (this need) really matters to you?" Mindfully aligning our words with our felt resonance, we may choose not to include feeling and need words at all. We might also use these later if we imagine that they would contribute to the other person's inner experience of connection. Our words are not so important as our heartfelt presence.

Reintegrating the Faculties

If we discover we are only guessing intellectually, we might first sit with this awareness, acknowledging the sensations in our own body. Do we feel uncomfortable? Are we inclined to make judgments of ourselves and others? Do we want to just sit with whatever we are feeling for a few moments? We can pause and reconnect with our body sensations and our breath. This deeper self-connection allows us to shift our attention and gently summon the other faculties for empathy. From this state of reintegration, we can direct our attention to empathically sensing into the experience of the other person from a consciousness of inter-being.

If we think it could contribute to relational repair, we may decide to name the momentary lapse in the energetic flow. Perhaps we share something like, "I notice that I was not quite present with you just now, and I want to fully grasp what you are telling me. Can I tell you what I got so far?" We can bring ourselves back into emotional sync by intentionally attuning ourselves to the other person again. Making eye contact, silently nodding, matching the speaker's tone and pace of speech, and mirroring the connecting⁵ nonverbal behavior (neuroscience refers to this as limbic synchronicity), if it feels genuine, may help us to find our way back to their heart.

SUMMARY

- ↺ This key distinction helps us to see that empathy is not *either* head or heart; integrating the two, we tap into the power of empathic attunement. Relying *only* on intellectual guesses limits this power and can move us away from the sensations that enable a fluid, empathic response.

- ↺ While we may intellectually guess based on the story we are told or by imagining how we might feel if that happened to us, we can then integrate our thoughts with our other faculties, including sensing, for resonant empathy.

- ↺ Intellectually, we can acknowledge to ourselves any limitations on our capacity to listen due to traumatic experiences whether personal or collective. Empathically, we can make peace with the degree of spaciousness we can achieve.

- ↺ In the space of integrated empathic attunement, we directly grasp an energy that contributes to connection and resonance with another, with or without words.

WALKING THE TALK:
A LIFE EXAMPLE FROM THE UNITED STATES

BY KRISTIN COLLIER

Tonight after dinner my family is immersed in conversation. The air has a crackle to it as I turn to an internet search related to our conversation. My son and parenting partner begin to wash dishes, as our dog, Leo, presses his face into my keyboard. I guess that he wants to be seen. "Hi," I tell him, looking into his eyes. "I see you." I push his silvering muzzle away gently as I scroll down. Leo's black nose nudges my hands off the keyboard again. "I see you," I say. "What's going on?" I rub his shoulder, guessing he wants to be near me, maybe wanting some company, and I let him stay.

Leo thrusts his head onto the keyboard and this time rests it there, gazing up at me with liquid brown eyes.

"Hello, honey, you want some love?"

And then I get it. Nothing I've said or done has satisfied Leo. He's telling me, bluntly now, that I'm not showing up for our relationship. Sighing, I realize that I haven't put my heart into any one of the things I've said to my dear companion who has been trying to connect. I close my laptop.

"My gosh," I say, taking his head in my hands, feeling his tension, and holding it intensely with my own energy. Opening my heart, and breathing in, I feel my body relax. As I focus on Leo, everything else in the room fades away, I feel more like myself, softly touching the love between me and my dog. His eyes lock with mine, and I realize he is afraid. I feel his fear and his desire to be right next to me, where he imagines he's safest. He feels the possibility of movement—big movement—afoot, I guess.

"Leo," I say, "you're afraid, aren't you? We are talking about big things and there's a lot of uncertainty." His eyebrows shift back and forth, but his head doesn't move. I hold his gaze and breathe quietly and slowly, my heart full.

"You want some reassurance?" I ask. Leo looks up. I express myself then. "I love you," I tell him. "You are precious to me, and we are all going to work this out, you included." Leo gazes at me, quietly and long, offering his empathic attention back to us in this time of uncertainty. I stroke his head and chest as he melts to lie down at my feet.

PRACTICE

Being Present With Another

As we increase our skill set to sense into and be present with our bodies, we enhance our capacity for empathy. Expanding upon the practices from Chapters 1 and 12 with respect to sensing and experiencing the body and feelings in the present moment, this practice is designed to support you in extending that presence and awareness to include another being. This practice calls on the ability to direct attention so that it integrates the heart/mind. This is an empathy practice. We estimate that this practice will take ten to thirty minutes.

This empathy practice can be done formally or informally, nonverbally, or accompanied by verbal guessing, according to your growing edges. If helpful, feel free to consider offering empathic presence to an animal or a small child before an adult. Usually, we are less likely to stay in our mental stories when no significant story is being told. Empathy is powerful both in moments of celebration and in times of grief or frustration. Empathically engaging with a companion during everyday conversation can nourish heart-to-heart connections. The following are guidelines that can be adapted to formal or informal settings.

∼ Start by grounding yourself, noticing sensations in the body. Observe if there is tension and what happens when awareness is directed to that space. Invite some relaxing, if possible, and visualize yourself "emptying the vessel." Acknowledge thoughts that arise and allow them to pass, if they will. Slowly ground yourself in your body, bringing attention to physical sensations.

~ Open awareness now to embrace the other person, listening with all the senses. Observe movement, tone of voice, verbal pacing, and the general quality of their energy.

~ Now invite your awareness to open to the relational space of shared energy. Sense the space between you. Sensing into this energy, allow the heart to be moved and the body to mirror movements of the "speaker" if and when it feels genuine.

~ Remember that we are being and not doing. Breathe. Experience the body. Sense. A shift may occur naturally between the two of you.

~ Take a moment to give thanks for this practice time.

REFLECTION

~ Did you notice the energy in the shared space affecting your body?

~ How did you experience the energy of empathy? What were some of the sensations? Did you enjoy them?

~ If you feel moved to, check in with the other being. How did they experience this empathic exchange?

~ Is there a relationship in your life that might benefit from more of this empathic attunement? Do you have any specific requests of yourself to develop your practice of empathy?

14

SELF-EMPATHY AND ACTING OUT, REPRESSING, OR WALLOWING

If your compassion does not include yourself,
it is incomplete.

—JACK KORNFIELD

This key distinction invites us to cultivate self-empathy as compassion in action that starts with ourselves. Pausing to relate to ourselves with care allows us to recognize the space between the stimulus (observation) and our response. Self-empathy empowers us to choose how we respond, so as to reduce reactive behaviors—such as acting out, repressing, or wallowing in our feelings—which tend to create more suffering.

Within the NVC process, self-empathy is a path to connection with our experience, with a focus on feelings and needs. This transformative process is foundational for nonverbal or verbal empathy and self-expression. As the practice

> **Self-empathy empowers us to choose how we respond, so as to reduce reactive behaviors—such as acting out, repressing, or wallowing in our feelings—which tend to create more suffering.**

deepens, it may include an inquiry into our thinking and into the power-ful driving forces of internalized messages from family and society. By uncoupling feelings from thoughts and observations from evaluations, we may find the spaciousness and power to choose our response.

Self-empathy allows us to approach challenging moments as well as savor pleasant ones. This differentiation focuses on self-empathy's gift of empowering us to become aware of, allow, and befriend emotions, whether pleasant or unpleasant, and needs, whether we experience them as "met" or "unmet." As a mode of sustained self-awareness, it allows us to acknowledge the interconnection among emotions, thoughts, condi-tioning, and values. We can then make requests, as much as possible, from expansion rather than resistance.

The Options of Overwhelm

Within the dominant culture, acting out, repressing, and wallowing in feelings are conditioned ways of coping with our emotional life. We act out, repress, or wallow in our feelings when we are overwhelmed by pain and do not have the skills or spaciousness to deeply connect with our feelings and needs. Perceiving the "demands" of life to be greater than the resources we have at our disposal, the stress response sets in—fight, flight, or freeze. Acting out of habit, we blame and induce guilt or shame, whether targeting ourselves or others, in a paradoxical effort to relieve some of our own suffering. These behaviors, survival mechanisms often reinforced by conditioning, may unconsciously aim to protect us from facing unresolved pain or trauma or from being flooded by emotions. In these moments, we don't find the courage or capacity to experience the ache long enough for us to awaken into compassion.

We *act out* (the fight response), by identifying with and taking action from our reactive mind, judging, criticizing, or blaming others. Or we might express emotions without connecting them to our own needs. We may act out physically, perhaps fighting, throwing things, or hurting ourselves. Or we might make rash decisions, like thinking, speaking, and acting from a paradigm of separation. We may be unaware of our interdependence and are not open to considering the possible impacts of our reaction. We might say things like, "What's the matter with you? How many times have I told you . . . ?" Conversely, we might direct anger inward, leading to self-hatred, depression, and despair.

We act out, repress, or wallow in our feelings when we are overwhelmed by pain and do not have the skills or spaciousness to deeply connect with our feelings and needs.

We believe our own thoughts and feelings, unable to see that we have abdicated responsibility for them. Our attention is focused on survival. While "acting out" is a tragic attempt to connect with power, we are unlikely to reconnect with our own sense of empowerment.

We might *repress* (the flight response) our feelings out of fear, hoping to protect ourselves or someone else. Perhaps we do not trust that we will experience acceptance or self-acceptance if we express ourselves authentically. Fearful of being overwhelmed by our emotions, we might attempt to avoid feeling them. This compromises our ability to take ownership of our emotional experience. Moreover, when we believe that some event or person causes our emotions, we don't see how our thinking colors our perception of needs. Feelings are often less intense but more persistent when we repress rather than compassionately owning them. Repression disconnects us from the life within and outside ourselves. And sadly, because we cannot selectively numb emotions, such repression also compromises our capacity to experience pleasurable emotions.

Perhaps we learned to repress our feelings in childhood when our parents accepted some of our emotions but not others. Anger, sadness, and grief may have been discouraged or even disapproved of. We might have heard things like, "Look at the bright side of this." "Big boys don't cry!" or "Don't you dare talk to me like that!"

The Western historical denigration of affect and exaltation of reason leads us to seek "control" over our feelings. We fear that we will be unable to pull ourselves back together after an emotional release. Having internalized this dynamic of repression, we might say things like, "It doesn't matter, let's not make a big deal out of this."

When we *wallow* in our feelings (a form of self-absorption typical of the freeze response), we invest attention in what we do not enjoy, typically with a sense of unfulfilled needs. Instead of witnessing our discomfort around perceived unmet needs until we gracefully connect with the power of what we value, we fall into a negative spiral. Our habitual thinking and conditioning wedge us in, as if things would never change, while we experience an ongoing sense of lack.

> STEPHANIE: As the novel coronavirus spread rapidly through Northern Italy, where my eighty-nine-year-old mother resides, I felt increasingly scared, because I care for her life and well-being. Looking deeper, I touched a sense of powerlessness. Thoughts percolated into my awareness. What if she gets sick? Do I leave my family here in the United States and go to Italy? The hospital would not even allow me to see her. Were she to die, I would not even be able to say goodbye. I realized my thinking was spiraling me into increasingly scary places. As I identified with my thoughts, my body contracted and the fear expanded. I paused. I reminded myself to come back into the present moment. This being human is so complex and so fragile. I tenderly held myself, realizing I was at a choice point: "Do I want to focus my attention on power as an unmet need or on its energy living in me which may then help me to recognize what actually is in my power?" As I connected more deeply with my longing for my mom's well-being, I chose to ask my brother to give her a smartphone so that we could see each other through WhatsApp. I could give her the gift of my presence more often and more joyfully as we looked into each other's eyes.

Wallowing in our feelings may also indicate that we are not truly allowing ourselves to touch our pain and grieve. As clinical psychologist

John Welwood writes, "What we fail to grieve turns into grievance."[1] Having a grievance becomes a protective strategy born from the fear of touching the depth of our needs. Wallowing in grievance, we identify with what is missing instead of opening ourselves to peace amid unmet needs and finding courage in the power we do have to meet our needs.

We might notice this is happening if we can't relate to our emotions in ways that empower us to sense beauty and fullness in our need. Or we may be able to connect with our needs but still be inclined to blame or judge something or someone, even ourselves, as wrong or responsible for why our need is not met. We may feel "stuck," unwilling or unable to shift into an empathic space.

It is not uncommon, even after years of practicing NVC, to find ourselves paralyzed in our feelings and perception of needs not met. While we all have power to relate to our unmet needs in life-giving ways, our practice is in no way a substitute for seeing that everyone's basic human needs are met. Nor will such a practice in and of itself address systemic inequalities that prevent such needs from being met.

Wallowing in emotions, repressing emotions, and acting out are unlikely to lead to a nourishing sense of connection with self or others. All three stem from a paradigm of domination, in which we are likely to see ourselves as a victim—alone, pitying ourselves, and not trusting in our own wholeness. The thoughts we think are focused on what we do not want, what we do not like, and what needs are not met. The results typically are physical tension, contraction, despair, anger, and depression as we long for a sense of inner relief and understanding.

The Value of Self-Empathy

We can set a formal time daily for self-empathy around celebration or mourning. Taking a few breaths can give us space to listen to our thoughts or judgments and then, with curiosity, connect with our feelings and needs. Or we might practice informally by pausing for a brief moment in the midst of activities to empathize with ourselves.

Self-empathy can support the rebalancing of what neuroscientists call the "negative bias" of the brain. Our brains focus predominantly on threats—events we experience as unpleasant or dangerous. Neuroscientists posit that this bias served evolutionary purposes by priming us to spot possible perils in time to save ourselves. This trait has been essential to human survival.

> Self-empathy can support the rebalancing of what neuroscientists call the "negative bias" of the brain.

Our unrecognized collective traumatic retentions, due to socialization, also interfere with how we think, feel, and respond to situations. Those unmetabolized aspects of trauma can wreak havoc on our relationships, communities, and nations.

When we neglect to acknowledge the impacts of intergenerational and historical trauma, we might mistake "culture" for what really are traumatic retentions. "Culture," writes Resmaa Menakem, "is how our bodies retain and reenact history."[2] When we ignore four hundred years of Black bodies being whipped by overseers on plantations, parents spanking ("whupping") their children may be interpreted as a cultural habit in many African American families. Likewise, when we ignore the widespread use of torture for centuries in Europe, we may interpret lynchings as an American phenomenon.

Focusing on needs in self-empathy can nurture a safe space within, a space of self-understanding and self-compassion that allows us to be resilient and make choices despite biological biases and historical traumatization.

Self-empathy also helps us to recognize choice in where to place our attention. Studies in positive psychology, according to psychologist Barbara Fredrickson, suggest that it takes between three and five positive interactions to rebalance one negative experience.[3] The consensus appears to be that up to a certain point, a higher positivity ratio is predictive of flourishing and a lower positivity ratio is linked to languishing. Our tendency to focus on the negative is natural; psychologist Rick Hanson shares that "the brain is like Velcro for negative experiences, but Teflon for positive ones."⁴ In our experience, self-empathy can help the brain become a little more Velcro-like for the positive. Giving ourselves empathy for celebrations allows us to treasure our experiences and be nourished and strengthened by them. Shawn Achor, author of *The Happiness Advantage*, says that, based on his studies at Harvard, "it's not necessarily the reality that shapes us, but the lens through which your brain views the world." After twenty-one days of writing down three things you are grateful for each day, he says the "brain starts to retain a pattern of scanning the world not for the negative, but for the positive first," raising levels of intelligence, creativity, and energy.⁵ If we regularly and intentionally ground our self-empathy in gratitude, this practice will likely take hold as a life-giving habit. As we attune to savoring what nourishes us, we expand our heart and our awareness, amplifying joy for ourselves and others. Self-empathy for celebrations and gratitude may, in this way, proactively counterbalance the times we perceive our needs not being met. Even in difficult times, we can then shift our brain response by leaning on this practice and finding authentic celebrations.

Sitting With Big Emotions

When we recognize that we are in a state of high reactivity, imbalance, and disintegration, we can pause and be mindful, acknowledge stress and suffering. Reminding ourselves that we are not alone, and that suffering, to varying degrees, is part of the human experience, we reconnect with a sense of belonging. We can then hold ourselves with compassion. Bringing our hands to the heart and feeling their warmth may support additional soothing when experiencing intense emotions.

> STEPHANIE: The following practice, called the "Self-Compassion Break," is one of the core practices that Christopher Germer and Kristin Neff offer in their Mindful Self-Compassion program. Since I attended their pilot training, I have found this practice very powerful as a precursor to the formal self-empathy practice.

Repeating to myself, "This is a moment of suffering. Suffering is part of life. May I be gentle with myself," supports enough self-regulation to enable me to deepen my self-connection and with compassion identify specific feelings and related needs beneath the stress I experience.

In the space we create between stimulus and response, we can consider the thoughts and beliefs that might contribute to the intensity of our suffering. Our cognitive assessments of needs met or unmet are filtered through layers of thinking, constructed and informed by personal experiences and social conditioning. Staying aware that our personal and social narratives shape our present experiences is a key to freedom. Our past experiences then have less power to define us in ways at odds with our values.

Self-regulation practices, such as the "Self-Compassion Break," allow us to dive beneath the waves of strong emotions and explore the rich and diverse ocean below. Underneath intense emotions are powerful needs that matter to us. Allowing the emotional energy to rush through us without acting on it in the moment will support us in discerning the values that are at stake. From that clarity, we may take conscious actions.

Focusing on Fullness Rather Than Deficit

Self-empathy can often be an alchemical process, turning the lead of our painful reactions into the gold of life energy. It is said that when we resist our pain, it tends to persist, and what we focus on tends to grow. Uncoupling observations from evaluations and stimuli from responses, we learn to mindfully allow our distressing or uncomfortable feelings to be known and seen. From that place of acknowledgment, we have the resources to intentionally direct focus toward the needs beneath the emotions. We can find the freedom to respond in new ways. Social conditioning affects which needs we perceive in the moment. We can offer a compassionate presence to our perceptions as they relate to emotions, sensations, and thoughts, thus regaining our center of power. We sit *with* our experience rather than *in* our experience, witnessing rather than identifying with our physical sensations and emotions.

Rushing to eliminate the discomfort of a need "not met" can make it last longer; allowing it simply to *be* as it is can lead to organic shifts toward what matters to us most. Over time, self-empathy becomes a practice of relating to our needs and letting go of the cognitive assessment of them as met or not met and even of the attachment to meeting them. We meet ourselves in such a moment of presence, knowing we may encounter the "not met" sense again. This practice may save us from the powerlessness and suffering of scarcity. Connecting to the life force within may be a cathartic relief, or even a powerful, mobilizing force. That vital energy arrives in its own time, like a seed sprouting from the earth in the spring, slowly growing roots in our consciousness. Bringing unconditional love to ourselves and all that arises is key.

Checking In and Requests

Finally, to ensure that we do not act out of unprocessed emotions or further repress them, we can check if we are in a state of contraction or expansion in regard to our perception of a situation. A sense of tenderness and openness, sometimes with a sigh, can reassure us that we have touched some of our core needs. At that point, we may determine whether a request of ourselves or someone else arises in our mind and heart.

Entertaining the possibility of a request to ourselves allows us to acknowledge growing edges and invites us to stretch. For example, if we perceive ourselves to be quick in responding in ways we later regret, we can ask ourselves to pause before talking. When we consider making a request of another person, we may notice whether we feel grounded in compassion enough to take our request to the parties involved. If we experience a tightness while considering the matter, we might need more empathy to fine-tune being conscious of interdependence, holding everyone's needs with care. This is a gradual process, and a request is where the rubber meets the road. The question of whether and how to formulate a request helps us harness relational qualities such as clarity and compassion for self and others.

Self-Empathy as a Foundation of Personal and Collective Healing

Self-empathy is a foundational practice for inner healing. Empathizing with ourselves helps us discover and connect with conflicting parts in our minds. By extending compassion to the parts of ourselves that have not healed from personal and collective wounds, we actively integrate those parts. Such healing allows us to reconnect to our power more fully and reduce the likelihood that our past pain will spill onto others.

Practicing self-empathy may also support us in learning how to receive empathy from others more skillfully. As we learn to sustain ourselves with awareness of needs, our self-responsibility will lessen the likelihood that we will enter the empathic space expecting someone else to validate our narratives or "show us the way." Otherwise, we may find ourselves seeking empathy for the same issue over and over, missing the power of self-connection. While seeking empathy may be associated with our desire to explore the complex layers of a situation, it may also relate to a fear of letting go of our interpretations. That is when balancing a request for empathy with a willingness to receive feedback can support us in recognizing where our power and responsibility lie. That clarity can move us into effective actions, personal and collective.

Holding needs with aliveness and compassion empowers us to take responsibility for our own experience and honor the same capacity in others. Receiving empathy from others as we integrate these qualities may be a powerful way to return to our own heart in self-empathy.

Self-empathy supports a healing journey that is not linear. With practice and repetition, we can allow past pain or trauma to arise, witnessing our reactive behaviors and holding them with tenderness, as a mother holds her child. Over time, self-empathy supports us in living with greater authenticity, integrity, and compassion.

SUMMARY

- This key distinction supports us in self-awareness. Our ability to distinguish between self-empathy and other responses affects our experience of the flow of life energy.

- In self-empathy we shed light on our intentions. As we integrate those with the potential and real impacts of our responses empowers us to make more life-giving choices personally and collectively.

- Distinguishing between self-empathy and other responses can help us understand and potentially increase our capacity to recognize deep-seated conditioning and unhealed pain. As these are slowly unearthed, we may touch the power and wholeness of our universal needs.

- In self-empathy, any request we make of ourselves or others comes from a place of expansion rather than constriction.

WALKING THE TALK:
A LIFE EXAMPLE FROM THE UNITED STATES

BY STEPHANIE BACHMANN MATTEI

I see video footage on the news of a White[6] police officer kneeling into the neck of George Floyd, a Black person who repeatedly says, "I can't breathe," and pleads for help until he stops breathing.

My heart aches beyond words. I am in shock. I think: "This cannot be true! How can we be so blind to another's humanity as to be deaf to the plea for air? This is not the world I want my children to grow up in. And what about my African American daughter?"

The ache is overwhelming. I take a few breaths and bring my mind back to my sensory experience: I feel my feet on the ground. My body is shaking. My breathing is heavy. Checking in with my mental state, I sense total disbelief.

Looking deeper, I realize I feel brokenhearted. Speechless. Flooded by despair. I continue to breathe, making space for my reactions so I can allow them to just be, without judging them. Resting in the body, I observe but do not act on forceful impulses to do something. I want to run. I want to scream. I want to pack our bags and move out of the country.

Rage swells inside, then tears wet my eyes. I let them flow as I feel an overwhelming sense of powerlessness.

I breathe, continue to connect with my sensory experience, my thinking process, and my emotional roller coaster of the moment. I slowly allow myself to touch the fear and grief underneath the anger, not resisting it. I pause. I wait for my body and mind to regain some fragile sense of balance in this world of inequity.

I witness the downward spiral of thoughts, "This is sickening . . . this is so wrong . . . this country will never change." Then the self-referencing patterns kick in: "I made a mistake moving here . . . I messed up . . . I should know how to protect my daughter. There is something wrong with me." I am now at a moment of choice. If I believe this unbridled proliferation of the mind, I will fall further into a state of being overwhelmed and paralyzed.

I patiently redirect my mind to the self-empathy anchors—body sensations, feelings, and needs.

Attention regulation leads to emotional regulation, I remind myself. I keep focusing on my breath, allowing for the body and mind to settle a bit.

I patiently wait to regain enough balance to continue the self-inquiry process. What is the need that is present in me? I whisper quietly: "Safety for all human beings. A sense of security. Valuing life. Always staying connected to the humanity of one another."

I let attention rest on those needs. I invite myself to live those needs in relation to the police officer. I want to see his humanity too. I stay with that until I sense some balance in me.

I move to the last anchor of the NVC process, the request. To stay in my integrity, I ask myself how I can embody those needs as my values. How do I own and manifest my values right here, right now?

I recommit to continue learning about racism and the weight of our social conditioning. I will grow my awareness around the immense impact of power inequalities on human beings so as to be able to facilitate those hard conversations and support the evolution of consciousness.

I think of the Zen tradition of "bearing witness" to what feels overwhelming and impossible to hold.

PRACTICE

Deepening Self-Empathy

How we experience and relate to our needs plays an important role in deepening our empathy and self-empathy. This practice invites us to approach our perception of unmet needs with compassion to lessen the likelihood that we will stay attached to them (wallowing). We can then deepen our self-empathy by cultivating an awareness of the fullness of our needs. This is a meditative self-reflection practice. We encourage you to make either a formal space for this practice by setting aside a minimum of fifteen minutes for focused self-empathy or finding a routine time to practice during a daily activity that doesn't require careful mental focus, such as brushing teeth, taking a shower, washing the dishes, or waiting for a website to load.

Ask yourself the questions below, as time and focus allow.

- How am I feeling at this moment? What matters to me?
    - Notice sensations in the body while making this inquiry and whether they expand or contract as feelings and needs are named. Restriction may be related to a perception of an unmet need.

- Bringing my focus to feelings and needs, can I allow my (possibly) unmet sense of the need while inviting a sense of wholeness?

- While holding the "not met" assessment of this need with great compassion as a parent holds their child, also acknowledge that this need is much more expansive and that there are multiple possibilities to meet it.

∿ Do my sensations change as I hold my need warmly, with a greater sense of possibility and presence?

  ◦ Do I have a request for myself and/or others?

∿ Notice whether asking this question brings renewed tension or restriction, and if so, offer further empathy if you feel so moved.

15

GIRAFFE HONESTY AND JACKAL HONESTY

*By nature, we are relational beings,
born with a voice—the ability to communicate
our experience—and with the desire to
engage responsively with others.*

—CAROL GILLIGAN AND NAOMI SNIDER

Nonviolent Communication is based on the understanding of nonviolence as drawn from the Sanskrit word *ahimsa*, meaning "not harming," which can also be captured as "a heart so open it knows no enemies." As we consider this key distinction that examines jackal and giraffe honesty, we root ourselves in the knowledge that all expressions—our own or those of others—can lead us to a life-giving transformation at personal and collective levels.

We are all capable of an expression based on our judgmental thinking—jackal honesty—especially when hungry, tired, or overwhelmed. Such expression could be viewed as shortsighted and defensive, qualities often associated with jackals, due to their size and carnivorous nature. Giraffe honesty, on the other hand, is firmly grounded in the wider perspective and connected to a giant heart. Engaging in giraffe honesty, we understand that our expression, or lack of it, has an impact on ourselves and others. With giraffe honesty, we commit to a practice in which everyone's needs matter.

Inner clarity about our own needs allows us to discern what we want to say and then to convey our truth skillfully. We can choose to share our honesty while

> **By practicing with patience and humility, moment by moment, our approximations of giraffe honesty come closer to holding compassion for everyone, including ourselves, and trusting in our interdependence.**

holding an awareness that our words affect the listener. Exploring this key distinction, we clarify the difference between these two perspectives of honesty and discuss preparation for expressing ourselves with awareness. By practicing with patience and humility, moment by moment, our approximations of giraffe honesty come closer to holding compassion for everyone, including ourselves, and trusting in our interdependence.

Jackal Honesty

In "jackal honesty," we speak our thoughts, judgments, and beliefs about our own or another person's behavior in ways that often end up stimulating fear, shame, or guilt. "I think that's sexist!" may be an honest expression, but it conveys an evaluation without awareness of feelings and needs, nor consideration of impact. At times, we even comment on others' intentions—"You did this just to hurt me!"—though we have no real access to the intentions of others. We rarely mean to be unkind when we talk this way; our words usually stem from the same fear, shame, and guilt that they are likely to activate. Rooted in a sense of scarcity and worrying that our needs don't matter, we lose the trust that human beings enjoy contributing to one another when they can do so freely. Acting out of fear, we frequently become single-minded and unintentionally exert power over others to reach our desired goals.

Understanding Jackal Honesty

"Jackal honesty" often arises from a lack of self-connection and clarity about our own needs. It could stem from stress or illness, or we might speak from a position of privilege, having little awareness of impact or empathy for others. Our confusion and urgency might also stem from childhood experiences in which some of our basic needs were not tended to with care. It is not uncommon for an inner jackal to take a stand for the wounded child within, though we are typically unaware of it at the time. We might find ourselves demanding exactly what we want, unaware of what needs we are trying to meet and the many options available.

Sometimes we express ourselves with jackal honesty when we are focused on a host of other concerns and are momentarily oblivious of the feelings and needs of others. While we fully intend to hold awareness of the needs of all involved, we are not always able to track the complexities of being in relationship.

At times, we may prioritize focusing on ourselves at the expense of others. Such a focus may spring from unresolved trauma and unexamined pain. Also heralded as "independence," this perspective could result from a lack of experience with interconnection in relationships.

The factors that lead to jackal honesty are often unseen, and in some cases the consequences are hidden too. In this vein, our jackal honesty may surface because we suffer from shortsightedness due to social conditioning to focus on ourselves or to make life-disconnecting assumptions about others. Expressing ourselves with an intention for mutual understanding, we can miss the other likely impacts of our words if we fail to grasp others' perspectives.

> STEPHANIE: When a White friend says to my African American daughter, "I don't see color when I look at you," he likely intends to connect with my daughter and convey a sense of care. Unfortunately, color blindness is one layer of White privilege; Black people do not have the luxury to walk around the United States of America and say, "I don't see color," because every

moment of their lives is filled with reminders that they are perceived as "less than," and that their safety is at risk.

My White sons have a very different experience in the world than my African American daughter. For example, my boys had such fun learning to drive. There was no need for me to warn them that if they got pulled over, it could be a life-or-death situation. The first driving lesson I taught my daughter was that when she is stopped by police, she is not to move her hands from the wheel until the officer tells her to do so.

Jackal honesty may also be related to automatic survival mechanisms. When we find ourselves activated—out of fear for our survival or finding our core sense of identity threatened—the brain typically responds by going into fight, flight, or freeze mode. Jackal honesty could take a fight stance: "What's the problem with you? Can't you figure it out on your own?" Or a flight response: "Just do whatever you want," we might say, leaving. Operating in freeze mode, we might find ourselves speechless and dissociating, dumbfounded.

We may have learned to rely on one of these strategies—fight, flight, or freeze—more than others. It has become a default mode, often linked to what we witnessed and experienced in our families of origin or due to gender-based conditioning. For example, women tend to freeze or flee and men tend to fight. We may rely on different responses depending on the relationship: We may fight with our partner, submit to our children, distance ourselves from our mother, or underfunction with a colleague.

Our thinking can sometimes hijack our ability to feel. Our logic and analysis can create obstacles that block the connection we would find in honest giving and receiving. When this happens, our jackal honesty takes the form of "feedback" that conveys a sense of deficiency to the person we are speaking to. We might say something like: "That is the problem. When people say they 'don't see color,' they actually contribute to racism!" Our jackal expression may consequently stimulate fear, guilt, and especially shame in them.

Children are particularly vulnerable to our honest jackal "feedback" as it often gets internalized with painful and at times lifelong consequences. Sometimes, as adults, we silently recycle these jackal expressions, judging ourselves with the same words that others targeted at us when we were children. It can take years, maybe even a lifetime, for the pain from such expressions to heal. We might also repurpose these expressions aloud, directing them toward others as a tragic way to ease our own pain.

> **Our jackal honesty can take the form of "feedback" that conveys a sense of deficiency to the person we are speaking to.**

Jackal in a Giraffe Suit

Our jackal expression may also be our conscious attempt to show up honestly while following the NVC process, even though we have not yet integrated the part of giraffe consciousness that is based on partnership.

We might even use "jackal honesty" to defend ourselves in the giraffe suit of OFNR. Using observations, feelings, needs, and requests, the "jackal lawyer" in us may seek to definitively prove our own righteousness with "exceptional" communication skills. Or we may use our skill to prove that our point of view is correct, especially focusing on observations that can serve as "evidence." In that moment, our consciousness is rooted in the right/wrong, worthy/unworthy dualistic paradigm. Without the presence of compassion and awareness of interdependence, this expression is unlikely to be in alignment with NVC's overarching intention to build connection. Sometimes we play the jackal lawyer when we have the conscious desire to embrace the NVC process, while subconscious pain still urges us to prove ourselves right.

Transforming Jackal Honesty: Listening to the Howl

Jackal honesty points to needs that have been overlooked and are now crying out to be heard and cared for. We can greet our jackal honesty with compassion, welcoming and loving the part of us that is in pain.

It is kindest to ourselves and others if we do this internally or ask for empathic support from a third party, rather than directing our jackal honesty outward toward the people involved.

All communication is an attempt to meet a need. If we repress the honest jackal expression in our own minds without honoring the underlying needs, we may become chronically angry or depressed with no clear path to well-being. What we most need is compassionate listening and deeper self-understanding.

> **All communication is an attempt to meet a need.**

We all want to speak our truth, whether out of discomfort or delight. Rosenberg used to say that all communication is either a *please*, or a *thank you*. Jackal honesty howls "please!" as it directs us to the heart of the matter.

"Never hear what another person thinks . . . especially . . . what they think of you," Rosenberg says,[1] encouraging us to listen for feelings and needs rather than hearing the judgments. Pausing to mentally reframe a jackal expression as a "please" helps us to not take it personally. We remember then it is more about what the speaker longs for than it is about us. This is true when we deliver jackal honesty as well—our expression tells us more about what we value than about the other person. Remembering this can help us return to self-compassion and self-responsibility. Hearing the jackal expression as a cry for help can open our hearts to compassion. This allows us to hold space for whatever is present, even if painful, as we further inquire into the nature of that "please." Whether in nonverbal or verbal empathy, our listening may contribute to healing.

Loving Our Jackals

We can transform the moralistic judgments in jackal honesty and create more spaciousness by touching the values and needs at their source. Self-connection is key as we consider the possible impacts of our statements before talking. Checking in with ourselves if our heart is open enough to empathize will give us clues on whether we are ready to self-express with care and an awareness of interconnection.

Sometimes we are oblivious to the possible impacts of statements we have made because of our cultural or personal biases. If connection is our priority, then we learn

> Sometimes we are oblivious to the possible impacts of statements we have made because of our cultural or personal biases . . . The consequences of jackal expressions, spoken unconsciously from a place of privilege, are significant, but we cannot address them unless we first recognize them.

to listen with undefended curiosity, opening ourselves to the possibility of being moved by how our words affect others. In the above discussion of racism, facing the reality that people of color (POC) are still systematically mistreated due to racist policies can be excruciatingly painful for a White person to take in. Yet raising awareness is the only way we know to address the pervasive social conditioning that perpetuates and institutionalizes White supremacy. The consequences of jackal expressions, spoken unconsciously from a place of privilege, are significant, but we cannot address them unless we first recognize them. The toll of racism is taken in lives and dignity. In addition, racism sets groups of people against each other, severs human connections, and leaves us with the herculean task of unearthing one another's humanity. That is a weight we all carry, regardless of what racialized group we are part of. Tragically, this burden is added to the heft borne by those who are directly targeted by racism. Our persistence in deep healing work and willingness to join the conversation will benefit all. Personal and collective work can also seed the transformation of systems.

"Taming" Our Jackals With Empathy

One way to grow self-awareness and self-empathy is by distancing ourselves a bit from identifying with the narratives and judgments we carry. This playful suggestion comes directly from Rosenberg. He invites us to "enjoy the jackal show." Rosenberg's insight suggests that we listen to and observe the jackal honesty "show" inside our heads without *believing* it. When we do this, we have the opportunity to witness ourselves in the panorama of our personal experiences, conditioning, family culture, and social location.

The more we tend to our own jackals, the more compassion we will have for the jackals that others present to us when in pain. Each time we receive someone with an open heart and mind when they express themselves by howling, our compassion offers us a small sense of peace which may in turn soothe the other's heart as well. Such compassion spreads its warmth through everyone who is touched by it, whether they are trained in NVC or not. In our gratitude for this peacemaking, we can thank our jackals; their howls show us what needs healing.

Giraffe Honesty

"Giraffe honesty" is an authentic expression, grounded in a partnership model where everyone's needs are held with care. This consciousness is nurtured step by step. Reaping some freedom from our past patterns of response as well as freedom from fear of another's emotional response opens us to be truly present to needs. Caring about the impact of our actions without taking responsibility for others' feelings, another balancing act in its own right, we support their autonomy and ours. Moving toward shared power, we do not claim more power than we have; nor do we give our power away. Our giraffe authenticity, progressively emerging, invites us to express what's important to us in the moment, making requests that honor the needs of all and amends whenever needed.

> **Moving toward shared power, we do not claim more power than we have; nor do we give our power away.**

Stepping Into Freedom

In order to speak our truth, it is essential to discern it from our habitual reactions. Judgments, demands, "deserve" thinking, and denial of responsibility are often linked to unresolved pain and generally also have systemic roots. Brain science tells us that our prefrontal cortex gets disconnected when we are stimulated. In other words, when we are enraged, our ability to think and self-regulate is reduced. Our practice of seeking to connect with the source of our pain rather than moving away from it—or letting it run the show—slowly leads us to greater spaciousness, self-acceptance, and awareness of our potential.

By cultivating unconditional self-compassion, we may heal those parts of our psyche that still operate in survival mode. It is a lifelong process. As long as we are afraid of losing something, such as acceptance, belonging, or our very lives, then we are likely impaired in our efforts to discover and express what is truly alive for us.

As we surrender our self-protective masks, we break free and more easily connect with the life energy. We feel gradually more at ease showing up transparently, taking responsibility for our words and actions, and empathically engaging. As we become progressively more liberated, the likelihood of acting out of a desire to please, to hide, or to get even diminishes.

Incrementally disentangling ourselves from our emotional reactivity, we also find freedom from taking responsibility for others' reactions. Having arrived at greater self-acceptance, we may be able to bear witness to the humanity of another rather than taking their words personally or replaying our stories about them. Self-examination gives us greater capacity to recognize that we all share the same life force.

Cultivating Awareness of Impact

While we are not responsible for how others feel or interpret our words, awareness of how our actions impact others—on individual, interpersonal, and community/social levels—is part of a compassionate consciousness and commitment to do no harm. We can listen to their jackal or giraffe expression, resting in the life energy in and between us, with our "giraffe ears" on, hearing only "please listen—this is important to me!" In our deep listening, we show that we are open to hearing the impact of our actions by allowing our heart to be moved by their expression, whether or not we agree with it. In this willingness to be moved lies the dance of inner peace and outer partnership. Once our heart is attuned with another by empathically receiving their expression, we can better determine how to make amends when needed. In partnership, we can consider whether some tangible offering would be welcomed to support the reconnection.

> **In this willingness to be moved lies the dance of inner peace and outer partnership.**

STEPHANIE: In the example where my friend tells my daughter that he does not see color, I move toward giraffe honesty by first pausing to feel how painful it is for me to hear, yet again, the implication that not noticing race solves racism, and conversely that noticing race is racist. I would love to support greater awareness in the world.

I slowly turn to my daughter who is looking down at the floor, her fingers playing with her hair. I imagine she feels torn between her desires for connection and self-protection. I breathe and wait until her eyes meet mine. I take another deep breath and choose to actively step into the role of ally. I believe that our White unawareness plays a key role in maintaining the structures that result in racial injustice, so I reach to find my voice, knowing that the conversation may become uncomfortable. Stepping into this, I consider my friend's perspective, needs, and motivations for having used this expression.

"Paul, I'm guessing you really want to convey that you care about my daughter, right?" He smiles in agreement. "I appreciate that. Are you open to hearing what's happening for me right now?" I ask. When Paul expresses his willingness, I share further. "When I hear you say that you don't see color, I am touched because what I hear is an attempt to contribute to some ease for all of us. I am also keenly aware that you and I, as White people, navigate the world very differently from people of color. For instance, I have never been followed in a store by a clerk. Is the same true for you?" Paul nods. I nod back and continue.

"For my daughter, as for many African Americans, being followed in the store is a common experience. I worry that subscribing to a color-blind approach contributes to denying the structural and systemic inequalities linked to racism. I am brokenhearted in recognizing that my daughter's reality is very different from mine or my sons'. I want to pause and hear how it is for you to hear me say that?"

When I ask this, I am genuinely curious and grateful for my friend's willingness to engage in this dialogue. Even giraffe honesty, when imposed, can be violent. It takes skillfulness to navigate when and how to share our truth with sufficient care for others' needs so that it can actually be received. And sometimes we feel called to voice a truth that has been silenced more than we can tolerate. In the course of further discussion, I open my heart and mind again and again to sit with his confusion and respond only when I am in touch with my heart rather than out of defensiveness. Such discussions play a pivotal role in changing our dominant culture so that it better holds the needs of all.

Clarifying Our Intention

Giraffe honesty is born from partnership—a way of living and being that fully acknowledges the humanity of all and has faith in the human intention to contribute. Bearing witness to our truth with compassion, we may set an intention to enrich ourselves and another when choosing self-expression. This gift of love is based on the desire to show up authentically to nourish the relationship rather than based on some form of conditionality—if you do this, then I'll do that. In giraffe honesty, our intention is to connect our energy with someone else's, offering our truth with the most care possible. We do not seek to change the other person in any way, only to offer ourselves in our vulnerability. Living from this intention, we implicitly invite others through our modeling to join us in this state of empowerment for everyone's benefit.

Finding Our Authentic Giraffe Honesty

Rosenberg described NVC as a process based on two basic questions: What is alive in me in this moment? And, how can I make life more wonderful for myself and for you? The question of what is alive in us in the moment depends first and foremost on our ability to be connected and authentic with ourselves. The second question engages us with the quality of interconnection inherent in giraffe honesty. To answer these questions, we attend to physical sensations, feelings, and needs—first in ourselves and then as we understand them in others. We move toward congruence by aligning our thoughts with our words and our words with our actions. There is no perfect or static giraffe prescription for honesty, because the very nature of communication is dynamic. We express ourselves with our best approximation of giraffe honesty in the moment and return to a state of presence over and over again to compassionately navigate the responses of our conversation partner.

In general, our awareness of interdependence leads us to query the willingness of the listener before we express. Nevertheless, there are times when what matters to us is so powerful—perhaps related to safety and human dignity—that we choose to express, even if our message is less than welcome.

> STEPHANIE: Had my friend repeatedly said no to my offerings in response to his "see no color," then, eventually, I would likely have expressed my honesty in alignment with "protective use of force," grounded in compassion. Rosenberg calls that forceful yet protective self-expression "screaming in giraffe."

Our sustained practice of NVC invites us to transcend the polarity of self and others. "Others" pertains not only to the person in front of us but also to the rest of humanity and all life. Domination systems are unlikely to voluntarily share power, redistribute resources, or invest in the transformation of our structures and policies without the strength of expression rooted in protective use of force. Expressions that insist on being heard can be sustained by an awareness of interdependence. Holding no threat nor ill will, this expression is still fully within the framework of nonviolence as long as we continue to ground in caring for all needs, including those of the person(s) whose actions we aim to influence. Frequently checking in with ourselves to gauge a cost-benefit analysis of potential consequences, for others as well, can help us decide whether expressing giraffe honesty when unwelcome is, in fact, upholding interdependence.

Focusing our attention on continued growth, we bear witness to the opening of our hearts and minds as we connect with the needs within any expression. Giraffe honesty calls us to embrace and find love for the life energy in all of us.

SUMMARY

- ☙ This key allows us to meet our jackals' howls with compassion, deeply listening to discern the needs underneath.

- ☙ Our willingness to become more aware of the quality of our expression supports us in clearly conveying what matters to us most. Speaking authentically and fearlessly with intentions of mutuality grows with practice.

- ☙ Cultivating awareness of the impact of our actions can help us understand how our expression can come from and contribute to reinforcing fear-based, systemic conditioning.

- ☙ Gradually, our practice of giraffe expression more fully acknowledges interdependence. Our incremental approximations of giraffe honesty stretch us toward holding compassion for everyone.

WALKING THE TALK:
A LIFE EXAMPLE FROM BRAZIL

BY SANDRA CASELATO, CNVC TRAINER CANDIDATE

It is deeply important to me to transform the domination systems I've internalized throughout my life. Over the years, I have walked the path of NVC and devoted myself to living this consciousness daily. I have learned to practice being kind and gentle to myself when jackal thoughts arise in my mind and when I use jackal language. The more I learn to receive my own jackal thoughts with acceptance and empathy, the easier it gets to translate them into feelings and needs. Because my expressions blossom from my thoughts, I want to notice what is happening in my heart and mind before I speak. This helps me engage more choice and care for connection, which I value.

I once worked in a place where I had lunch every day with my male colleagues, because I thought my female colleagues were "too shallow, they only talked about soap operas and gossip." When I expressed that to the men at lunch, I immediately felt guilty and started judging myself: "I'm a bad person for thinking like that!" So, in addition to the jackal thoughts I had toward the women, I piled them up on myself as well. I felt shame and regret for perpetuating stereotypical thoughts about women that contribute to sustaining patriarchy and misogyny. (I value these words for naming and thus making visible complex beliefs, narratives, systems, and actions that belittle, oppress, and harm women, and often are normalized out of sight.)

Instead of getting stuck in the jackal judgments toward myself, I tried to receive my feelings and thoughts with empathy. I realized that behind those thoughts and feelings were important needs and values I cherished that were not being met, namely, respect and care for women.

In seeking to understand the needs I was trying to meet when I had those thoughts toward my female colleagues, I realized that I longed to have meaningful conversations at lunch and deep connections *with the women* in my workplace.

This discovery supported me in translating my jackal thoughts into giraffe language:

Jackal thoughts: "Women are shallow; they only talk about soap operas and are always gossiping."

Giraffe translation: "I'm sad because I long for meaningful conversations and connection with my female coworkers."

After doing this translation exercise, my disposition toward the women changed. The enemy images I held of my female colleagues dissipated, and I felt my heart open to new possibilities of deepening connection and conversation with them.

I started having lunch with the women from time to time and would express what was going on with me: "I'm frustrated. I don't watch soap operas, so I can't keep up with your conversation. Would you be willing to talk about something else?" Then I would suggest a different topic that I expected would interest me and them both. I might say to one of them, "I hear your daughter got a scholarship, is that right?" Taking action to meet my own needs while honoring mutuality, I stepped into my power. The conversation became engaging for all of us, and it was a joy for me to be in their company. From then on, I sometimes had lunch with my male colleagues and sometimes with my female colleagues. And all these relationships benefited from my translation of jackal thoughts to giraffe language.

PRACTICE

Perspective-Taking

Taking the perspective of another can support us in expanding awareness in general and in considering how our expression may be received
in particular. This practice invites us to take a different perspective from
the one we are most conditioned to. This is a journaling practice. We
invite you to gather two sheets of paper and a pen. We imagine this practice will take about thirty minutes.

We invite you to use your imagination to prepare the heart and mind to
be open and receptive to experiencing the viewpoint of another person.
We will then reflect on whether and how our words or actions might
shift given this new awareness.

On the first sheet of paper, draw four columns.

- In the first column, write down as an observation something
  you said that stimulated some disconnection in an interaction
  that you had recently.

- In the second column, describe the body sensations and
  emotions that arose as you were talking. Were you aware of
  them when you spoke?

- In the third column, identify some of the possible needs that
  were alive for you in the moment, whether you were aware of
  them or not.

- In the fourth column, write what you experience in your heart
  and mind right now, as you write about this event.

On the second paper, draw two columns. Imagine being that other person and hearing the sentence that you wrote down in the observation section above. Acknowledge to yourself that this other person may have lived different experiences and may hold different cultural beliefs than yours that affect their feelings, thoughts, and needs.

Perspective-taking skills are particularly important during cross-cultural interactions. Invite yourself to see the world through their eyes. How might they understand the situation? How might your words impact their experience? Get into their mind frame as much as possible before you aim to cultivate an understanding of their feelings and needs, so you can really sense their possible feelings and needs from within rather than from a list that isn't connected with that person's experience.

- In the first column, write what body sensations and emotions they might feel in this experience.

- In the second column, write down what needs they might experience in this situation.

- Pause and, with spaciousness, take in the possible experience of the other person. What do you notice now?

- Finally, go back to the observation (your initial remarks) and see if and how you would like to change it, now that you have given greater attention to the possible impact of your words on the other person.

REFLECTION

What could be the value in considering your own feelings and needs before taking the perspective of the other person?

PART IV

OPTIONS FOR POWER

In this section, you will find three keys examining the options for using power. Our relationship with power at the intrapersonal, interpersonal, and collective levels is intrinsically connected to our sense of well-being. Conditioning within domination systems over millennia has impaired our abilities to relate to power in healthy and life-giving ways. These keys help us shift our relationship with power. By better understanding the dynamics around authority, force, power-over, and power-with, we are less likely to misuse or abuse power.

The following key differentiations give us the opportunity to consider how we relate to our personal power and integrity vis-à-vis authority roles and to investigate what motivates us to use the power we have.

16

PROTECTIVE AND PUNITIVE USE OF FORCE

Love is the only force capable of
transforming an enemy into a friend.

—MARTIN LUTHER KING JR.

A n exploration of the key distinction that distinguishes protective and punitive use of force[1] allows us to examine our actions and align them with the intention of preventing harm and supporting life. Force can be understood as energy, power, and strength as well as coercion, oppression, and violence. While force may be punitive and threatening to life, there are also times when it becomes a direct path to protecting life.

Punitive use of force, according to Rosenberg, "is the root of violence on our planet."[2] This force punishes, coerces, and prevents access to what is needed. Sometimes it is employed with the intention to "teach" a valuable lesson, without awareness of impact and consequences. Punitive use of force is based on the assumption that guilt, shame, and fear effectively motivate changes in behavior. And they may . . . but at a price in terms of personal and relational well-being. "Punitive use of force tends to generate hostility and to reinforce resistance to the very behavior we are seeking,"[3] Rosenberg reminds us. In the practice of NVC, it is essential to consider the long-term consequences of punishment and coercion as they stem from a paradigm of domination.

Protective use of force, by contrast, is implemented only when we perceive there is an imminent threat to life, safety, and basic human needs. In these cases, the least amount of force is used for the shortest amount of time to restore safety. We only utilize such force when there is no opportunity or willingness for a dialogue to take place. According to Rosenberg, "the intention . . . is to prevent injury or injustice, never to punish or to cause individuals to suffer, repent, or change."[4] As we intervene to prevent someone from harming themselves or others, we do so with as much awareness of impact as we can muster, with the intention of restoring connection. Our actions are rooted in compassion. Careful discernment is continually called for, to ensure that this force has the smallest possible negative impact. As soon as safety is reestablished, we seek dialogue to attend to everyone's needs, repairing the relationship as needed. When our protective use of force has resulted in pain, we may mourn unmet needs and hold with care the needs we sought to meet.

Punishment—It's for Your Own Good!

Punitive use of force is based on power differential and is upheld unilaterally by the person, group, or institution with greater power. When punishing, we *do* something *to* someone rather than *being with* someone. Force may take physical form, like spanking, or be psychological, such as shaming—or anything in between. Love, attention, care, and respect may also be withdrawn as a form of punitive force based on power differential. The other person is transformed in our minds from person to object, with no say about how they are being treated. Any interpersonal or collective tension is perceived as a conflict rather than as a dilemma to explore together.

The consciousness behind punitive force is one of dualism (either/or, my needs/your needs), fueled by moralistic judgment. In Rosenberg's words, "Punitive action . . . is based on the assumption that people commit offenses because they are bad or evil, and to correct the situation, they need to be made to repent."[5] Reward, the flip side of the coin, is a more subtle way to coerce and is related to punitive force.[6] When human beings are viewed as inherently evil, external restraint is perceived as necessary for safety. Punitive use of force justifies violence as a way to educate and control people "for their own good" and/or for the well-being of society.

Do the ends ever justify the means? Rosenberg's words offer some insight: "When we submit to doing something solely for the purpose of avoiding punishment, our attention is distracted from the value of the action itself. Instead, we are focusing upon the consequences, on what might happen if we fail to take that action."[7] Many studies show that extrinsic motivators in general, and punishment in particular, are not merely ineffective, but are actually counterproductive in terms of nurturing intrinsic human qualities, such as connection to our personal power, integrity, and responsibility. Decades of studies tragically indicate that prison does not rehabilitate, reducing recidivism. Instead, it may actually have a criminogenic effect, increasing the likelihood that people who have been convicted of a crime will commit another crime.[8] Because we are interdependent, a society that engages in punitive force will actually be less safe, as it escalates the cycle of violence and disconnects us from one another.[9]

> Punitive use of force justifies violence as a way to educate and control people "for their own good" and/or for the well-being of society.

Punitive Force in Systems of Domination

Evidence suggests that punitive use of force has been a dominant child-rearing practice historically around the world in patriarchal societies. As psychohistorian Lloyd deMause writes, "The history of childhood is a nightmare from which we have only recently begun to awaken. The further back in history one goes, the lower the level of child care, and the more likely children are to be killed, abandoned, terrorized, and sexually abused."[10] Punitive use of force makes its appearance in sometimes elusive ways. In mainstream Western societies for example, withdrawal of "privileges" is perceived as a benign form of guidance rather than a punishment.

Unexamined power dynamics related to punishment can be found within interpersonal systems such as parenting, institutional contexts such as education, and social action realms, such as armed struggle. Let's consider the institutional context of the prison system. In these settings, someone in a more powerful role can threaten to take away a preferred object or activity as a consequence of "bad" behavior. This same dynamic appears in adult-child relationships whether in parenting or educational arenas. Yet, in the US prison system, additional levels of punishment emerge: Incarcerated individuals lose many basic rights, including the "privilege" of voting. These examples of punitive use of force are pervasive because they are rarely questioned.

In our quest to move away from punitive force toward protective use of force at the systemic level—shifting from retributive justice to restorative justice, for example—Rosenberg's two provocative questions can support us in gaining deeper clarity: "What do I want this person to do that's different from what he or she is currently doing?" And secondly, "What do I want this person's reasons to be for doing what I am asking?"[11] Self-determination as well as awareness of our shared humanity are born of intrinsic motivation. Such internal purpose will direct us to engage more meaningfully with one another on the personal, interpersonal, and collective levels, inspiring greater understanding and care. This is not a simple or swift transition. Individually, along the way, we are likely to encounter many situations that will appeal to our punitive habits. Systemically, much will need to change before restorative paradigms become the norm.

Protective Use of Force

The consciousness of partnership and interdependence permeates protective use of force. Whether arising from individual or collective action, it uses the least amount of force to protect vital and urgent needs, typically life and safety, for oneself, for others, for large numbers of people, or for life as a whole. As little force as possible is applied for the shortest amount of time possible. This use of force is followed with an attempt to restore dialogue, connection, and mutual respect.

The consciousness of partnership and interdependence permeates protective use of force.

Let's consider the relationship between force and nonviolence. Rosenberg tells us, "There are two things that distinguish truly nonviolent actions from violent actions. First, there is no enemy in the nonviolent point of view. You don't see an enemy.[12] Your thinking is clearly focused on protecting your needs. Second, your intention is not to make the other side suffer."[13] Reflecting on these points before action is taken, we retain a clear awareness of our own needs and supportive intentions. We also appreciate Miki Kashtan's definition of nonviolence as it relates to protective and utilitarian (see below) use of force: "Nonviolence is a way of being and living that orients, in thought, word, and deed, towards integrating love, truth, and courage in individual and collective action aimed at preserving what serves life and at challenging what doesn't to transform itself so the human family can realign with life."[14] One can never be certain that what was intended nonviolently will be received as nonviolence. While experiencing force is always impactful, when it is used within the parameters of protective use of force, there is more of a chance that our nonpunitive intentions will invite the recipient to awareness. Also, the care put into the intervention and reparation may mitigate any pain triggered by the action.

Protective use of force can be used on both interpersonal and global fronts. Yet its concrete applications vary depending on the context. Protective use of force is an effective nonviolent resistance to structures and policies that are perceived as life-serving for some, while they are utterly life-disconnected for others. When violence and injustice unfold before us and dialogue is not a viable option, our inaction becomes implicit consent. Protective use of force empowers us to have a voice in nonviolent civil disobedience when our silence would equate to compliance.

On a large scale, Mahatma Gandhi capitalized on collective power to drive nonviolent change by guiding people to march together and illegally (according to British rule) harvest salt from the seaside. This noncooperation movement "forced" government officials to make concessions. The people of India reclaimed access to their salt, and the impact was transformative. They had experienced their internal and communal power. It was seventeen years before India was granted independence, yet the effects of this nonviolent shift rippled across a century as other leaders such as Martin Luther King Jr., Nelson Mandela, Leymah Gbowee, and Greta Thunberg applied those same principles of noncooperation in various social justice settings. As David R. Hawkins, author and director of the Institute for Spiritual Research writes, "When the will of the people is so united and aligned with universal principles, it is virtually unconquerable."[15]

The Skills of Protective Use of Force

The consciousness that upholds protective use of force is solely grounded in the protection of life. Our movement to engage force is not based on a moralistic judgment of badness or wrongness. In order to embrace protective use of force, we are called to examine and shift our view of human nature. Our patriarchal narratives condition us to see humans as inherently evil and violent, needing to be controlled and deserving of punishment. Recognizing that as humans we have the potential capacity for love as well as for violence empowers us to use force in a protective rather than punitive way. There have been enough studies on childhood development to confidently state that violence is a learned social behavior. When raised with empathy rather than punishment, evidence indicates that children will not grow to resort to violence.[16] In the words of Bruce Perry and Maia Szalavitz: "We are indeed born for love. But at birth, we are not yet fully loving. Infants' brains are the most malleable—and vulnerable—that they will ever be outside the womb. . . . As with so many other human potentials present at birth, empathy and love require specific experiences to develop."[17]

From that basic paradigm shift, our decision to act, even when there is an immediate concern for safety, is connected to love and care. Such determination to act from our hearts requires a paradigm shift from conditioned distrust in human nature to unconditional positive regard—even toward those who have harmed others—based on interconnection. Discernment is needed in the moment to determine the quality of energy that moves us to use force. Proactive inner work is called upon in preparation for such events. In order to embrace protective use of force, we are called to heal the places in our heart-mind system where we have internalized beliefs based on domination. Only with such healing well underway can we consciously choose to take action in the face of harm rather than unconsciously reacting to the implicit sense of emotional hurt echoing from our past. There is not a linear path from personal to collective healing; our paths intertwine and support one another. As educator and philosopher Paulo Freire tells us, "We cannot say that . . . someone liberates someone else, nor yet that someone liberated himself, but rather that human beings in communion liberate each other."[18]

> To embrace protective use of force, we are called to heal the places in our heart-mind system where we have internalized beliefs based on domination.

Throughout the duration of what we deem to be the "least amount" of force necessary to restore safety, we mindfully check in with ourselves, moment by moment. The use of force will often be directly proportional to the power differential; the more asymmetric the relationship is, the more internal or external force is used. Force can also trigger an opposite reaction in whomever we are forcing. This can, at any time, prompt a rush of adrenaline that escalates in tandem with the energy of those around us. When that happens, awareness of our intention is critical—do we aim to protect or to punish? Are we still connected to love or are we coming from anger and judgment? Committed to doing no harm to life or dignity, we observe ourselves, individually and collectively, with care before, during, and after our actions.

Seeking feedback, whenever it is available, is crucial to discern whether we walk in alignment with our values. In community, we may be better guided to discern what amount of further force, if any, would restore safety. Such a feedback loop is also essential to prevent and/or repair unintentional misuse or abuse of power.

Awareness of the power differentials in every relationship is important, as these affect the dynamic of giving/receiving feedback. Whenever we play a role as teachers or mentors, for example, we hold greater power and responsibility. We may be idealized, feared, and/or anything in between. As in the story "The Emperor's New Clothes" where none of the monarch's subjects wanted to tell him that he was naked for fear of having their heads chopped off, so those around us may not want to share their truth or may assume that our behavior models a nonviolent approach, possibly amounting to collective delusion. Punitive use of force has the potential to lead to a reduction in feedback, resulting in diminished growth, learning, and well-being for all. When we are unwilling to challenge ourselves by engaging in a healthy feedback loop, then we are no longer engaging in protective use of force.

After the use of protective force, and as soon as safety is reestablished, dialogue is sought with all affected. We begin with empathy, listening deeply for how our choices affected those on whom we used force. Then we may speak about what is important for us, owning our choices, acknowledging the impacts, expressing regrets for not having seen another strategy, and mourning unmet needs. If the other person is open to it, we may also share what needs we were attempting to meet with our actions.

Utilitarian Use of Force

Another important aspect of power is the utilitarian use of force, a concept articulated by CNVC certified trainers Inbal and Miki Kashtan. This use of force, also called "functional," includes a unilateral decision that is neither specifically in protection of life and safety, nor fueled by punitive energy.

Longing to uphold an awareness of interconnection, at times we find we have exhausted our resources, skills, and creativity to find solutions that address the needs of all involved. We may choose in these moments to use our role power, perhaps as parents or organizational leaders, while at the same time expressing our intention and sadness about not having other resources and/or not seeing other strategies to draw upon. Inbal Kashtan called such moments a "crisis of imagination," noting how little capacity we have to find strategies that work for us in a global built environment that is not set up to meet needs. In this setting, our "muscles" to think of requests have atrophied, especially after offering many pathways that have been declined. We simply find ourselves stuck. From such a point of exhaustion, we can acknowledge the impact we are aware of. Moving through the same skill set above that led us to effectively navigate protective use of force, we will engage in a heartfelt dialogue as soon as spaciousness arises to support this.

> STEPHANIE: I remember that while I usually took into consideration my then three-year-old daughter's desire to "drive" at the wheel before climbing into her seat, sometimes I did not succeed in taking time for her to make this joyful transition on her own. In those moments, the need for responsibility around time agreements with a third party (perhaps appointments or visiting friends) would arise. When sharing my concerns did not prompt movement, I would pick up my daughter lovingly and settle her into her car seat, applying the least amount of force possible to accomplish this. I let her know that I was aware she wanted to play some more, and I did not know how to give her more time and maintain the agreement with others. While doing this, I expressed my sadness and regrets that I could not see another way to support her in exploring and playing in that moment. Later, I initiated dialogues with myself, with my empathy buddy Kristin, and with my daughter about how to better navigate such dilemmas in the future.

Acknowledging the Impact of Force

As children, most of us experienced a disconnection from our own agency when adults, even out of care, made unilateral decisions that affected us. The lifelong impacts of such force on our well-being, especially when applied punitively, depends on whether repair happened and in what measure.

Over decades of working with parents, the two of us have consistently seen how the perception of scarcity around time can lead to punitive force. This is especially true in Western cultures where parenting happens in isolation. Lack of systemic support—having extended family and community at home for childcare, for one—drastically reduces access to external resources. It erodes our inner resources as well, such as patience and self-connection. The fewer options that we perceive ourselves to have, the less access to power we experience, and the more likely we are to rely on punitive force and violence as a tragic attempt to leverage power and agency.

Force in its many forms, including reward, is leveraged ubiquitously and often invisibly throughout the course of raising our children. Whether our use of force is engaged around hygiene or use of technology, the dialogues that follow use of force have dramatically different outcomes when we acknowledge and mourn any negative impacts. As we embrace a new parenting paradigm, we might carefully consider the possibility of using such functional force. It can be tempting to give ourselves permission to fall into old patterns of using punitive force by simply labeling it as utilitarian. It is our hope, as writers, that this newfound understanding never "justifies" violence.

Yet we would like to hold ourselves with compassion in the use of utilitarian force as our culture catches up to support a partnership paradigm in parenting. We often experience loneliness and a dearth of resources when we are at the leading edge of such a movement. Perhaps our Western individualistic family units will someday again integrate extended family and community support with greater ease, so more compassionate options for partnership will be ever present.

While force can be punitive and life-threatening, sometimes it also serves to protect life. Understanding the various ways to use force helps us foster compassion for ourselves and others, while exploring nonviolent ways to meet needs.

SUMMARY

- ↔ This key distinction supports us in understanding why and how we use force as a strategy to meet needs. As we come to understand that punitive use of force stems from ingrained systems of domination living within us, we can seek to meet our own and others' inclination to use force with compassion whenever possible.

- ↔ When we engage in protective use of force, we intentionally seek to meet the most vital of human needs—safety, health, and well-being—while holding everyone's needs with love.

- ↔ This key supports us in understanding that internalized beliefs based on domination call for healing of our heart-mind system in order for us to shift from punitive to protective use of force.

- ↔ When engaging in protective use of force, as soon as safely possible, we seek dialogue with those affected and repair any harm done.

- ↔ Distinguishing protective from punitive use of force entails allowing ourselves to be moved. We honor our intentions, take in the impact of our choices, mourn unmet needs, and hold with care the needs we sought to meet.

WALKING THE TALK:
A LIFE EXAMPLE FROM INDIA

BY MANASI SAXENA, CNVC CERTIFIED TRAINER

Following violence in North East Delhi in February 2020, three volunteers from my organization are in the field trying to rebuild six Muslim slum dwellings that were burned down. The slums belonging to Hindu neighbors were left untouched. I receive a distress call from a volunteer who says that the local people are threatening violence.

These slum dwellings are located on a strip of land next to a large concrete pipe. Arriving at the site, I see that thirty to forty people from the permanent concrete residences on the other side of the pipe are shouting and threatening to burn down anything we build. There is anger on both sides of the pipe.

I physically wedge myself in between the groups and stand on the pipe. My ears are filled with the angry voices, threats, and challenges from my team, the slum dwellers, and residents of the permanent concrete homes. I notice that some have projectile weapons in their hands and pockets. I fear that violence will break out and lead to loss of resources or worse.

I raise my hands and voice and *demand* my team stop speaking. I do this until I am heard, and they stop. I then turn to the people who are outraged and raise both my hands and my voice to match their energy: "This is escalating. Please stop shouting. We will come and speak to you. Please help us to control the escalating violence." I say this again and again until I am heard. It takes five minutes before two to three people register my words and then others begin to attend as well. The voices lower.

I spend five minutes reassuring my team and the slum dwellers. A team member and I embark on the short walk down to the concrete houses. I breathe and anchor myself in my intention, which is protection and safety for all.

Thirty people meet and surround us in the street. They are shouting protests. I stand in one place and do not move my feet. I actively listen and offer empathic reflection. They share their struggles with the slums, addressing social problems like crime and hygiene. I focus my energy on their words, paraphrasing and sensing what is important. When voices are raised, I raise mine in volume *only* to ensure I am heard over the sound.

I consciously do not bring up my own thoughts. Right now, it's not about shared reality; it's about de-escalation and safety.

Twenty minutes in, there is a breakthrough when I say to the man speaking the loudest, "So, you must be really *irritated*."

He stops, seemingly taken aback. A moment passes.

He says, "Yes, I am *so irritated*."

There is tangible relief in his being heard, and it ripples through the crowd. Voices lower. Some people smile. Bodies relax. I take this moment to ask that they not escalate to violence; we are given reassurance. I also offer reassurances that we will not do anything without consent from everyone. They hear this.

When they bring tea and ask us to come in and listen some more, I relax too. The violence, for now, has calmed.

PRACTICE

Discerning Use of Force

A wareness of body sensations associated with punitive force can help us awaken to our use of it, so that we can more intentionally align with our values. This practice aims to support you in identifying what kind of force you used in a past incident. This is a practice of meditative self-reflection, possibly with a journaling component. We invite you to find a quiet and comfortable space, and a pen and paper or keyboard if you feel moved to write. We encourage you to set aside fifteen to thirty minutes for this practice.

Think of a time when you felt moved to or actually did use force to achieve an end. As you think about the situation and the moment of choice, what sensations arise in the body?

- Is it relaxed? If you experience a tightening, you might direct curiosity to what thoughts are present. Is there a judgment?

- What do you notice about your experience in terms of feelings and needs?

- Do you notice a sense of clarity?

- Do you feel yourself connected to love?

- How easy or hard is it to discern the type of energy behind the force you used?

Are you open to the possibility of checking in with the other person to see how they received your intervention? Do you have a request of yourself? Repeat this exercise with a few situations and compare your responses.

17

RESPECT FOR AUTHORITY
AND FEAR OF AUTHORITY

Nothing strengthens authority so much as silence.

— LEONARDO DA VINCI

This key explores the distinction between respect for and fear of authority, to help us examine power differentials within our relationships. The notion of authority is inescapable in our world, and thoughts and feelings about hierarchies permeate our subconscious. This key distinction can support our growth toward personal and communal empowerment.[1]

Fear of authority prompts a reaction to someone's real or perceived greater power, experience, or resources, to name a few variables. We might fear punishment or a loss of "privileges" on one hand, or seek their counterparts, rewards and approval. Either way, when we comply out of fear, we lose touch with personal power, authenticity, and choice.

By contrast, respect for authority is grounded in an awareness of equal dignity and personal or collective empowerment.

Respect for authority is grounded in an awareness of equal dignity and personal or collective empowerment.

We choose to offer respect, maintaining an awareness of interdependence. We recognize the role of the authority within the structure of a functional hierarchy[2] and have a clear understanding of the needs we aim to serve in the relationship. We stay rooted in our dignity, recognizing that our needs matter, even when in a lower position linked to role, status, and/or systemic power differential. We respect both the person who has authority and ourselves, even as we may experience fear related to internalized powerlessness and learned helplessness.

In this key, we will consider the dynamics of roles and ranks, then explore how our conditioned fear of authority affects us personally and socially. Being connected to our inherent dignity and authenticity enables personal and collective empowerment. Cultivating that empowerment can help us grow our capacity for respecting, rather than fearing, authority. We can then choose to entrust another (or be entrusted) in a leadership role. Respecting ourselves and the person in a role of authority, we engage in a dynamic relationship that involves personal responsibility, awareness, and compassion.

Where Authority Comes From

Engaging with this key differentiation, we considered whether the concept of authority per se is intrinsically steeped in the patriarchal paradigm. We discovered that the word *authority* evolved from Latin to Old French.[3] Since the thirteenth century, the concept of authority has become linked to having "legal validity." In Middle English, authority came to be understood as having the power to influence people based on good reputation. As authors of a book on the key distinctions, are we automatically to be considered authorities on the subject? Does the fact that this book is being published by the official NVC publishing company, PuddleDancer Press, add validity to its content?

How we relate to the concept of authority and how we use its intrinsic power seem to determine whether authority is life-giving or life-alienating. In broad strokes, fear of authority is linked to operating within a top-down dynamic. Respect for authority is linked to a bottom-up approach.

> STEPHANIE: Both Miki Kashtan and I are CNVC certified trainers. This means that a recognized organization, the Center for Nonviolent Communication, conferred upon us this title (top-down). This label can be held with a sense of entitlement or as a responsibility. Yet I, and other certified trainers as well, confer upon Miki a position of additional authority around NVC, because we value her knowledge, experience, and wisdom. I recognize I can learn a great deal by engaging in dialogues with her—like this one on authority (bottom-up)!

There is a difference between authority based on hierarchy and authority based on love and justice. As Martin Luther King Jr. said, "power without love is reckless and abusive and . . . love without power is sentimental and anemic. Power at its best is love implementing the demands of justice."[4]

History teaches us that any system that depends solely on fear of authority to continue functioning will sooner or later collapse from overuse of resources, internal strife, or too many wars. Only systems which function based on respect for authority, absent any fear, have the capacity to continue functioning indefinitely. Prior to patriarchy and the establishment of states, humans lived mostly in peace for most of the three hundred thousand years that it is now posited that we have existed as a species. Even after settling and creating cities, matriarchal societies were stable for centuries and sometimes millennia until the horrific events that led to the expansion of patriarchy, mostly through invasion.[5]

Our Social Selves: Roles and Ranks

We are constantly negotiating power in relationships, whether consciously or subconsciously. We outrank some and are outranked by others, depending on our roles and the systemic environment we are in. Roles are the parts we play or functions we perform, and they come with social expectations. We play many roles at once, each one with different qualities of power, influence, and responsibilities. As we change social context, our roles shift too. If we are unaware of these shifts, we may misuse or abuse the power related to a specific role.

Rank, or caste, is a somewhat fluid status or position within our socially constructed hierarchy based on historical circumstances within culture. Rank is a manifestation of the domination mentality. Rank leverages a combination of different kinds of power: personal, status, and systemic. It is tied to roles and depends on others' perceptions

We are constantly negotiating power in relationships, whether consciously or subconsciously.

(the "power" of reputation). Titles, credentials, and labels signal power inequalities and clarify who is on a lower rung of the ladder. The higher our social rank, the less we notice all the privileges that come with it.[6] Benefiting from a sense of belonging and often entitlement at or closer to the top of the pyramid, we experience comfort and ease, which we often take for granted as high priority needs.

The incremental differences between ranks may be subtle and shapeshifting. Children have less access to inner and outer resources, so, less power than adults. Additionally, spoken and unspoken beliefs that reinforce a negative view of children consolidate their lower status. When more closely examined, we find variations: a male or older child may have higher rank than a female or younger child in certain settings. Depending on the family and broader cultures—the degree to which patriarchy is embedded in economic, religious, and educational systems—status can shift so that a younger male child may be ranked higher than an elder female child. These ranks are rarely acknowledged publicly, but can be ascertained by the respect, privileges, benefit of the doubt, and/or kindness given or withheld. And while we all depend upon people who have more resources than we do in certain circumstances, it is important to recognize that roles of authority depend on many for acknowledgment, value, and power.

Power dynamics unfold explicitly and implicitly whether we are aware of this or not. "Rank is linked to power, and power protects those who hold it," physicist and social reformer Robert W. Fuller notes.[7] Such power may be directly or indirectly bestowed. We might experience our status by simply being a citizen or by achieving a certain rank in the military, in our career (being a tenured professor, for example), or as a title in religious leadership—a priest, rabbi, or imam.

"To bemoan power differences is like bemoaning the fact that the sun is brighter than the moon,"[8] Fuller writes. This key differentiation may point us toward a healthy relationship with authority (beyond just positional) within a functional hierarchy, rather than the eradication of authority in general.

Our ranks may appear solid, particularly when based on visible features like physical prowess or skin color—or they may shift according to different circumstances and settings. Labels, such as young/old, rookie/expert, trans/cisgender, are wittingly or unwittingly embedded in the fabric of our social dynamic. This is an intricate dynamic; one may wonder if we can ever truly be ourselves in this social arrangement.

Rank based on skin color, for example, differs according to geographical/historical contexts. Pulitzer Prize-winning journalist and author Isabel Wilkerson describes an insight shared with her by a Nigerian-born playwright: "'Africans are not black,' she said. 'They are Igbo and Yoruba, Ewe, Akan, Ndebele. . . . They don't become black until they go to America or come to the U.K.'"[9] Without comparison to the lighter-colored skin of those with European heritage and the ranking that grew out of this distinction which began in the 1600s, black skin would be unremarkable as a means of rank. Without a tie to the domination mentality and its embedded ranking system, skin color, as well as other physical features, would not reflect on a person's worth.

Our social status is related to our economic circumstances, age, gender, physical and psychological abilities, geography, appearance, education, religion, sexual orientation, marital status, ethnicity, race, and interests, among others. Ranking is complex, and it is important that we view it through the lens of intersectionality. Accordingly, people who experience low rankings in many areas, such as queer/trans women of color, consequently find themselves with severely limited access to resources. Those who experience low status in one area and high status in others may encounter fewer barriers to empowerment. In these cases, our myriad statuses can leave us navigating confusion, uncertain of where power gives us a foothold.

Rank not only subliminally informs how we act, but also dictates the treatment we receive. Studies show, for example, that by third grade, many girls in the United States have internalized the belief that they are not adept at math and sciences.[10] Their performance and joy of learning often plummets. This is not surprising after being given few opportunities and little support from teachers who subconsciously rank them lower than boys.[11]

The more ranks and their related hierarchies are unacknowledged, the more powerful they become. "How others treat us, and we them, hinges on relative rank more than we care to admit," Fuller notes.[12] When we benefit from and do not see the power we have in our daily lives, we are less likely to consciously consider impact and rebalance it.

Fear of Authority

Fear exacts a price on both personal and societal levels. Collectively, fear of authority cries out from needs related to safety and security. In fact, wherever there is social discrimination, fear of authority is viscerally linked to survival. Fear impacts the part of the brain responsible for higher executive functions such as being in relationship, modulating emotions, and problem-solving. The neurobiology of fear freezes the creative freedom related to needs-based awareness.

Wherever there is social discrimination, fear of authority is viscerally linked to survival.

In the parenting arena, "respect for authority" and "obedience to authority" often appear dangerously interchangeable, as obedience is based on fear of those with higher rank. Authority figures, from politicians to "parenting experts" lament a "breakdown of authority" that they believe contributes negatively to children, family, and society. Generations who have grown up fearful find themselves wielding external power later as parents themselves, thus continuing the cycle.

The power of such authority is based on control—punishment and reward—rather than guidance and trust in the relationship. As such, it serves to perpetrate patriarchal narratives. As CNVC certified trainer Sura Hart and her coauthor Victoria Kindle Hodson write, "Human beings have been operating in a fiercely competitive mode for over ten thousand years—exerting power over others. . . . As parents learn to foster co-operation in families, they become models of change for their children, for other parents, and for community members. They also become active participants in creating an evolutionary shift toward global peace and sustainability."[13] Such a shift is grounded not in fear, but in mutual respect.

High Rank: Impact, Misuse, and Abuse

Higher status offers social recognition as well as greater and easier access to resources. Authority is a gatekeeper on the path to success. When we occupy roles of authority we get easily attached to our status as "somebody," and we defend it as part of our identity.[14]

In a high-rank position, we are less likely to see the impact of our choices on others even when these choices tend to affect many people. If we rely on power to enforce our will, rather than earning trust to influence, we behave from a power-over paradigm. Having greater access to resources, we may be tempted to misuse or abuse our role power to satisfy personal needs. We may not step up to the responsibilities of service that come with the position.

We might also be tempted to please others and use our role to seek appreciation and acceptance, particularly in the short term. We may resist saying no to anyone, regardless of the consequences. Afraid that we may be perceived as abusing power when assertive, we can end up misusing power by failing to channel it according to the group's purpose. As author and public speaker Charles Eisenstein points out, "To shrink from leadership in an effort to conform to fashionable ideals of inclusivity and egalitarianism is not an act of compassion at all; it is an act of cowardice; it is an abdication of one's duty to serve a calling."[15]

With less accountability, a de facto wider sphere of influence, and the sense of protection that often comes with high-rank status, we are more likely to do significant harm without intending or even knowing it. Here is an apt metaphor: The larger the vehicle we drive, the safer we feel, and the more damage we are likely to do to others in the event of a collision. Decreased inhibition, decreased empathy, and increased sense of control make roles of authority susceptible to sometimes catastrophic misuse and abuse of power. These dynamics are antithetical to reciprocity, equality, and equity. Furthermore, the aggrandizement of any one person or group (heterosexuals, Whites, or men, for example) at the expense of those in oppressed ranks (such as gay people, Indigenous people, or women), is an abuse of authority status, and tragically so. It can even be lethal.

We may find fault in those of lower rank in order to defend our own higher status. Our identification with and misuse and abuse of these roles and ranks, with or without awareness of what we are doing, deeply impacts the lives of many people.

There are downsides for authority roles, too, aside from challenges to integrity. The full humanity of people in high-rank power roles is often not seen. As a CNVC assessor, Stephanie has experienced being inadvertently skipped in sharing in circles with candidates; as a school administrator, Kristin is rarely invited to socialize with teachers and staff.

Role power changes how people relate; those in a role of authority often get stereotyped and are either criticized and seen as "less than," or seen as being somehow "more than" and socially inaccessible. Conversely, we may enjoy popularity in high-ranking roles, only to discover that when we shift roles, our popularity does not follow. Whether holding a position of authority or not, it is important to remind ourselves that we are human beings, first and always, not the roles we play.

Low Rank: Impact and Forfeits of Power

The negative impacts of low rank are many. Inhabiting a low-rank status affects our limbic system and puts our brains into survival mode. When we perceive somebody as using their power over us, the body-mind system floods with stress hormones. We might also find ourselves the target of rank-based discrimination if the authority figure exerts coercion rather than seeking to influence.[16] While a position of authority is not stress-free, its impacts on health and survival within a domination system are not as consequential as the impacts related to being on the low end of the power differential.

In low-rank roles, fear may lead to disconnection from ourselves. Doubt about our own sense of mattering and hopelessness about our ability to contribute may hinder our capacity to stay connected with our personal power. "The most common way people give up their power is by thinking they don't have any," says Alice Walker.[17] We may not stand up for what we value because we prioritize our safety and security, among other needs. Sadly, our future abilities may be shaped by self-fulfilling expectations based on social rank.

Fear of authority may emanate from the violence and trauma within the process of socialization, leading to fears of being unworthy or unlovable . . . ultimately of not belonging. Systemic factors such as knowing that our grandparents were beaten for speaking their Indigenous language may give birth to or reinforce this fear. Seeing people who resemble us being jailed, assaulted, and murdered by law enforcement at far higher rates than people of a different skin color understandably leads us to avoid and fear authority.

We may fear for our lives and see ourselves as a "nobody"—invisible, powerless, vulnerable, and disconnected from resources . . . a psychological state matching the disempowerment many of us likely experienced as children. We may feel scared, helpless, and "not as good as" the authority, and so we silence ourselves. Unwilling to negotiate, we give our personal and collective power away by not giving voice to our individual and/or community needs.

Fear may not be the only feeling we experience around authority figures and systems of domination. Another powerful emotion that leads us toward action rather than the often debilitating effects of fear, is "dignified anger."[18] The energy of anger is channeled to bring life-giving societal changes rather than being used in harmful ways. Dignified anger allows us to stand up, protect needs, and act in the world in ways that influence systems while respecting authority.

Respect for Authority

Power is a universal need. Rank as human construct entails ideological justification of how that power is used. Learning to engage respectfully with the notion of authority from both high- and low-rank roles is a step toward collective empowerment. Rosenberg's emphasis on interdependence advocates mutual empowerment that would eliminate a rank or caste system as a social construct that infringes on dignity. The core of this key differentiation directs us toward a healthy relationship with authority and its associated power within the web of interdependence.

> This key differentiation directs us toward a healthy relationship with authority and its associated power within the web of interdependence.

When respecting authority, we value the expertise, knowledge, experience, training, and resources a person holds. Rosenberg said, "I choose to do what this person says because I respect their authority. I really see them as having something to offer in serving life, so I choose to do it. One of the first things we teach kids in our [NVC] schools is never to give authority the power to tell you what to do. It's the *first* thing we want to teach them. . . . But respect authority, hear what authority has to offer, learn from them."[19]

Often our position of authority is conferred, whether explicitly or implicitly through cooperation and agreement of others.[20] Distinct roles offer clarity about what people are likely to contribute and who may be approached for specific forms of help. We recognize equal personal power and share it mutually in our individualized capacities. Respect for authority is not an abolition of authority, but rather an intentional redistribution of power based on a mutual agreement according to areas of expertise.[21] When positions of authority are exercised with an awareness of interdependence and a commitment to nonviolence, they embody social change and can become powerful tools to support social equity and justice too.

Power-With in a Functional Hierarchy

The power of authority is acknowledged with transparency, honesty, and life-connection in a functional hierarchy. In such a configuration, someone with more expertise might make decisions that affect those with less expertise. Roles are respectfully based on function rather than gender, religion, or other types of social status. At the core of this mutual respect is the inherent, unshakable value of every human being rooted in personal power. The role of authority is understood as being at the service of the community, therefore tightly linked to the relational model of power-with rather than power-over. In functional hierarchies there is a place for vulnerability and dialogue related to purpose. Information and resources are accessible as needed to fulfill the purpose within the system. Feedback is offered and received. *We*, rather than you and I, serve a shared purpose.

"Shifting constantly in and out of high- and low-ranking roles benefits our emotional and social development. . . . It helps us develop empathy and insight into others," writes Julie Diamond. "The conflict

The role of authority, when understood as being at the service of the community, is tightly linked to the relational model of power-with rather than power-over.

between roles increases our overall relational abilities, broadens our perspective of ourselves in the environment, and increases self-awareness."[22] As we step into and out of specific role power throughout our day, we always have the opportunity to connect with the personal power we carry within.

Power-With in Personal and Collective Empowerment

Connection with our own dignity and authenticity is a taproot of personal empowerment. When respecting authority, our personal truth provides a consistent connection with the life energy within and may become important feedback for the person in authority. We listen to the voice of external authority while remaining connected to our own voice, a sense of internal authority.[23] Both voices are held with care. Empowered to express ourselves, we are also connected with a humble desire and openness to grow and learn. Because our internal voice is not censored but free to speak, a dynamic relationship is nourished as we uphold a respectful awareness of the role power between the parties.

This quality of respect calls us to consciously engage with the personal/collective power that low-rank roles do offer. One of the perils of lower-power positions is to misuse our personal/collective power by believing that we have no power at all. Mahatma Gandhi awakened people in low-rank positions to their own inherent power and harnessed this power in nonviolent resistance. "The English have not taken India; we have given it to them,"[24] he said. The power of authority depends on people's willingness to follow.

Founder of the Right Use of Power Institute Cedar Barstow writes with Reynold Ruslan Feldman, "In a down-power role, one may even have opportunities to influence a system in which power is not being used well toward better use of power."[25] In low-ranking roles, we are in an optimal position to monitor power misuse or abuse. At times, the risk of not acting is greater than the risk of acting.

Individuals find greater power by working within a collective. For example, small farms make up the livelihood of most people in the subcontinent of India. When the Indian government progressively promoted deregulation and privatization of agribusiness, small farmers organized "the single largest proletariat uprising in world history."[26] In November of 2020, tens of thousands of farmers marched to New Delhi as 250 million Indians joined in solidarity by participating in a twenty-four-hour strike. Self-responsibility to inner authority and collective empowerment on a large scale can influence massive change.

Entrusting Leadership With Respect

Aligned with our inner compass, we maintain a sense of full choice when entrusting leadership positions to others. Relating to authority from an integrated brain, we are less likely to underestimate our power or overestimate the power of people with higher rank.

> **Relating to authority from an integrated brain, we are less likely to underestimate our power or overestimate the power of people with higher rank.**

Respect for authority is grounded in honoring needs. We are ultimately responsible for the degree to which we stay in our power, exercise awareness of ourselves and others, and hold an intention to treat all parties—ourselves included—with fierce compassion. If we find ourselves repressed systemically, seeking to touch this power collectively can support us in finding our way to personal empowerment.

The ability to voice our truth with awareness of interrelationship, even vis-à-vis a disagreement, indicates respect for, rather than fear of, authority. We are free to agree or disagree, while being aware of the needs that could be met by either approach. Such respect indicates a sense of balance and equal dignity for all involved even as the skills and expertise are not equal between parties. In a functional hierarchy, all needs are held with care. From a systemic perspective, we offer more care to the people who historically have had less access to leadership positions and resources as a way of rebalancing systemic power.

Respect for authority supports those in up-power roles as well as down-power roles. "Quis custodiet ipsos custodes?" ("Who will guard the guardians?") asked the Roman poet Juvenal.[27] The mutuality derived from a respectful relationship with authority benefits the integrity of all, as well as many other needs on both sides. If those in low-ranking roles stay in their personal power instead of giving it away, their feedback could benefit the entire system. The empowerment of many will secure collective visibility and provide a balancing act within all power dynamics.

The distinction in this key invites us, in all roles, to maintain a needs-based awareness. The differentiation between respect for and fear of authority unlocks our abilities to use our personal/collective power whatever our rank or role in the moment, freeing us to respect one another's humanity.

SUMMARY

- ⤴ This key distinction helps us understand how and why our sense of personal empowerment shifts when we move from fear of authority to respect for authority.

- ⤴ Discerning when we are fearful of authority can support us in pausing to inquire into our needs. Such a pause empowers us to intentionally choose to use our voice freely.

- ⤴ This key distinction calls for self-awareness when we are trusted or entrust another in a role of authority. Respect, in regard to this key, points to a relationship built on trust and choice rather than control and submission or rebellion.

- ⤴ Fostering mutual respect in up- and down-power roles, we can engage in a dynamic relationship that touches personal responsibility, awareness, and compassion.

- ⤴ This quality of respect for authority promotes equal dignity rather than equality of expertise.

WALKING THE TALK:
A LIFE EXAMPLE FROM INDIA

BY RANJITHA JEURKAR, CNVC CERTIFIED TRAINER

Some years ago, I worked for a corporate organization with a clearly defined hierarchy. As one of the younger and less-experienced executives, I had little or no say in decisions that were made.

When a conflict arose between me (a ground-level executive) and a creative head (a few levels above me in the hierarchy), I approached the regional manager for support. When I informed him about what had transpired between me and the creative head, he responded: "Let it go. You need to understand that worse things happen, and focus on your work."

I felt shocked and afraid. Here I was, a young, inexperienced executive, offering feedback about someone higher up the ladder than me, which took a considerable amount of courage. I experienced his reply as a dismissal of my concerns.

After I left the meeting, I realized that my fear had kept me from standing my ground and asking how we could achieve more safety in the work environment. I wondered if I were making a fuss out of something insignificant and thought about letting it go.

It took some reflection and support from friends to realize that my reactions were based in fear. Having grown up in a culture that repeatedly emphasized that I should obey those in authority, I found myself struggling to trust that my voice mattered, and that it would be heard. I worried that my word would not be taken as seriously as that of someone above me, that this would adversely affect the ease with which I was able to work, that I would be branded a troublemaker, and that I would be punished for speaking up, possibly even fired.

Being seen and heard by friends, my fear subsided and clarity about my next course of action emerged. I discovered other avenues in which to address my feedback, while still respecting the order that hierarchy brought to the functioning of our organization.

I approached the head of the Human Resources Department and raised a formal complaint about the situation I had experienced with the creative head, requesting their support in addressing the issue, and my larger needs for ease and safety at work. Throughout this process (which took around six weeks), I had the support of friends to remind myself to engage with authority from a space of clarity about my own intentions, rather than fear of punishment.

Acknowledging and exploring my fear helped me see that while the distribution of power in the organization aimed to meet many needs, it was not serving me in this situation. I felt grateful that NVC had supported me in taking action to address my needs rather than obeying or being resigned to my supervisor's way of dealing with the situation.

PRACTICE

Respecting Authority With Personal Empowerment

Our ability to respect authority is enhanced by our connection to personal power. This exercise is designed to support awareness of and possible reconnection with our personal power as we explore our relationship to authority figures retrospectively. This practice can be self-reflective, journaled, or explored through mindful dialogue with a friend (turn-taking clarifies speaker/listener roles). We encourage you to find a comfortable space where you will not be interrupted and writing implements if you need them. We imagine this practice can be completed in about thirty minutes.

Think of a relationship you have with someone in a role of authority.

- ∼ What support is this role (not person) intended to provide? What needs does the role intend to meet?

- ∼ Are these needs indeed being met within the relationship?
  - ○ Observe thoughts/judgments without identifying with them.
  - ○ Notice your feelings with compassion.

- ∼ How can the role you play contribute to the relationship? Are you able to contribute in this role? What needs are met and/or not met in the way you play this role?
  - ○ Observe thoughts/judgments without believing that they are necessarily true.
  - ○ Notice your feelings with compassion.

- ∼ Is there anything you disagree with this authority about? What needs might be met in voicing this disagreement? What

needs may not be met? How do you feel about voicing this
disagreement?

- Meet these feelings with a compassionate presence and inquire
  within about the needs that are alive.
- Observe whether you feel connected to a sense of personal
  power and dignity. To the best of your abilities in this
  moment, get in touch with what matters to you while also
  holding the needs that are intended to be met within this
  relationship.
- Is it possible to savor this embodied awareness of needs,
  expanding it with the breath? If not, what keeps you from it?
- What is the precious value that calls to you from there?

18

SELF-DISCIPLINE AND OBEDIENCE

You are personally responsible for becoming more ethical
than the society you grew up in.

—ELIEZER YUDKOWSKY

The key distinction that juxtaposes self-discipline and obedience explores how we stand in relationship to our personal power. The energy that prompts us to take action affects our trajectory as well as those around us. Bringing attention to our relationship with personal power can support us in thinking, speaking, and acting in alignment with our values.

Acting out of obedience, we may not be conscious about what needs we are attempting to meet; instead, we may blindly do what others want us to do.[1] Disengaging from a wider awareness of our own values, we fearfully submit to a system of domination or a person who holds positional power. Obedience disconnects us from our personal power, our values, and our capacity for empathy.

Engaging in self-discipline, as seen from the perspective of nonviolence, we use our personal power to meet needs. Mobilizing our energies and resources, we choose to act in integrity with what we cherish. Our sense of choice flows from the clarity of needs we anticipate meeting with a particular behavior or practice.

Building awareness around the impetus for our actions—sometimes even our thoughts—can support us in moving into choice and empowerment. Stepping into self-discipline, we ground ourselves in needs-based intentions and an awareness of interdependence. With clarity, we make effective requests of ourselves and ask for support from trusted others, taking space and time for reflection before, during, and after acting.

> **Engaging in self-discipline, we use our personal power to meet needs.**

Strictly Obedience

Obedience is the kingpin of power-over in social systems of domination that have unfolded across millennia. The dichotomous thinking of "dominate or be dominated" fuels fear-based action. Scripts from this paradigm have served authoritarian systems for much of recorded history. This "either/or" mode of thinking directs us to submit to or rebel against perceived demands we experience as threats. In obedience, we acquiesce to external authority because we fear punishment, grasp for a reward, or feel shame, guilt, or a sense of obligation. These motivators are all extrinsic. Consciously or not, we conform to the will of those with power linked to their role. For instance, a student might submit to a teacher. We may defer to those with greater status—an immigrant to a citizen, for example. Or we may yield to abstract principles put forth by those holding societal or institutional power, as with White supremacy. Authoritarian systems praise obedience as morally valuable and accept violence as a means to an end because they are founded on and perpetuate a view of humans as inherently evil.

Rosenberg postulated that human beings thrive in connection and enjoy contributing to one another's well-being if they can do so freely. Self-discipline emerges when connection and contribution are chosen as a practice. Today, we reflect on substantial neuro-research that supports Rosenberg's proposal. Stephen Porges's theory of the social engagement system, unique to mammals, sheds light on the neural circuits that support social behavior. The experience of safety in connection and co-regulation is now considered a "biological imperative" that supports well-being and growth.[2]

Mirror neurons are considered key to social interactions and to our capacity for empathy. Mirror neurons create a "simulation" in the brain so we can, from our own perspective, "tap into" another's experience. Studies on altruism suggest that human beings do naturally enjoy contributing to one another's well-being.

The quest to uncover the root of human violence and its links to obedience persists. How is it that some human beings consciously engage in, justify, and even enjoy harming other people? If violence is a learned behavioral response, then we are called to focus our attention on the ways children are raised. "Since childhood shapes society . . . little wonder humanity has been so war-like,"[3] writes psychologist and author Robin Grille.

One powerful source of education springs from mythical stories about the creation of the world through acts of violence.[4] The Biblical doctrine on the human fall from grace links the presence of evil in humanity to an act of disobedience initiated by Eve.[5] The Augustinian Christian theory of the transmission of this defect postulates that sin is an inherited spiritual disease. These stories still inform prevalent Western theories about human nature and justify authoritarian-based use of power. The valorization of obedience, linked to a system of punishment and reward, leverages people and systems with greater positional and systemic power to control others through power-over dynamics.

The Value of Obedience

Obedience is typically endorsed in environments where self-determination, choice, and critical thinking are responded to on a continuum from subtle discouragement to open banning. To this day, there remains a general expectation of obedience in most settings including family cultures,[6] mainstream schools, and the military. Obedience is perpetuated in corporate, institutional, national, and global systems of domination. Civil disobedience and nonviolent resistance are examples of collective power that counterbalance the perpetration of this domination on a large scale.

While obedience within such systems may provide safety, order, and even productivity, these "benefits" come at a price. Miki Kashtan writes that "[obedience] is an act of submission to another's will, of giving up our own feelings, needs, intuition, moral judgment, and anything else that would constitute our own choice, so as to follow something external and often dissonant. Whether we obey based on fear, calculation of risks, or loyalty and respect, this act of disengaging from our own inclination in order to follow another's is foundational to what it means to obey."[7] Any accomplishment delivered within such a system compromises self-connection and self-responsibility.

The Habits and Cycles of Obedience

This disconnect from our thoughts, feelings, and actions is manifested and reinforced by habitual ways of speaking. Words like "I had to" or "they made me" allow us, especially when in "down-power roles,"[8] to psychologically escape personal responsibility.[9] Discussing the impact of blind obedience, Miki Kashtan writes, "When people focus more on doing a good job and following orders than on the impact of their actions, their innate capacity for empathy ceases to function as a guide to moral action."[10] The fear embedded in these systems impacts our ability to connect, be creative, and tap into collective power. Divided among ourselves, we have no collective power. "Divide and conquer" is a strategy to break down relationships so people do not unite against a dominating force. The higher the level of obedience we are expected to meet, the greater the risk for misuse and abuse of power by the authority. When one person or small group "wins" over others, we all lose.[11]

Obedience may also manifest as resignation—a disconnection from personal power due to internalized oppression. Founding director of the Greater Good Science Center Dacher Keltner writes, "powerlessness is the most robust trigger of stress and cortisol ... [and] undermines the individual's ability to contribute to society."[12] The chronic stress of reduced personal and systemic power sustained over centuries may lead to conformity as a survival strategy. For example, women backing down in conflicts with men relates to, among other disparities, their voice having been and continuing to be silenced in many ways all over the world. Obedience may also be an indication of fatigue, apathy, and disengagement in the face of systemic inequality. "Threats that devalue a person's social identity are particularly potent triggers of cortisol release and elevated cytokine levels. They activate the biology of defense,"[13] according to Keltner. Worse yet, through transgenerational stress inheritance, our hardwired reactions and disease can be passed on epigenetically, further entrenching us in cycles of domination/oppression.

Self-Discipline

The motivation behind self-discipline comes from a completely different psychological context than that of obedience. While obedience calls attention to an external focus of authority, self-discipline draws its power intrinsically. We become our own authority. Self-discipline stems from an intentionality of the heart-mind and is based on a model of partnership internally with ourselves and externally with others. Self-connection leads to clarity about what needs or values are arising in us. From there, we

> Obedience may manifest as resignation—a disconnection from personal power due to internalized oppression. Obedience may also be an indication of fatigue, apathy, and disengagement in the face of systemic inequality.

can make requests of ourselves or others to address them. The decision is completely self-directed, even when uncomfortable. Tapping into the power of self-discipline, we reflect, choose, learn, and self-correct. Committed to such a practice, we come to know ourselves more deeply and trust in our inner resources and those we access communally. We value respecting ourselves and others. Connection manifests at different levels—with self as personal freedom, with others as belonging, and with the earth as trust in the sufficient resources offered.

The brain's internal reward system lights up with pleasure as we engage with our personal power and attend to self-care. We matter to ourselves and draw courage from living in integrity with our values. Expanding this experience of partnership outward, self-discipline grows exponentially as collective power. The act of gathering motivation, strength, and influence from a group's resources in service to a common interest can be extremely catalyzing. Peer support groups such as those related to addiction, grief recovery, or stress management are all examples of drawing on power in community to restore freedom and choice. Nonviolent social change movements demonstrate self-discipline on a collective level, as they subvert habitual power dynamics in order to address more needs.

> **Nonviolent social change movements demonstrate self-discipline on a collective level, as they subvert habitual power dynamics in order to address more needs.**

What Is Invisible to the Eye

While our actions appear to be the same externally, our internal experience will differ if we are engaged in self-discipline rather than blind obedience. For example, we may write reflections on our experience in clinical notes at work out of care for our clients and our own desires around competency and growth, or we might write the same notes *for our supervisor* because we are "supposed to." What we write and how we feel about the connection with ourselves, our clients, and our supervisor are affected by whether we act from self-discipline or obedience.

Dichotomous thinking may seep in and, catching us unaware, direct our day-to-day actions. In parenting, for example, permissiveness is not the only alternative to obedience. Neither honors the intricacy of needs involved in the relationship and its inherent power dynamics. Labeling behavior as right or wrong and attempting to control it based on moralistic judgments clearly perpetuate the same system of domination most of us were raised in.

Giving in and giving up on our needs is another form of submission from the same paradigm. In an attempt to distance ourselves from the obedience model, we may end up obeying our children's strategies! We can break the status quo by incrementally embracing a partnership model in parenting and family life, learning to honor the needs of all involved—including our own. As adults we can initiate honest, needs-based dialogues, honoring interdependence.

Intentions and Needs Awareness

We nurture self-discipline with short- and long-term intentions toward needs-based partnership. Whenever we discover that we have, instead, been acting or thinking along the well-worn paths of obedience, we can be compassionate with ourselves.

When we are in an up-power role, we often strive to maintain obedience for the sake of safety, order, belonging, responsibility, and contribution, among others. Serving obediently, when in a down-power role, we typically connect with safety, acceptance, belonging, love, and self-preservation. Awareness of needs supports us in shifting from obedience to choice and self-discipline. Maintaining awareness of interdependence can direct us to first uncover our own needs in self-empathy or in empathic relationships with others. When activated, we may find that our own needs are all we have access to. Self-empathy, or receiving empathy from another, may be the starting point that supports us to naturally open with curiosity to our feelings and needs and those of others. From there we touch inter-being.

Clarity about our deepest values supports us in crafting doable, present-tense requests that honor our own values with awareness of the needs of others. Making such requests of ourselves brings our hearts forward with vulnerable clarity. Self-discipline is a labor of love for which only we are accountable. If we find that we lack capacity or willingness to find strategies that are aligned with our values, we may regard our choice with care and curiosity.

> **Self-discipline is a labor of love for which only we are accountable.**

Whether or not we find such pathways to care for our needs in ways that attend to our own values, a possible next step toward self-discipline is to self-reflect and elicit the accompaniment or support of others in this self-inquiry. What needs did we attempt to satisfy in our action or inaction? Are we, in fact, content at this moment? Examining the outcomes of our actions upon ourselves and others while holding intentions for partnership will guide us in movement or stillness. Dissatisfaction may be greeted with compassion and warmth toward ourselves. We engage in self-inquiry with a commitment to take responsibility for our actions—self-discipline—while maintaining our dignity intact, thus transforming any sense of blame, shame, or guilt. If we notice that others have suffered a negative impact from our choices, we may feel sadness, regret, or mourning at not effectively holding their needs with the care that we so treasure. We recognize our "limitations" without spiraling all the way down the path of believing we were "bad." We commit to learning from the experience. Our intentions call us to lean in, touching our personal dignity, and lean out, requesting support or reflection as needed from others.

Cultivating an awareness of interrelationship invites us to confront fundamental beliefs about wrongness and violence in human nature. By shifting our understanding of those myths, we increase our capacity to embrace and nurture the compassion that lives within us. We may revisit and reinterpret the mainstream iteration of creation stories and bring awareness to ways that domination systems like patriarchy have interpreted those narratives to benefit some at the cost of others' well-being for millennia.

Holding ourselves, our collective history, and our creation stories with compassion, we can align ourselves with a new model where there is freedom, agency, and well-being for all. Self-discipline can then emerge and thrive. When dignity and self-responsibility are upheld, we set our intention beyond right and wrong and contribute to a world where all beings can stand in their integrity and embrace interdependence.

SUMMARY

- ✎ In discerning between self-discipline and obedience, we can observe our connection to personal power.

- ✎ Awareness of body sensations and feelings supports us in discerning the energy we come from. Stepping into self-discipline, we ground ourselves in clarity about short- and long-term intentions around needs-based partnership with the awareness of interdependence.

- ✎ In self-discipline we become our own authority.

- ✎ Taking responsibility for our own needs, we make effective and doable requests of ourselves and others.

- ✎ Differentiating obedience from self-discipline at the systemic level, we might notice a shift from collective despair to collective empowerment.

WALKING THE TALK:
A LIFE EXAMPLE FROM AUSTRALIA

BY JEAN MCELHANEY, CNVC CERTIFIED TRAINER

M y energy is heavy as I walk toward the bedroom. I feel weary, with a touch of resentment. I do not want to make the bed again! Checking in, I notice the thought, "I have to make the bed." I remember my parents—especially my mother—telling me to make the bed every day before going to school. I was trained to be "a good girl," and that meant obeying the rules.

Realizing that I have internalized a message about obedience, I step into choice. Instead of unconsciously continuing this behavior (or rebelling against it by refusing to make the bed ever again!), I want to consciously take responsibility for my short- and long-term intentions. Short-term: I will decide for myself whether I am willing to make the bed or not, with awareness of needs. Long-term: I will become more aware of other situations where my actions are based on habitual patterns of obedience rather than self-discipline based on needs, intentions, and choice. Ultimately, my short- and long-term intentions are about "making life more wonderful!"

Focusing on needs, I realize that I like when the bed is made during the day. It gives me a sense of order and beauty, especially seeing my favorite colors of turquoise blue, purple, and teal in the duvet cover over it. Making the bed also allows me to demonstrate care and contribute to the household in a way that is small but which my partner has said he values. With an awareness of interdependence, I appreciate that something I can do so easily is received as a gift, rather than being demanded as an obligation or a sign of obedience. Being received in this way in turn becomes a gift to me, reminding me that my actions matter; I matter.

With my intentions and needs in mind, making the bed regularly becomes an act of self-discipline that contributes to my life rather than an act of habitual obedience to rules imposed long ago. It's a quick chore that I can do willingly, with a light heart and gratitude for having a home and a bed to sleep in. On days when I am not feeling so willing, I can make a different choice!

While seemingly small, I am aware that making the bed is loaded with societal expectations relating to the roles of children, women, and men. Such simple chores also involve positional and relational power and privilege. I consider the cultural context in which I was raised— "middle-class," the Midwestern United States, of White European ancestry—and the needs that my parents may have been trying to meet when they told me to make the bed daily. Given the dominant paradigms and assumptions surrounding them, they probably thought this was part of being "good parents" and made the request out of love. They, too, may have valued order, beauty, care, contribution, and self-discipline. Contemplating this, my heart opens with more compassion and gratitude toward them.

PRACTICE

Shifting From Obedience to Self-Discipline

Our obedience, or call for it, is often mindless. The first step in valuing self-discipline in ourselves and others is awareness of when we are unintentionally doing what we are told or asking obedience of others without connection to needs. This practice is intended to help us discern where we experience obedience. This is a self-reflective practice, perhaps journaled, that may be done alone or with a friend. We invite you to find a comfortable space where you will not be interrupted. We anticipate that this practice will take twenty to thirty minutes.

Review your day-to-day life. In which tasks do you experience tension, boredom, and/or irritation? Consider the following questions:

~ Am I connected to an awareness of interdependence and intention for partnership as I take this action?

~ Am I clear about what needs I could meet if this action is accomplished?

~ Am I taking responsibility for addressing my own needs? Am I considering the needs of others involved?

  ○ Whether your answer is yes or no, if tension is still felt, we encourage you to review Chapter 14, on self-empathy, as a support for potential grieving and greater clarity. Empathy from a skillful friend could also be of help.

  ○ What needs are you trying to meet by acting out of or demanding obedience? This inquiry may help you make a request of yourself or others to support a shift from obedience as you move toward self-discipline.[14]

PART V
FURTHER APPLICATIONS

I n this section, we have gathered seven key differentiations that support deeper integration of the NVC practice
both internally and externally.

As we learn to discern the ways in which we have been
habituated to think and to relate to ourselves and others,
we step toward choice in our thoughts, words, and actions.
In this cluster, we will examine some of the ways we have
been taught to express our needs and learn how to increase
the likelihood of satisfying them.

Ultimately, we bring closure to this exploration by
coming full circle and returning to the core of NVC. Rosenberg
envisioned the process of Nonviolent Communication as a
strategy to manifest love. This last key, centered on love, is
the culmination of our journey.

19

NATURAL AND HABITUAL WAYS OF BEING

It's very dangerous to mix up the words natural *and* habitual.
*We have been trained to be quite habitual at communicating
in ways that are quite unnatural.*

—MAHATMA GANDHI

When Gandhi suggested that some of our habitual communication is quite unnatural, he pointed out the gap between our nature and the ways in which we have been habituated for millennia otherwise. The key distinction that compares habitual to natural communication asks us to consider whether our attempt to connect is conscious or unconscious, life-serving or life-alienating. Awareness of and understanding around these two modes of communication can support us in compassion for self and others.

Communicating out of habit is familiar because it is what we are used to, even if it leaves us out of touch with our humanity. Living out of habit,[1] we are unaware of our own needs and everyone else's. Rosenberg invites us to bring attention to our thoughts, words, and actions and notice that often, what we believe feels natural may in fact be what we have been habituated to.

> Millennia of conditioning keep us from knowing for certain what is natural.

Millenia of conditioning keep us from knowing for certain what is natural. And the practices of NVC help us connect with what is beyond our conditioned experience: the life-giving energy of needs. As we peel away layers of conditioning, we uncover, little by little, what may be part of our nature. Gradually, we come to feel more in touch with our authentic being. We surrender with growing ease to experiencing and expressing our truth in the moment, touching the life force in and around us. This key distinction, informed by the words of Gandhi, invites us to learn where our habits lie, offer empathy to our habitual expressions, and consciously align our thoughts, words, and actions.

Communicating More Naturally

"Natural" points to a way of being that lies beneath millennia of social conditioning. While we do not know for sure what is natural, one way of perceiving and understanding our essential nature, unaffected by socialization, is by looking at a baby. Human beings are born with an innate trust that their needs will be cared for and with the capacity to fully express those needs. Babies live fully within the flow of life.

What we know for sure is that we become our practice.[2] Language is a social construct that reflects our collective consciousness. When we align our speech with need-based consciousness, our communication becomes less and less affected by the norms of socialization. The process of NVC is one path to restore that quality of communication. One basic NVC principle, or orientation of the heart, is the faith that all human beings carry the innate capacity for compassion and the desire to contribute to life, when free to do so. When living with an awareness of inter-being, life isn't so much about us anymore, as we are about life. While we don't know what is natural, we have mounting evidence[3] that giving from the heart is entirely within our repertoire. When we come into the world and are surrounded by love, love will be nourished as our primary mode of being. Out of generosity, we speak and act within the integrity of who we are in each moment. Such authentic expression occurs when we live from our fullest potential rather than how we were programmed by domination systems that have guided us to think and speak in the static language of moralistic judgment.

And there's the rub. It turns out that it is not so easy to undo social conditioning and restore our capacity to live from the heart. Community support to reclaim this authenticity is crucial, given the continued influence of patriarchal systems in our lives. Here is where the strategy of Nonviolent Communication can help. The core intention of this process is to connect with life energy in the moment. Such awareness supports our incremental shift from feeling fear as a habitual reactive response to experiencing a state of love. Spiritual traditions generally aim to rediscover this capacity, pointing to it as a part of our nature. In our practice, we move from unconsciously participating in a paradigm of power-over and instead consciously engage our personal and collective power. NVC principles of needs awareness, interdependence, and choice, when lived in community, can gradually help us transform conditioned patterns of judgment and rigidity in thought and communication.

Communicating Habitually

Perhaps the most common way that we use language habitually is in words of dichotomized judgment—good/bad, right/wrong, nice/mean, to name a few. Our language is rooted in such dualities because we have been trained to think that way. Those polarities are so familiar that it often seems the words define us. Habits of communication arising from socialization shape our minds and influence our experience of the world.

When we are in habitual, reactive mode, we typically live in the future or the past. Our interactions are shaped and driven by circumstances linked to our historical, social, and personal conditioning. Our unexamined core beliefs, whether personal or collective, can feed our survival personalities. "Habit energy" is how we will refer to our words, actions, and emotional responses to the world shaped by programming.

This habit energy compromises our capacity for being fully present and making choices, as it is directed by our filters and learned responses.[4] We operate from a sort of autopilot, rather than awareness and choice. One example of such habit energy is within the natural survival response of fight-flight-freeze. These survival responses are natural, but habit informs when we default to them. These habitual responses may or may not be in alignment with our values of living consciously and compassionately. Another example of such habit energy can be found in women who are in the habit of withdrawing whenever experiencing conflicts with men. This habitual flight response is due to socialization by which women are programmed to defer to male authority.

> KRISTIN: The following is an example that I have heard iterated in many forms before, and it is also an experience familiar to many other women. I recall an instance when a man, after sharing his perspective for several minutes, declined my request for two minutes to express my point of view. I felt frustrated, a response compounded by repeated historical incidents of not "being heard" by men. When I expressed my frustration and requested reflection back of what I'd said, he told me I was making a big deal out of nothing. I felt ashamed, probably because I have been well-socialized to accept male authority and here, I had persisted in asking to be heard. He had likely responded in keeping with the same gender-based conditioning from the other side of the coin: Perhaps he deflected my request while subconsciously trying to hide the discomfort he experienced.
>
> While it is understandable to feel annoyed and frustrated when we do not have a sense of being heard the way we would like, the intensity of my feelings as well as the host of uncomfortable emotions being felt by my companion are more reflective of our conditioning than of the event itself.

The social costs of habitual communication such as this across the board are real. Women, for example, are not being equally represented in management and governance.[5] These are costs absorbed not just by individuals, but by families, communities, and society at large.

Such conditioning—related to gender, race, socio-economic status, and countless other "norms" reflecting social imbalance—has been transmitted to us across generations. Conditioning and trauma that are not transformed within us are then unintentionally passed down to our children. When unconscious habit energy floods our body-mind system, it usually brings suffering to ourselves and others. At times, we perceive this energy as stronger than our resources. Bringing awareness to our habits, even in hindsight, empowers us to create some inner spaciousness and choice.

> **Conditioning and trauma that are not transformed within us are passed down to our children.**

When we think and speak in the ways we have been educated, we follow the habits of judgment, blame, and sometimes a sense of righteousness.[6] We confuse stimulus with cause, mix evaluation with observation, and misconstrue strategies as needs. Most of us can recall times that we have felt driven to say and do things we later came to regret. Some habits of speech are incredibly difficult to transform, particularly when talking to children. "I told you so," and "Haven't I told you a million times . . ." are phrases that, with awareness, leave us biting our tongues.

Even a quality of speech that we find naturally life-giving, like empathy, can become habitual. When that happens, empathy is not a choice to be present and alive to the reality of another, but becomes rote.

Making the Shift: Habitual to Natural

We can gradually recognize, embrace, and transform life-disconnecting habits by cultivating and sustaining an awareness of our moment-to-moment experience. Because every behavior is an attempt to meet a need, when we are acting out of habit, we still unconsciously seek to meet needs. Practicing needs awareness, we deconstruct these habits and return to our natural awareness, listening deeply and sharing from the heart. Cultivating a consciousness that is connected to life, we form new ways of relating and communicating which encourage greater authenticity, clarity, and accuracy. We experience a more authentic and deliberate way of being, living from a state of compassion, connection, and choice. Converging discoveries of interdisciplinary research indicate that these qualities are more natural.

Finding Where Our Habits Lie

The mind is experience-dependent. What flows through the mind sculpts the brain. Neuroplasticity—the ability of the brain to change throughout life—allows us to realign our trajectory. Taking time and space to discern the patterns of our thoughts, emotions, actions, and reactions, we may discover the source of our habits. This self-reflection is a distinct shift from that habit energy. Cultivating self-awareness in the moment, and in larger blocks of time—as we do by engaging in the readings and the exercises of this book, for example—helps us remember our natural energy. Self-awareness, whether momentary or sustained, puts the brakes on habitual thinking patterns and builds a foundation for a more compassionate expression. Relying on the NVC process of communication, we can break out of habits of judgment, directing our attention to observations, feelings, and needs instead.

It is not always easy to discern where and when we are acting out of habit, because our actions are not consciously directed. We operate on autopilot. Becoming aware of our habits is the first step to cultivating the human qualities that make us more humane, and which may be more aligned with our evolutionary makeup. They can be observed in the few remaining pre-patriarchal cultures and in stories about first contact with such cultures in the early stages of colonization.

In this quest toward the natural, we learn to observe ourselves closely, inside and out. We might notice when we have "softer" feelings hiding behind the initial "harder" feelings that we habitually notice more easily.

We may think that it is "natural" to get angry when someone skips the line and bypasses us. What lies beneath the hard feeling of anger? The tender feeling of fear that we do not matter? Sadness for how we each live in a bubble of separation? Embracing this level of vulnerability can melt away the conditioning and bring us closer to an aware, soft choice. With persistence, we may slowly discover more direct ways to relate to our feelings and needs.

With a kind, yet firm commitment to noticing what is going on, we can seek awareness in all our undertakings. Once we are caught in the momentum of habit energy, we are likely to react in countless habituated ways. When we go about our business, for example, scrolling through emails on our cell phone, checking text messages, and popping over for a peek at social media, we are doing out of habit in all its glory. We might try to accomplish all this between tasks at the office, or while running a household, balancing the needs and expectations of our coworkers and families. Mindless doing rather than choiceful being is a strong habit energy that blindly drives most of us through our days. We may experience physiological sensations linked to stress—tightness and constriction—that could indicate we are not fully present.

Intentionally considering where and when in our day we experience such sensations of constriction can be a first step in noticing this habit energy, realigning the heart/mind with choiceful awareness. Recognizing that our busy-ness is a hotbed of habit energy can cue us to build in time and space for self-reflection. Successive approximations of connection to our natural state of being may offer us the opportunity to shift if we wish.

Self-Empathy for Habit Energy

When we discover where our habit energy lies, we can approach it gently. "Hello, my little habit energy, I know you are there. I will take good care of you,"[7] Buddhist monk Thích Nhất Hạnh says, and this is an apt model for self-compassion. Fighting or resisting the energy of habit only strengthens it further. We can take care of habit energy by mindfully stopping, recognizing it, and then compassionately connecting with the needs underlying our own behavior. Self-empathy can leverage us out of habitual ways of seeing, feeling, and behaving. When we notice ever more subtle physiological changes, we might pause and fully experience the sensations. Asking ourselves, "What needs am I attending to right now?" can bring us back into our natural awareness, and intentional behavior is likely to follow.

Learning to notice when we are operating from autopilot, coming to care for our habitual energy, can sustain awareness and choice. Our new behaviors gradually replace the unconscious learned behavior. Learning new behavior entails

> **The question "What needs am I attending to right now?" can bring us back into our natural awareness. Intentional behavior is likely to follow.**

an awkward period of integration, until with practice and repetition it becomes much easier. At a certain point, we become fluent and the new behavior becomes second nature. The question is: Which behaviors will we gain fluency in? Will they be habitual behaviors which separate us from the life within ourselves and others, or will they connect us to the life energy that flows among us all? Will we learn to wake up to ourselves, individually and as communities, or will we walk in our sleep?

Expanding Our Awareness

Another factor that can support us in understanding and compassion for ourselves and others is knowing that about 95 percent of our emotions, thoughts, and actions are not conscious, but occur at tremendous speed as a programmed response to a stimulus, shaping our conscious feelings and thoughts.[8] Amid this barrage of conditioned responses 5 percent is left for conscious activity. The implications are massive . . . who are we 95 percent of the time?

And here is why the pattern thrives: We encounter a situation which leads to a particular set of entangled thoughts and emotions. We can repeat and reinforce the same reactions ad infinitum. Those reactions inform our words and actions as well. It is a negative feedback loop. Yet we are so familiar with our habitual ways that we resist letting them go. Psychotherapist Virginia Satir has often been credited with saying that "people prefer the certainty of misery to the misery of uncertainty."[9]

Psychologist Rick Hanson says, "The natural state of the brain when not threatened by illness, pain, hunger, or disturbed by chemicals is typically calm, caring, and creative. In its natural mode, our brains are responsive rather than reactive."[10] According to the Center for Compassion and Altruism Research and Education at Stanford University,[11] scientific evidence increasingly suggests that we are compassionate beings at the core.

The paths that bring us toward our true nature are as unique as we are. Awareness of habit alone begins to break the cycle; sensing ourselves frees us to more effectively sense others as well. Choosing to exercise the compassion "muscle" to counterpose our habitual postures toward life incrementally liberates our energy, allowing us to live in alignment with our values. Caring for that process brings healing on the individual and collective levels.

SUMMARY

- ✧ The distinction of habitual from natural rests on the trust that all human beings carry the innate capacity for compassion and the desire to contribute to life, when free to do so.

- ✧ As we learn to recognize our habits—whether personal, familial, or societal—we can cultivate awareness of needs. From that deeper self-connection, deliberate behavior is more likely to follow.

- ✧ Giving ourselves compassion, we can offer empathy to our reactive habits.

- ✧ Expanding our awareness, we can discern personal, collective, and systemic conditioning from choice and become agents of life-giving social change.

WALKING THE TALK:
A LIFE EXAMPLE FROM THE UNITED STATES

BY STEPHANIE BACHMANN MATTEI

One day, when my kids were ages nine, five, and one, they were playing in the family room while I was cooking dinner in the kitchen. I saw they were starting to fight over a toy. I tried to redirect their play in a way I hoped would satisfy them (or me?) better. Before long, I found myself at a loss. They kept fighting. As my discouragement mounted, a sense of powerlessness overtook me. I stepped back and said: "Whatever! Do whatever you want." And I stalked off to the kitchen.

In that moment, I remembered the words of an adoption educator I was studying with: "When we don't get our kids to do what we want them to do, how do we react? Do we tend to get angry or do we tend to withdraw emotionally? In other words, what takes us out of relationship—fight or flight?"

I realized I had just emotionally withdrawn myself from my children. In shock, I saw that I had recycled the behavior I had been on the receiving end of as a child whenever my own mom had not been happy with something I'd done. In those moments, at her wits' end, she would convey her disapproval, retreat, and then become emotionally unreachable (in my experience as a child). My mother has lovingly shared with me many times since then that her mom had done the same, to an even greater extreme.

Recalling how painful it had been for me to experience my mother's momentary emotional withdrawals as I grew up, I decided that I did not want to pass on this habitual wound. I paused, took a few breaths, and gave myself some empathy. "Oh, Stephanie, it's so hard at times, isn't it? You just want to be heard and support them in playing together so that everyone has fun." I took a few more deep breaths. "And you value authentically conveying all the love you have in your heart for each one of them, regardless of their behavior." I breathed deeply again and then chose to speak from the natural inclination of my heart. I walked toward my children and gave each one of them a hug before kneeling down to talk with them. "I am here for you," I said. "I love you. Can I help?"

PRACTICE

Bringing Habits to Light

Acting in ways that align with our values and intentions rather than from habit can contribute to many needs being met. This exercise is intended to offer support around awareness of when, why, and how we are behaving habitually. This is a self-reflection practice. We encourage you to set a timer for a few times a day as a formal reminder to pause and reflect on these questions briefly. The more we make such intentional space for self-reflection, the more likely we are to informally reflect on our thoughts, words, and actions as well. We imagine that these points of reflection will take about five minutes each.

Several times during the day pause *before* acting/speaking and ask yourself:

- Do those actions/words come out of habit energy?
- What is the need I am trying to care for right now by behaving or speaking this way?
- And given this new awareness, do I want to take a different action?

Several times during the day, pause *while* acting/speaking and ask yourself:

- Am I driven by habit energy, or am I connected to life energy and its qualities (needs) in the moment?
- Do I want to pause and reconnect to my authenticity?
- Do I want to change the course of my behavior?

Several times during the day, pause *after* you did something or spoke, and ask yourself:

~ What was the energy behind that thought, word, or action?

REFLECTION

Each time that you engage in this exploration, we invite you to take a few minutes to notice how this practice is affecting you.

~ Any sensations and/or feelings?

~ Any needs that you are wanting to celebrate or mourn?

20

VULNERABILITY AND WEAKNESS

---

*That visibility which makes us most vulnerable is that which
also is the source of our greatest strength.*

—AUDRE LORDE

The key distinction between vulnerability and weakness asks us to acknowledge the moralistic judgment in "weakness" and the value judgment in "vulnerability." When we are vulnerable, we are capable of being wounded physically, psycho-emotionally, and spiritually. Weakness is defined as a lack of strength or having the likelihood of yielding or breaking. Embracing vulnerability can increase authenticity and a willingness to be moved. These facets of connection are at the heart of NVC.

When we practice vulnerability, we commit to and benefit from acknowledging and experiencing ourselves authentically before discerning whether, when, and what parts of ourselves to express. Through it all, we embrace ourselves compassionately, cultivating a sense of wholeness that touches the beauty of interconnection in giving and receiving.

The Perception of Weakness

Dictionary definitions of weakness as a state or condition of lacking strength stem from a model of deficiency. Labeling a person as "weak" typically stimulates resistance and shame, because it implies a sense of being "less than." On the contrary, strength, associated with independence, is highly valued in Western mainstream cultures. If we assume the moralistic judgment of weakness is a static truth about us, we may hide ourselves in shame or wish we didn't exist, so strong is the connotation of unworthiness.

Weakness can also be ascribed to and then internalized by target groups who have been systematically oppressed and discriminated against for centuries. Their reduced access to external resources makes it harder to cultivate the necessary inner resources to withstand the dominant perception of being "less than."

Those of us who have taught the process of NVC for a while have bumped into the widespread notion that even acknowledging our universal human needs can be perceived as a sign of weakness or being "needy." We might catch ourselves behaving from this domination paradigm that abhors weakness by noticing a sense of constriction in our bodies related to the experience of shame. Exploring further, we may find that we ourselves are contributing to this static judgment.

In the dominant culture, we place high value on a person's ability to maintain control of the circumstances in their lives. In the context of this cultural predisposition, both vulnerability and weakness are associated with a lack of control and therefore

> **Reduced access to external resources makes it harder to cultivate the necessary inner resources to withstand the dominant perception of being "less than."**

powerlessness—and hence, weakness and vulnerability are often seen as interchangeable. Yet, as with all the key differentiations, mindful investigation can help us discover for ourselves the felt difference this key directs us to. Our cognitive understanding then settles into an experiential knowing.

Vulnerability: Befriending Ourselves Deeply

Vulnerability can be held as a value judgment—an intention to acknowledge and experience our deepest feelings and needs authentically, even when it is uncomfortable. To be open to ourselves in this way, we become aware of and relinquish defensiveness. We remain connected to our inherent dignity. We learn to recognize our triggers and mourn interactions with ourselves and with others when they do not contribute to meeting essential needs. We experience and may share our truth nakedly, feeling our pain and discomfort. We take care of our feelings so as not to discharge them with words or actions that induce or reinforce blame or guilt in ourselves or others.

In interpersonal relationships, we experience vulnerability by opening our hearts and allowing ourselves to be moved. We may also share transparently what is going on inside of us and make space for the others' vulnerability as well.

We want to acknowledge that, as two White writers, it is relatively easy to celebrate vulnerability, because we are in a position of enough privilege to enjoy its benefits and risk less in being vulnerable. At the same time, in our patriarchal world, touching vulnerability can be a challenge for us too. Female voices have been silenced for centuries. Males are also socialized against being vulnerable as it is associated with weakness—the opposite of the stereotypical masculine "toughness."

It is important to acknowledge that while there is personal courage involved in stepping into vulnerability, there are also intricate societal dimensions of conditioning involved. We wish to name and honor the complexity and risk of moving toward vulnerability, especially in its relationship to transparency. Other survival-oriented needs may be in play. For example, the more a power differential is experienced in the relationship, the more complex it is to step into vulnerability and transparency, potentially for both parties. The need for protection may supersede the need for authenticity in a down-power role, and the perception of strength or professionalism may be seen as threatened in an up-power role.

Vulnerability is an inner orientation inclined toward deep listening rather than an expectation that we express our process aloud to anyone or everyone. In consideration of others' feelings and needs, we may well express our truth in the moment transparently, holding it as our experience rather than "the truth" of how things are. Vulnerability in relationships calls for a certain degree of non-identification with our views allowing for a different perspective to move us.

If we think that our expression may not contribute right now, particularly around needs for connection in the long term, we may decide to take some alternative course of action. Experiencing the rawness of our feelings, we may be uncertain whether we have cared for our own reactivity enough to enter the dialogue with an awareness of interdependence. Sharing our truth in such moments could result in more pain rather than supporting understanding and intimacy. It could even contribute to an irreparable rupture. In such instances, our ability to pause and discern are fundamental.

Discernment Grounded in Awareness of Interconnection

When uncertain about whether to share transparently, we might listen, give ourselves empathy, or make a request of ourselves that is in alignment with what we value. If we choose not to share, we can check in with ourselves to determine what needs are prompting our decision. Western socialization leads us to believe that we should either withhold nothing and speak our truth bluntly, or fully repress our truth, self-censoring. Both extremes are actually weaknesses in the paradigm of interdependence and may harm us or someone else in terms of over- or under-sharing. Is our fear actually survival-related? Or, is it about losing what we believe is our identity? Or are we perhaps concerned about the other person or people involved and whether their needs will be met? We may take some space or get empathy to help discern this.

Some of us see vulnerability as a play-by-play sharing of whatever emotions are present. Others hold vulnerability as first and foremost a deep connection within ourselves so that our words and actions are grounded in a place of integrity, self-responsibility, and care for the impact rather than in reactivity. Self-regulation is not antithetical to vulnerability and authenticity. While we might acknowledge our judgments aloud, naming them as judgments— "I'm thinking that what you said was mean-spirited, and I know that is a

Self-regulation is not antithetical to vulnerability and authenticity.

judgment. I'm longing to have understanding . . ."—such transparent expression can leave its mark on individuals and relationships in ways that do not contribute to health, well-being, and connection. Our emotional responses to secondhand information may invite even deeper consideration before sharing. We always have the choice about whether or what to share, and when or with whom we speak.

Vulnerability, Fragility, and Interdependence

The gift of vulnerability is that it is grounded in the awareness of our shared humanity. In tandem with self-empathy, vulnerability empowers us. We come to know ourselves and sit with an awareness of the agency we have to express or act upon what is true for us. Any intentional response we make from a place of ever-deepening vulnerability will more effectively address that truth with love. Such a vulnerable response gifts us and our community with clarity about our authentic feelings and needs.

We may be socialized to equate vulnerability with expressing our reactivity "unabridged," and authenticity with expressing the full range of our feelings with the intensity we feel them and the sense of urgency that prevents self-connection. Paradoxically, this reactivity may stem as a self-protective strategy to shield us from the fear of vulnerability.[1] With self-connection, we can tap into choice about whether to share our vulnerability transparently in the moment.

Vulnerability implies a willingness to let go of our self-protective structures. Incrementally, we become more aware of and take responsibility for our emotional reactions and the influence of our worldview on our perceptions. As we experience genuine feelings, our intention to be vulnerable calls us to discern whether urgency is present and to what degree. If we have an urge to express ourselves, a curious inquiry into the quality of this energy may support choice. Are we seeking relief? Urgency can point to an underlying sense of scarcity, whether birthed by trauma or social conditioning. Mindful that we are reacting emotionally, even if we don't fully understand why, we can hold ourselves with care and self-empathy. With this awareness, our next steps can be determined with a greater sense of freedom. Will we step away from the event and seek empathy or support, or make a plan to do so later? Meeting our reactions with compassion, we free our energy and our hearts, touching vulnerability.

> Vulnerability implies a willingness to let go of our self-protective structures.

When discerning the degree of transparency we want, many factors come into play, and we may not be conscious of them all. In particular, the power differential within the relationship may influence our willingness to be transparent and vulnerable.

> KRISTIN: Two years after knee surgery, I thought I was fully healed and took a job supporting neurodivergent preschoolers. Within a month, my knees felt very sore, I supposed from bending down and getting up so often. Hoping they would improve and knowing that such movement was an expected part of my work, I did not tell my supervisor, for fear that they would fire me.

The relationship we have with our fear influences the degree to which we allow ourselves to experience vulnerability. Choosing to transparently share our vulnerability calls for a discriminating awareness of who our listening partners are and what kinds of power differential—historical or structural, for example—are in play.

STEPHANIE: I recall a training in South America where the Black people present at the event—fewer than 10 percent of the participants—shared in the larger community their pain about racial discrimination. A White elderly woman started to cry. She said that their sharing touched a deep concern she had for one of her family members who had married someone from a religious minority group. She worried about the couple's children, who could face discrimination. The whole group turned its attention to this woman and gave her empathy. The needs of the people with Black bodies and the courage they showed in transparently sharing their pain were effectively forgotten. I recall this with great sadness now, remembering that I was not skilled enough to contribute to them being heard in the moment. In my ignorance, I unintentionally supported the reenactment of a historical dynamic in which the pain of Black people becomes invisible or deemed less important than the pain of White people.

This dynamic plays out often and points to how we unconsciously operate in ways that contribute to maintaining the racial hierarchy we have internalized. Robin DiAngelo has named this "White fragility" and explains that as White people, we inadvertently seek to counterbalance any threat to our often unconscious sense of entitlement. Resmaa Menakem denounces some of the manifestations of White fragility that can be particularly relevant to our practice of NVC: "The deadliest manifestation of white fragility is its reflexive confusion of fear with danger and comfort with safety."[2] Menakem brings attention to the difference between what we perceive as emotional safety, often related to fear and comfort, and actual, physical threat linked to danger and safety. Here, as writers, we extend the usage of "fragility" to include any and all attempts to maintain unexamined personal assumptions and social constructs in order to protect our identity and our worldview. Whether in relationship to race or not, we see fragility as being in direct juxtaposition to vulnerability. In vulnerability, we make every effort to recognize and surrender our self-identity and any structures that protect it. We set aside our worldview to openheartedly listen and share, with a willingness to be moved.

Vulnerability implies a willingness to acknowledge and take responsibility for the ways our worldview influences our perceptions.

Sharing transparently with someone from a perspective of self-responsibility and awareness of impact can be a powerful way to enhance the resilience and resources within a trusting relationship. There are many voices within us. Greater clarity about all the needs present will likely support everyone in finding strategies that encompass these needs.

Embracing Ourselves With Compassion

As we show up in our truth, we are called to embrace ourselves with compassion. We can learn to be with the pain, accepting our sensations without judgment, and trusting that discomfort is part of the path. Taking responsibility for our thoughts, words, and actions, we gradually come to terms with the sobering fact that we ultimately have no control over life.

From this place of gentle self-awareness, we cultivate authentic presence. We see our perceived limitations or mistakes as part of our humanity rather than as a threat to our sense of mattering and belonging. Embracing our "imperfections," we may then find ourselves more open to an awareness of the impact of our words and actions. It can take courage to remain vulnerable and not close our hearts when exposed to pain, whether ours or someone else's. Loving ourselves and others without guarantees of return, we let go of our static defensive structures. If the choice to close one's heart serves needs for protection, security, and, paradoxically, acceptance, we can hold this, too, with compassionate awareness.

We might ask ourselves, "How can I step toward vulnerability while supporting favorable conditions for another person who may have less access to inner and outer resources to do the same?" That is interdependence in action: knowing that our flourishing in vulnerability depends on that of others.

Opening our hearts to vulnerability meets needs around letting ourselves be known, which may contribute to a sense of belonging and love. As authenticity fosters connection, so vulnerability fosters intimacy. Experiencing and sharing ourselves in this way opens our hearts tenderly to give and receive from a place of integrity and reciprocity.

> **As authenticity fosters connection, so vulnerability fosters intimacy.**

From that place of openheartedness, together, and with great care, we can begin to transform domination systems within and without. We recognize and name the barriers those systems have created to being in the flow of life. Whether we acknowledge a limitation of ours to a friend or step into a leadership position examining the cultural norms that push us to hide behind so-called professionalism, we take one step closer to vulnerability. As more of us do so, we move toward collective liberation.

Wholeness and Interdependence

The vulnerability of NVC practice roots us in an unshakable sense of mattering and belonging. Relationships are a fertile ground for exploration. In relationships we get hurt, and in relationships we can heal. By letting ourselves be seen for who we are, we touch our truth and beauty. It is in our vulnerability that we sense ourselves connected to those we love. In the microcosm of our vulnerability, we intentionally let go of rigid self-images. In the macrocosm, our vulnerability contributes to collective compassionate awareness as we unravel domination systems and structures that do not serve us in interdependence. In this progressive deconstruction, deeper layers of conditioning and trauma will emerge. That is when we may return to and rest in our individual and collective practice. This is the interplay of the microcosm and macrocosm in vulnerability, each stimulating and inspiring us to open further into experiencing ourselves and community.

With an open heart, we find our place. We belong. As do all life-forms. We all belong to life. Even the distinction between human and "nature" begins to fade.

Whatever we say or do from our hearts may be viewed as weak in the dominant paradigm. Yet further integration of a conscious-ness rooted in wholeness and compassion empowers and grounds us when we show up vulnerably. Choosing to embrace our full, authentic humanity, including the complexity of our feelings and needs, can be a source of integrity.

This gradual connection with and manifestation of one's own power facilitates connection between ourselves and others as we align with our values and take responsibility for our responses. Practicing vulnerabil-ity, we are willing to reach out for help and ask for what we want. We may give and receive from a place of being honestly connected with our needs and curious about others'. We are aware that everyone's needs matter. In this way, vulnerability brings interrelationship to life. We lean on one another more effectively and joyfully by maintaining greater clarity about who we are, what we offer, and how we would like to receive.

SUMMARY

- ✺ While Western culture equates both weakness and vulnerability with a lack of power, mindful investigation can help us discover for ourselves the felt difference this key directs us to. Our cognitive understanding may then settle into an experiential knowing. We connect with the power of vulnerability.

- ✺ Vulnerability implies a willingness to let go of our self-protective structures. It calls us to embrace ourselves compassionately as we are, perceived weaknesses and all.

⌀ In vulnerability, we commit to and benefit from acknowledging and experiencing ourselves authentically *before* discerning whether, when, and what parts of ourselves to express.

⌀ Exploring this key differentiation, we find that power differentials may influence our willingness to be transparent or vulnerable to others and even to ourselves.

⌀ In vulnerability we become incrementally more aware of and take responsibility for the influence of our worldview on our perceptions.

WALKING THE TALK:
A LIFE EXAMPLE FROM THE NETHERLANDS

BY CHRISTIAAN ZANDT, CNVC CERTIFIED TRAINER

Dorje, my youngest son, was diagnosed with leukemia when he was five years old, setting off a roller-coaster ride that invited us time and again to step into the unknown. It has become a practice of trust.

In my practice, I vulnerably lean into an emotion without asking it to leave. I am always surprised as my feelings shift, and my heart grows ever more tender. One night, I remember crashing onto a hotel bed, crying, "No, no, no . . ." Children don't die, I thought. They go to school, grow old, and enjoy a fulfilling life. And we all live happily ever after, with me as gray-bearded grandfather. These stories, which reflected my privileged, sheltered life as a White European male, crumbled like sandcastles before the tide. I was shocked at the possibility that my son might not adhere to this storyline. I sobbed for a while, releasing my hold on outward circumstances and relaxing into my grief.

Slowly, I began to sense myself coming to terms with a different reality, one without anything solid to stand on. Peace welled up in me as I opened to these uncomfortable emotions again and again.

Caring for a child with cancer has become a practice of broken-heartedness—seeing Dorje, weakened by chemotherapy, wrestle his body up the stairs; hearing that a particular treatment didn't work out the way the doctor had hoped.

One evening, Dorje and I were lying in his bed. He suddenly said, "When I die, I want to be buried beside you." It felt as if my heart stopped beating for a moment. I swallowed my urge to console him as fear and sadness flooded my body. Silently, I affirmed myself as one might reassure an animal panicking: "Stay . . . stay . . ." Time stood still, and I said softly, "I would like that too."

In 2020, we found out that Dorje's leukemia had returned, and I reached out to people around us. Asking for prayers and kind thoughts, I intended to meet my needs for support and an uplift of energy. Sometimes, however, I received messages from people who needed empathy themselves: "Oh, we're so worried! I read about special stem cells to boost immunity. It would be good to investigate that."

I felt furious and tired, reading it. Connected with my intentions and needs, I sent out a message: "It takes more energy than I have now to respond to medical suggestions. I receive them, but will not respond, to protect my energies so as to be present for Dorje. Okay?"

Sometimes I feared that vulnerably sharing my honesty would negatively impact short-term connection. Yet I trusted that becoming clear about my intention and what I needed would help me navigate these exchanges in a way that served connection and many other needs in the long term. Sustaining my presence to care for Dorje has become a practice of trust, courage, and vulnerability as we face the unknown in all its intensity, day by day.

PRACTICE

Choosing When to Share Vulnerably

Consciously discerning when it would meet needs to share vulnerably and to what degree can support us in all our relationships. This practice of self-empathy helps us decide the degree of transparency we wish to embrace. Discernment requires a level of awareness about our core needs, and this practice can help us ground ourselves in presence before expressing. This is a meditative self-reflection practice. We encourage you to find a quiet and comfortable space. We imagine this practice will take thirty minutes to an hour.

Think about a situation you feel uncomfortable about that involves another person. You may want to begin with a lower level of discomfort and expand the practice to include larger conflicts as you gain confidence and skill.

Give yourself empathy by inquiring about your feelings and needs layer by layer, breathing into each. Then, attending to the body, notice whether there is tightness, constriction, or some sense of opening and expansion. If you notice physical constriction or emotional resistance, allow it to be. Just acknowledge your experience with compassion. If inclined to a deeper self-inquiry, observe what thoughts are tied to this sense of constriction or resistance. Do these thoughts relate to some idea of yourself you want to uphold, a self-protective force within you? Or is there some sense of concern about your or the other person's needs in the bigger picture? Inquire into your experience with curiosity and pause when it becomes more than you feel ready to explore.

If, on the other hand, there is a sense of openness, savor that. Slowly, let curiosity arise, guessing the needs that may be up for the other person.

∼ How might you share your feelings and needs transparently
with that person (if there are more than one to choose from,
consider each individually with the following questions)?

  ○ Letting yourself be heard this way, how do you imagine this
    could foster connection to your own needs in the short run?
    What about for the other person?
  ○ How might your expression affect the other person and/or
    your relationship in ways you would not enjoy in the short run?

∼ Now imagine the same questions in relation to the long run.

  ○ How do you imagine sharing your truth this way would foster
    connection to your own needs? What about for the other
    person?
  ○ How might your expression affect the other person and/or
    your relationship in ways you would not enjoy?

∼ Holding an expansive awareness of all these short- and long-
term needs, what do you choose? And how do you choose to let
your words emerge from this self-connection?

∼ Reflecting on what you have written, is sharing transparently
something you imagine yourself doing? When and where would
be a setting conducive to this dialogue? Do you have a request of
yourself in this moment?

21

STIMULUS AND CAUSE

What we contact we feel.

What we feel we perceive.

What we perceive we think about.

What we think about we proliferate about.

What we proliferate about we dwell upon.

What we dwell upon becomes the shape of our mind.

—CHRISTINA FELDMAN

The key distinction between stimulus and cause invites us to examine the all-consuming sense of powerlessness that occurs when we believe that our experience is caused by outside forces. Whenever we believe we are acted upon, we perceive ourselves to be the victim of other people or circumstances. The process of NVC supports us to navigate life with greater freedom by uncoupling stimulus and cause.

All information that reaches the brain through the sense organs comes in as stimuli. We are constantly flooded with sensory input that the brain decodes, interprets, organizes, and makes predictions around. Stimuli can also be internal. A thought or a memory, just like an external stimulus, spurs a cascade of biochemical reactions, physical sensations, emotions, and further cogitation. While the stimulus activates the body-mind system to respond, it is not in itself the cause of our emotional responses. The cause of our reaction or response is internal. The brain processes experiences, storing them as mental maps in its neuro database. As the brain arranges new experiences, it matches them to those available maps. These mental models are part of our implicit (unconscious) memory and are the cause of our reactions.

Understanding the difference between stimulus and cause supports us in recognizing and owning our emotional reactions and responses. This owning offers us true autonomy and responsibility. Whenever we believe external forces "make" us feel something, we don't experience ourselves as having a choice. By learning to pause whenever we perceive something outside of ourselves to be the "cause" of our emotions, we step toward freedom. Noticing uncomfortable physical sensations and emotions helps us to recognize them so we can pause more often in the moment. Exploring our thoughts and beliefs with curiosity, we empower ourselves to touch the underlying needs at the "root." As we take responsibility for our inner experience as well as our external behavior, we free ourselves to discover greater compassion, authenticity, and empowerment.

Stimulus

As soon as sensory information touches us, an automatic, mostly unconscious process of appraisal takes place in the brain. Complex computations determine whether this information is pleasant, unpleasant, or neutral, with the intention of maximizing our chances for survival. This primal emotional appraisal, which we are largely unaware of, directs us to approach, withdraw from, or ignore the stimuli.

Herein lies the confusion: in a fraction of a second and without conscious awareness, the stimulus gets compounded with this initial response which is biased toward avoiding threats rather than approaching opportunities. An emotion-driven impulse to action quickly follows. During a scientific dialogue with His Holiness the Dalai Lama, Buddhist scholars and Western brain scientists gathered together. Psychologist and professor emeritus Paul Ekman[1] affirmed that awareness of this secondary response, "impulse awareness," can be cultivated by mindfully[2] monitoring physiological feedback. We can also increase this awareness by befriending our triggers and the sensory cues that activate them. Anticipating possible triggers allows us to live more at ease and with choice.

After the initial appraisal stimulates an emotional impulse, a behavioral response quickly follows. Ekman calls this "action awareness." Here is the choice point most available to us—where we can learn to interrupt the habit energy and modulate our recurring behaviors and speech patterns. In so doing, we allow ourselves to reshape our response to match our values.

When Stimuli Become Triggers

By definition, a stimulus activates a physiological response. Sensory organs signal the thalamus and the sensory processing areas of the neocortex where this information is appraised. There is also a direct neural shortcut between thalamus and amygdala, the part of the brain that scans the environment for threats. When the amygdala sets off an alarm, all available energy is redirected, bypassing the higher executive functioning part of our brain, the prefrontal cortex. Since the amygdala is also a storehouse of emotional memory, psychologist Daniel Goleman points out that "the amygdala can trigger an emotional response before the cortical centers have fully understood what is happening."[3]

In these moments, sensory stimuli become "triggers," spawning intense emotional reactions, impulsive behaviors, and distortions in our perceptions. The automatic appraisal compounded with the matching of stored mental templates activates the amygdala to set off the alarm. The amygdala associates a fear response with a specific stimulus. Sensory stimuli awaken subconscious memories of past events.

While we may not be conscious of how those templates were first created, we can compassionately observe their impact on our daily lives.

STEPHANIE: My daughter was bitten by a small dog when she was three years old. While she does not have a conscious memory of the event, for years when a dog approached her body would contract with fear and she would seek refuge in my arms. While responding to her need for safety in the moment, over time I also explained to her that her fear was a normal reaction linked to being bitten at age three. My daughter came to understand her knee-jerk reactions and gradually learned to stay more present around dogs, thus reducing unconscious reactivity.

Amygdala activation within us can also rouse our moralistic judgments and limiting core beliefs. That is when our NVC practice of pausing to distinguish observations from evaluations supports self-regulation. As we reframe an event, we engage the brain's higher executive functions.

All experiences shape neural connections, yet the amygdala is hardwired to focus on negative information. The more emotionally charged and traumatic an event is for us, the earlier it happened in our life, and the more it has recurred impacts the frequency, duration, and intensity of amygdala arousal and consequent shutting down of the higher processing capabilities of the brain. Past personal and collective trauma amplifies our reactivity. Negative core beliefs about ourselves and the groups we identify with, others in general, and the world develop

Past personal and collective trauma amplifies our reactivity.

around these triggers. It is often challenging to disentangle our true temperaments from our responses to the experiences that have shaped the structure and function of our brains and, accordingly, our minds. Healing may happen by recognizing and naming those deeply ingrained reactions within an empathic relationship. Investigating our stories and the systemic landscape we are born into helps us understand our collective reactivity.

Cause

To understand the cause of our feelings, we turn again to the development and evolution of the brain. In order to maximize the chance of survival for our species, the human brain processes experiences conservatively, ordering, labeling, and storing them as mental templates with established patterns of neural firing. New sensory input is juxtaposed with previously determined patterns of neural activation—filtering models—to classify experiences and predict likely outcomes based on past records.

Although the brain reaches maturity at around age twenty-five, 90 percent of its growth happens within the first five years of life. Prenatal brain science has discovered that "the amygdala achieves a high degree of maturity by the 8th month of gestation, allowing it to associate a fear response to a stimulus prior to birth."[4] This implies that some number of those mental templates are created prenatally. Our early childhood experiences determine which neural connections (synapses) are established, thus shaping the structure of the brain and significantly impacting its functions.

Cultivating curiosity whenever stimulated allows us to grow awareness of these filters and to incrementally expand our understanding of how they color our perceptions, thoughts, and emotions. Rosenberg reminds us that "our feelings result from how we choose to receive what others say and do, as well as from our particular needs and expectations in the moment."[5] The actual *cause* of our feelings is to be found in how our brains have been shaped by experience, specifically in our initial unconscious appraisal and historical reactions to stimuli (emotional impulse and behavioral response).

There are also momentary contextual preconditions that play a role in transforming a stimulus into a trigger.

The actual *cause* of our feelings is to be found in how our brains have been shaped by experience, specifically in our initial unconscious appraisal and historical reactions to stimuli.

Physical states such as hunger or tiredness, and emotional states such as melancholy, fear, or stress, reduce the brain's ability to access needed inner resources or reach out to mobilize external resources.

Part of our biological makeup is to approach what we find pleasant and move away from all we deem unpleasant. Whenever we feel anything from a mild discomfort to full blown suffering, we tend to blame circumstances and other people for our feelings. Sometimes we even blame ourselves. In these instances, we are likely seeking protection from experiencing dysregulating emotions.

How we relate to an event is determined by whether we assess our inner resources to be adequate to face the challenge. Rosenberg suggests that "anger, depression, guilt, and shame are the product of the thinking that is at the base of violence on our planet."[6] Likewise, when we deem anything outside of us (pleasant or unpleasant) to be the "cause" of our emotions, we experience our feelings as being more connected to the environment than they are to us. Whenever we become aware that we are attributing the cause of our emotions to outward causes, we can redirect awareness within, owning our experience. This redirection of our attention will contribute to greater freedom and autonomy.

Shifting Awareness From External to Internal

The cause is always within us and is related to how we make meaning of the stimulus, which is influenced by many elements, including unexamined issues, unresolved personal and collective trauma, and loss. The cause of other people's emotional reactions is about how they make meaning of the stimulus—including the actions we have taken. Again, this meaning-making process is influenced by what they have experienced, how they have made sense of their experiences, and whether or not they have had support in the journey. While we are not responsible for their reactions, each and every action of ours has impacts. And so does our level of presence or lack of it at the time of their reaction. Regardless of what we did, regardless of our intentions, regardless of the meaning we make of our actions, the impact would not have happened without our actions, even if we didn't cause it. This is a delicate and complex understanding of interdependence: we neither cause others' reactions, nor are we unrelated to them.

It is important to notice that this key distinction can be used as a self-protective strategy to bypass taking responsibility for our actions and their effects. This is especially true of people in positions of power and privilege in

This is a delicate and complex understanding of interdependence: we neither cause others' reactions, nor are we unrelated to them.

relation to those without it. Ironically, often in NVC circles, people from marginalized contexts are implicitly or explicitly asked to make sure they are using an observation and not blaming when they try to point to behaviors from those in dominant groups that have impacts on them. After all, so goes the reasoning, the cause of their reactivity is internal . . .

Here is one of the instances in which stepping out of the either/or mentality can determine whether we in the dominant culture (where the NVC practice originated) contribute to harm or to repairing harm. Can we hold ourselves with compassion for inadvertently stimulating patterns of pain in people of the global majority and receive their feedback as a gift for greater awareness? And can we hold the enormity of their compounded pain with the utmost care? Can we receive their expression without judging them or attempting to "educate" them? It takes great humility to practice NVC as our unilateral practice and live it to the best of our abilities without expecting or demanding that others practice NVC the way we do.

Coming to understand our emotional reactivity, regardless of our roles and ranks, we may notice that we have abdicated power to external circumstances. Even after a full emotional blowup, it is never too late to pause and give ourselves empathy. Whenever we experience intense, unpleasant feelings in relation to something others do or don't do, we can investigate how the external structures of domination live inside of us and contribute to unresolved patterns of reactivity and pain. When we observe our own emotional reaction and notice that it is incongruent with the event itself, we may recognize that we are in reactive mode. In that moment of awareness, we have the power to uncouple the stimulus from the cause.

Cultivating a quality of curiosity and openness to a wider perspective invites the executive functions of the prefrontal cortex to operate at their best, allowing for reframing to happen. Looking at the stimulus from another perspective may help us clarify that it is not the cause of our feelings. Stepping back to garner a different viewpoint may help us take responsibility for our own reactivity.

Sensations and Emotions

With practice, we increase our capacity to observe our impulses (impulse awareness) and choicefully intervene (action awareness). Fostering self-understanding, we revisit reactive behaviors. By cultivating the ability to monitor our behavior, we create spaciousness and become present to a wider repertoire of possible responses. Additionally, we may gradually increase our awareness of physiological feedback. Attuning to subtler cues around bodily sensations in unstressful situations, we learn to listen to the messages of the body. Then we can expand our mindful impulse awareness to include more challenging situations. In doing so, we enhance our potential to live with greater freedom from the reactivity that arises from personal and social conditioning, and we experience more choice.

We can learn to recognize early signs of stress in the body as our minds enter a state of chaos or rigidity. We might notice tension in our throat, jaw, or shoulders, or perhaps some heaviness in the chest as our breathing rhythm changes. In fact, we might notice a host of unpleasant bodily sensations. Fine-tuning our attention, we prime ourselves to notice physical discomfort or emotional uneasiness as it unfolds. Opening ourselves to the experience of sensations in our bodies, our feelings, and our needs, we actually interrupt habitual reactive thinking patterns in the moment. With patient introspection, we learn to discover what lies between the stimulus and our responses to it.

Thoughts

Once present with the sensations and feelings of our inner experience, we can continue the journey to greater self-understanding by exploring the thoughts behind them. Examining our patterns of thinking, we create new neural pathways that will become more accessible over time, eventually even in the heat of the moment.

We may observe the mind revisiting the past or predicting the future based on our past experiences, rather than staying in the present. A few mindful breaths can help us regulate our nervous system, especially if we lengthen the exhalation. Then, when we feel ready, we can use the thinking mind as an ally to deconstruct our experience, engaging in a deeper self-empathy process that encompasses a gentle, yet persistent, self-inquiry.

Becoming aware of how thoughts affect our perceptions, we can redirect the flow of mental processing toward needs. Self-empathy can support us in noticing how our mind assesses some needs as met or unmet in relation to a situation.[7] We can remind ourselves that this assessment is influenced by our personal and societal conditioning. What we place our attention on, how we interpret the situation, and expectations we may be holding dictate how we will perceive our needs.

When we become aware of our thoughts, we can sort them from the stimulus, and remind ourselves that the stimulus itself is not the cause of our pain. We might question ourselves: What is the observation linked to that thought? Can the situation be observed from different angles? Am I missing something here? Exploring and evaluating these patterns of thinking in hindsight supports us in recognizing them as they emerge in the moment. This awareness allows us to befriend and anticipate possible triggers.

Responsibility for Our Inner World

Holding ourselves with compassion whenever we give up our personal power, whether in denial, in escape, or in self-protection, we can regain responsibility for our inner experience. Tenderly, we hold our fears with care. Acknowledging that the root of our emotional responses and reactions is to be found in our own needs is a revolution of Copernican magnitude. Instead of seeing ourselves at the center of the universe, taking everything personally, we connect with the most important source of life—universal needs.

The decision to take ownership of our inner reality and consequent experience by awakening needs awareness seamlessly shifts us away from right/wrong or punitive thinking. Resting on life-connected awareness, we enter and act from a different paradigm.

Taking responsibility for our inner world as a practice affords us a point of choice. With greater frequency, we find we can interrupt habit energy by deconstructing our thoughts and then reconnecting with what matters most to us. With that clarity, we may choose our course of action. If we don't catch ourselves when we experience the impulse to action (impulse awareness), the choice point might lie in catching ourselves as we notice our behavioral response (action awareness). At the beginning, we may become aware of our reactions only in hindsight. Consciously tapping deeper into the energy of what inherently motivates us, we get to the root of our emotional reactivity, attend to it with compassion, and make new choices henceforth.

> **Taking responsibility for our inner world as a practice affords us a point of choice.**

Strategies to Get to the Root

In order to empower ourselves to uncouple stimulus and cause, and connect with the root (our needs), we can cultivate strategies to lower reactivity and bring the prefrontal cortex back online. Additionally, we can increase self-awareness and self-responsibility as we step toward greater integrity and authenticity.

We may practice the following strategies to support changes in the body physiology from high arousal to a low arousal state, settling the stress response:

- Deep exhalation (perhaps breathing eight seconds out for every four seconds in)
- Mindfulness of breathing
- Mindfulness of the body
- Conscious relaxation of the body
- Intentional yawning, sighing, laughing, or touching the lips
- Sipping water

Stepping Into Our Power

Perhaps the ultimate crash course in self-empowerment is to take full responsibility for our internal experience, as well as our actions and their impact on other living beings. Owning these sheds light on the path to self-empowerment. If we blame others, we deny ourselves the possibility of self-discovery. Moments of reactivity present us with the golden opportunity to connect consciously with our unconscious world.

As we take responsibility for our own reactions and responses, we may begin to heal. Uncoupling stimulus and cause empowers us to stay receptive to the impact of our behaviors without taking responsibility for others' feelings and habitually spiraling into guilt and/or shame. This key frees us to move from the dependency mode of seeing others as the cause of our feelings, and our behavior as the cause of their feelings, to a paradigm of care. Self-responsibility does not

> **Uncoupling stimulus and cause empowers us to stay receptive to the impact of our behaviors without taking responsibility for others' feelings and habitually spiraling into guilt and/or shame.**

reinforce separation but is balanced with the awareness of interdependence by acknowledging impact.

Maintaining awareness of the differentiation between stimulus, cause, and root (needs) empowers us to live in partnership rather than domination. Self-empathy supports us in taking responsibility for ourselves while we make space for others by not laying blame. In that spaciousness, it is possible that they may join us on our voyage to self-responsibility, empowerment, and compassion. As we shift our relationship to our experiences, our efforts ripple out from intrapersonal and interpersonal relationships to impact the collective.

SUMMARY

- ⌇ Exploring this key distinction, we learn to notice uncomfortable physical sensations and unpleasant emotions. In this acknowledgment, we can pause to distinguish stimulus from cause.

- ⌇ Differentiating stimulus from cause, we achieve deeper self-understanding. We can take responsibility for our inner experience as well as our external behavior and discover greater compassion, authenticity, and empowerment.

- ⌇ By exploring our thoughts and beliefs with curiosity, including assumptions about cause, we empower ourselves to discern how these contribute to the sensory input becoming a stimulus. Then, we can touch the underlying needs at the root.

- ⌇ Uncoupling stimulus and cause supports us in staying receptive to the impact of our behaviors without taking responsibility for others' feelings.

WALKING THE TALK:
A LIFE EXAMPLE FROM THE UNITED STATES

BY STEPHANIE BACHMANN MATTEI

Many years ago, I became determined to look into the anger growing within me. I remember one incident in particular when, filling out a long form over the internet (to offer an NVC-based training!), I was unsure about whether it would automatically save before being submitted. My boys were still very young, and I was accustomed to working with a lot of interruptions. I emphatically asked my husband to keep the internet open even if I was not sitting at my desk. After a break, I returned to my work only to realize with horror that he had closed the browser!

I stormed into the kitchen where he stood cooking and spoke from my pain. "Didn't I ask you to keep the browser open? I spent hours filling out that form, and now I have to start all over again!" (I was not even sure that was the case.) "Can't you listen to me for once?" And then came the core belief, chiming in from beyond my conscious awareness: "Do I even matter to you?"

When I heard myself say that (action awareness), I woke up, as if from a trance. I decided to look more deeply into this core belief around mattering. In self-empathy and in empathy with trusted others, I came to realize that while I feared not mattering to the person closest to me, deep down I actually did not matter to myself enough to function from a place of wellness and wholeness. That awareness marked a turning point for me.

I gave myself time to breathe into my fear and breathe out stillness. Once the body-mind system regained some soothing balance, I recognized that my disproportionate reactions were actually telling me something about myself. I chose to acknowledge and honor the energy of the needs that flowed within me and stepped further into my power by reaching out for empathic support.

When I realized I was telling myself that I didn't matter to my husband, I became aware that this belief prevented me from taking in the myriad of ways in which he poured his love into me daily. Once I compassionately realized that I wanted to matter to myself, I started to care for myself in new ways and asked for support from my husband and kids to help me do so. As a result of that inner work, the reactivity ultimately linked to that particular need drastically diminished.

PRACTICE

Self-Regulating at the Stimulus Gate

Awareness of body sensations at the moment of stimulation can support us in attuning to our internal process and caring for the needs at hand. This practice is designed to support you in identifying the sensory gate of the stimulus in retrospect as a preparation for future stimulation. This is a meditative self-reflective process, possibly with a journaling component. We invite you to find a quiet and comfortable space and pen and paper if you feel moved to write. We imagine this practice will take fifteen to thirty minutes.

Recall a moment of dysregulation and, with curiosity, try to identify the specific stimulus.

- ∼ What moved you out of the present moment and into a state of dysregulation?

- ∼ Which senses were involved? After identifying the stimulus and the sensory gate, recall which emotions that were most prominent in that moment of activation: Was it a boiling anger? A rush of embarrassment? Debilitating shame?

- ∼ Owning thoughts as the "cause" of feelings, mindfully inquire, "What was I thinking?" Did an image or a word emerge?

Now, imagine yourself in the same situation. Picture the stimulus happening and breathe, witnessing the sensory experience in your imagination. Observe your experience, as best you can, without judgment. Inquire with curiosity about the needs present in that moment. What is important to you? What does your heart long for?

As we move through these layers of self-connection, we reframe our experience. The more we hold ourselves with compassion, the more the trigger becomes a doorway to deeper self-understanding and healing.

22

PERSISTING AND DEMANDING

We can do anything we want to
if we stick to it long enough.

—HELEN KELLER

The key distinction between persisting and demanding juxtaposes two extreme expressions on a continuum of methods people use to satisfy needs. Discerning the energy of demands from the energy of persistence allows us to stay in our power without using it to dominate others. Learning how and when to persist can support us in sharing power to meet many needs.

Persistence—determination despite challenges and obstacles—is a dynamic force for change. In the Western world, we tend to persist for

> **Persistence—determination despite challenges and obstacles—is a dynamic force for change.**

ourselves, by ourselves. When grounded in a core value of inter-relationship, persistence is not a lonely job, but one that grows out of collective power. Because our well-being is directly linked to the well-being of others, persistence is born from a commitment to honor our values while caring for the needs of all. Demands, in contrast, typically come from a place of fear that we alone can investigate in order to find out what's important to us. In extreme cases, demands might also reveal a desperate cry to be heard and seen.

The more we practice NVC, the more we realize that persistence is interwoven with the intention to nurture connection and understanding. We tend toward strategies that maximize the possibility of satisfying everyone's needs, including our own. Even when strategies are not readily imaginable, all needs are held with care and a sense that they matter. There is a clear aim to engage with another person in the paradigm of partnership, not giving up, not giving in, nor using power-over. We trust in and rely on the process of giving and receiving even when it becomes, as Rosenberg calls it, "dogging for our needs."[1]

We can enhance our persistence by clarifying and staying connected to needs. At the same time, we intend to maintain awareness of the impact of our preferred strategies on others. Tuning in to what might keep others from persisting—especially in the case of a power differential that favors us—we can support them in staying in their power. Grounded in a sense of multiple possibilities, our creativity and partnership can be honed to find strategies that support the needs of all.

> **Tuning in to what might keep others from persisting—especially in the case of a power differential that favors us—we can support people in staying in their power.**

Making Demands

We make demands when we insist on getting our needs met, or met in a particular manner, even when the other person is not willing to support us. Demands relate to an attachment to outcome. Our intention and focus is on what matters to us alone, either individually or as a group. On the individual level, demands may reveal our disconnection from personal power; we do not see another way to meet our needs. Counterbalancing this sense of powerlessness, we leverage our status or role to get what we want.

Demands are especially likely to arise when we temporarily lose access to envisioning more than one strategy. There are, of course, also structural realities that concretely impact connection and access to more strategies. Or demands may occur

On the individual level, demands may reveal our disconnection from personal power.

when we confuse strategies with needs. This happens when we do not find the courage or do not trust our skills to honor and speak up for what matters to us. Or we may live in a social context where it is dangerous to do so. Whenever we hear our inner or outer dialogue infused with urgency, despair, or an "I have to have it!" energy, we might step back and observe whether we are experiencing a crisis of imagination regarding possible strategies. Our ability to stay connected to the energy of life will empower us to compassionately mourn when we do not see a way to manifest our needs in the world at this time.

Underlying demands, there is often a fear that our needs do not matter or that we cannot get them met. This fear arises from the framework of scarcity and separation many of us have internalized through patriarchal socialization or experience on a daily basis due to social discrimination. The deeper the fear, the stronger the "demand energy" that builds up within us. People from cultures geared toward collective power rather than individual power—or perceived lack of it—tend to trust that their personal needs are held by the community. The urgency behind a demand might stem from a lack of space to hold our own needs with compassion.

Demands in the Face of Structural Inequities

The urgency of demands is often directly proportional to the chronic experience of systemic violence. When all hope for a heartfelt mutual giving and receiving has been exhausted, the desperate call to be seen can take the form of demands. When there is a daily awareness that one's life is endangered, the anguish cannot be contained and may seek expression in demands as a tragic attempt to restore personal and collective power. With no leverage on the role, status, and systemic levels, we might wonder: how can power be collectively held onto?

Historically, public demands have been used as strategies to address structural violence and the abuse of power against so-called social minorities (which are in fact the global majority!). For example, the global present-day Black Lives Matter movement[2] and the Zapatista Uprising in Chiapas,[3] Mexico, in 1994, demanded that the needs, rights, and dignity of Black Americans and Indigenous Peoples respectively be recognized after hundreds of years of discrimination and social invisibility.

In these cases, the intensity of demands contributed to global awakening, sparked discussions on the alarming living conditions of certain groups, and mobilized resources. The demands "worked," up to a point. Yet the very act of presenting a list of "demands"—as both movements framed them—raises questions about what would happen if such movements were to gain power. Without an active commitment to nonviolence, many previously oppressed groups have, upon gaining power, tragically turned to oppressing others. The issues are complex, well beyond what this chapter can explore with sufficient care and depth, and so we leave these to the reader as questions. What would happen if, instead of demands, which arise from the domination mentality that underlies violence and inequity, a different kind of language could be used, emphasizing the intensity of the challenges without the separation mentality? For example, what would happen if the language were, "Unless these needs are attended to, we don't see any change possible in our conditions and lives. Without making the changes we are pointing to, life will continue as is, which will ultimately lead all humanity to extinction"? These kinds of questions take us into thorny territory regarding what power the disenfranchised hold. Many have indeed resorted to armed struggle. Controversy abounds in terms of both efficacy and spiritual morality of different approaches.

When in a position of systemic disempowerment, how do we use the power we do have to raise awareness of the inequities that have been experienced for centuries? While the options available for using the power we do have may seem limited to either power over others (and making demands) or spiraling into a powerless rage, we want to include here a well-known but rarely used pathway.

The civil rights movement offers us sundry examples of non-negotiable use of force to protect life and to have basic human needs acknowledged. From February to July 1960, African American students refused to leave after being denied service in the Greensboro sit-ins. As these students continued to sit at the lunch counters despite being told to leave, being harassed, and sometimes being physically attacked, we could interpret their actions as demands. Yet they were also determined to uphold the dignity and humanity of their "oppressor." They had been intentionally trained to absorb the violence without striking back. Furthermore, they sat immovable, resolutely unwilling to let themselves be dehumanized. Interdependence informed their actions.

Dogging for Our Needs

Persisting allows us to stand up for our own needs and also to support others in not giving up or giving in. When we open ourselves to the world of possibilities, we let go of attachment to specific people taking specific actions. In doing so we touch a sense of freedom. When we release a preferred strategy and stay connected with life-serving energy, we concretely seek solutions in partnership.

Persistence is rooted in a paradigm of mutuality and trust that our needs matter, first and foremost, to ourselves. This trust is the foundation for persistence. The process of learning to trust that our needs matter is a journey in its own right. We often struggle on the individual level, and many of us wrestle

Persistence is rooted in a paradigm of mutuality and trust that our needs matter.

on the systemic level as well, to trust that our needs matter. Childhood and social experiences have often taught us the opposite, sometimes subtly and sometimes blatantly. For those of us whose access to safety and resources has been obstructed, such trust is slim to nonexistent. We often long for companionship on this journey from others who have themselves managed to restore their own sense of trust. Greater access to resources will provide an easier path to restoring trust.

When persisting, our body may experience tension, as we are venturing into unknown waters. Yet we might also touch a sense of clarity, knowing that we are ultimately responsible and generally capable of caring for our own needs in relationship with others. Our mind focuses on persevering for our needs rather than against someone else's strategies or even needs. The brain operates within the window of stress tolerance, and the social circuitry is actively engaged to be in relationship.

Our ability to persist in the paradigm of interdependence stems from self-awareness and a sense of agency. We invite others to share power as they engage with us (power-with). If we wonder whether someone is leaning toward compliance or compromise as we persist, we may choose to refocus on the relationship before addressing the issue at hand. We might support mutuality by making a request like, "Do you have any specific strategies in mind?" Or we could direct our curiosity to making connection requests that contribute to further understanding and mutuality, such as, "Can you help me understand what is preventing you from . . . ?" Whatever the challenge, we seek to hold it as a dilemma to solve together rather than a conflict that separates us. Recommitting moment by moment to making requests rooted in mutuality, we draw deeply from a source of goodwill within so that we may persist without attachment to outcomes.

If we wonder whether someone is leaning toward compliance or compromise as we persist, we may choose to refocus on the relationship before addressing the issue at hand. . . . Whatever the challenge, we seek to hold it as a dilemma to solve together rather than a conflict that separates us.

Developing the Skills to Persist

The primary components of persisting with compassion include awareness of our own needs, valuing the other person's needs, and free choice. Committed to dialogue, we remain open to hearing a no; we seek strategies that work for everyone. We advocate for our needs boldly and hold our preferences lightly. In discerning whether we are persisting or demanding, we might ask ourselves the following questions:

- Am I holding the other person's needs as fully as I'm holding my own?
- Am I open to hearing no?
- Am I clearly differentiating my needs from the strategies I envision would meet my needs?
- Am I willing to let go of any strategy I'm envisioning?

If we answer no to any of these questions, we are likely experiencing an underlying sense of separation and scarcity that will convey the energy of a demand. Finding compassion for this space just as it is, we can step into an empathic field by ourselves or with a trusted friend, turning our persistence inward, toward self-care.

In persistence, we dig deeper to clarify our needs and the needs of others. Our determination conveys the sacred intention to prioritize connection and uphold a consciousness of interdependence.

Mindful attention toward potential impact is upheld to the best of our ability, as we welcome the possibility of our persistence transforming into a shift. Life-alienating impact may arise when we harbor judgments that value some needs over others or when we operate under the systemic conditioning that has us prioritize the needs of some people over the needs of other people.

This subconscious dynamic is commonly seen in the relationship between adults and children. "Cut it out, will you?" is a message that many children hear. As adults, we are often pained to see the determination with which a child connects to needs, such as play, that we have long since set aside. Disconnection from our own needs and lack of awareness of impact can lead us to make demands of our children when they persist. We might tell them that they need to be quiet while we are working . . . or else! Making such demands will likely contribute to their desensitization to the needs of others, too, continuing the cycle.

Ironically, the very persistence that we often seek to shut down in our children is seen as an asset when exercised between adults on a level playing field. Our demands as parents may stunt our children's abilities to stand up for their needs as adults. It is easy, potentially mindless, and socially acceptable to leverage power to prioritize our needs over a child's or to insist on the valuing of some needs over others, all in the guise of educating them. Awareness of this dynamic invites us to pause when we experience resistance with a person younger than ourselves. We can ask ourselves whether our efforts would qualify as persisting or demanding, given this power differential. For example, do we actively query about the needs of a young person while persisting to meet our need for peace? Or do we assume they know we are open to hearing their needs as we focus on speaking about our own? In the case of a power differential, when we are in the up-power role, how do we transmit openness and seek clarity about others' needs, rather than assuming that those with less power will ask to be heard?

In an up-power role, how do we transmit openness and seek clarity about others' needs, rather than assuming those with less power will ask to be heard?

With awareness, especially when we have role or status power—as we do when in the role of parent or simply by being male—we may tune into the possibility that those around us may not have the skills, willingness, or ability to persist. Perceived and real power differentials can have a significant impact on our ability to be creative and exercise choice.

Opting Not to Persist

Persistence is grounded in a sense of personal and communal power. Those of us who have role, status, or systemic power will find it easier to persist. For those who experience less power in certain arenas, the effort to persist can feel overwhelming. Internalized messages, especially at the systemic level, condition us to either trust in or give up on our personal and collective power, depending on our social status.

Persisting may also put us in the path of danger. People whose gender identity does not match the sex they were assigned at birth, for example, may be endangered when they persist in stating the pronoun they use. Tragically, this attempt to honor their own dignity increases their risk of being harmed.[4] Those in a more powerful social location can support those who are not, enhancing partnership.

Whenever our energy is free from attachment or resistance (internal, external, or both), we can tap into fuller creativity and a world of possibilities. The untethered mind can take in new ideas, supporting power-with and nurturing what we value most.

SUMMARY

- ↶ Making a distinction between persisting and demanding helps us to clarify our mind frame and connect with our needs when we notice strong energy around what we want.

- ↶ When we focus our awareness on interdependence, persisting allows us to stand up for our own needs and also support others in not giving up or giving in.

- ↶ If we wonder whether someone is leaning toward compliance or compromise as we persist, we may choose to refocus on the relationship before addressing the issue at hand.

- ↶ Whatever the challenge, this key distinction invites us to hold it as a dilemma to solve together rather than a conflict that separates us.

WALKING THE TALK:
A LIFE EXAMPLE FROM CHINA

BY LIU YI, CNVC CERTIFIED TRAINER

My partner and I have divergent habits of spending money, likely shaped by different upbringings. In short, I hear her express joy in spending money for things she deems important, while I am more likely to say, "Please reconsider if you really need this."

I always thought I was making requests when it came to spending, because I saw myself being open to hearing her no at any time. Then I realized she rarely says no. In fact, it had been some time since I'd checked the energy that I'd been attaching to these messages or asked how she received them.

When I learned she often felt guilty hearing my "requests," I realized there was more work to be done on my side. Indeed, there is a perceived power imbalance in this area between us. I earn more money, while her contributions to sustain the family are less quantifiable.

I asked myself how I would truly feel if she continued her trajectory of spending. I saw that my frustration might turn toward anger, and that I held blame and judgments about my partner and her actions. I noticed that the energy I carried left little space to honor her needs behind spending. I awakened then to the consequences of a power imbalance intensified by our Chinese culture where no is not easily expressed. The one playing a more powerful role in these circumstances is called to be extra conscious when persisting, in order to truly honor needs on both sides.

I did more inner work to connect to the needs we *shared* around money—long-term sustainability and trusting our own resourcefulness. Thereafter, during a conversation about money, I honestly expressed my longing for contributing to predictability. I shared that my persistence was linked to supporting us both in living the life we dreamed of by nurturing more teamwork. I proposed she try tracking expenses so that we could make financial plans for the future together.

When I asked how she received this, she said she was feeling sad and afraid I would judge her. She shared that she couldn't find the app I recommended for bookkeeping. I felt relieved to hear her honest response and appreciated the opportunity to be present with her. With curiosity, I asked to hear more about her concerns around acceptance and what needs she sought to meet in spending money. She explained she felt joyful spending—secure, and valuing herself.

Grounded in trusting both my partner and our resourcefulness together, I felt grateful that we truly heard each other. I chose to let go of my strategy request and just enjoyed our connection, waiting to see what would unfold. Interestingly, a shift occurred. In the days that followed, I embraced our differences, and my partner announced that she had started to track her expenses and our income! I am happy to celebrate with her my persistence and willingness to shift gears. We both cherish our connection and are not attached to an expectation around what happens next.

PRACTICE

Persisting Toward Creative Strategies

Empathy can support us in connection, clarity, and creativity as we navigate a dilemma in search of strategies that serve many needs. This exercise is designed as a playful practice in partnership that supports awareness of needs based on persisting rather than demanding. If a partner is not available, it may be done as a journal entry with the writer playing two roles alternately. We invite you to find a comfortable, quiet space with a partner or a pen and paper. We imagine that this practice will take twenty to thirty minutes.

Decide together what the fictional dilemma is. We encourage choosing a challenge that could come up when you are doing something you both perceive as fun, such as discussing how to make dessert together, deciding what to visit in another city, or determining how to paddle a tandem canoe. Decide who is Person A and who is Person B and what strategies you each want that don't align.

Now, for Person A to practice persisting:

~ Consider and ground yourself in the needs linked to your strategy of choice. Then imagine what the needs of your partner might be. Check to be sure that you are holding their needs with the same quality of care as your own. How does that feel in the body?

~ Express yourself (using observations, feelings, needs, and requests) to begin a dialogue.

~ Offer empathy to clarify and care for the needs of the other person, making sure you are maintaining an embodied connection to your needs as well.

~ Now connect again with your needs. Has there been a shift?

~ Notice your body. Are you feeling tense or relaxed? Is your heart open or closed? Do you sense the capacity and self-responsibility to touch your needs regardless of outcome (personal empowerment)?

~ If there has not been a shift, notice what is present in terms of body sensations. Inquire into the needs that you see are in play, yours and theirs, and with a connection request, invite Person B to join in finding possible solutions with you.

~ Without choosing a solution strategy, check in with yourself: Are you experiencing a greater sense of abundance than you think you might if you had not engaged with yourself and Person B this way?

~ Invite Person B to share their experience.

Now, switch roles, and have Person B practice persisting.

23

SHIFT AND COMPROMISE

Don't compromise yourself.
You're all you've got.

—JANIS JOPLIN

The key distinction that explores shifting and compromising sheds light on some possible choices when our preferences are at odds with someone else's. An exploration of this key supports awareness of needs in this situation. Appreciating the needs present can contribute to understanding and mutuality.

Will we give up on what we want or attempt to convince them to do what we like? Will we seek to get at least part of what we want, as they seek to do the same in a compromise?[1] Or will we look for a shift[2] by opening ourselves to the deeper needs behind our desire and listening with like attention to what matters most to them? If we engage in such a shift, then, in the words of Marshall Rosenberg, "we do not look for compromise; rather, we seek to resolve the conflict to everyone's complete satisfaction."[3] The willingness and ability to shift rather than compromise stems from awareness of interconnection—tracking the needs at stake for all involved in the situation, assessing potential impacts of the strategies considered, and courageously attending to power differentials within the relationship.

Our willingness to shift often has a mysterious effect on the energetic field between or among people. An openhearted disposition is physiologically transmitted to the other parties. Registered by the brain as a basic sense of safety, this experience creates a nonthreatening space that allows them the possibility of shifting as well. Such shift in the relational space also assists us in tapping into deeper levels of creativity that make it possible to find solutions that work for everyone.

Compromise: A Win-Win Solution?

When two people or groups are in conflict over strategies, they often seek a compromise. One or both decide to give up on some of their needs by prioritizing other needs, or by giving in to some parts of another's strategy, even though they are not completely satisfied with this arrangement. We might decide to compromise because we are socialized to view compromise as essential to peaceful living or as the only option for collaboration. Or we may suffer a crisis of imagination due to trauma, cultural prohibition, or a lack of role or status power. We usually compromise while earnestly attempting to satisfy needs, such as those for peace or partnership. Yet over time we might feel resentful or have regrets because we have given up on some of our own needs when we answered with a partial rather than a wholehearted yes. And we may even make ourselves or others pay for it!

> We might decide to compromise because we are socialized to view compromise as essential to peaceful living or as the only option for collaboration.

Compromise stems from a paradigm of separation rooted in scarcity and the idealization of individuality. (It is either my needs or yours, or we "split the difference.") Within that model of scarcity, our urge to compromise can also stem from systemic violence compounded by intersectionality. For example, a First Nations woman is both racially discriminated against and faces disadvantages as a woman. Consequently, she is likely to have substantially less access to resources. As her needs are neither socially recognized nor valued, compromise may be a strategy that does support her survival within a patriarchal system. This paradigm of separation and individuality also heralds sacrifice and selflessness as tools for harmonious living. In this mode, we usually believe we are dependent or independent, and may see people as instruments for or obstacles to meeting our needs. Our ability and willingness to recognize our interdependence is numbed, and our quality of connection with all living beings and ourselves is compromised in this mode.

Shift: The Willingness to Be Moved

When operating from the paradigm of interdependence, we are aware of being linked by universal human needs, by our actions always affecting one another, and by having finite resources we all share with the rest of life. We have the capacity to connect inside ourselves with what deeply matters beneath our preferred strategy. In this exploration, we begin to free ourselves from conditioned preferences and the protective structures that may have served us until now. Reaching a greater dimension beyond the boundaries of our skin, we experience both the heart of who we are and the universal energy of life.

We may begin by holding our subjective personal experience with compassion. If we find ourselves navigating challenging situations while feeling depleted and confused, among many other possible uncomfortable feelings, we can open ourselves to this experience with acceptance and love. We can sit with discomfort and notice how it feels in the body, in the breath. By allowing our feelings to just be, we can slowly connect to the needs within. Feeling into our experience, we give ourselves the opportunity to grow, to contribute to the conversation, and to authentically support our relationships. Considering the power imbalances in play in every relationship, we can make an extra effort to return to our values at times when we are in a position of benefiting from a role or status that confers us more power. At times, denying parts of our own experience, whatever they are, in favor of upholding some spiritual value such as compassion or equanimity may seem tempting. Yet whenever we attempt to rise above our experience and deny our emotions, we escape into a spiritual bypass. It is only when we embrace ourselves fully that we empower ourselves to reengage with others more compassionately and creatively. An undefended heart is nurtured with care and patience and is rooted in self-knowledge.

It is essential that our willingness to shift be born from this self-connection, embedded in the wholeness of life. NVC as an approach to life offers clear processes to support us in deeply attuning to ourselves as we experience the life energy within and around us. A sense of being grounded in what matters to us stems from our clarity about which specific needs we are experiencing and the quality, depth, and intensity of our feelings. This comprehension supports us in deciding moment by moment how much to persist in conversation with another while also making space for shifts to emerge in either of us. Our overarching intention is to honor our needs, including the needs for contribution and acknowledgment of our interdependence.

While we may be conditioned to hold compromising as a relational gesture of love or social justice, in compromising, we may lose sight of our own personal or collective needs. Self-empathy can support us in honoring who we are and in slowly unveiling the experiences and socialization we have been shaped by. This modality invites us to connect with and establish needs-based limits.

> STEPHANIE: When my son and I were in Macau, we found it more challenging than anticipated to find vegetarian food. One night, some of our NVC group wanted to try a restaurant that was renowned for its crab dishes. We sat down at the big round table, only to realize that the restaurant did not have any vegetarian food. Because my son and I have a nonnegotiable, needs-based limit to not eat animals, we told the group as a relational gesture that the two of us could go somewhere

else while the group enjoyed their crab. Socialization, after all, has taught us not to be a burden on others! But as NVC practitioners, we all decided to look together at the needs we were valuing the most—enjoying one another's company and sharing some food. One person suggested we could look for a different restaurant where everyone could find something to eat. Those who wanted crab could eat less and then go for some crab later on that evening.

NVC practices allow us to be grounded in our experience while also opening up to the relational encounter of the other person or people. When we recognize our common humanity, we allow ourselves to be moved by the needs of others. This shift stems from staying firmly connected with our own needs and graciously acting from that power.

> When we recognize our common humanity, we allow ourselves to be moved by the needs of others. . . . We don't experience conflict so much as a shared dilemma held jointly.

Listening with curiosity to the other person's feelings and needs, their dreams and their fears, we allow our minds to reframe the conflict differently. Practicing perspective-taking,[4] we grow our ability to imagine how a situation appears to another person. Understanding how they emotionally relate to and cognitively make sense of the situation supports us in releasing attachment to our views. This allows for a true shift to emerge. Our awareness moves from separation to interdependence, from aloneness to companionship. We don't experience conflict so much as a shared dilemma held jointly. Together, we may look at the needs, resources, and impacts we have on one another and seek a solution that cares for all of these.

Connecting to the needs perceived as being in conflict, we are likely to gain clarity about which strategies would meet most needs, perhaps mourning some while still holding them with a consciousness of care. In this way, we can accept what is rather than resisting what we deem unpleasant and clinging to what we enjoy. Mourning then becomes a practice of resilience,[5] as we connect energetically to what matters most. We might relate to needs in a way that acknowledges them as unmet in the moment, while still appreciating their aliveness. Our minds and hearts may touch peace in the midst of unmet needs. Within the process of shifting, our priority is connection, and we remain openhearted and vulnerable to ourselves and the other person or people involved. Our eyes and hearts are open to expand into this new reality emerging moment by moment. We become aware that we don't have to give up on our needs and give in to the other person's wishes in order to offer support for another.

If we are rooted in self-connection and release our attachment to a particular strategy, we may find ourselves willing to shift after hearing the needs of someone else, while also harboring a clear understanding of which needs of ours will be met by shifting to a different strategy. We might shift because we hear and take to heart the impact that our initial strategy would have on another person or people. When we realize that their yes would come at a cost, our compassion may awaken, and we can find ourselves moved effortlessly.

From the outside, our shift may appear to be a compromise. Sometimes it will result in a completely new strategy that neither party could see before, and sometimes it may look like going along with the other person's proposed strategy. The difference between compromise and shift is what motivates our actions, not about which strategy we employ. The inner experience of a shift is very different from the inner experience of compromise. Because we began the process by listening deeply to ourselves while also listening to someone else—which does not equate with agreement—compassion and creativity have been our guides. A shift toward peace naturally follows when we have anchored ourselves in the needs for choice and care for the relationship. We maintain connection with both ourselves and the other person, and this in itself may generate joy.

Mind the Half Yes and Half No!

Whenever fear of repercussions, a sense of obligation, duty, guilt, or shame leads one of the parties to say yes to a strategy without feeling entirely satisfied with it, everyone ends up paying the price. Resentment seeps in as unresolved pain surfaces. While giving or receiving such a yes offers temporary relief, in the long run, submission comes at a cost. The more we feel disconnected from a sense of agency, the more likely we are to experience stress and potentially trauma, particularly in the absence of external support and self-compassion. Through the practice of NVC, we are invited, when feeling ambivalent, to engage in dialogue. With curiosity, we can explore possibilities in partnership until there is a sense that both parties are fully behind a strategy.

We might find ourselves giving a mixed yes to a request for a variety of reasons. We may feel fatigued and disconnected, or we might feel restless and anxious to move on. We could be driven by an energy to please or by a fear of exposing ourselves. Whatever our patterns or specific situations might be, we can learn to pause to consider whether we are defaulting to a habitual response without connecting to needs. If we tend to tip toward the consideration of others' needs, we might try exercising the opposite muscle, cultivating spaciousness outside of our regular habit, thus contributing to the possibility of a shift. If we tend to respond in ways that please others in order to contribute or to keep the peace, we might ask, "Would you be willing to give me twenty-four hours to return with an answer on that?"

On the other hand, we may be prone to giving a half no for an answer. If we notice we instinctively protect ourselves without awareness of interdependence, we could ask for some space to think before responding, to allow us to connect with a wider perspective of the needs involved and possibly shift. Similarly, if we notice another person's body language retracting as they verbally agree to our request, we can invite them to take some time before responding and let them know we are open to hearing a no. Receiving a half no, we might use the opportunity to arouse our curiosity and continue the dialogue.

A Consideration of Power Differentials

Explicitly naming our openness to hearing a no is crucial when we are in a position of power in the relationship. While we all share the same universal needs, we have different levels of access to resources. Equality and equity are not one and the same. Even when people in up-power roles and status aim to engage in sharing power, the reality of their structural power affects the relationship.

It takes a tremendous amount of courage to say no to someone or to an entity such as the government or church, whose structural power is greater than our own. If we experience less power than another person or system, the courage to say no may entail working with our fears first, so we are not reactively driven by them. We may feel called to do the inner work of dissipating enemy images around the person(s) with more power, individually and collectively. We may also do the inner work of releasing the fear of consequences, as many humans have done in times of collective struggle. That transformation frees us to share energy with groups that promote social change. Participating in these efforts can then help mobilize resources to transform the very structures that perpetuate inequalities of power.

The Southern Christian Leadership Conference led by Martin Luther King Jr. to fight segregation in Birmingham, Alabama (1963), actively trained high school and college students to stand up for civil rights by sitting with determination and dignity at segregated lunch counters while being denied service. Even when their safety was threatened, the students' training allowed them to stay connected with the humanity of all involved. In the words of American statesperson and chair of the Student Nonviolent Coordinating Committee John Lewis, the students used their bodies as nonviolent instruments of change.[6] Resistance with dignity—whether to our own habits that no longer serve or to authority in the name of social change—takes courageous and disciplined practice. Opening our hearts fully allows us to retrieve energy once lost to resistance, whether to uphold enemy images or to keep the fear of consequences at bay. Once integrated, this energy allows us to focus on what matters most, effecting the change we wish to see in the world.

Conversely, if we find ourselves at the top of a hierarchy, whether perceived or real, it can take rigorous determination to be open to hearing a no when an existing social structure typically supports us in getting what we want. In Western mainstream parenting for example, we are conditioned to expect compliance and to try to control our children, especially when they tell us no. When we want to shift from control to connection, from fear to love, it is essential to let our children know that their needs and free will matter to us. As we have more role power, we can tell them we will find a different way if they decline, and we can partner with them to come up with different strategies that hold everyone's needs with the utmost care. This may call us to step out of our comfort zone and exercise greater creativity. It takes time to establish trust when our children are habituated to thinking their needs don't matter. As we attend to that sense of deep mattering, the possibility of solving dilemmas together from a place of mutual care emerges.

Shifting toward partnership in holding dilemmas together, we learn to assess potential impacts for all involved. We also find ourselves better able to care for our own needs while simultaneously supporting others with theirs. Tending to power differentials with awareness, we compassionately allow for a shift to emerge. Alternatively, we may mourn our limitations to meet all the needs present. Creativity expands as we tap into the universal energy that flows through all life and multiplies our resources exponentially.

SUMMARY

- ↢ This key distinction highlights that our willingness and ability to shift rather than compromise stems from our awareness of interdependence.

- ↢ The capacity to access and cultivate this willingness is affected by our status and systemic power.

- ⮑ When discerning a shift from a compromise, we can track the needs at stake for all involved in the situation, as well as any inequalities.

- ⮑ Leaning into a shift, we allow ourselves to be moved while grounded in our needs.

- ⮑ Courageously, with openness to shift, we can attend to power differentials within the relationship.
  - If we find ourselves with less access to power and resources, we might cultivate self-compassion, love for our "enemies," and the willingness to face consequences.
  - If we find ourselves with more access to power and resources, we may cultivate compassion by mindfully considering the potential impact of our choices and actions and holding other peoples' needs with greater care.

WALKING THE TALK:
A LIFE EXAMPLE FROM NIGERIA

BY FRANCA N. ONYIBOR, CNVC CERTIFIED TRAINER

I, Franca, was part of a team in Nigeria involved in a dialogue between the farmers and the herders, who have been in conflict for years over land. Both parties expressed willingness to meet after we, the facilitators, visited the leaders of each three times, offering them the space to tell their stories of deep pain. Farmers held the land as more precious than their lives, and herders held their cows in the same regard. Crops, property, and land had been destroyed. The death of people and cows compounded this great pain, and the livelihoods of both groups were damaged and/or threatened. We, the facilitators, listened without judgment to the leaders on both sides, our deep empathy touching what mattered most. By the end of the third visit, I witnessed a shift in each of the leaders as they agreed to move from the strategy of killing and destroying property to using a dialogue process to resolve their conflict.

On the first day of the dialogue, the two groups separated and the participants in each group were given the opportunity to express their experiences in this conflict in a safe environment and receive from the facilitators deep empathic listening for their pain. This gave all participants an opportunity to experience firsthand the quality of listening that they would later offer to each other during the dialogue. Next, the two groups came together in a circle.

This phase began with a face-to-face dialogue with each participant given the opportunity to speak to three guiding questions, one at a time, beginning with this one: "How are you right now as you think about the conflict and its consequences?" This question, which addresses both interdependence and the impact of each party's actions on the other, guided the dialogue for the remainder of the day. As each person spoke, they chose someone in the circle to listen to them and this listener was invited from time to time to say back the main message of what they heard the speaker say. All those who chose to speak were deeply heard. This experience of mutual sharing, listening, and reflecting back continued for three days. As each side was given the space to share and to listen to one another's stories and pain, I witnessed frozen hearts melting. This shift was expressed through their words to one another, some of which I share below:

"I have come to realize that when we understand each other and know the pain we each carry, these go a long way in helping to resolve conflicts."

"What I have learnt through this dialogue cannot be quantified; if we'd had this kind of dialogue earlier, the conflicts in our communities would have been minimal."

"I am happy that together we are close to a solution that would work for each group. I did not know this would be possible."

Once this miraculous shift happened, both parties continued to explore together strategies that would resolve the conflict in a way that attended to the needs of all.

PRACTICE

Cultivating Awareness of Shift and Compromise

Awareness of body sensations can alert us to our tendency to compromise, thus creating space for conscious choice. This kinesthetic practice invites you to experientially connect with the need that comes up for you during a conflict with another person as you open to the possibility of shift. You may record and play back this meditation practice or read through it once in preparation for engaging with the material more slowly on a second read through. We invite you to find a comfortable, quiet space. We imagine this practice will take fifteen to twenty-five minutes.

Choose a situation that is about a four or a five on a ten-point scale, where ten is the most challenging. Connect with your needs and imagine the needs of another person before beginning this exercise. Take a moment to acknowledge to yourself the power differentials in the relationship. Feel free to pause as you explore what you feel drawn to.

Prepare yourself by coming to a standing position, or any position in which you experience a sense of balance, with your feet parallel, hip-width apart. Relaxing your shoulders away from your ears, draw your chin slightly back. And finally, align your head over your torso.

And now, bring awareness to bodily sensations. Feel into the subtle movements of your body that maintain its upright, balanced position. Remember that it took each of us about a year to learn to get up and stand.

Now direct awareness inward, to the body breathing. Become aware of the natural flow of the breath:

- *Breathing in, I am aware I am breathing in.*
- *Breathing out, I am aware I am breathing out.*[7]

Invite awareness to focus on the feet. Feel them fully rooted to the earth, gravity drawing you down. The earth supports your existence by supporting your feet. Feel the touch points between your feet and the earth.

From this center of clarity, you may witness all that is occurring in the mind and the body . . . in you and around you.

And now, invite awareness of the challenge you have chosen. Connect with what need you hold dear and breathe into it, feeling the sensations that this awareness brings to the body. Experience these sensations for several breaths, in and out. If you become aware of a different need, allow the shift to occur naturally as you witness sensations in the body. Notice thoughts and emotions without intentionally following them with more thought. Allow all of it to be.

Is there a shifting of the weight forward, backward, or side to side as you touch the need? If so, notice how any such movements affect the whole body and the overall sense of balance. Check if and when your feet lose full contact with the ground.

Now consider the needs of the other person. Imagine yourself touching these needs lightly, as you remain grounded in the experience of your own needs.

If you notice resistance, return your attention to the experience of what matters to you until your full attention is with the sensations in your body. Then touch the needs of the other person, perhaps just for a second, before returning to your own needs. If your needs shift, follow this shift, and breathe into the energy there.

Allow yourself to touch these alternative needs again, listening to your body's feedback about its groundedness. Explore this balancing point, taking all the time you want.

REFLECTION

~ Was it possible to discern when you began to lose touch with what you value deeply? What body awareness, if any, contributed to this knowing?

∼ How did you find your balance again? What feelings did you experience as you endeavored to reestablish balance and self-connection?

∼ How might this practice be of value to you in your daily life?

24

APPRECIATION AND
APPROVAL/COMPLIMENTS/PRAISE

Compliments and praise, for their part,
are tragic expressions of fulfilled needs.

—MARSHALL B. ROSENBERG

This key distinction—exploring the difference between appreciation and approval, compliments, or praise—acknowledges that our words carry conscious and unconscious meanings that impact the receiver on multiple levels. How we express what we enjoy matters, as our sharing manifests and reinforces relational dynamics. Mindful feedback in intra- and interpersonal relationships contributes to cultural shifts toward a paradigm of power-with.

> How we express what we enjoy matters, as our sharing manifests and reinforces relational dynamics.

Compliments and praise are typically intended to encourage and help people feel good about themselves. We might enjoy offering praise and compliments, as we value contributing to what we imagine is others' well-being. On the receiving end, we may be happy to be praised, hearing that someone is pleased with our behavior. We may experience the body softening and pleasurable feelings arising, from relief to joy. Needs to "be seen" and "appreciated" might be fully alive in our heart.[1]

While the energy behind praise and compliments is most often one of celebration, the language can give away some unexamined assumptions about power differential in relationships and convey unintended moralistic judgments. We are socialized to communicate within a framework of dichotomies, and praise/compliments/approval fall into that category. The shadow of praise is criticism, compliments are the opposite of reprimands, and approval is the reverse of disapproval. All can trigger discomfort and powerlessness as they intentionally or unintentionally leverage structural power. Dignity, freedom, and connection may be compromised by a well-intended compliment.

Rosenberg's approach is grounded in an understanding that human connection is based on joyful giving and receiving. Unlike praise, compliments, and approval, NVC's appreciative feedback is rooted in a paradigm of partnership and mutuality. In this model, we become aware of the feelings and needs we are touching and share them with specific observations. When praised, we aspire to learn to elicit clear, appreciative feedback as well as give ourselves the appreciation that joyfully nourishes us.

To Praise or Not to Praise?

Rosenberg's work passionately examines the relationship between language and violence. "Perhaps you are surprised that I regard praise and compliments to be life-alienating," he says. "Notice, however, that appreciation expressed in this form reveals little of what's going on in the speaker; it establishes the speaker as someone who sits in judgment. I define judgments—both positive and negative—as life-alienating communication."[2] Most praise is couched in the verb "to be," followed by an adjective the speaker uses to describe the receiver, as in, "You are awesome/smart/beautiful!" In the practice of NVC, these adjectives are considered static labels—moralistic judgments born from the right/wrong mentality. Subconsciously, praise may contribute more to distance than connection. It separates the person praising from the one receiving praise. The former uses their power over the other to define them. The latter is the recipient of the judgment. This power differential unfolds even with positive judgments. A subjective sense of powerlessness is unwittingly reinforced in the receiver.

Approval, compliments, and praise may be internalized into a "fixed" identity—intelligent, beautiful, cute, or cheerful, for example—rather than contributing to what psychologist and Stanford researcher Carol Dweck calls a "growth mindset," in which traits and abilities can be developed and improved.[3] Praise discourages risk-taking by implicitly sending a message that setbacks and failures are shameful (fixed mindset), rather than learning opportunities (growth mindset). And this is just one hidden cost.

"You picked up that new music piece so quickly—you are really smart!" unintentionally suggests that if one does not learn quickly, one is not smart. Coupling success with perceived cognitive abilities reinforces the fixed mindset that performance is a reflection of identity.

Praise stimulates a host of complex responses. Receiving compliments may awaken in us a sense of dependency on praise or even entitlement, shifting our focus from an intrinsic to an extrinsic point of reference. Instead of staying connected to what pleases us, we focus on pleasing others or working for a reward. Praise and compliments encourage us to "make choices dependent on external sources of approval or disapproval rather than on an awareness of our own needs," write CNVC certified trainers Raj Gill, Lucy Leu, and Judi Morin in the *Nonviolent Communication Toolkit for Facilitators.*[4] We can choose to relate to our search for external approval with compassion, understanding that our attempts to please others likely stem from an intention to meet needs for acceptance, security, belonging, and love. This dynamic puts the giver of praise in a role of authority, reinforcing how we should behave and impairing self-determination.

Writer and speaker on human behavior and education Alfie Kohn aligns evidence to attest that "a good deal of research has found that intrinsic motivation does indeed decline as a result of praise."[5] Conversely, fear, insecurity, and performance anxiety may rise as we seek to live up to the compliment. While praise is likely intended to boost self-esteem, it can ironically erode unconditional acceptance and reduce creativity and self-expression. Internalizing an evaluation of what we "are" renders us vulnerable to receiving other evaluations. As Kohn reminds us, "every verbal reward contains within it the seed of a verbal punishment."[6] For this reason, we may receive praise by tightening inside, guarding ourselves against shadowy messages that threaten to haunt us. When our starting point is one of self-doubt, praise will not support us in becoming more confident, as we will likely disregard it. In fact, whenever the mind is offered information that contradicts its existing point of view, it quickly generates counterarguments to further disprove what does not align with its beliefs.

> While praise is likely intended to boost self-esteem, it can ironically erode unconditional acceptance and reduce creativity and self-expression.

Another layer of separation and anxiety arises when praise is framed as a comparison.

> KRISTIN: A supervisor once told me "You are so much better at that than the last person who worked here!" My relief and joy at having contributed collided with self-consciousness in the present and fear of failure in the future: What if other employees overheard, thought there was favoritism, and started to avoid me? And would those exact words be spoken to the employee who would someday take my place?

Not only is connection with ourselves jeopardized by comparisons, but also our connection with both the speaker and the person we are being compared to. Praise and comparison, especially when public, are more likely to breed rivalry than collaboration.

A Paradigm Apart

Praise leverages authority and power differentials. Moralistic judgments such as "you are a fantastic helper," or "good work!" are often delivered with pride and care, yet inadvertently support right/wrong and "should" thinking. These judgments also imply that where

Praise that perpetuates stereotypes, discrimination, and societal oppression reinforces the power of the dominant group.

there are rewards, there are also punishments in the form of disapproval, criticism, or withholding praise. Praise, and its potential absence, can paradoxically amplify the idea that we are not innately connected with love and may actually be deficient in our very nature.

Praise, approval, and compliments are powerful tools to uphold and transmit systemic beliefs, as in the case of Western patriarchal culture. Praise that perpetuates stereotypes, discrimination, and societal oppression reinforces the power of the dominant group. Praise can also be used as a tool to ensure behavioral conformity, further marginalizing many who do not fit into the conventional parameters. Intersectionality exacerbates grave power imbalances entrenched in praise, and the inherent dignity of every person's participation in community goes unrecognized. Some examples:

Reinforcing Systemic Beliefs	Praise	Hidden Systemic Message
Traditional gender role stereotypes	"He is a good father; he spends time with his kids."	A woman is expected to care for her children; she is just fulfilling her "normal" role. No more nor less is expected of her.
Individualism and meritocracy	"You had a humble start and have really worked your way up to senior manager!"	Success equates to personal achievement without any help or benefit from structural access to resources.
A worldview based on domination	"I am so proud of you! You got first place! You are the best!"	There is only room for a few to be successful, so it's a race to the top.

Racial stereotypes: Ascription of intellectual inferiority	(To a Black person) "You are so articulate!"	What a surprise, since Black people do not have the same intellectual capacity as White people!
Sexist stereotypes/ sexual objectification.	"I'm in love with the shape of you."	Humans are seen as sexual objects.

Praise as a Socialization Strategy

Praise can be a powerful extrinsic motivator for living beings, and it has long been held as an effective tool in enhancing performance and in shaping behavior where positional power imbalances exist. Such dynamics are in place in a parent/child, teacher/student, and employee/ manager relationship. Praise can also be leveraged for effect, even if inadvertently, according to socio-structural imbalances around gender, age, class, and race.

In the evolution of child-rearing, the rise of what psychohistorian Lloyd deMause calls "the socializing mode" in the late nineteenth and twentieth centuries prioritized raising children to conform to social expectations. One of the three main strategies for behavioral control in children became praise as a form of psychological manipulation—the other two being corporal punishment and shaming.[7]

Approval, compliments, and praise are sometimes given in an attempt to control behavior through a verbal reward, or with an agenda beyond the intention to connect, as when "productive" behavior is "reinforced" on a work team or self-esteem is "built" in kids. Compliments intended as a gift are also often leveraged to extrinsically motivate behavior. A parent may convey approval with a compliment, hoping the behavior will continue if reinforced. They might also convey conditional love and acceptance: If you do what I want, I will show you positive attention/ warmth, but if you don't, I will ignore or reprimand you.[8]

People often feel uncomfortable receiving such praise without knowing why.

KRISTIN: I remember one of my sons bristling at praise for his new haircut that was shorter than he'd wanted it to be. Adult friends and relatives likely intended to express their comfort with his choice and encourage him to keep his hair a length that was socially acceptable for boys. The praise conveyed no sense of curiosity about how my son felt about his hair.

All of us have given and received approval, compliments, and praise. In reflecting on that, we can celebrate the values these strategies were meant to meet, while mourning any unintended consequences such as reducing connection, emotional safety, and self-determination. In this way, we can deepen our self-compassion as we practice new skills.

Specific, Appreciative Feedback, NVC Style

The NVC process of appreciation is aimed at fostering an authentic sense of partnership. Giving and receiving is valued and celebrated in mutuality and shared power. Our appreciation intends to celebrate how life has been enriched by sharing specific, nonevaluative information and encouragement that honors self-determination for the receiver.

The NVC process of appreciation is aimed at fostering an authentic sense of partnership.

NVC-style appreciation conveys the same enthusiasm as praise, while also offering specific observations to support the receiver in understanding what has contributed to the speaker's experience. The structure of such appreciation is in the same format that we learned earlier for self-expression: observation, feelings, needs, and possibly a connection request (OFNR). For example, "Oh my gosh! You're cooking three different dishes for my birthday. I feel so nourished by the care!"

Such an expression of gratitude can help the receiver clearly understand what they did to contribute and how it positively impacts the speaker; the celebration is shared and enhanced. Such expression speaks to what is happening in us in the moment. This appreciative feedback contributes to a mindset where abilities are perceived as qualities to be cultivated instead of tenuous signs of our worthiness, subject to change. It invites self-reflection both for the person giving and for the person receiving the feedback. Expressing such heartfelt appreciation rather than approval, praise, or compliments leaves the person's intrinsic motivation intact, as well as their dignity and self-determination to contribute joyfully in the future or not.

> STEPHANIE: My fifteen-year-old daughter passes the entry exam to study in college while still in high school. My mind is conditioned to say, "I am so proud of you!" But I realize such a statement suggests that my feelings are directly linked to her success. I pause before speaking and then say, "Wow, I bet you are proud of yourself. Yes?" She cracks a big grin, her eyes twinkling. I smile back and add, "You know, when I hear you passed the exam (external observation), I am guessing it has to do with how you organized yourself in order to track deadlines and manage your time between studying and your other passions (internal observation). And I feel so delighted (feeling) because I value self-responsibility and persistence (needs). How is that for you to hear?" (request). She puts her arms around my neck and kisses me. "I touch a sense of peace (deeper need) because I believe these are values that will serve you well in life," I say.

While integrating the practice of NVC, we learn to examine how we have been conditioned, to intentionally redirect our mind, and to shift our language, especially with children. We can support youth more effectively with appreciation than with the praise that is often used to reinforce control in domination structures, such as school systems. As Dweck points out, such praise is at odds with creating an environment "where kids feel safe from judgment, where they understand that we believe in their potential to grow, and where they know that we are totally dedicated to collaborating with them on their learning."[9] Partnering with teachers and other students supports growth that is self-determined and lasting, as it is motivated from within. As Rosenberg highlights, "NVC is interested in learning that is motivated by reverence for life, by a desire to learn skills, to contribute better to our own well-being and the well-being of others."[10]

Appreciation offers an opportunity to touch more deeply what is meaningful for us and name it with gratitude. Observations, feelings, and needs are tools that support us in greater vulnerability with ourselves and others. Sometimes pausing the flow of action to connect with such depth can be daunting, yet still we feel inclined to express and to touch briefly and truthfully what matters to us. Letting go the language of praise, we can contribute to a system of nonjudgment, owning our appreciations in brief vernacular.

The following are abbreviated statements of appreciation that do not touch the full expanse and depth of what is true for us, nor do they include a request. Yet the words in these examples are forms of appreciative self-expression and can support a high-energy connection that is not hierarchical. Becoming fluent in such translations (idiomatic language) can help us make a doable request of ourselves to shift from praise to appreciative feedback, enjoying a meaningful depth while keeping a natural flow in conversation. Imagine what it would be like to both give and receive the following for a felt sense of praise versus appreciation:

PRAISE	APPRECIATIVE FEEDBACK ON THE FLY
• You are such a good driver!	• I feel relaxed with you at the wheel. (feeling/observation)
• Nice work!	• I love the vibrance of these colors you used! (observation of inner experience)
• You're so smart.	• I'm glad one of us thought of that! (inner observation + feeling)
• That's gorgeous.	• Whoa! I really like the curve here and how it meets this angle!
• Your dress is so pretty!	• Your dress just floats on the air! (feeling of wonder implied in tone and word choice + observation)

In keeping with the primary intention of NVC, connection is key in conveying appreciation rather than approval, praise, or compliments. One may "do giraffe" and use the formula of OFNR, yet come from an unexamined assumption of hierarchical order and communicate approval. Conversely, one might "be giraffe" and have a heart grounded in mutual respect with words related to a model of hierarchy and approval. Within the context of a trusting relationship, these words may still communicate a clear appreciation.

Receiving Praise, Compliments, and Approval

When we are the recipients of praise or approval, we can choose how to receive what is behind the initial statement in order to better support ourselves and nurture a deeper sense of connection with the person offering praise. We can activate our curiosity and make an empathic guess as to what values were touched in witnessing our action: "Are you excited because when you heard me share that parenting story you touched a sense of being in this together (needs for companionship and shared reality)?"

If we are uncertain as to what we did specifically to contribute, we also have the option of an observational guess: "I want to make sure I'm following you . . . are you referring to the moment when I said, 'Let's all pause and reconnect with our shared purpose for this meeting?'" Once we have clarity around the observation, we can nourish the connection further by asking, "I'm curious . . . would you be willing to tell me how that contributed to you?"

Even when we receive an appreciation that informs us of how our actions contributed to someone else, how they felt and what needs they touched, it may be challenging for us to fully savor the appreciation. We have been socialized to think we don't deserve appreciation and resist accepting it for fear of becoming arrogant. Either way, our preoccupation is with ourselves rather than celebrating the positive impact we can have on one another. Actively receiving appreciation is an opportunity for interdependence in action!

Appreciating Ourselves

Empowering ourselves further, we can tap into our innate ability to appreciate ourselves, offering unconditional love and acceptance to our own heart. With compassion and acceptance for how the process of socialization has contributed to often painful hierarchies, we can slowly transform and heal the relationship with ourselves, embracing the pleasure of our own company.

> STEPHANIE: I have kept a self-appreciation journal for years, and my children decided to get journals for themselves to do the same! Our personal practice often kindles powerful shifts in those who witness and partner with us too.

Appreciating ourselves with clear observations and awareness about which unique aspect of life energy we are touching within, we contribute to a sense of well-being, joy, and self-empowerment. From that place of inner abundance, we can contribute to greater connection in interpersonal relationships and support collective shifts toward a paradigm of power-with.

SUMMARY

- ⊸ Differentiating between appreciation and approval, compliments, or praise, we bring awareness to subterranean power dynamics, clarify our intentions around engaging with them, and cultivate awareness of impact.

- ⊸ The NVC process for appreciation includes sharing specific observations of what a person did that contributes to us, which needs are touched, and how we are feeling, possibly followed by a connection request.

- ⊸ This key supports us in learning to receive praise as a gift. We can kindly elicit clear, appreciative feedback by tracking the context, making empathy guesses, and inviting deeper self-expression.

↬ Intending to connect, we can become aware of, but not contribute to, socialized hierarchies. We can share appreciation and respond to praise in ways that contribute to greater clarity and more fulfilling relationships.

↬ Turning the exploration of this key inward, we can direct the NVC components of appreciation to ourselves, sustaining joy and unconditional love with meaningful feedback.

WALKING THE TALK:
A LIFE EXAMPLE FROM JAPAN

BY YUKO GOTO, CNVC CERTIFIED TRAINER

As a small child, I valued myself when my parents felt happy about what I had done. I enjoyed their praise and tried harder. Yet now I see that I learned to focus more on praise than on what I had done or *why* it had been enjoyed. Sometimes now I struggle with a desire to seek approval and praise; it takes great effort to overcome the habit of giving and receiving praise when raised in such a system. I wish I had been given the opportunity to understand and connect with what needs my actions met for others and even for myself.

I recall once playing a recorder flute at home when my grandfather visited. "Wow! You are such a good player," he told me, in front of our other family members. The excitement and joy of that moment filled me. Every time he visited our home after that, I played the flute in hopes of receiving praise again. It never happened, and I felt disappointed. Looking back now, I see that I lost the pure joy of playing the flute, so focused was I on receiving praise.

I wonder what would have happened if my grandfather had said something like, "I enjoy listening to you play the flute and find it very relaxing. Do you like playing your recorder?"

Had I heard this expression linked to my grandfather's needs and been asked how playing the flute made life wonderful for me, I think things would have gone differently. I would probably have expressed how much I love playing, regardless of whether there is an audience or not, and taken the opportunity to explore why. I imagine this exchange would also have been a gift in my relationship with my grandfather.

And perhaps I would find it easier today to connect with what I value in myself, seeking and giving praise and approval less often.

PRACTICE

Savoring Appreciation

In the book *Nonviolent Communication: A Language of Life*, Rosenberg shares how his grandmother did not think in terms of what a person "was," but rather "she thought in terms of what people feel and what they need."[11] This key distinction supports a frame of mind that focuses on appreciation based on feelings and needs. This practice aims to help you connect mind and body as you appreciate something in retrospect. This is a self-reflection practice with a possible journaling component. We invite you to find a quiet space with pen and paper or keyboard if you feel moved to write. We anticipate that this practice will take about fifteen minutes and suggest doing it at the end of the day.

We invite you to review an event from the day. Focus attention on one instance in which someone did or said something that contributed to your well-being and sense of joy.

- ∾ What happened exactly (observation)?
- ∾ How did you feel in the moment?
- ∾ What nourished you? In other words, what needs did you connect with in that moment?
- ∾ What feelings come up for you now revisiting the event?
- ∾ What do you notice in your body right now?
- ∾ Do you notice an inclination of the heart to share that celebration/appreciation with the person?
    - ○ If yes, how do you imagine expressing it?

~ Would you like to share it verbally?

~ In writing? In art? In a song?

o If no, what is keeping you from expressing your appreciation?

~ Are you telling yourself that the person already knows it? Or, is it awkward to stretch into a degree of transparency that you are not used to?

~ Are you feeling apprehensive about how you may be received?

~ Are you willing to explore the needs you are trying to meet by resisting the idea of sharing the appreciation?

~ Can you touch a place of self-compassion in the midst of it all?

∼ Does anything change for you right now around the idea of expressing the appreciation?

25

LOVE AS A FEELING
AND LOVE AS A NEED

Thus, when enemies or friends
Are seen to act improperly,
Remain serene and call to mind
That everything arises from conditions.

—SHANTIDEVA

The key distinction that juxtaposes love as a feeling and love as a need[1] supports an exploration of the nature of love as a transient emotion and an ever-present force. The ways in which we place our attention on love impacts our personal empowerment, connection, and intimacy.

Love, when expressed as a feeling, however deep and meaningful it is in the moment, is transient and at times, conditional. It may fade when the person or being is no longer meeting our needs. Holding love as a need allows us to take responsibility for "meeting" this universal need within us and manifesting it in the world.

> The key distinction that juxtaposes love as a feeling and love as a need supports an exploration of the nature of love as a transient emotion and an ever-present force.

415

Seeing love as a need, we are empowered to make connection or action requests of ourselves and others. These requests support us in moving toward a greater sense of aliveness and flow.

The transformative power of love shapes how we perceive the world and our experience of it. "Nonviolent Communication really came out of my attempt to understand this concept of love. . . . I came to the conclusion that it was not just something you feel, but it is something we manifest, something we do, something we have. . . . It is giving of ourselves in a certain way,"[2] says Rosenberg. Experiencing love as a need grants us a giraffe's view of our core humanness, supporting us in bridging the conditioned gap of separation and touching our inherent wholeness.

Love as a Feeling

Much of Western mainstream culture considers love to be a feeling, and a feeling that is primarily seen through a romantic lens. The stories we tell our children, pop songs, books, and movies—all powerful instruments of socialization—often depict the yearning of an incomplete heart that is trying to fill a void. The feeling of love within this understanding often relates to needs for comfort, security, and belonging. When we look for proof of love solely outside of ourselves to "fulfill" these needs, we reinforce habitual patterns of self-doubt and fear related to being socialized in a society in which our needs are routinely denied.

The Western notion of romantic love is still prevalently heteronormative (exclusive of love experienced by lesbian, gay, and pansexual people, for example) and portrays an asymmetric power relationship between men and women. The view of romantic love we are enculturated to limits women's influence to private and family life, while men dominate the public sphere. Subscribing to this point of view cements gender roles that do not support women's safety and humanity. A 2018 United Nations study reports that every day, 137 women are killed by their partners or family members worldwide, usually at home. This accounts for 58 percent of female homicides.[3] Those are staggering phenomena in the name of love.

Feelings Go With the Flow

In addition to the safety risks surrounding the patriarchal view of romantic love, our *feeling* of love can shift and change within moments. According to neuroscientist Jill Bolte Taylor, emotions shift about every ninety seconds.[4] Comparing the physiological lifespan of an emotion with our cultural perception of love as a static and unchanging feeling is bewildering. When we tell someone we love them or ask them if they love us, we generally seek to give or receive reassurance of love's solidity. When Rosenberg was asked if he felt love for someone, he famously replied: "No. But try me again in a few moments."[5]

When we define love as an ever-present feeling, we are likely to make demands around how we want others to "satisfy" our needs. We might say, "If you really loved me, you would (fill in the blank)." Leveraging love to get what we want is a desperate conscious or unconscious attempt to meet our needs . . . a weaponization of love. Sadly, if there is no discernment between feelings and needs, and between needs and strategies, we may unquestioningly believe our assumptions and "shoulds."

As human beings, we constantly experience emotions. We may be amazed to feel the warmth of a surge of love, the tenderness of our heart, a tingling of delight, or however else we experience the enchantment of these sensations seeking expression. We touch the mystery of loving. Intentionally savoring and cultivating feelings of loving-kindness, gratitude, joy, compassion, or affection can empower us to create new neural pathways that support connection to love as a fundamental need, a current of life.

Love as an Immanent and Transcendent Need

When we shift from the idea of love as a feeling to love as a universal need, we turn our attention to the energy inherent in all life. While love is always available for us to tap into, our awareness of and access to it fluctuates. There is a relational quality to this need; it is a life-giving energy between and within us that has the potential to free the heart.

The liberating power of this need is astronomical when harvested collectively. Mahatma Gandhi believed that "power based on love is a thousand times more effective and permanent than the one derived from fear of punishment."[6] Here is where we see love as a need intersecting with love as an action. This notion was well represented in the Chipko movement in the 1970s, when rural people, mostly women, from the Himalayan region of India embraced trees to impede corporate logging. The Hindi word "Chipko" translates as "to hug," an expression that spawned the notion of "tree-huggers" in later environmental movements in North America. Connected to love and the need to protect the earth that sustained their people, nonviolent Chipko protests initially resulted in regional success, and a decade later, their efforts culminated in a fifteen-year ban on the commercial felling of trees.[7]

The need for love is rooted in interconnection. It can be found in our vulnerability—joy and pain—whether acknowledged intrapersonally or transparently shared with others. "It's a gift when you reveal yourself nakedly and honestly, at any given moment, for no other purpose than to reveal what's alive in you. . . . To me, that is a way of manifesting love,"[8] wrote Rosenberg. Love can be experienced in the way we receive a message from others too, he tells us. When we "receive it empathically, connecting with what's alive in them, making no judgment,"[9] we lean into love.

> Love is a life-giving energy between and within us that has the potential to free the heart. The liberating power of this need is astronomical when harvested collectively.

When we commit to cultivating love, we tend to the needs it relates to in all our relationships. We value understanding and listen with attunement to empathize with ourselves and others. Building trust, we take responsibility for our own feelings and needs and share them authentically, mindful of potential impacts. We respond with all the care and compassion that we can muster to those around us. Even with a heart broken open, we may cultivate the qualities related to unconditional love.

When we hold love as a need, we are empowered to manifest it to the best of our abilities in the moment. Whenever the answer to a request of ours is no, we are less inclined to see this response as proof that the other person doesn't love us. Rather, we treasure a dance of partnership which allows enough flexibility to find strategies that consider the needs of all. If there is no willingness on the part of another, we can turn our attention inward and get in touch with the vibration of love within. Just enjoying the sensations of connecting with this quality may be enough. Or we might be inspired to make a request of ourselves or someone else to further actualize love in the world.

Rooting in integrity and self-determination, we connect with the giving and receiving nature of love. Empowered, we can experience this quality and offer it to the world regardless of our circumstances or conditioning. Even when we experience less access to external options and resources, we may still courageously cultivate the internal experience of choice informed by love.[10]

Heaven and Earth

Within the practice of NVC, we can meet and feel our feelings and the needs beneath, rather than staying locked in a story of grievance. Regardless of whether our experience in the moment is pleasant or unpleasant, it has value as we are living it and it points to what matters to us. It is an intrinsic part of the whole, and we can honor our individual truth in the moment, while also nudging our hearts to open to the universality of needs.[11]

While we experience glimpses of a boundless sense of transcendent love (heaven), we are limited in the ways we manifest it concretely (earth). This is part of the paradox which stems from the paradigm we are socialized into; we long for unconditional love while we perceive ourselves limited by our conditional fears. Our access to love as a need has been greatly impacted by the narrative of domination.

> **We can honor our individual truth in the moment, while also nudging our hearts to open to the universality of needs.**

The authenticity of love Rosenberg points to has been acutely compromised in all of us; women experience that predominantly as a conditioning not to self-express, and men as a conditioning not to empathize.[12] Our nature as relational beings with voices has been sacrificed for the sake of maintaining a social order that isn't conducive to human thriving. Rosenberg's vision of the process of Nonviolent Communication as a manifestation of love has the potential to shake the foundations of the hierarchical structures of patriarchy in all its current manifestations. This compassionate giving and receiving of one another's voices and hearts restores our capacity to align with life.

In traditional Chinese philosophy explicated in the Yi Jing[13] and following commentaries, as well as in the philosophies of martial arts such as Aikido, the cosmological place of human beings is between heaven and earth (*Ten-Jin-Chi*). Human beings are seen as the unifying factor between these two polarities, the link that allows for heaven and earth to be harmonized and their relation perfected. In that vision, human nature is prone to being conditioned by its internal and external environments while also being part of something more expansive. As such, personal liberation from societal conditioning and collective liberation from social oppression are both essential to tap into our inherent need to love and be loved. Undoing the effects of patriarchy (separation and powerlessness) and transforming the causes and conditions that sustain it (scarcity) are of paramount importance if we want to survive as a species and manifest the power of love.

Love as Divine Energy

Most if not all contemplative and devotional practices point to love as an energy of life, aiming to kindle this power within and manifest it without. Love is considered a path to awakening. The NVC lens reflects this energetic quality as the universality of needs. CNVC certified trainer and author Robert Gonzales writes, "We feel it as the warmth of love and compassion. . . . We invoke divine energy to be present. What is transcendent has become immanent."[14]

Using NVC as a spiritual practice supports us in awakening to the divine energy of love. We are all, even when grounded in strong universal needs, prone to experiencing the earthly duality of a need being "met" or "unmet." As practitioners, we are elated and awed by how much we find the process of NVC to be rooted in this way to the earthly, human experience. In that sense, practicing NVC offsets the temptation of a spiritual bypass: Instead of denying feelings and needs and escaping into transcendence, we learn to reclaim the fullness of our human experience. Placing our attention on the emotions that arise from sensory stimuli and the thoughts and perceptions that are linked to those emotions, we increase our capacity to be aware and choose love. Noticing how we relate to the universal need for love also helps us touch our common humanity beyond the many ways we have been conditioned to see one another as separate.

Honoring our earthly experience is at the foundation of large-scale social change. By deeply listening to the human experience of those from different social locations, we become aware of the impacts of systems of oppression. We can then mobilize energies and resources to follow Martin Luther King Jr.'s invitation to see that "power at its best is love implementing the demands of justice, and justice at its best is love correcting everything that stands against love."[15]

Our Need for Love

While devotional communities consistently emphasize the universal energy of love, when we embrace NVC as a life practice, we learn to

first acknowledge and care for our human suffering with all the judgments attached to it. We can then learn to skillfully make space for our
experience as it is while also growing an awareness that extends beyond
domination structures. Embracing NVC supports us in acknowledging
our experience while also inviting awareness to broaden and touch the
universality of needs.

If we fail to pursue the space of nonseparation, we may get trapped
in a psychological bypass, protecting the self and denying that the
experience of freedom in love is available to us. As we integrate the consciousness underlying the NVC process, we experience a more consistent
connection with the "Beloved Divine Energy," as Rosenberg refers to it.
From that perspective, we welcome our howling jackals as reminders of
our human experience under cultures of domination. In cultivating love
as a need, we choose to direct our attention toward an unrestricted felt
sense of this energy.

Mind the Gap: Falling Into Separation

Recalling the sensations of universal, ever-present love, we are better
prepared to meet the sense of lack when we tumble into our conditioned
separation. Turning away from parts of ourselves that experience fear,
anger, anxiety, and judgment, we unwittingly contribute to this pattern
of separation. Divided within, we are unable to give and receive love
freely. In our limited, conditioned understanding of love, we can easily
contribute to harm within ourselves and in each other. Tara Brach calls
this state of separation "the trance of unworthiness."[16] John Welwood
refers to it as the "mood of unlove."[17] As we confront our fear of being
unlovable and not belonging, we may connect more deeply to our own
and others' humanity. While relationships may open us to pain, they
also provide an opportunity for deep and expansive healing. The more
we undo the limitations we have been conditioned to place on our vulnerability, the more relationships among humans and with nature will
help us restore our reverence for life.

We might fall into the painful cycle of longing to be loved. Perceiving this longing as a weakness, we may not allow ourselves to touch our vulnerability. Tragically, we might try to silence or ignore these parts of ourselves. Disconnected from love, we may find ourselves at once desperate and fully armored. Unwilling to let ourselves be nourished by the love we long for and think ourselves unworthy of, we wither.

Paradoxically, fear then emerges in our pursuit of love. Habituated to express our needs as grievances that focus on what's missing, we remain trapped in unhealed core wounds. We succumb to the messages of socialization that teach us we are fundamentally unlovable. Often our grievances show up in the form of moralistic judgments, suggesting some sense of security. At the heart of the grievance is unhealed pain. This grief is often linked to not experiencing love in the way we needed it, because those who were entrusted with our care were themselves socialized into the same systems. The distress is thus passed on from generation to generation. The loss of connection with life in and around us leads to our emotional shutdown.

Born from personal, family, and societal conditioning, there is a historical context behind patterns of reactivity and wider forces in play. Recognizing the systemic roots of these behavioral patterns can help us understand the needs beneath and cultivate compassion for ourselves and others. Clearly naming the current internal and external manifestations of the domination systems Rosenberg referred to empowers us to recognize the myriad of ways in which we perpetuate collective core beliefs and implicit assumptions that reinforce systems of oppression and subordination. The establishment of patriarchy was a process that came into being about five thousand years ago,[18] and we still collectively sustain ways to negate the basic trust in life we are born with.

Personal power and liberation are prerequisites to collective power and

The vision to manifest the power of love in the world summons us to transform how we relate to ourselves, one another, and the existing social order in which we operate.

liberation. Nurturing a vision to concretely manifest the power of love in the world summons us to transform how we relate to ourselves, one another, and the existing social order in which we operate.

Peace With "Imperfections"

"Find the antidote in the venom. Come to the root of the root of yourself," writes the thirteenth-century Persian poet Rumi.[19] The unifying aspect of love as a need has the power to envelop separation in an embrace of oneness. Looking within, we can ask ourselves what it will take, personally and in terms of support, to love our self-protective structures and behaviors and progressively lay them down, as we open our hearts.

"Your task is not to seek for love, but merely to seek and find all the barriers within yourself that you have built against it," writes Helen Schucman in *A Course in Miracles*.[20] Surely, a cultural movement toward greater awareness and an embrace of interconnection would support such shifts at the personal and societal levels.

As we welcome our experience of duality, unity begins to move through us. At first we might experience tension in the dichotomies, an opposing push and pull. Sensing ourselves as separate from others, we can embrace the tension and this experience of separateness. Bringing attention to the universality of needs, togetherness emerges. This perception of inter-being is not static; movement and change is the norm. We tip and balance between I, you, and we, time and again.

Held with love, our tendencies toward scarcity and separation still "belong" to the vastness that we are. Leadership consultant Mukara Meredith, a teacher of Stephanie's, reminds us that "love belongs to us, and we belong to love."[21] Love is presence, aliveness, and expansion. When we open to it, giving flows, and we begin to see with new eyes. We become attuned and responsive. Gonzales writes: "As long as we are alive, we can have some sense of our essence. Because our essence is life itself, it is life energy."[22] When we look through the eyes of love, we see with the heart. The integration of our conditioned perception of love into love energy as a universal need can lead us toward authentic aliveness.

When we look through the eyes of love, we see with the heart.

As Rosenberg puts it, "Nonviolent Communication helps me stay connected with that beautiful Divine Energy within myself and to connect with it in others."[23] The NVC practices of self-empathy, empathy, and self-expression help us grow our capacity to reconnect, celebrate, and grieve.

Love bridges the two different sides of ourselves—our constricted, conditioned, habitual patterns and the expansive presence within us that is connected to all life. We humans meet our needs for love in countless ways, each as unique as we are. Gratitude and giving from the heart, for example, are practices we can cultivate to generate the energy of love. It is within our capacity to touch the source of ever-present love, flowing beneath its limited manifestations in societies based on domination.

The energetic quality of love extends to and beyond the caring closure of a relationship as well. Cultivating our connection with love allows us to change the form of our relationship with another being, or even end the relationship, without closing our hearts.

Sometimes, as we transition out of a relationship or role, we may choose to engage in protective use of force, perhaps disconnecting from someone on social media. "Just because our heart is open does not mean that we must set aside all caution," writes Welwood.[24] Sometimes, even bringing closure through dialogue may be at odds with our safety. Even then, we can still cultivate a heart broken open, acknowledging to ourselves all the needs behind our thoughts and actions. In this case, love supports us in staying away from using force punitively.

By engaging with love as an inherent need, we find love within to give to the world.

Deconstructing judgments by unearthing the needs embedded in them, we can move behind the veil of our evaluations and connect with what matters to us most. Then we can ask ourselves moment by moment what resources we need, inner and outer, to cultivate and mobilize love. Reawakening to interdependence in action, love might manifest as making time for ourselves to relax in nature, cook dinner for a neighbor, or stand in solidarity with those of us who most experience powerlessness due to systemic oppression. By engaging with love as an inherent need, we find love within to give to the world.

SUMMARY

- ⟿ This key distinction supports us in clarifying how we want to experience the flow of giving and receiving love moment by moment.

- ⟿ Our perception of love as a feeling carries different qualities and expectations than love as a need. There is a relational quality to love as a need; it is a living process between and within us that has the potential to free the heart.

- ⟿ In learning to discern between love as a feeling and love as a need, we embrace our personal experience with the presence and flow of universal love. We can gradually make peace with unmet needs and allow ourselves to cherish our values in their wholeness. This supports us in manifesting change in the world with the power of love.

- ⟿ The liberating power of love as a need is astronomical when harvested collectively.

WALKING THE TALK:
A LIFE EXAMPLE FROM INDIA

BY SUDHA SHANKAR, CNVC CERTIFIED TRAINER

"**C**ome back! You'll get lost! Somebody will take you away . . . you are wearing so much gold!" I heard my voice grow shrill as I revved up into a panic. My eighty-nine-year-old mother kept plodding along, looking for her dear dog Blake, who has been dead thirty-five years.

At my mother's first signs of dementia years ago, I persuaded my parents to live with me. Our home is located beside a busy road. Fearing that my mother would wander, we had kept the gate locked at all times. Until that morning.

I was working when the woman who supports me in the household reported that my mother had walked off and was calling for Blake. I sped outside, gripped by fear, and spotted her at the intersection. I caught up to my mother, took her by the arm, and pulled her homeward. She resisted, pleading that Blake was just around the corner.

Visions flashed through my mind of her wandering lost or being run over. Worse still, I imagined her being bundled away by someone so they could steal her jewelry. She was wearing her *mangal sutra*—the heavy gold necklace, which signaled that she was a married woman. By custom in South India, most women of my mother's generation wore these adornments every day of their lives.

Pushing these thoughts away, I tried to drag her home. When I repeated, "Ma, you are wearing so much jewelry; it's dangerous to be walking about," the warning took hold. She turned back with me. I sat her on a chair on the porch and told her she mustn't go out because it is unsafe. She squared her jaw. "Then bring Blake to me," she said. Exasperated and trembling, I stood up and walked into the house.

I had barely taken ten steps when I thought, "What am I doing?" A part of me was still angry that we had had this public display of our tussle and, thereby, her dementia. I so longed to guard our privacy. I felt a pit of unease in my belly, knowing that the situation called for more vigilance, and I wanted reassurance that mum would be safe. I felt helpless because I wanted to contribute to her joy of finding her beloved dog . . . to see her eyes light up again. And that would never be. I deeply mourned all she had lost—her dog . . . her memory . . . her functionality.

I took a deep, slow breath and touched the love that both held and transcended my fears. "I need to connect with her in her world," I thought. I swiveled around and came to kneel in front of her chair. "You want to look for Blake?" I asked. Her eyes lit up.

"Can we?" she whispered. I nodded. Ever since, when my mother asks me to find Blake, I play along. Feeling a little foolish, I walk up to the intersection and call out for him while she looks on, hoping, hoping . . .

PRACTICE

Connecting With Love

Welcoming both our experience of love as a feeling and love as a need, we can deepen our understanding of and nurture a more consistent connection with the energy of love. The intention of this practice is to offer a felt sense of universal love, while also holding the experience of love as we have been conditioned to perceive it. This is a meditation practice. You may record and play back this meditation or read through it first before reading again slowly during the experience. We invite you to find a quiet and comfortable space, and we encourage you to set aside at least twenty minutes for this practice.

Standing still, feet hip-width apart, invite your body to relax; close your eyes, if it feels comfortable. Bringing awareness to your heart, open yourself to the energy of love, however you experience it. Allow this energy to radiate from the heart center outward. In your kinesthetic experience, notice any effort you make to hold yourself up. Invite more relaxation, if possible, allowing yourself to be held by love.

What quality of holding do you need at this time? If helpful, repeat to yourself with or without speaking it aloud, "It's okay to long for what I need and open myself to this inner source of love."

Invite yourself to be held in love, by love, in whatever way feels right to you at this moment. What are some of the qualities of this energy that you touch? What is your experience of love? Is it a sensation of stillness? Is it moving through you? Savor whatever arises, with no expectations, remembering that inner experience of love.

Take a few deep breaths. When you are ready, think of a situation in which you perceive or perceived your need for love as "unmet." Notice what sensations arise now. Attend to them with compassion. Allow feelings to move in the body—anger, shame, frustration, sadness. What is present? The pain of separation, however you perceive it, is part of the human experience. Take as much time as needed for the energy of grievance and scarcity to move through you.

Now, rekindling the quality of love you bookmarked earlier, offer it to the part of yourself that is experiencing lack. How does that feel? Breathe into this ever-present love, holding your entire experience with compassion. Perhaps internally or speaking it in words, offer a wish: "May I be compassionate with myself." What sensations arise? How does love move in you now? How does it feel to shine unconditional love where conditionality is being experienced?

Honor your full humanity with the awareness that there is a beloved divine energy that embraces from within and without. Rest here as long as you enjoy. And then, before bringing this practice to a close, see if a request of yourself arises in relation to this practice.

CONCLUSION

There is no end to our unfolding. Every moment is an opportunity to nurture the consciousness of our choosing and a chance to practice NVC as a way of life. The key differentiations move with us like a kaleidoscope as we cultivate personal, interpersonal, and systemic awareness. They support our spiritual expansion in ways that naturally move us toward social change.

Rosenberg's practice evolved throughout his lifetime. The maturation of our individual practices shapes this work as a collective. Our growing number of mindful interactions touches the lives of others and society at large. "NVC is a way of keeping our consciousness tuned in moment by moment to the beauty within ourselves," Rosenberg wrote.[1] As we integrate the process of NVC, we inevitably share it, living it in a flow of giving and receiving.

Moving toward vulnerability while exploring these keys and reckoning them with our lives, we can speak from our authenticity in the moment, realizing that our understanding develops as we change and grow. In the course of writing this book, the two of us consistently challenged our thoughts and investigated our perspectives on the keys, particularly related to their systemic repercussions. We know beyond a shadow of a doubt that our views will evolve with each and every new interaction and life experience, if we stay open to living with awareness and cultivating self-inquiry.

It takes a tremendous amount of courage to stand in our integrity in the moment, knowing that our understanding and consequent expression is ever-changing. "I am not at all concerned with appearing to be consistent," says Gandhi. "In my search after Truth I have discarded many ideas and learnt many new things."[2] May we explore and discard, meeting ourselves and others with compassion as we move toward our truth.

NVC provides a simple process that supports us in returning to our inner experience for clarity and guidance. Understanding and tending to needs brings healing and inspires greater vitality, thus enhancing our ability to care for humanity and the earth. Self-empathy, empathy, and self-expression stem from personal groundedness. Skillfully persisting with these three core practices, we slowly transform our intrapersonal and interpersonal relationships.

With growing freedom of heart and mind, we empower ourselves to address the systems of domination. We become more willing to expand our sense of personal responsibility to actively engage with others in the sacred work of social transformation for the greater good. We become nonviolent agents of systemic change, restoring community and moving together toward a more equitable world.

Promoting needs and life-giving strategies, the spiritual integrity of NVC fuels our efforts to transform mechanisms of violence and the misuse and abuse of power toward a sustainable and peaceful global future.

Our commitment to social change begins as we attune to a different narrative, a vision of possibility. We can shift our attention to what Isabel Wilkerson calls "radical empathy . . . putting in the work to educate oneself and to listen with a humble heart to understand another's experience from their perspective, not as we imagine we would feel." This, she writes, "is the kindred connection from a place of deep knowing that opens your spirit to the pain of another as they perceive it."[3]

We open ourselves to jointly hold this pain, connecting, understanding, and together turning the tide toward systems based on the organizing principles of caring for all needs. This would mean, for example, revamping our justice system and shifting from retributive to restorative justice. It would mean creating economic systems that are oriented toward needs rather than profit. It would mean rethinking every single one of the systems that govern our lives so we can create societies based on life-giving policies for all.

Equally important, we cultivate joy in our lives—"the joy of a little child feeding a hungry duck," Rosenberg used to say.[4] For it is this joy, this deep peacefulness and satisfaction, that is needed to establish a culture of connection, awareness of interdependence, and care for the impact of our actions. Such joy leads us toward greater aliveness, curiosity, and clarity about what we most wish to contribute to.

This joy, we imagine, is born from pure love. "Nonviolent Communication is just a manifestation of what I understand love to be,"[5] wrote Rosenberg. And so, it is our wish that these keys be a love offering. Let us open the door of compassion together, for ourselves and all creation.

ACKNOWLEDGMENTS

We celebrate the interconnection we experienced in relation to writing this book, and we want to thank the many people who have graciously contributed to it. Our heartfelt gratitude goes to Meiji Stewart, founder of PuddleDancer Press; Kyra Freestar, our PuddleDancer Press editor; and Virginia Herrick, copyeditor. Both Kyra and Virginia encouraged us and fielded our questions including on evenings and weekends. It is thanks to the three of them, and the whole team at PuddleDancer Press—Shannon Bodie, Palma Odano, and Ruth Prado—that you now have this book in your hands.

Our gratitude goes out to CNVC certified trainer Jean McElhaney, who supported us in finalizing our initial manuscript, and to Elisabetta Schiavon, one of Stephanie's trainer candidates, whose reflections as a European living for decades in the Global South expanded our awareness of the systemic impacts of patriarchy and colonialism.

Many more readers offered feedback and supported us in fine-tuning ideas. We are immensely grateful to Giuseppe and Giacomo Mattei, Seda Collier, Kerstin Kristen, and CNVC certified trainers Filipa Hope and Christine King, all of whom enriched our understanding with their unique perspectives and feedback.

We have been and remain moved in heartfelt ways by the breadth and depth of Miki Kashtan's participation in this project. Her feedback, in many different forms, truly inspired us. When our dialogues with Miki started, she shared with us fourteen additional key differentiations that she and her sister Inbal had compiled, which point to further restoring our individual and collective capacity as humans in a world in crisis. As Miki engaged with this book, she fleshed out these keys and, generously making resources available to all, posted them online at *The Fearless Heart*: https://thefearlessheart.org/miki-kashtan-and-inbal-kashtans-additional-nvc-key-differentiations/.

Stephanie is profoundly grateful to her friends, colleagues, and mentors, who wholeheartedly shared their expertise. She values their contribution to this book beyond measure. Fellow CNVC trainers including Lucy Leu, Marion Little, Roxy Manning, Jim Manske, and Oren Sofer supported the investigation of particular topics related to the NVC process. Christopher Germer, cocreator of the Mindful Self-Compassion program, offered Stephanie his perspectives on crucial aspects at the intersection of NVC and brain science. Julia Corley, certified teacher for the Hakomi Institute and teacher with the Right Use of Power Institute, provided feedback on the practices for each chapter.

A deep, deep bow of gratitude goes to our families for their unwavering support and concrete contributions toward creating space and helping us find countless hours to investigate, study, write, and rewrite this book. In this vein, Kristin humbly thanks Seda, Sam, and Trinidad Collier, close friends (human, canine, and feline), and the forests, owls, coyote, and bear she shared paths with in this journey. Stephanie's beloved husband, Giuseppe, and their three children, Giacomo, Simone, and Desiree, brought patience and kind understanding to Stephanie's absorption with this book, encouraging her to pursue her dream even as it revealed itself to be more labor-intensive than initially anticipated. Stephanie also wants to express her gratitude to her Italian- and English-speaking CNVC trainer candidates for their unwavering encouragement.

Many, many others have supported us to be who we are today. Among them, we honor and celebrate the late Inbal Kashtan, our first cherished NVC teacher. The loss of her mentoring and companionship we mourn beyond words. Stephanie also celebrates the influence the late Robert Gonzales had on her life and her understanding of the spirituality of NVC: he is another of her main teachers whose absence she now mourns.

We are immensely grateful to all of these people, and so many more, who have helped bring this book into being.

RECOMMENDED READING

Adolphs, Ralph, and David J. Anderson. *Neuroscience of Emotions: A New Synthesis*. Princeton, NJ: Princeton University Press, 2018.

Barrett, Lisa Feldman. *How Emotions Are Made: The Secret Life of the Brain*. New York: First Mariner Books/Harcourt, 2018.

Barstow, Cedar. *Right Use of Power: The Heart of Ethics*. Boulder, CO: Many Realms, 2005.

Buber, Martin. *I and Thou*. New York: Scribner's, 1970.

Chenoweth, Erica, and Maria J. Stephan. *Why Civil Resistance Works: The Strategic Logic of Nonviolent Conflict*. New York: Columbia University Press, 2012.

Dahl, Robert. *Polyarchy: Participation and Opposition*. New Haven, CT: Yale University Press, 1972.

deMause, Lloyd. *The History of Childhood: The Untold Story of Child Abuse*. Oxford, UK: Rowman & Littlefield, 1974.

Diamond, Julie. *Power: A User's Guide*. Santa Fe, NM: Belly Song Press, 2016.

Dweck, Carol S. *Mindset: The New Psychology of Success*. New York: Penguin Random House, 2006.

Eliot, Lise. *What Is Going On in There? How the Brain and Mind Develop in the First Five Years of Life*. New York: Bantam Books, 1999.

Frankl, Viktor E. *Man's Search for Meaning*. Boston: Beacon Press, 2006.

Fuller, Robert W. *Somebodies and Nobodies: Overcoming the Abuse of Rank*. Gabriola Island, BC, Canada: New Society Publishers, 2004.

Germer, Christopher. *The Mindful Path to Self-Compassion: Freeing Yourself from Destructive Thoughts and Emotions*. New York: Guilford Press, 2009.

Gilligan Carol, Naomi Snider. *Why Does Patriarchy Persist?* Cambridge, UK: Polity Press, 2018.

Gladwell, Malcolm. *Outliers: The Story of Success*. New York: Back Bay Books, 2008.

Grille, Robin. *Parenting for a Peaceful World*. New South Wales, Australia: Longueville Media, 2005.

Hanson, Rick with Richard Mendius. *Buddha's Brain: The Practical Neuroscience of Happiness, Love, and Wisdom*. Oakland, CA: New Harbinger Publications, 2009.

Kashtan, Inbal. *Parenting From Your Heart: Sharing the Gifts of Compassion, Connection, and Choice*. Encinitas, CA: Puddledancer Press, 2004.

Kashtan, Miki. *Reweaving Our Human Fabric: Working Together to Create a Nonviolent Future*. Oakland, CA: Fearless Heart Publications, 2015.

———. *Spinning Threads of Radical Aliveness: Transcending the Legacy of Separation in Our Individual Lives*. Oakland, CA: Fearless Heart Publications, 2014.

Keltner, Dacher. *The Power Paradox: How We Gain and Lose Influence*. New York: Penguin Books, 2016.

Kohn, Alfie. *Punished by Rewards: The Trouble with Gold Stars, Incentive Plans, A's, Praise, and Other Bribes*. New York: Houghton Mifflin Harcourt, 1999.

Lipton, Bruce. *The Biology of Belief: Unleashing the Power of Consciousness, Matter & Miracles*. Carlsbad, CA: Hay House, 2005.

Mandela, Nelson. *Long Walk to Freedom: The Autobiography of Nelson Mandela*. New York: Little, Brown, 1994.

Menakem, Resmaa. *My Grandmother's Hands: Racialized Trauma and the Pathway to Mending Our Hearts and Bodies.* Las Vegas, NV: Central Recovery Press, 2017.

Neff, Kristin. *Fierce Self-Compassion: How Women Can Harness Kindness to Speak Up, Claim Their Power, and Thrive.* New York, NY: HarperCollins, 2021.

Neff, Kristin. *Self-Compassion: Stop Beating Yourself Up and Leave Insecurity Behind.* New York, NY: William Morrow, 2011.

Neff, Kristin. *Self and Identity.* 2: 85–101, Psychology Press, 2003. https://self-compassion.org/wp-content/uploads/publications/SCtheoryarticle.pdf

Nhất Hạnh, Thích. *Interbeing: The 14 Mindfulness Trainings of Engaged Buddhism,* 4th ed. Berkeley, CA: Parallax Press, 2020.

———. *No Mud, No Lotus: The Art of Transforming Suffering.* Berkeley, CA: Parallax Press, 2014.

———. *Nothing to Do, Nowhere to Go: Waking Up to Who You Are.* Berkeley, CA: Parallax Press, 2007.

Nkrumah, Kwame. *Neo-Colonialism: The Last Stage of Imperialism.* Bedford, UK: Panaf Books, 1987.

Peyton, Sarah. *Your Resonant Self: Guided Meditations and Exercises to Engage Your Brain's Capacity for Healing.* New York: W. W. Norton, 2017.

Porges, Stephen W. *The Polyvagal Theory: Neurophysiological Foundations of Emotions, Attachment, Communication, and Self-Regulation.* New York: W. W. Norton, 2011.

Romesin, Humberto Maturan, and Gerda Verden-Zöller. *The Origin of Humanness in the Biology of Love.* Exeter, UK: Imprint Academy, 2008.

Rosenberg, Marshall B. *The Heart of Social Change: How to Make a Difference in Your World.* Encinitas, CA: Puddledancer Press, 2004.

———. *Nonviolent Communication: A Language of Life,* 3rd ed. Encinitas, CA: PuddleDancer Press, 2015.

———. *Practical Spirituality: Reflections of the Spiritual Basis of Nonviolent Communication.* Encinitas, CA: PuddleDancer Press, 2004.

———. *Speak Peace in a World of Conflict: What You Say Next Will Change Your World.* Encinitas, CA: PuddleDancer Press, 2005.

———. *Speaking Peace: Connecting with Others Through Nonviolent Communication.* Louisville, CO: Sounds True, 2003.

Siegel, Daniel. *Mind: A Journey to the Heart of Being Human.* New York: W. W. Norton, 2016.

Simard, Suzanne. *Finding the Mother Tree: Discovering the Wisdom of the Forest.* New York: Knopf, 2021.

Treleaven, David A. *Trauma-Sensitive Mindfulness.* New York: W. W. Norton, 2018.

Wilkerson, Isabel. *Caste: The Origins of Our Discontents.* New York: Random House, 2020.

Wineman, Steven. *Power-Under: Trauma and Nonviolent Social Change.* Self-published, 2003. Available from http://www.traumaandnonviolence.com/.

Wink, Walter. *Engaging the Powers: Discernment and Resistance in a World of Domination.* Minneapolis: Augsburg Fortress, 1992.

———. *Naming the Powers: The Language of Power in the New Testament.* Minneapolis: Fortress Press, 1984.

———. *Unmasking the Powers: The Invisible Forces That Determine Human Existence.* Minneapolis: Fortress Press, 1986.

NOTES

INTRODUCTION

1. Nine White people and twenty-five African Americans were killed in the riots, with seven hundred more reportedly injured. Of the twenty-five African Americans killed, seventeen were killed by the police. None of the nine White people were killed by the police.
2. Marshall B. Rosenberg, *Speak Peace in a World of Conflict: What You Say Next Will Change Your World* (Encinitas, CA: PuddleDancer Press, 2005), 14.
3. William Blake, "The Argument," *The Marriage of Heaven and Hell*, plate 3, 1790.
4. Although the list has changed over time, understanding and integrating the key differentiations has long been part of the journey toward certification with CNVC.
5. "Marshall Rosenberg's NVC Quotes," PuddleDancer Press (website), 2021, https://www.nonviolentcommunication.com/resources/mbr-quotes.
6. Regulation is defined as the ability to experience and maintain stress within one's window of tolerance. A regulated state is generally experienced as calm, focused, or relaxed. Dysregulation is the experience of stress outside of one's window of tolerance. When this happens, the brain is unable to regulate the flow of energy and information and consequently goes into chaos or rigidity. This experience is often referred to as being "stressed out" or in distress.
7. Trauma is defined as any direct or indirect exposure to an event or series of events that involve death, injury, or a threat to physical integrity and result in physiologic changes and complex psycho-emotional adaptations. These responses to trauma are due to intense fear, horror, and helplessness, which in turn depend on the proximity of support or lack of support available. Many events fall into a gray area in terms of the level of emotional and psychological threat someone will experience. The determining factor in trauma is a person's subjective assessment of how helpless they felt. Trauma responses are clearly linked to adverse health impacts in ways that vary depending, again, on the support available.
8. Rosenberg, *Speak Peace*, 9.
9. This is from a slide presented during the courses Stephanie took with Bruce Perry in 2007.
10. The roots of Western civilization and education are in Hebrew monotheism, ancient Greek philosophy (especially the writings of Aristotle), and Christianity.
11. Various versions of this story label the two wolves differently—one of love and one of hate; one good and one evil; one of hope and the other of despair. The main idea is that we live in a subjective world of dichotomies.
12. Robert W. Fuller, *Somebodies and Nobodies: Overcoming the Abuse of Rank* (Gabriola Island, BC, Canada: New Society, 2004), 61.
13. Rosenberg, *Speak Peace*, 172.
14. Marshall B. Rosenberg, *The Heart of Social Change: How to Make a Difference in Your World* (Encinitas, CA: PuddleDancer Press, 2005), 43.
15. This quote from Rosenberg comes from participants' notes from a special session on NVC and social change at a workshop held in Switzerland in 2005; these notes were documented by Miki Kashtan in "Can the Social Order Be Transformed Through Personal Practice? The Case of Nonviolent Communication," *The Fearless Heart (blog)*, September 6, 2019, https://thefearlessheart.org/?s=Can+the+Social+Order+Be+Transformed+Through+Personal+Practice%3F+The+Case+of+Nonviolent+Communication/.
16. Rosenberg, *Heart of Social Change*, 7–15.
17. Justice, in the way we define it, includes responsiveness to basic needs, equitable access to resources, restoration for historical harm, and restorative rather than punitive practices.
18. Lisa Feldman Barrett, *How Emotions Are Made: The Secret Life of the Brain* (New York: First Mariner Books/Harcourt, 2018), 146.
19. Fuller, *Somebodies and Nobodies*, 3.
20. Here, and throughout this book, we refer to race only as a social construct. There are no biological distinctions that relate to the human race; the social construct of race exists and has real effects.
21. We use the definition of patriarchy as a system of domination and a set of cultural

assumptions, codes, and scripts based on gender separation and hierarchy. To be clear: All forms of life suffer under this system, men included. Other forms of domination, based on separation among humans as well as between humans and nature, stem from this initial stratification. For a comprehensive article on the ramifications of patriarchy, we recommend Miki Kashtan, "From Obedience and Shame to Freedom and Belonging: Transforming Patriarchal Paradigms of Child-Rearing in the Age of Global Warming" (Oakland, CA: *The Fearless Heart*, 2017), https://thefearlessheart.org/wp-content/uploads/2017/12/From-Obedience-and-Shame-to-Freedom-and-Belonging.pdf.

22. See Walter Wink's books *Naming the Powers: The Language of Power in the New Testament* (Minneapolis: Fortress Press, 1984); *Unmasking the Powers: The Invisible Forces That Determine Human Existence* (Minneapolis: Fortress Press, 1986); and *Engaging the Powers: Discernment and Resistance in a World of Domination* (Minneapolis: Augsburg Fortress, 1992).

23. Center for Partnership Systems (website), accessed November 15, 2021, https://centerforpartnership.org.

24. See Marshall B. Rosenberg, "Anger and Domination Systems" (excerpt from a slightly edited manuscript from a workshop on anger that Rosenberg led in England in May 1999), Center for Nonviolent Communication (website), accessed November 15, 2021, https://www.cnvc.org/what-nvc/articles-writings/anger-and-domination-systems/anger-and-domination-systems.

25. The mind is not the brain. The brain is the central organ of the nervous system, protected by the skull. The mind involves consciousness, subjective experience, and information processing. Daniel Siegel's working definition of the mind is "an embodied and relational, self-organizing emergent process that regulates the flow of energy and information both within [one's own experience] and between [relational space]." Daniel Siegel, *Mind: A Journey to the Heart of Being Human* (New York: W. W. Norton, 2016), 37.

26. Brain plasticity is the capacity of brain cells to grow and reorganize, through new neural connections and cortical remapping, in response to intrinsic and extrinsic stimulation. Self-directed neuroplasticity is the intentional use of the mind to change the brain.

27. We explain the references to giraffes in the introduction to Part 3, Options for Connection.

28. The Parent Peer Leadership Program (website), accessed November 15, 2021, www.nvc-pplp.com.

CHAPTER 1

1. Marshall Rosenberg referred to this key distinction as *life-connected* and *life-alienated*. In the course of our exploration, we found that the word *alienated* carries such an intense sense of disconnection that it is difficult to use the term without casting the shadow of right/wrong thinking. In this chapter, we avoid the term and use synonyms such as *disconnected* instead. We use both *disconnected* and *alienated* in other parts of the book to honor Rosenberg's legacy.

2. Marshall B. Rosenberg, *Nonviolent Communication: A Language of Life*, 3rd ed. (Encinitas, CA: PuddleDancer Press, 2015), 23.

3. Lloyd deMause, "The Evolution of Childhood," in *The History of Childhood: The Untold Story of Child Abuse* (Oxford, UK: Rowman & Littlefield, 1974), Chapter 1.

CHAPTER 2

1. Peggy O'Mara, *Natural Family Living: The Mothering Magazine Guide to Parenting* (New York: Atria Books, 2000).

2. Michelle Montgomery and Jon Sharpe, *Fast Facts About Indigenous Cultural Autonomy: Decolonizing Autonomy to Transform Research Practices* (Seattle: University of Washington Center for Ecogenetics and Environmental Health, 2013), https://depts.washington.edu/ceeh/downloads/FF_Decolonizing.pdf.

3. Practices of infanticide, child sacrifice, mutilation, slavery, sexual abuse, and abandonment have been documented universally with but a handful of exceptions. See Lloyd deMause, *History of Childhood*, 51–53; Robin Grille, *Parenting for a Peaceful World* (New South Wales, Australia: Longueville Media, 2005), 21.

CHAPTER 3

1. From an evolutionary standpoint, individual survival is tightly linked to being part of a group.

2. Marshall B. Rosenberg, *Practical Spirituality: Reflections on the Spiritual Basis of Nonviolent Communication* (Encinitas, CA: Puddle-Dancer Press, 2004), 3.

3. Suzanne Simard, *Finding the Mother Tree: Discovering the Wisdom of the Forest* (New York: Knopf, 2021).

4. "World Hunger: Key Facts and Statistics 2021," Action Against Hunger (website), accessed November 15, 2021, www.actionagainsthunger.org/world-hunger-facts-statistics.

5. In the dominant paradigm, giving and receiving are framed within an economic transaction model. Giving is usually tied to

expectations, even if expecting just a sign of gratitude. Receiving is intertwined with the idea of becoming indebted toward the other.

6. Miki Kashtan, *Spinning Threads of Radical Aliveness: Transcending the Legacy of Separation in Our Individual Lives* (Oakland, CA: Fearless Heart Publications, 2014), 102.

7. Kerry Lotzof, "Are We Really Made of Stardust?" Natural History Museum (website), accessed November 15, 2021, https://www.nhm.ac.uk/discover/are-we-really-made-of-stardust.html.

8. Malcolm Gladwell, *Outliers: The Story of Success* (New York: Back Bay Books, 2008), 67.

9. An example of these dynamics is the Global North's explicit or implicit control of the Global South through economic, political, cultural, and other strategies of pressure. See Kwame Nkrumah, *Neo-Colonialism: The Last Stage of Imperialism* (Bedford, UK: Panaf Books, 1987).

10. Bright Alozie, "How Igbo Women Activists Influenced British Authorities During the Colonial Rule of Nigeria," *Quartz Africa*, August 7, 2020, https://qz.com/africa/1889847/how-nigerias-igbo-women-influenced-british-colonial-rule/.

11. Inga Kim, "The 1965–1970 Delano Grape Strike and Boycott," United Farm Workers (website), March 7, 2017, https://ufw.org/1965-1970-delano-grape-strike-boycott/.

12. Oscar Lopez, "Factbox: Where Latin American Women Are Fighting the World's Highest Murder Rates," Reuters (website), March 6, 2020, https://www.reuters.com/article/us-latam-women-protests/factbox-where-latin-america-women-are-fighting-the-worlds-highest-murder-rates-idUSKBN20U095.

13. "Across Latin America, Women Fight Back Against Violence in Politics," UN Women (website), November 14, 2018, https://www.un women.org/en/news/stories/2018/11/feature-across-latin-america-women-fight-back-against-violence-in-politics.

14. "HeForShe Launches #YearofMaleAllyship Campaign," HeForShe (website), March 1, 2020, https://www.heforshe.org/en/heforshe-launches-yearofmaleallyship-campaign.

15. Humberto Maturana Romesin and Gerda Verden-Zöller, *The Origin of Humanness in the Biology of Love* (Exeter, UK: Imprint Academic, 2008), 214.

16. Lise Eliot, *What Is Going On in There? How the Brain and Mind Develop in the First Five Years of Life* (New York: Bantam Books, 1999), 303.

17. Howard Bath, "Calming Together: The Pathway to Self-Control," *Reclaiming Children and Youth* 16, no. 4 (Winter 2008): 44–46.

18. Martin Buber, *I and Thou* (New York: Charles Scribner's Sons, 1970), 14.

19. Thích Nhất Hạnh, *Interbeing*.

20. Some of the aspects of this relationship that are beyond the scope of this chapter are awareness, denial, guilt, defensiveness, and meritocracy.

21. This quote is drawn from conversations among the community of CNVC certified trainers.

22. "Do We Know the Full Extent of Juvenile Recidivism?" *MST Services* (blog), November 1, 2018, https://info.mstservices.com/blog/juvenile-recidivism-rates.

CHAPTER 4

1. "Marshall Rosenberg's NVC Quotes," Puddle-Dancer Press (website), 2021, https://www.nonviolentcommunication.com/resources/mbr-quotes.

2. For more on this topic, see Chapter 8.

3. Steven Wineman, *Power-Under: Trauma and Nonviolent Social Change (published online by author)*, 2003. Available from http://www.traumaandnonviolence.com/.

4. Wineman, *Power-Under*, 99.

5. Wineman, *Power-Under*, 47.

6. Julie Diamond, *Power: A User's Guide* (Santa Fe, NM: Belly Song Press, 2016), 80–81.

7. Miki Kashtan, *Reweaving Our Human Fabric: Working Together to Create a Nonviolent Future* (Oakland, CA: Fearless Heart Publications, 2014), 154.

8. For more on this topic, see Chapter 17.

9. Diamond, *Power*, 53.

10. Viktor Frankl, *Man's Search for Meaning* (Boston: Beacon Press, 2006), 66.

11. We use the terms up-power and down-power as defined by Cedar Barstow and the Right Use of Power Institute (https://rightuseofpower.org).

12. Cedar Barstow, *Right Use of Power: The Heart of Ethics* (Boulder, CO: Many Realms, 2005), 23.

13. For an in-depth exploration of the powers of role and rank, see Chapter 17.

14. For more on intersectionality—a concept that points to the interconnected nature of the personal characteristics and social categorizations that contribute to our identities and how those factors intersect to create compounded modes of discrimination and privilege—please refer to the work of professor Kimberlé Crenshaw. Lafayette College, "Kimberlé Crenshaw Discusses 'Intersectional Feminism,'" YouTube video, October 15, 2015, 9:56, https://www.youtube.com/watch?v=ROwquxC_Gxc.

15. Diamond, *Power*, 14.

16. Inbal Kashtan, *Parenting for the Present and Future: The Path of Nonviolent*

Communication in Family Life (Oakland, CA: Fearless Heart Publications, 2013), 7. Available from https://thefearlessheart.org/item/parenting-for-the-present-and-future-packet/.

17. For inspiration and information about a decision-making process rooted in the partnership model, see Miki Kashtan, *The Highest Common Denominator: Using Convergent Facilitation to Reach Breakthrough Collaborative Decisions* (Oakland, CA: Fearless Heart Publications, 2020).

18. Examples of collective trauma include wars, genocides, famine, pandemics, slavery, terrorist attacks, and shootings, as well as institutionalized trauma such as discrimination based on race, gender, and sexual orientation.

19. David A. Treleaven, *Trauma-Sensitive Mindfulness* (New York: W. W. Norton, 2018), 17–19.

20. Dylan Wiliam, "The Half-Second Delay: What Follows?" *Pedagogy, Culture & Society* 14, no. 1 (2006): 71–81.

21. Bruce Lipton, *The Biology of Belief: Unleashing the Power of Consciousness, Matter & Miracles* (Carlsbad, CA: Hay House, 2005), 173.

22. Teresa Romero, "Mexico: Poverty Rate 2018, by State," Statista (website), July 5, 2021, https://www.statista.com/statistics/1036147/poverty-rate-mexico-state/.

CHAPTER 5

1. Our collective patriarchal/colonial mindset tends to order these responses hierarchically, giving the fight response (more often associated with men) a higher value than the flee or freeze responses (more often associated with women and children).

2. Diamond, *Power*, 57.

3. The third survival response, a freeze reaction, is usually misinterpreted not as submitting but as passive-aggressive or defiant.

4. Robert Dahl, *Polyarchy: Participation and Opposition* (New Haven, CT: Yale University Press, 1972), 45.

5. Erica Chenoweth and Maria J. Stephan, *Why Civil Resistance Works: The Strategic Logic of Nonviolent Conflict* (New York: Columbia University Press, 2012), 10.

6. Rosenberg, *Heart of Social Change*, 17.

7. Nelson Mandela received the Nobel Peace Prize jointly with F. W. de Klerk (then president of South Africa) in 1993.

8. Nelson Mandela, *Long Walk to Freedom: The Autobiography of Nelson Mandela* (New York: Little, Brown, 1994), 621.

9. Christopher Germer, *The Mindful Path to Self-Compassion: Freeing Yourself From Destructive Thoughts and Emotions* (New York: The Guilford Press, 2009), 65.

10. "Marshall Rosenberg's NVC Quotes," Puddle-Dancer Press (website), 2021, https://www.nonviolentcommunication.com/resources/mbr-quotes.

11. William E. Henley, "Invictus," *101 Famous Poems*, ed. Roy J. Cook (New York: McGraw-Hill Education, 2003), 95.

12. The sympathetic nervous system prepares the body for the fight-or-flight response during any perceived potential danger. The parasympathetic nervous system restores the body to a calm, balanced state (homeostasis) that is often referred to as the relaxation or rest-and-digest response.

13. This double meaning of the word *meet* as both *encountering* and *filling* is rooted in the English language and does not relate to how the word is used in other languages.

14. When basic survival needs are unmet, no amount of self-connection will shift realities such as hunger or homelessness.

15. M. K. Gandhi, "Training for Non-violence," Comprehensive Website by Gandhian Institutions—Bombay Sarvodaya Mandal & Gandhi Research Foundation, accessed November 28, 2021, https://www.mkgandhi.org/momgandhi/chap23.htm.

16. Transforming enemy images is a core value within the vision of nonviolence in all spiritual traditions.

CHAPTER 6

1. See Rosenberg, *Nonviolent Communication*, 28.

2. For more information on pausing for self-empathy, see Chapter 14.

3. The scientific term for this phenomenon is *inattentional blindness*. See Trafton Drew, Melissa L. H. Vo, and Jeremy M. Wolfe, "The Invisible Gorilla Strikes Again: Sustained Inattentional Blindness in Expert Observers," *Psychological Science* 24, no. 9 (2013): 1848–1853.

4. The term *neuroception* was coined by Stephen W. Porges, "Neuroception: A Subconscious System for Detecting Threats and Safety," *Zero to Three* 24, no. 5 (2004): 19–24.

5. Deb Dana, *Polyvagal Exercises for Safety and Connection* (New York: W. W. Norton, 2020), 24.

6. This quote has been attributed to the Talmud, Kant, Anaïs Nin, and others. In other words, the origin and translation are uncertain; the version we collected most likely comes from a text on oration published by Harvard in 1891.

7. This is what Rosenberg called "enjoying the jackal show." By playfully calling it a "show," we can choose to watch it rather than be an actor in it. See more about the jackal show in chapter 15.

8. "Anti-Muslim Hatred Has Reached 'Epidemic Proportions' Says UN Rights Expert, Urging Action by States," *UN News: Global Perspectives, Human Stories*, March 4, 2021, https://news.un.org/en/story/2021/03/1086452.

9. Cynthia Griffith, "Crimes Against Homeless People Increase Again in 2021," *Invisible People*, March 5, 2021, https://invisiblepeople.tv/crimes-against-members-of-the-homeless-population-increase-again-in-2021/.

10. Wineman, *Power-Under*, 42.

11. Recognizing this goal allows us to ask ourselves: "With this interpretation of the components of NVC, who is included?"

12. Rosenberg, *Nonviolent Communication*, 26.

13. Mary-Frances Winters, *Black Fatigue: How Racism Erodes the Mind, Body, and Spirit* (Oakland, CA: Berrett-Koehler, 2020), 71–72.

14. Rosenberg, *Heart of Social Change*, 10–11.

15. Roxy Manning, "Unpacking Observations" (unpublished article, quoted with permission).

16. Roxy Manning, "Unpacking Observations" (unpublished article, quoted with permission).

CHAPTER 7

1. For more on perceptions as they relate to observations, feelings, and needs, see Chapter 6.

2. Survival and social behavior are inextricably intertwined.

3. Ralph Adolphs and David J. Anderson, *Neuroscience of Emotions: A New Synthesis* (Princeton, NJ: Princeton University Press, 2018), 282.

4. Ken Wilber, *The Essential Ken Wilber: An Introductory Reader* (Boston: Shambala, 1998).

5. Moods differ from feelings: moods are a prolonged experience of a particular emotion that can last from hours to years. We are often uncertain about what stimulates a mood. Like emotions, moods can significantly affect the cognitive processes of memory, attention, and decision-making.

6. Adolphs and Anderson, *Neuroscience of Emotions*, 289.

7. Please see page 460 for Some Basic Feelings and Needs We All Have.

8. Joseph LeDoux, "Feelings: What Are They and How Does the Brain Make Them?" *Daedalus* 144, no. 1 (Winter 2015), 97.

9. Joseph LeDoux, "Rethinking the Emotional Brain," *Neuron* 73, no. 4 (2012), 665.

10. What is considered "innate" vs. "learned" remains uncertain, as learning starts in utero. Studies point to last-trimester fetuses processing sounds and learning and remembering words. See Beth Skwarecki, "Babies Learn to Recognize Words in the Womb," *Science News* (blog), August 26, 2013, https://www.sciencemag.org/news/2013/08/babies-learn-recognize-words-womb.

11. Barrett, *How Emotions Are Made*, xii.

12. Adolphs and Anderson, *Neuroscience of Emotions*, 83.

13. Barrett, *How Emotions Are Made*, 40.

14. Diamond, *Power*, 100.

15. Shari Klein and Neil Gibson, *What's Making You Angry: 10 Steps to Transforming Anger So Everyone Wins* (Encinitas, CA: Puddle-Dancer Press, 2004), 4.

16. For more on stimulus and cause, see Chapter 21.

17. Cognitive behavioral therapy encourages us to look at our unspoken scripts; to ask ourselves, "What is the story I am telling myself?"

18. Marshall B. Rosenberg, *The Surprising Purpose of Anger: Beyond Anger Management: Finding the Gift* (Encinitas, CA: Puddle-Dancer Press, 2005), 11.

19. Barrett, *How Emotions Are Made*, 31.

20. Adolphs and Anderson (*Neuroscience of Emotions*, 310) denounce the anthropocentric bias of many studies on emotions.

21. Those of us raised in Western cultures continue to systemically transmit our distrust of emotions each time we invite our children to think about what they did rather than inquire into their felt experience.

22. In his book *Descartes' Error: Emotion, Reason, and the Human Brain* (New York: G. P. Putnam's Sons, 1994), Antonio Damasio outlines how damage to brain structures that are linked to the ability to process emotion also disrupts the ability to carry out day-to-day responsibilities and to make sound decisions, even while other cognitive abilities remain intact.

23. We cannot numb emotions selectively. When we attempt to numb unpleasant emotions, we also decrease our ability to experience pleasant emotions. The experience of numbness can also be the result of trauma, whether personal or collective.

24. Meenadchi, *Decolonizing Non-Violent Communication*, 2nd ed. (Mexico City: Co-Conspirator Press, 2021), 71.

25. Audre Lorde, *Sister Outsider: Essays and Speeches* (Berkeley, CA: Ten Speed Press, 2007), 115.

26. For a List of Physical Sensations, please see page 458. And for Some Basic Feelings and Needs We All Have, please see page 460.

27. Matthew D. Lieberman, professor and director of the Social Cognitive Neuroscience Lab at UCLA, researched the effects of affect labeling and showed how naming feelings contributes to soothing the limbic system; see Matthew D. Lieberman, Naomi I. Eisenberger, Molly J. Crockett, et al.,

"Putting Feelings Into Words: Affect Labeling Disrupts Amygdala Activity in Response to Affective Stimuli," *Psychological Science* 18, no. 5 (2007): 421–28.

28. James J. Gross, "The Emerging Field of Emotion Regulation: An Integrative Review," *Review of General Psychology* 2, no. 3 (1998): 271–99.

29. Sarah Peyton, *Your Resonant Self: Guided Meditations and Exercises to Engage Your Brain's Capacity for Healing* (New York: W. W. Norton, 2017), 29.

30. We see needs as comprising two major categories: survival needs, such as food and water, and thriving needs, such as play and learning. Perception plays a greater role in how we assess needs as met or unmet for thriving needs, and a lesser role (or none at all) for material survival needs. Some people do not have access to adequate food, or any at all, because of the systems we sustain in the world, and this is not a perception; it is a fact.

31. Elizabeth Johnson and Leah Olson, *The Feeling Brain: The Biology and Psychology of Emotions* (New York: W. W. Norton, 2015), 290–91.

32. For more on such internal feedback loops, see Chapter 6.

33. For more on the brain's experience of pain, see Naomi I. Eisenberger, Matthew D. Lieberman, and Kipling D. Williams, "Does Rejection Hurt? An fMRI Study of Social Exclusion," *Science* 302, no. 290 (2003): 290–92, available from https://www.wisebrain.org/papers/RejectionHurt.pdf.

CHAPTER 8

1. Most NVC teachers and trainers offer "needs lists" to help people cultivate a cognitive awareness of needs. On page 460, please see Some Basic Feelings and Needs We All Have.

2. Much of mainstream Western culture is founded on the statement "Cogito, ergo sum," from *Discourse on Method* (Leiden, Netherlands, 1637) by René Descartes, father of early modern philosophy. Translated as "I think, therefore I am," this declaration prioritizes the individual mind.

3. The acronym PLATO—Person, Location, Action, Time, Object—is a useful tool for distinguishing needs from strategies: while strategies often include PLATO elements, needs do not.

4. For more on formal and informal expressions of needs, see Chapter 10.

5. Statistic from "World Hunger Key Facts and Statistics 2021," Action Against Hunger (website), accessed November 15, 2021, https://www.actionagainsthunger.org/world-hunger-facts-statistics.

6. This quote comes from the memories of CNVC trainers who attended Rosenberg's in-person workshops in the 1990s and early 2000s.

7. For more on this topic, see James Gilligan, *Violence: Our Deadly Epidemic and Its Causes* (New York: G. P. Putnam, 1996).

8. Jean Liedloff, *The Continuum Concept: In Search of Happiness Lost* (Cambridge, MA: Perseus Books, 1977), 80.

9. Thích Nhất Hạnh, *No Mud, No Lotus*.

10. For a deeper exploration of the dynamics of wallowing in our feelings, see Chapter 14.

11. Carl Rogers, *On Becoming a Person: A Therapist's View of Psychotherapy* (New York: Houghton Mifflin, 1995), 17.

12. Chimamanda Ngozi Adichie, *Dear Ijeawele, or A Feminist Manifesto in Fifteen Suggestions* (New York: Knopf, 2017), 30–31.

CHAPTER 9

1. For more on up-power roles, see Chapter 4.

2. "Marshall Rosenberg's NVC Quotes," PuddleDancer Press (website), 2021, https://www.nonviolentcommunication.com/resources/mbr-quotes.

3. Rosenberg, *Nonviolent Communication*, 73.

4. Stephen W. Porges, *The Polyvagal Theory: Neurophysiological Foundations of Emotions, Attachment, Communication, and Self-Regulation* (New York: W. W. Norton, 2011), 12.

5. Needs as universal life energy are never in conflict. Our perceptions of our needs may well conflict, however.

6. Dacher Keltner, *The Power Paradox: How We Gain and Lose Influence* (New York: Penguin Books, 2016), 7.

7. We define *work* as achieving mutual willingness, not compromise.

8. Resmaa Menakem, *My Grandmother's Hands: Racialized Trauma and the Pathway to Mending Our Hearts and Bodies* (Las Vegas, NV: Central Recovery Press, 2017), 102–3.

CHAPTER 10

1. We explain the references to giraffes in "On Jackals and Giraffes" on page 192.

2. For support in cultivating idiomatic NVC, we recommend Miki Kashtan's learning packet *Naturalizing the Language of NVC* (Oakland, CA: Fearless Heart Publications, 2021), available on a gift-economy basis at https://thefearlessheart.org/item/naturalizing-the-language-of-nvc-packet/.

3. Rosenberg, *Practical Spirituality*, 2.

4. Over the past twenty years, we have witnessed increased numbers of books and trainings that value observations, feelings, needs (often

using various other terms), and requests, and we are pleased to see this evidence that the vocabulary of Western dominant culture is slowly shifting.

5. Social location includes gender, race, social class, age, ability, religion, sexual orientation, and geographic location. It is particular to each person and is rarely the same for any two people.

6. Rosenberg, *Nonviolent Communication*, 2.

PART III

1. The NVC Tree of Life diagram is available at https://thefearlessheart.org/nvc-reference-materials/the-nvc-tree-of-life/. Inbal Kashtan's *NVC in the Body* learning packet (Oakland: Fearless Heart Publications, 2021) includes a comprehensive explanation of the practice supported by this visual diagram and can be found at https://thefearlessheart.org/item/nvc-in-the-body-packet/.

CHAPTER 11

1. Robert Gonzales, *Reflections on Living Compassion: Awakening Our Passion and Living in Compassion* (Bloomington, IN: Balboa Press, 2020), 13.

2. This quote was shared with us by Miki Kashtan, who heard it from Kit on many occasions.

3. Rosenberg, *Speak Peace*, 15.

4. The distinction between long-term and short-term intentions is frequently discussed among NVC practitioners. This specific description of overarching, time-specific, and moment-to-moment intentions comes from Gregory Kramer, founder of Insight Dialogue and one of Stephanie's teachers.

5. "Marshall Rosenberg's NVC Quotes," Puddle-Dancer Press (website), 2021, https://www.nonviolentcommunication.com/resources/mbr-quotes.

6. Fred Mazelis, "Harry Belafonte Provides an Historical Insight Into the Civil Rights Movement's Decay," *World Socialist Web Site News & Commentary*, May 25, 2012, https://www.wsws.org/en/articles/2012/05/king-m25.html.

7. Expressing curiosity about someone else's behavior through empathy guesses or through a request for help in understanding may be more connecting than asking "why" questions, which often point the listener toward thought and analysis.

8. Stephanie learned this practice from Christopher Germer, one of her meditation teachers.

9. Stephanie learned this practice of learning to pause before, while, and after talking from her spiritual teacher Gregory Kramer of Insight Dialogue.

CHAPTER 12

1. We want to acknowledge that these two words have varied definitions both historically and today, depending on the disciplines, and sometimes people use *sympathy* for what we here call *empathy* and vice versa.

2. This chapter focuses on interpersonal empathy. The process for self-empathy (recognizing, naming, and holding with care our own feelings and needs), mirrors the process of creating empathic space for another. Considering how few people in the world today have the capacity to offer empathy, and the enormous need, learning to be in compassionate connection with ourselves even as we seek support is essential.

3. Rosenberg, *Speak Peace*, 80.

4. Miki Kashtan and Inbal Kashtan, unpublished reference materials from the LP Leadership Program/PPLP Parent Peer Leadership Program (Oakland, CA: The Fearless Heart, 2015), 90); there are plans to make these materials publicly available in the future as a learning packet at https://thefearlessheart.org/store/learning-packets/.

5. "Marshall Rosenberg's NVC Quotes," Puddle-Dancer Press (website), 2021, https://www.nonviolentcommunication.com/resources/mbr-quotes.

6. This formal spoken guess is a practice template. In actual speech, we flow with language that resonates more easily. For more on this, see Chapter 10.

7. For the sake of clarity, we refer to "giving" and "receiving" empathy based on conscious choice around who will be the speaker and the listener. We acknowledge the limitation of this language, which points to doing the practice rather than to a way of being that dissolves the static boundaries of separation between you and me. The process of empathy involves no actual sense of separation; it invites the listener, through an act of imagination, to connect with the humanity of the speaker. Our belief is that empathy is a state we enter, like a source of light, that we can then direct at self or other.

8. Rosenberg, *Nonviolent Communication*, 91.

9. Hermann Hesse, *Siddhartha* (New York: Bantam, 1982), 104.

10. Thích Nhất Hạnh, *Nothing to Do, Nowhere to Go*.

11. Rosenberg, *Speak Peace*, 16.

12. Rosenberg, *Practical Spirituality*, 22.

13. Empathy therefore differs from coaching, where an explicit leadership agreement is in place.

14. Rosenberg, *Speak Peace*, 88.

15. Miki Kashtan, learning packet *Empathy for Self and Others, A Compendium* (Oakland, CA: The Fearless Heart, 2021), 7–8, https://

thefearlessheart.org/item/empathy-for-self-and-others-a-compendium-packet/.

16. This is especially relevant when leading NVC groups. There is a tendency to put the whole purpose of the gathering on hold and default to empathy as soon as someone is in distress. (Sometimes the person in distress is one of the trainers themselves!)

17. "Marshall Rosenberg's NVC Quotes," Puddle-Dancer Press (website), 2021, https://www.nonviolentcommunication.com/resources/mbr-quotes.

18. Black, Indigenous, and People of Color.

19. Roxy Manning, "Cross Privilege Dialogues: Avoiding the Trap of Centering Yourself When You Have More Privilege," Roxy Manning, PhD (website), accessed December 7, 2021, https://www.roxannemanning.com/avoid_centering/.

20. Rosenberg, Nonviolent Communication, 91.

21. We can decolonize our minds by recognizing and unlearning ideologies linked to colonialism, Eurocentrism, and Western-centrism that reinforce the superiority and consequent privilege of Western thought, society, literature, history, and education, to name a few. We can also acknowledge and address how the dominant culture continues to promote power dynamics and economic disparities between the Global North and the Global South.

CHAPTER 13

1. We want to acknowledge the influence of Miki Kashtan's insights that support detecting the many subtleties within the paradigm of either/or. A consciousness of power-with aims at integrating our human capacities rather than holding them in opposition. When we contrast mind with heart, we lose the possibility of mobilizing the mind to operate in partnership with the heart.

2. Rosenberg, Nonviolent Communication, 91.

3. John B. Furness, Brid P. Callaghan, Leni R. Rivera, and Hyun-Jung Cho, "The Enteric Nervous System and Gastrointestinal Innervation: Integrated Local and Central Control," in Microbial Endocrinology: The Microbiota-Gut-Brain Axis in Health and Disease, ed. Mark Lyte and John F. Cryan (New York: Springer, 2014): 39–71.

4. We may instead decide to attend to our other needs and communicate that to our conversational partner.

5. When mirroring nonverbal communication, it is important to specifically notice and embody connecting behaviors and not disconnecting ones such as rolling the eyes, crossing the arms, or physically distancing oneself.

CHAPTER 14

1. John Welwood, Perfect Love, Imperfect Relationships: Healing the Wound of the Heart (Boulder, CO: Shambhala Publications, 2006), 76.

2. Menakem, My Grandmother's Hands, 245.

3. Barbara L. Fredrickson, Positivity: Top Notch Research Reveals the 3-to-1 Ratio That Will Change Your Life (New York: Crown, 2009). Different ratios have been recommended at different times—for example, Gottman recommended a ratio of five to one in marriage (John Gottman with Nan Silver, Why Marriages Succeed or Fail, New York: Simon & Schuster, 1994). Fredrickson herself updated her thinking on the positivity ratio in 2013.

4. Captured in Stephanie's notes from a retreat with Rick Hanson at the Barre Center for Buddhist Studies, 2010.

5. Shawn Achor, "The Happy Secret to Better Work," TedxBloomington video, May 2011, 12:04, https://www.ted.com/talks/shawn_achor_the_happy_secret_to_better_work/.

6. We capitalize White and Black with the understanding that these terms refer to race identities and not a color. To not name White as a race would reinforce the assumption that White is the norm, which is a privileged perspective.

CHAPTER 15

1. Marshall B. Rosenberg, "Be Careful What You Hear During the Holidays," Puddle-Dancer Press (website), accessed November 16, 2021, https://www.nonviolentcommu-nication.com/resources/articles-about-nvc/holiday-conflict-mbrosenberg/.

CHAPTER 16

1. This exploration of the key distinction also includes Inbal and Miki Kashtan's concept of a "utilitarian use of force," toward the end of the chapter.

2. "Marshall Rosenberg's NVC Quotes," Puddle-Dancer Press (website), 2021, https://www.nonviolentcommunication.com/resources/mbr-quotes.

3. Rosenberg, Nonviolent Communication, 193.

4. Rosenberg, Nonviolent Communication, 193.

5. Rosenberg, Nonviolent Communication, 186.

6. For more on this, see Alfie Kohn, Punished by Rewards: The Trouble with Gold Stars, Incentive Plans, A's, Praise, and Other Bribes (New York: Houghton Mifflin Harcourt, 1999).

7. Rosenberg, Nonviolent Communication, 188.

8. Jarryd Bartle, "We Know That Prison Doesn't Work. So What Are the Alternatives?" The Guardian, August 15, 2019, https://www.

theguardian.com/commentisfree/2019/
aug/16/we-know-that-prison-doesnt-work-so-
what-are-the-alternatives.

9. For more on restorative justice as an alternative to punitive justice, see the Winter 2012 issue of *Tikkun* magazine, at https://www.tikkun.org/winter-2012-table-of-contents/.

10. deMause, *History of Childhood*, 1.

11. Rosenberg, *Nonviolent Communication*, 189.

12. Seeing another as an "enemy" is typically linked to clusters of moralistic judgments we hold "against" the "other," often subconsciously.

13. "Marshall Rosenberg's NVC Quotes," Puddle-Dancer Press (website), 2021, https://www.nonviolentcommunication.com/resources/mbr-quotes.

14. Miki Kashtan, "Is Nonviolent Use of Force an Oxymoron?" Medium post, May 7, 2020, https://medium.com/@MikiKashtan/is-nonviolent-use-of-force-an-oxymoron-210e48d0ae83.

15. David R. Hawkins, *Power vs Force: The Hidden Determinants of Human Behavior* (Carlsbad, CA: Hay House, 2012), 174.

16. For a detailed history of child-rearing and social evolution, see Robin Grille, *Parenting for a Peaceful World* (New South Wales, Australia: Longueville Media, 2005).

17. Bruce D. Perry and Maia Szalavitz, *Born for Love: Why Empathy Is Essential—and Endangered* (New York: HarperCollins, 2010), 5.

18. Paulo Freire, *Pedagogy of the Oppressed* (New York: Continuum, 1993), 114.

CHAPTER 17

1. For more on up-power and down-power roles, see Chapter 4.

2. Functional hierarchy is recognized as a configuration of a complex system (uncoupled from rank and status), rather than automatically identified as a domination structure. For more on power with hierarchies, see Kashtan, *Reweaving Our Human Fabric*, 153–59.

3. "Authority," Online Etymology Dictionary, accessed November 28, 2021, https://www.etymonline.com/word/authority.

4. Martin Luther King Jr., *Where Do We Go From Here: Chaos or Community?* (New York: Harper and Row, 1967), 37.

5. How the initial patriarchal societies emerged is a topic of much debate. For a summary of some of the literature, see Miki Kashtan, "From Obedience and Shame to Freedom and Belonging: Transforming Patriarchal Paradigms of Child-Rearing in the Age of Global Warming" (Oakland, CA: *The Fearless Heart*, 2017), https://thefearlessheart.org/wp-content/uploads/2017/12/From-Obedience-and-Shame-to-Freedom-and-Belonging.pdf.

6. Most White people, for example, are conditioned not to recognize White privilege, as men are not taught to recognize male privilege.

7. Fuller, *Somebodies and Nobodies*, 63.

8. Fuller, *Somebodies and Nobodies*, 4.

9. Isabel Wilkerson, *Caste: The Origins of Our Discontents* (New York: Random House, 2020), 53.

10. Dario Cvencek, Andrew Meltzoff, and Anthony G. Greenwald, "Math-Gender Stereotypes in Elementary School Children," *Child Development* 82, no. 3 (May/June 2011): 766–79.

11. It's worth noting that higher rank usually means more financial power, and careers in math and science are often well paid.

12. Fuller, *Somebodies and Nobodies*, 45.

13. Sura Hart and Victoria Kindle Hodson, *Respectful Parents, Respectful Kids: 7 Keys to Turn Family Conflict Into Co-operation* (Encinitas, CA: PuddleDancer Press, 2006), 18.

14. In this famous experiment, roles that were randomly assigned to twenty-four college students were quickly internalized: The experiment was halted because the "prison guards" became increasingly sadistic and the "prisoners" distressed. For more on this dynamic, see Philip G. Zimbardo, The Stanford Prison Experiment (website), 1999–2022, https://www.prisonexp.org/.

15. Charles Eisenstein, "From Nonviolence to Service," *Essays by Charles* (blog), December 2015, https://charleseisenstein.org/essays/from-nonviolence-to-service/.

16. The more the authority uses unilateral force, the more we might question its legitimacy, as legitimacy can only be conferred.

17. "Alice Walker Quotes," BrainyQuote.com (website), accessed November 16, 2021, https://www.brainyquote.com/quotes/alice_walker_385241.

18. Examples of dignified anger in relation to authority figures can be seen in the international network called ATTAC, which works toward alternatives to the globalization process in the social, environmental, and economic levels of democracy.

19. Rosenberg, *Heart of Social Change*, 15–16.

20. We say this with awareness that meritocracy is a myth; we earn nothing alone. Meritocracy as a social construct is very real and serves the purpose of maintaining up-power roles. Whatever position of authority we hold is so because of the support of many others and favorable circumstances. For more on this topic, see Malcolm Gladwell, *Outliers*.

21. Distribution of power can take many forms. Apprenticeships and rotation of roles based on abilities and interests are structural strategies.

22. Diamond, *Power*, 46–47.

23. Attending to our internal voice in care for our body and personal well-being is especially important.

24. Mahatma K. Gandhi, *Hind Swaraj or Indian Home Rule* (Ahmedabad, India: Navajivan, 1933), Chapter 7.

25. Cedar Barstow and Reynold Ruslan Feldman, *Living in the Power Zone: How Right Use of Power Can Transform Your Relationships* (Boulder, CO: Many Realms, 2013), 42.

26. Nitish Pahwa, "India Just Had the Biggest Protest in World History: Will It Make a Difference?" *Slate*, December 9, 2020, https://slate.com/news-and-politics/2020/12/india-farmer-protests-modi.html.

27. Juvenal, *Satires*, Satire 7, lines 347–48.

CHAPTER 18

1. For more on cooperation with entrusted leadership, see Chapter 17.

2. Porges, *Polyvagal Theory*, 51.

3. Grille, *Parenting for a Peaceful World*, 19.

4. The ancient Babylonian epic *Enuma Elish* is considered the oldest written creation story, perhaps from the second millennium BC. The story tells of the great battle between gods Marduk and Tiamat that resulted in the creation of the Earth and mankind. See Joshua J. Mark, "Marduk," World History Encyclopedia, December 9, 2016, https://www.worldhistory.org/Marduk/.

5. Genesis 3: 1–24.

6. It is hard to distance ourselves from patriarchy, in any family culture, so ingrained are the narratives and stereotypes *and* our responses to them.

7. Miki Kashtan, "The Freedom to Disobey" (Oakland, CA: The Fearless Heart, 2016), 3, https://thefearlessheart.org/wp-content/uploads/2013/12/The-Freedom-to-Disobey-by-Miki-Kashtan.pdf.

8. For more on power roles, see Chapter 4.

9. Nazi war criminal Adolf Eichmann reported that he and fellow officers called such language "Amtssprache." This "bureaucratese" (loose translation) denies choice and responsibility. "Superior orders" allowed Eichmann to help organize and carry out the Holocaust without interference from personal feelings (Rosenberg, *Nonviolent Communication*, 19, citing Hannah Arendt, *Eichmann in Jerusalem: A Report on the Banality of Evil*, edition unknown). The inner voice that guides was conveniently silenced by upholding obedience.

10. Miki Kashtan, "The Freedom to Disobey"

(Oakland, CA: The Fearless Heart, 2016), 8, https://thefearlessheart.org/wp-content/uploads/2013/12/The-Freedom-to-Disobey-by-Miki-Kashtan.pdf.

11. For one of the many examples of the costly psycho-social consequences of being in the dominant position in an unjust, hierarchical system, see Lisa B. Spanierman, Nathan R. Todd, and Carolyn J. Anderson, "Psychosocial Costs of Racism to Whites: Understanding Patterns Among University Students," *Journal of Counseling Psychology* 56, no. 2 (April 2009), 239–52.

12. Keltner, *Power Paradox*, 141.

13. Keltner, *Power Paradox*, 149.

14. We acknowledge that for people who are meeting needs for safety and sustainability by acting in obedience, addressing this can carry risks. If you are in this situation and choosing to make the shift from obedience to self-discipline, we encourage you to explore every possible resource in your community to find adequate support.

CHAPTER 19

1. We are creatures of habit, and habits can be functional in our daily lives. But when habit is coupled with unawareness, we are not making a conscious choice.

2. The scientific explanation for this is found in the concept of neuroplasticity.

3. Summer Allen, *The Science of Generosity* (Berkeley, CA: Greater Good Science Center, May 2018), https://ggsc.berkeley.edu/images/uploads/GGSC-JTF_White_Paper-Generosity-FINAL.pdf.

4. In fact, we are always learning. The crucial question is whether our learning increases or decreases our awareness.

5. According to World Bank data, in 2019 women held 38.8 percent of national parliament seats in Ethiopia, 32.0 percent in the UK, 30.5 percent in Australia, 27.9 percent in Afghanistan, 23.5 percent in the US, 15.0 percent in Brazil, and 10.1 percent in Japan.

6. The "need" to be right often stems from the fear of punishment if wrong. It is a by-product of domination education.

7. Recorded during a weeklong retreat that Stephanie and her family attended with Thích Nhất Hạnh in 2013.

8. Jan E. Stets and Jonathan H. Turner, eds., *Handbook of the Sociology of Emotions* (Berlin: Springer, 2006), 51.

9. "52 Thought-Provoking Quotes by Virginia Satir on Family, Relations, Living, and More," The Famous People (website), accessed November 16, 2021, https://quotes.thefamous-people.com/virginia-satir-4012.php.

10. Stephanie heard Rick Hanson, author of *Buddha's Brain: The Practical Neuroscience of Happiness, Love, and Wisdom* (Oakland, CA: New Harbinger, 2009), say this in a retreat she attended.

11. For more, see Stanford Medicine: The Center for Compassion and Altruism Research and Education, http://ccare.stanford.edu.

CHAPTER 20

1. When we do not experience a choice to act differently, our action is usually a trauma response.

2. Menakem, *My Grandmother's Hands*, 99.

CHAPTER 21

1. In Daniel Goleman, *Destructive Emotions: A Scientific Dialogue with the Dalai Lama* (New York: Bantam Dell, 2004), 145.

2. Mindfulness of breathing, in particular, supports attunement to other automatic processes.

3. Daniel Goleman, *Emotional Intelligence: Why It Can Matter More Than IQ* (New York: Bantam Dell, 1995), 19.

4. Louis Cozolino, *The Neuroscience of Human Relationships: Attachment and the Developing Social Brain* (New York: W. W. Norton, 2006), 56.

5. Rosenberg, *Nonviolent Communication*, 49.

6. "Marshall Rosenberg's NVC Quotes," Puddle-Dancer Press (website), 2021, https://www. nonviolentcommunication.com/resources/ mbr-quotes.

7. Again, we want to clarify that owning the mind's perceptions does not change the reality that some basic needs may not be met.

CHAPTER 22

1. Rosenberg coined this term to describe the persistence with which a dog goes from person to person to be pet or have its ball thrown, without ever implying any wrongness toward anyone who says no.

2. For more, see the Black Lives Matter website, https://blacklivesmatter.com/.

3. For more, see "Al pueblo de México: las demandas de EZLN," Enlace Zapatista (website), March 1, 1994, https:// enlacezapatista.ezln.org.mx/1994/03/01/ al-pueblo-de-mexico-las-demandas-del-ezln/.

4. Nine percent of the respondents to the 2015 US Transgender Survey reported being attacked for being transgender. "Violence Against Trans and Non-Binary People," VAWnet (website), accessed November 28, 2021, https:// vawnet.org/sc/serving-trans-and-non-binary-survivors-domestic-and-sexual-violence/ violence-against-trans-and.

CHAPTER 23

1. This situation can bring in the dynamic of submitting or rebelling, as well as raise an opportunity for shift or compromise. For more, see Chapter 5.

2. A shift can also emerge in relation to ourselves (intrapersonal), when we experience an inner conflict where one part of us seems to want one thing and another part wants something else. Our energy can shift; we suddenly find ourselves capable of viewing the situation from a different vantage point; a way forward opens up. This chapter specifically addresses shifts in relational and collective conflict, but we also want to acknowledge that the ability to cultivate a shift in general will support us intrapersonally as well as interpersonally and in community.

3. "Marshall Rosenberg's NVC Quotes," Puddle-Dancer Press (website), 2021, https://www. nonviolentcommunication.com/resources/ mbr-quotes.

4. Empathy entails sharing others' emotions while being able to differentiate between oneself and the other. Perspective-taking relates to the cognitive ability to understand others' viewpoints. Perspective-taking and empathy are linked to distinct neural circuits.

5. Resilience can also come from practices that cultivate gratitude, joy, and playfulness.

6. National Museum of American History, "Reflections on the Greensboro Lunch Counter," YouTube video, January 30, 2020, 6:32, https://www.youtube.com/watch?v=u FQ3ZCAgAA0.

7. Stephanie learned this Gatha (a short poem that helps to cultivate mindfulness) at a retreat with Thích Nhất Hạnh in 2013.

CHAPTER 24

1. We may perceive needs in the passive form, such as "to be" seen, appreciated, or loved. However, this mindset usually does not support us in being in our own power. Instead of waiting or expecting to be seen, loved, or appreciated, we can *let ourselves be seen* for who we are, learn to love ourselves and others, and value appreciation as something we enjoy giving *and* receiving.

2. Rosenberg, *Nonviolent Communication*, 209.

3. For more on this, see Carol S. Dweck, *Mindset: The New Psychology of Success* (New York: Penguin Random House, 2006).

4. Raj Gill, Lucy Leu, and Judi Morin, *Nonviolent Communication Toolkit for Facilitators: Interactive Activities and Awareness Exercises Based on 18 Key Concepts for the Development of NVC Skills and Consciousness* (Encinitas, CA: PuddleDancer Press, 2022), 287.

5. Kohn, *Punished by Rewards*, 101.

6. Kohn, *Punished by Rewards*, 103.
7. deMause, *History of Childhood*, 51–53.
8. Selective reinforcement, whether verbal or tangible, is based on the same theory of motivation. For more, see Kohn, *Punished by Rewards*.
9. Dweck, *Mindset*, 217.
10. "Marshall Rosenberg's NVC Quotes," Puddle-Dancer Press (website), 2021, https://www.nonviolentcommunication.com/resources/mbr-quotes.
11. Rosenberg, *Nonviolent Communication*, 218.

CHAPTER 25

1. This key distinction is described as love as a feeling/need juxtaposed to an action in the most recent version of the CNVC certification preparation packet.
2. Rosenberg, *Practical Spirituality*, 5.
3. United Nations Office on Drugs and Crime, *Global Study on Homicide: Gender-Related Killing of Women and Girls* (Vienna: United Nations, 2018), https://www.unodc.org/unodc/site-search.html?q=Global+study+on+homicide%3A+gender-related+killing+of+women+and+girls.
4. Jill Bolte Taylor, *My Stroke of Insight: A Brain Scientist's Personal Journey* (London: Plume, 2009), 183.
5. Marshall B. Rosenberg, "Do You Love Me?" YouTube video, July 12, 2016, 4:33, https://www.youtube.com/watch?v=otynMEeMStg.
6. Mahatma K. Gandhi, quote from *Young India*, Aug. 1, 1925, 15, collected in "Essence of Democracy," Comprehensive Gandhi website by Gandhian Institutions: Bombay Sarvodaya Mandal & Gandhi Research Foundation, accessed November 28, 2021, https://www.mkgandhi.org/momgandhi/chap72.htm.
7. Melissa Petruzzello, "The Chipko Movement," Encyclopedia Britannica, updated May 24, 2021, https://www.britannica.com/topic/Chipko-movement.
8. Rosenberg, *Practical Spirituality*, 6.
9. Rosenberg, *Practical Spirituality*, 6.
10. Maximilian Kolbe offers a powerful example of liberation despite atrocious constraints (of a Nazi concentration camp, to choose an environment of extreme collective trauma). A Franciscan friar, Kolbe volunteered to take the place of another prisoner and be starved to death. After two weeks of starvation, he was killed by lethal injection. Ready to face any consequence, Kolbe was free to love.
11. For more, see John Welwood, "Double Vision: Duality and Nonduality in Human Experience," in The *Sacred Mirror: Nondual Wisdom and Psychotherapy*, ed. John J. Prendergast, Peter Fenner, and Sheila Krystal (St. Paul, MN: Paragon House, 2003), Chapter 6, http://www.johnwelwood.com/articles/DoubleVision.pdf.
12. For more, see Carol Gilligan and Naomi Snider, *Why Does Patriarchy Persist?* (Medford, MA: Polity Press, 2018).
13. A classic Chinese text from approximately 1000–750 BCE, with many published English translations.
14. Gonzales, *Reflections on Living Compassion*, 42.
15. Martin Luther King Jr., "Where Do We Go From Here?" (annual report, 11th Convention of the Southern Christian Leadership Conference, Atlanta, GA, August 16, 1967).
16. Tara Brach, *Radical Acceptance: Embracing Your Life With the Heart of a Buddha* (New York: Bantam, 2003), Chapter 1.
17. Welwood, *Perfect Love, Imperfect Relationships*, 4.
18. This was estimated to occur from approximately 3100 to 600 BCE; see Gerda Lerner, *The Creation of Patriarchy* (Oxford, England: Oxford University Press, 1986), 8.
19. Jelaluddin Rumi, *Love Is a Stranger: Selected Lyric Poetry*, trans. Kabir Helminski (Boston: Shambhala Publications, 1993), 16.
20. Helen Schucman and William Thetford, *A Course in Miracles* (Novato, CA: Foundation for Inner Peace, 2000), 338.
21. Mukara Meredith is the founder of MatrixWorks and author of *MatrixWorks: A Life-Affirming Guide to Facilitation Mastery and Group Genius* (Bloomington, IN: Balboa Press, 2017).
22. Gonzales, *Reflections on Living Compassion*, 38.
23. See Rosenberg, *Practical Spirituality*, 7.
24. John Welwood, *Journey of the Heart* (New York: HarperCollins, 1990), 41.

CONCLUSION

1. "Marshall Rosenberg's NVC Quotes," Puddle-Dancer Press (website), 2021, https://www.nonviolentcommunication.com/resources/mbr-quotes.
2. Mahatma K. Gandhi, *The Selected Works, Mahatma Gandhi, Volume 3: Satyagraha in South Africa* (Ahmedabad, India: Navajivan, 1997).
3. Wilkerson, *Caste*, 386.
4. time2matter, "Marshall Rosenberg—Mem Noon," SoundCloud audiofile, 58:30, accessed November 28, 2021, https://soundcloud.com/time2matter/marshall-rosenberg-mem-noon.
5. Rosenberg, *Practical Spirituality*, 6.

INDEX

BRAIN/MIND STATES

DYSREGULATED
(Disconnected From Life Energy):

- **Mode: Withdrawal**
- **Reactive Mind** (Focus on Self-Preservation)
- **Survival Mode**
- **Chaos/Rigidity**
  - **Self-Criticism** (Fight)
  - **Self-Isolation** (Flight)
  - **Self-Absorption** (Freeze)

- **Intention to Be Right**
- **Attention to Past/Future**
- **Cry for Love — Please**

- **Deficit**
- **Extrinsic Motivation** (Punishment & Rewards)
- **Submission/Rebellion**
- **Dichotomic, Extrinsic Needs** (Mine/Yours; Met/Unmet)
- **Perceives Feelings as Caused by Outside Forces**

- **Attachment to Observations as Objective**
- **Demand** (To Educate/Coerce)

- **Power-Over**
- **Domination/Dependence-Independence**
- **Safety Through Force & Obedience**
- **Punitive Use of Force**
- **External Authority**
- **Pyramidal Static Hierarchy**

- **Moralistic Judgments** (Focus on Right/Wrong, Good/Bad)

- **Fear-Based Communication** (Anger, Blame, Guilt, Compliance Seeking, Obedience, Defiance, Control, Arguing, Screaming, Resistance, Shame, Depression, Anxiety, Withdrawal, Disconnection)

REGULATED
(Connected to Life Energy):

- **Mode: Approach**
- **Responsive Mind** (Focus on Inter-Being)
- **Optimal Integrated-Functioning**
- **Self-Awareness & Self-Connection**
  - **Calm** (The Avoid System)
  - **Contented** (The Approach System)
  - **Caring** (The Attach System)

- **Intention to Be In Relationship**
- **Attention to Present Moment**
- **Expression of Love — Thank You**

- **Fullness**
- **Intrinsic Motivation** (Nonnegotiable Values)
- **Choice**
- **Universal Intrinsic Needs** (Needs as Values to Live By, Self-Responsibility)
- **Perceives Feelings as Caused by Our Perceptions, Thoughts, Needs**

- **Holds Observations as Subjective**
- **Request** (With Persistence to Protect/ Enrich Life)

- **Power-With**
- **Partnership/Interdependence**
- **Safety Through Connection**
- **Protective Use of Force** (When Needed)
- **Internal Authority** (Self-Discipline)
- **Functional Hierarchy**

- **Value Judgments** (Focuses on Needs Awareness)

- **Compassion-Based Communication** (Integrity, Responsiveness, Mutuality, Reciprocity, Connection, Empathy, Acceptance, Compassion, Presence, Reaching Out)

© 2023 Stephanie Bachmann Mattei. Inspired by the works of Marshall B. Rosenberg, Kristin Neff, Rick Hanson, Daniel Siegel.

LIST OF PHYSICAL SENSATIONS

This is a partial list of physical and energetic sensations that support us in labeling and describing what is going on in the physical and energetic body.

PHYSICAL SENSATIONS:
- Achy
- Bloated
- Bruised
- Blushing
- Breathless
- Burning
- Buzzing
- Chills
- Clammy
- Clenched
- Cold
- Congested
- Contracted
- Cool
- Cramped
- Damp
- Dizzy
- Dry
- Faint
- Flaccid
- Flushed
- Fluttery
- Fragile
- Full
- Goose bumpy
- Gurgling
- Heavy
- Hollow
- Hot
- Itchy
- Jagged
- Jumpy
- Limp
- Loose
- Moist
- Nauseous
- Nervy
- Numb
- Paralyzed
- Pounding
- Pressure
- Prickly
- Puffy
- Queasy
- Quivery
- Relaxed
- Sensitive
- Shivery
- Silky
- Smooth
- Soft
- Spasm
- Sore
- Sticky
- Stiff
- Stretchy
- Suffocating
- Sweaty
- Tender
- Tense
- Tickly
- Tight
- Tremulous
- Warm
- Weak
- Wobbly

ENERGETIC SENSATIONS:
- Airy
- Alive
- Blocked
- Bubbly
- Calm
- Closed
- Constricted
- Cozy
- Deflated
- Dense
- Drained
- Dull
- Electric
- Empty
- Expansive
- Floating
- Flowing
- Fluid
- Frantic
- Frozen
- Fuzzy
- Glowing
- Hard
- Inflated
- Intense
- Jittery
- Knotted
- Light
- Luminous
- Open
- Pulsing
- Radiating
- Releasing
- Shaky
- Shimmering
- Spacey
- Spacious
- Spinning
- Still
- Stimulated
- Streaming
- Thick
- Thin
- Throbbing
- Tingling
- Trembling
- Twisting
- Twitching
- Vibrating

Clearly expressing how **I am** without blaming or criticizing	Empathically receiving how **you are** without hearing blame or criticism

OBSERVATIONS

1. What I observe *(see, hear, remember, imagine, free from my evaluations)* that does or does not contribute to my well-being:	1. What you observe *(see, hear, remember, imagine, free from your evaluations)* that does or does not contribute to your well-being:
"When I (see, hear) . . . "	*"When you see/hear . . . "* *(Sometimes unspoken when offering empathy)*

FEELINGS

2. How I feel *(emotion or sensation rather than thought)* in relation to what I observe:	2. How you feel *(emotion or sensation rather than thought)* in relation to what you observe:
"I feel . . . "	*"You feel . . ."*

NEEDS

3. What I need or value *(rather than a preference, or a specific action)* that causes my feelings:	3. What you need or value *(rather than a preference, or a specific action)* that causes your feelings:
" . . . because I need/value . . . "	*" . . . because you need/value . . ."*

Clearly requesting that which would enrich **my** life without demanding	Empathically receiving that which would enrich **your** life without hearing any demand

REQUESTS

4. The concrete actions I would like taken:	4. The concrete actions you would like taken:
"Would you be willing to . . . ?"	*"Would you like . . . ?"* *(Sometimes unspoken when offering empathy)*

© Marshall B. Rosenberg. For more information about Marshall B. Rosenberg or the Center for Nonviolent Communication, please visit www.CNVC.org.

Some Basic Feelings We All Have

Feelings when needs are fulfilled

- Amazed
- Comfortable
- Confident
- Eager
- Energetic
- Fulfilled
- Glad
- Hopeful
- Inspired
- Intrigued
- Joyous
- Moved
- Optimistic
- Proud
- Relieved
- Stimulated
- Surprised
- Thankful
- Touched
- Trustful

Feelings when needs are not fulfilled

- Angry
- Annoyed
- Concerned
- Confused
- Disappointed
- Discouraged
- Distressed
- Embarrassed
- Frustrated
- Helpless
- Hopeless
- Impatient
- Irritated
- Lonely
- Nervous
- Overwhelmed
- Puzzled
- Reluctant
- Sad
- Uncomfortable

 # Some Basic Needs We All Have

Autonomy
- Choosing dreams/goals/values
- Choosing plans for fulfilling one's dreams, goals, values

Celebration
- Celebrating the creation of life and dreams fulfilled
- Celebrating losses: loved ones, dreams, etc. (mourning)

Integrity
- Authenticity • Creativity
- Meaning • Self-worth

Interdependence
- Acceptance • Appreciation
- Closeness • Community
- Consideration
- Contribution to the enrichment of life
- Emotional Safety • Empathy

Physical Nurturance
- Air • Food
- Movement, exercise
- Protection from life-threatening forms of life: viruses, bacteria, insects, predatory animals
- Rest • Sexual Expression
- Shelter • Touch • Water

Play
- Fun • Laughter

Spiritual Communion
- Beauty • Harmony
- Inspiration • Order • Peace
- Honesty (the empowering honesty that enables us to learn from our limitations)
- Love • Reassurance
- Respect • Support
- Trust • Understanding

Nonviolent Communication Research

You can find an up-to-date list of journal articles, dissertations, theses, project reports, and independent studies exploring various facets of Nonviolent Communication at: www.nonviolentcommunication.com/learn-nonviolent-communication/research-on-nvc/

Some of these are qualitative, some quantitative, and some are mixed methods. Together they begin to offer an evidence base. If you have completed NVC research and would like to add your paper to the list, please contact us at: www.nonviolentcommunication.com/feedback-form/

 # About Nonviolent Communication

Nonviolent Communication has flourished for more than four decades across sixty countries selling more than 7,000,000 books in over thirty-five languages for one simple reason: it works.

Nonviolent Communication is changing lives every day. NVC provides an easy-to-grasp, effective method to get to the root of violence and pain peacefully. By examining the unmet needs behind what we do and say, NVC helps reduce hostility, heal pain, and strengthen professional and personal relationships. NVC is being taught in corporations, classrooms, prisons, and mediation centers worldwide. And it is affecting cultural shifts as institutions, corporations, and governments integrate NVC consciousness into their organizational structures and their approach to leadership.

Most of us want the skills to improve the quality of our relationships, to deepen our sense of personal empowerment, or simply to help us communicate more effectively. Unfortunately, most of us are educated from birth to compete, judge, demand, and diagnose; to think and communicate in terms of what is "right" and "wrong" with people. At best, the habitual ways we think and speak hinder communication and create misunderstanding or frustration. And still worse, they can cause anger and pain, and may lead to violence. Without wanting to, even people with the best of intentions generate needless conflict.

NVC helps us reach beneath the surface and discover what is alive and vital within us, and how all of our actions are based on human needs that we are seeking to meet. We learn to develop a vocabulary of feelings and needs that helps us more clearly express what is going on in us at any given moment. When we understand and acknowledge our needs, we develop a shared foundation for much more satisfying relationships. Join the thousands of people worldwide who have improved their relationships and their lives with this simple yet revolutionary process.

461

About PuddleDancer Press

Visit the PDP website at www.NonviolentCommunication.com. We have a resource-rich and ever-growing website that currently addresses 35+ topics related to NVC through articles, online resources, handouts, Marshall Rosenberg quotes, and so much more. Please come visit us.

- **NVC Quick Connect e-Newsletter**—Sign up online to receive our monthly e-Newsletter, filled with expert articles on timely and relevant topics, links to NVC in the news, inspirational and fun quotes and songs, announcements of trainings and other NVC events, and exclusive specials on NVC learning materials.

- **Shop NVC**—Purchase our NVC titles safely, affordably, and conveniently online. Find everyday discounts on individual titles, multiple copies, and book packages. Learn more about our authors and read endorsements of NVC from world-renowned communication experts and peacemakers.

- **About NVC**—Learn more about the unique life-changing communication and conflict resolution skills of NVC (also known as Compassionate Communication, Collaborative Communication, Respectful Communication, Mindful Communication, Peaceful Communication, or Effective Communication). Find an overview of the NVC process, key facts about NVC, and more.

- **About Marshall Rosenberg**—Read about the world-renowned peacemaker, educator, best-selling author, and founder of the Center for Nonviolent Communication, including press materials, a biography, and more.

For more information, please contact PuddleDancer Press at:

2240 Encinitas Blvd., Ste. D-911 • Encinitas, CA 92024
Phone: 760-557-0326 • Email: email@puddledancer.com
www.NonviolentCommunication.com

The Center for Nonviolent Communication (CNVC) is an international nonprofit peacemaking organization whose vision is a world where everyone's needs are met peacefully. CNVC is devoted to supporting the spread of Nonviolent Communication (NVC) around the world.

Founded in 1984 by Dr. Marshall B. Rosenberg, CNVC has been contributing to a vast social transformation in thinking, speaking and acting—showing people how to connect in ways that inspire compassionate results. NVC is now being taught around the globe in communities, schools, prisons, mediation centers, churches, businesses, professional conferences, and more. Hundreds of certified trainers and hundreds more supporters teach NVC to tens of thousands of people each year in more than sixty countries.

CNVC believes that NVC training is a crucial step to continue building a compassionate, peaceful society. Your tax-deductible donation will help CNVC continue to provide training in some of the most impoverished, violent corners of the world. It will also support the development and continuation of organized projects aimed at bringing NVC training to high-need geographic regions and populations.

To make a tax-deductible donation or to learn more about the valuable resources described below, visit the CNVC website at www.CNVC.org:

- **Training and Certification**—Find local, national, and international training opportunities, access trainer certification information, connect to local NVC communities, trainers, and more.

- **CNVC Bookstore**—Find mail or phone order information for a complete selection of NVC books, booklets, audio, and video materials at the CNVC website.

- **CNVC Projects**—Participate in one of the several regional and theme-based projects that provide focus and leadership for teaching NVC in a particular application or geographic region.

For more information, please contact CNVC at:

Ph: 1-505-244-4041 • Email: cnvc@CNVC.org • Website: www.CNVC.org

Nonviolent Communication,

3rd Edition

A Language of Life

By Marshall B. Rosenberg, PhD

$19.95 — Trade Paper 6x9, 264pp
ISBN: 978-1-892005-28-1

What is Violent Communication?

If "violent" means acting in ways that result in hurt or harm, then much of how we communicate —judging others, bullying, having racial bias, blaming, finger pointing, discriminating, speaking without listening, criticizing others or ourselves, name-calling, reacting when angry, using political rhetoric, being defensive or judging who's "good/bad" or what's "right/wrong" with people—**could indeed be called "violent communication."**

What is Nonviolent Communication?

Nonviolent Communication is the integration of four things:

- Consciousness: a set of principles that support living a life of compassion, collaboration, courage, and authenticity
- Language: understanding how words contribute to connection or distance
- Communication: knowing how to ask for what we want, how to hear others even in disagreement, and how to move toward solutions that work for all
- Means of influence: sharing "power with others" rather than using "power over others"

Nonviolent Communication serves our desire to do three things:

- Increase our ability to live with choice, meaning, and connection
- Connect empathically with self and others to have more satisfying relationships
- Sharing of resources so everyone is able to benefit

Speak Peace in a World of Conflict

What You Say Next Will Change Your World

By Marshall B. Rosenberg, PhD

$15.95 — Trade Paper 5-3/8x8-3/8, 208pp
ISBN: 978-1-892005-17-5

Create Peace in the Language You Use!

International peacemaker, mediator, and healer, Marshall Rosenberg shows you how the language you use is the key to enriching life. *Speak Peace* is filled with inspiring stories, lessons, and ideas drawn from more than forty years of mediating conflicts and healing relationships in some of the most war-torn, impoverished, and violent corners of the world. Find insight, practical skills, and powerful tools that will profoundly change your relationships and the course of your life for the better.

Nonviolent Communication has flourished for more than four decades across sixty countries selling more than 7,000,000 books for a simple reason: it works.

7,000,000 Copies Sold Worldwide • Translated in More Than 35 Languages

Comunicación No Violenta, 3era edición

Un lenguaje de vida

By Marshall B. Rosenberg, PhD

$19.95 — Trade Paper 6x9, 272pp
ISBN: 978-1-934336-19-9

What Is "Nonviolent" Communication?
It is the integration of 4 things:

Consciousness: a set of principles that support living a life of compassion, collaboration, courage, and authenticity

Language: understanding how words contribute to connection or distance

Communication: knowing how to ask for what we want, how to hear others even in disagreement, and how to move toward solutions that work for all

Means of influence: sharing "power with others" rather than using "power over others"

Available from PuddleDancer Press, the Center for Nonviolent Communication, all major bookstores, and Amazon.com. Distributed by Independent Publisher's Group: 800-888-4741.
For Best Pricing Visit: NonviolentCommunication.com

ABOUT THE AUTHORS

STEPHANIE BACHMANN MATTEI is a certified trainer and assessor with the Center for Nonviolent Communication, a Mindfulness-Based Stress Reduction certified teacher through the Mindfulness-Based Professional Training Institute, Center for Mindfulness at the University of California, San Diego, and an affiliated teacher with the Right Use of Power Institute. She holds  a research degree in philosophy from the Universita' Degli Studi di Firenze, Italy. She wrote her dissertation on the sixfold system of Indian philosophy while living in ashram under Swami Yogamudrananda Saraswati.

Photo: Mason Storm

Stephanie travels the globe to share her understanding of Nonviolent Communication as a lifelong practice to emerge into wholeness and authenticity and to celebrate the humanity in one another. She weaves mindfulness into all her teachings, and also offers Mindfulness-Based Stress Reduction courses as a path to reduce reactivity, increase well-being and aliveness, and cultivate the natural human capacity for compassionate presence. Stephanie's organizational trainings in Right Use of Power raise awareness of the power dynamics intrinsic in all relationships and share a heartfelt approach to power.

Stephanie is the mother of three children, biological and adopted. She loves to stroll on Florida beaches, travel back home to Italy with her family, cook Italian meals with her husband, and pet her cats.

To learn more, visit
www.stephaniebachmannmattei.com

KRISTIN K. COLLIER has published poems, articles, and essays online and in magazines such as *The Sun*. Kristin's 2016 memoir, *Housewife: Home-Remaking in a Transgender Marriage*, won several awards, including a prestigious Nautilus Book Award. She and her parenting partner, Seda Collier, have been featured on NPR's *Snap Judgment*.

Photo: Guru Updesh Singh

Kristin has been developing and sharing her practice of Nonviolent Communication since 2004, with a special interest in parenting. She is a teacher and administrator for social groups that serve neurodiverse children and youth, including young people on the autism spectrum. In these roles, she teaches about relationships and sexuality, and integrates the skills and spirit of Nonviolent Communication into every curriculum.

Kristin continues to learn about courage and adventure from her now-adult sons and enjoys canoeing, backpacking, and dancing the Lindy Hop.

Her work, focusing on joy, can be found at
www.collierconnections.com